MEDIA, SPORTS, & SOCIETY

MEDIA, SPORTS, & SOCIETY

EDITED BY **Lawrence A. Wenner**

SAGE PUBLICATIONS
The Publishers of Professional Social Science
Newbury Park   London   New Delhi

Copyright © 1989 by Sage Publications, Inc.

For information address:

SAGE Publications, Inc.
2111 West Hillcrest Drive
Newbury Park, California 91320

SAGE Publications Ltd.
28 Banner Street
London EC1Y 8QE
England

SAGE Publications India Pvt. Ltd.
M-32 Market
Greater Kailash I
New Delhi 110 048 India

Printed in the United States of America

Library of Congress Cataloging-in-Publication Data

Main entry under title:

Media, sports, and society / edited by Lawrence A. Wenner.
        p.   cm.
    Bibliography: p.
    ISBN 0-8039-3243-X. — ISBN 0-8039-3244-8 (pbk.)
    1. Mass media and sports—United States.   2. Sports—social
aspects—United States.   I. Wenner, Lawrence A.
GV742.M33   1989
306.4'83—dc20   89-10214
                                                                CIP

FIRST PRINTING, 1989

Contents

Preface

I think I should admit something up front. I'm a sports fan. In reading the morning paper, I'm one of those people who can't quite face the worldly troubles of the front page over my morning coffee. I put the deficit, the homeless, and the latest flare-up in the Middle East aside and head for the somehow more satisfying world of sports.

The SportsWorld, as Robert Lipsyte has called it, is not just a place where athletes compete. For theologian Michael Novak and millions of others like myself, the SportsWorld is on sacred ground and the chapel to which we come to worship is more and more a mediated one. While many fans attend sporting events each week, many million more watch sports on television, listen on radio, and read about events in the sports pages. Those who do so are doing much more than merely finding out who won the big game or what the strategy is for the next one. We have chosen to celebrate sports culture, immerse ourselves in its values, and share in its fruits with others.

Many might see my indulgences in sport as shameless behavior, especially for a communication scholar. There are days when I think I should be concerned with "serious" media issues like news and politics or violence and children. Certainly, important media studies remain to be mounted about "agendas" to be set, "silences" to be spiraled, "cultivations" to be analyzed, and "uses" to be gratified.

In any academic area, the easier questions to pursue merely follow what others are doing. Too often, this is what "building on existing research" means. More difficult are questions about what we have *not* been doing. And we have not asked very many questions about relationships among media, sports, and society. It's difficult to say why this is the case.

In sociology, an adjacent field where communication finds much grounding for its inquiry, the study of sport has been institutionalized. Moreover, the sociology of sport is a congregating point for scholars not only in sociology, but also in physical education, recreation and leisure studies, and cultural studies. On a smaller scale, the fields of psychology and philosophy maintain traditions of research on sport. Yet, in communication, no such tradition has emerged.

Interestingly, this is in the face of some very visible evidence that mediated sport is a featured player in modern life. In the United States, the Super Bowl is regularly among the top-rated television events of the year. Among broadcasting and cable networks, the profits yielded by the Entertainment and Sports Programming Network (ESPN) are eclipsed only by those of NBC, the runaway ratings leader among the traditional broadcast networks. As I write this in 1988, ESPN, although it reaches little more than 50% of U.S. homes, yields greater profits than the CBS or ABC broadcast networks.

Communication scholars have seemingly asked about every variant in the modern media. Studies of news and mediated politics and their influences tend to predominate. Fueled by our concerns about children as a special audience, we have asked more than our share of questions about the relationship between media violence and aggression. We have asked many questions about soap operas, many related to gender portrayals or gratifications. We're worried about the effects of MTV, about cartoons, and certainly about commercials. Yet, for the most part, sport eludes inquiry.

This book is a maiden voyage for the communication of sport. As editor of this volume, I take responsibility for whether the vessel floats, the shape and color of its sails, and the course to be navigated. In charting this voyage, I have attempted to take into account the wide variety of perspectives and concerns that communication scholars have. Similar to many other fields in the social sciences, communication has recently been experiencing a time of conceptual ferment. In this volume, I have attempted to meld the competing concerns of the scientific and cultural camps toward an understanding of what the study of mediated sport can be about.

Toward this end, the opening essay that I have authored for the volume attempts to draw a research agenda illustrating how contributions can be made from a variety of perspectives. In that chapter, I suggest an organizing framework for the communication of sport. This model, which charts relations among the media sports production complex, media sports content, and the audience, also guides the organization of this volume.

I am well aware that my approach is not the only way to paint a big picture of the communication of sport. Consequently, I have complemented my overview with Robert McChesney's chapter on the history of sports coverage and Sut Jhally's introduction to the cultural studies agenda for the communication of sport.

The section on the media sports production complex features studies on the functioning of media organizations, sports organizations, and sports journalists. Looking at broadcast industry strategies, Susan Tyler Eastman and Timothy Meyer provide important background information in their analysis of sports as television programming. Robert Bellamy turns this question around in his analysis of sports organizations and the strategies they use to leverage the media marketplace. Finally, Richard Gruneau provides a unique inside look at journalistic practice through his analysis of decision making in CBC sports production.

I open the section on media sports content by looking at the political constructions used in the pregame show that sets the tone for the Super Bowl telecast. Michael Real follows this by analyzing the cultural-structural aspects of the Super Bowl game itself and contrasting them with another "football" mega-event, World Cup soccer. Leah Vande Berg and Nick Trujillo examine the fluctuation of values about winning and losing in an analysis of 25 years of sportswriting about "America's Team," the Dallas Cowboys. The last chapter in Part III, by Lewis Donohew, David Helm, and John Haas, examines how the sports pages handled stories about drug use among athletes before and after two tragic drug-related deaths of major athletes.

Leading into the closing section on the audience for media sports, Walter Gantz and I examine how experiences with sports on television differ by sport. The work of Jennings Bryant follows, with an update on a line of research examining spectators' enjoyment of sports violence. In the last chapter, Michael Roloff and Denise Solomon pursue an often-voiced concern about sports on television, the role of sports in male-female relational harmony.

As the reader considers each of the areas of inquiry in this volume, it should become clear that many important questions about media, sports, and society remain to be asked. A volume this size cannot be comprehensive. My goal is to provide a foundation for the study of the communication of sport. Thus one simple measure of the volume's success will be whether scholars come to think in terms of the communication of sport. Further, if the collected work stimulates questions about the role of mediated sport in culture that we have omitted, we will have succeeded.

There are many people to thank in the preparation of this volume. I owe thanks to Michael Real, Jennings Bryant, and Dolf Zillmann, whose pioneering work helped give my push for this volume much-needed legiti-macy. Ann West, my editor at Sage Publications, has provided encourage-ment throughout this project. Ann facilitated helpful reviews of the proposal for the volume from Jay Coakley, editor of the *Sociology of Sport Journal*, and James Frey, president of the North American Society for the Sociology of Sport.

My institutions have been very supportive of this project. In particular, Loyola Marymount University funded a Summer Research Grant and Faculty Development Grant to support this project. I owe a special debt of gratitude to Loyola's academic vice president, Fr. Albert Koppes, O. Carm., for providing release time and travel funds for my related research efforts culminating in this volume. My new academic home, the University of San Francisco, has been gracious in providing a base of support for the volume's completion.

Inspirational on a different level was my father, Sam Wenner, who taught me to appreciate almost any ball that was in play on the television screen. We didn't go to many games; we had better seats at home. My mother, Gerry Wenner, played such a strong role in my development here that I have no choice but to remain a Los Angeles Lakers fan, even as I live in the San Francisco area. Because of my mother, I appreciated the joys of Lakers' announcer Chick Hearn, who added Kareem Abdul-Jabbar, Magic John-son, and James Worthy to my family. Fortunately, my wife and my biggest fan, Susan Rice, enjoys this extended family with me. It was Susan who con-vinced me this book was important. I remain her number one fan.

Lawrence A. Wenner
Mill Valley, California

I

Overviews

1

Media, Sports, and Society: The Research Agenda

Lawrence A. Wenner

The numbers are startling. In 1988, the million-dollar minute seemed almost a bargain, as it cost $675,000 for 30 seconds of commercial time on ABC's broadcast of the championship game of American professional football – the Super Bowl. The three American television networks together broadcast approximately 1,800 hours of sports programming each year. One of cable television's most noteworthy success stories has been the Entertainment and Sports Programming Network (ESPN), which features sports programming almost 24 hours a day. Even with such abundance, sports organizations – both professional and amateur – are paid handsomely for the rights to broadcast this material. ABC and NBC's shared network rights contract paying Major League Baseball $1.2 billion for six years will be supplanted in 1990 by an exclusive three year pact costing CBS $.1 billion. The current contract the three major networks and ESPN have with the National Football League pays some $1.4 billion for broadcast rights over a three-year period ("Baseball Bags Almost $370 Million," 1988; Tedesco, 1987a, 1988).

And the network monies are a relatively small portion of the cash that flows between media and sports. Local station broadcast rights can be considerable, especially if they involve a good team in a large and desirable media market. For example, local broadcast rights for large-market teams like baseball's New York Mets are edging up toward $20 million a year ("Baseball Bags Almost $370 Million," 1988).

Sports teams and leagues are also subsidized by cable networks and satellite-distributed superstations. In addition to ESPN, each of the three major cable superstations – TBS in Atlanta, WGN in Chicago, and WOR in

New York—rely heavily on sports programming to fill out their schedules. Even on cable, sports does not come cheaply. TBS recently paid $30 million for five-year distribution rights for the Atlanta Braves baseball games (Taaffe, 1985).

The reason broadcast rights command so high a price is that they are a good business proposition. Audiences for sports programming offer desirable demographics for advertisers. The television sports audience is heavily composed of relatively hard-to-reach males between the ages of 18 and 49. It tends to be a well-educated audience, and one with considerable disposable income. Advertisers are willing to pay top dollar for this audience because they tend to make purchase decisions about big-ticket items such as automobiles and computers ("Broadcasters to Spend $536 Million," 1984).

Indeed, more men watch sports on television—90% of men watch, versus 76% of women—but there is evidence that the female audience for sports is growing, even for almost exclusively male sports like football and baseball. Some 6 million women watch a typical NFL game on network television, and about 30 million tune in to the Super Bowl game. Older women are beginning to make up a significant part of the audience for professional football and baseball (Miller, 1984).

Advertisers compensate the broadcast and cable outlets for their hefty outlay for the rights to cover events. While the $675,000 price tag for a 30-second spot during the Super Bowl is atypically astronomical, advertisers are willing to pay sizable sums for less colossal regular sports competitions. For an NFL regular-season game, a 30-second commercial spot broadcast on ABC's prime-time *Monday Night Football* costs in the neighborhood of $200,000, while an equivalent spot during a weekend daytime game costs $100,000 (Tedesco, 1987a). For an important NCAA Division I college football game, that 30-second network spot would cost only $30,000 (Fierman, 1984). Major League Baseball is more in line with college football, with a 30-second network spot running about $40,000 during regular-season weekend day games, but jumping to near $300,000 for the broadcast of World Series championship games ("Broadcasters to Spend $536 Million," 1984; "Baseball Bags Almost $370 Million," 1988).

The Appeal of Mediated Sport

What makes the sports contest on television so appealing to advertisers may be the relative intensity with which sports fans view the game. The sporting event is unscripted and live. Dramatic things may happen at any moment. The televised event is a colorful spectacle, resplendent with heroes who compete in active conflict guided by strategy, held to the rules of the game by officials, and cheered on by fans in the stadium.

The fan at home is aided and abetted in interpreting the contest by the television camera, which focuses on action deemed important. Announcers add to this focus, as their commentary reinforces and heightens the significance of the contest and its players. Technological supplementation such as the "instant replay" focuses the fan even more intensely and allows the most significant of the events to be dissected further and commented upon by the announcer. If the broadcasters have done their job well, the sports fan will be attentively viewing when a commercial message appears.

The sports pages of the newspaper reflect upon the significance of the events that are so often broadcast. The sports pages ready the fan for the event. The sporting event is heightened in importance by "insider's gossip" about the players, coaches, strategies, and historical context for the sporting event. After a contest has been played, the sports pages recap these same themes, placing the game and its heroes into a "fantasy world" that both sportswriters and readers have had a hand in creating.

In many ways, the sports press provides a socially sanctioned gossip sheet for men in America, a place where a great deal of conjecture is placed upon "heroes" and events of little worldly import. Indeed, a careful look at the content of the sports press reveals surprising parallels with the societally devalued "gossip" that appears on the "women's" or "society" pages of many metropolitan daily newspapers. The legitimized gossip for men is about sporting events rather than social events, but it is socializing nonetheless, as the debutante's male counterpart learns of the significance of the sporting world and its heroes. An uninitiated female entering this "alternate reality" of the male sports world may have much beyond "table manners" to catch on to in order to understand the significance of the sporting world. However, the sporting world — and the mediated representation of it — may be changing as well, as more women attend to it and report on it (Morse, 1983).

Approaching Mediated Sport

Sports sociologists seem to agree that the most common involvement people have with sports is through viewing them on television (Loy,

McPherson, & Kenyon, 1978; Snyder & Spreitzer, 1978). And these same people who watch televised sporting events listen to games on radio and read about contests and heroes in the sports pages and in sports magazines. This communication forms the basis of a shared sports culture in America.

This mass-communicated and highly commercialized sports culture is easily related to myriad issues concerning socialization, interpersonal communication, value formation, racial and gender assessments, and the balance of political and economic power. Whether a sports fan or not, every individual in America is to some degree influenced by the communication of sports culture. Mediated sports culture is an inescapable reality, forming part of the context of every American's life.

Even so, it is understandable that sports sociologists and others concerned with the role of sport in culture see media issues as peripheral. There are many sport issues of sociological, psychological, or anthropological import that have little to do with the media and sports relationship. Less understandable has been the limited interest from the field of communication, where inquiries about media and sports have been so few and far between that the present situation is one where a few unrelated studies exist and no ongoing research programs have been established.

Given that sports programming can be much more readily seen on American television on any weekend day than either political or children's programming—both areas of well-established traditions in mainstream effects research—it is ironic that sports programming has eluded the scrutiny of mass communication researchers. Indeed, research in mass communication is often initiated by that which is obviously visible in the marketplace. Hence we find the familiar foci on the repercussions of overtly sexual and violent content in television programs, stereotyping and "antisocial" behavior in children's programs, and deceptive and distorted messages in television advertising.

These issues and others are plentiful in the communication of sport—both in sportswriting for newspapers and magazines and in sports programming for television and radio. As such, the "communication of sport" has a natural lineage to other areas of communication inquiry and can further develop as unique issues are defined. This essay develops a theoretical model to characterize research and guide inquiry about the communication of sport. By looking first at approaches to sport in other social sciences, the unique contributions of a communicative approach may be understood as fitting into the larger body of knowledge about sports and society.

Sports and the Theoretical Battleground

By far the main line of inquiry into the significance of sport in American society has come from sociology's emerging subdiscipline, the sociology of sport. While the sociology of sport has largely charted a "normal science" course, a variety of critical approaches advocate navigating the waters differently. Such "battling" between dominant and emerging paradigms can be seen in many of the social science disciplines, and is particularly evident in the "ferment" in the field of communication. In various fields, the sides have faced off—behaviorism versus critical research, quantitative versus qualitative research, positivists versus humanists, administrative versus critical research, structural-functional versus conflict theory, and instrumental versus consummatory approaches. Taken in total, these battles characterize a somewhat windy and long-term disagreement about how best to go about the doing of social science. This disagreement is well beyond, but relevant to, the discussion here about how best to approach inquiries into the relationship of media and sports.

As I have outlined at length elsewhere, my approach lies at the intersection of this disagreement (Wenner, 1985a, 1985b). This "transactional" approach follows philosophically on arguments posed by Dewey and Bentley (1949), and is an attempt to cut across the somewhat artificial bounds between scientific and cultural views of communication, as the feuding camps have been characterized by McQuail (1985).

To many staunch supporters of either camp, such a compromise is not possible, and any attempt to make one merely waters down a tenable position. However, in the fields of both communication and sociology, recent theoretical discussion has aimed at such common meeting points. For example, the themes of the 1985 and 1986 meetings of the International Communication Association have focused on such paradigm dialogues. In sociology, the camps are talking as well, as can be seen in Alexander's (1985) volume, *Neofunctionalism*, where the word *critical* is quite up front in Sciulli's (1985) lead chapter, "The Practical Groundwork for Critical Theory: Bringing Parsons to Habermas (and Vice Versa)." Rothenbuhler (1987) has eloquently translated these concerns to the communication research agenda.

My approach to the communication of sport is most similar to the positions outlined by Melnick (1979) and Rose (1982) with regard to the sociology of sport. Their critiques find the mainstream's "value-free" descriptive research of values and functions a useful starting point, but its relative lack of critical or "normative" positioning tending by default to enlist sport in the service of the status quo in a culture rather than aiming to pinpoint and solve problems to which sport may be contributing in society.

While in this essay I am not advocating any one particular critical position, I believe critical positions in conjunction with the so-called value-free methods of "normal" social science may uncover the kind of answers about the relationship between media and sport that can benefit both the audience and policymakers. Also, such critical positioning is necessary to traverse the macro and micro views needed to make sense of the media, sports, and society relationship.

A Place to Start for Mediated Sports Inquiries

Most social science inquiries that consider mediated sport see the process of mediating sport as a peripheral issue. Often, the main focus has been on the playing of the sports contest and what it means for the participants rather than what it means for the spectators. Nevertheless, this research is of considerable heuristic value to mediated sports inquiries, serving as a point of departure in looking at how sport is translated into the language and setting of mass culture products designed for consumption on a much larger scale.

In fact, a significant amount of preliminary inquiry into mediated sport might center on how the culture of sport is changed as it is mediated. From there, research may logically proceed to what implications those changes in content and scale have for the society at large. To get started on this task, media research might well look to some basic generalizations about why people engage in sport and the values that are attached to such engagement. Some implications of these generalizations for mediated sports inquiries are considered in the following two sections.

Extending the "Why of Sports" to Mediated Sports

Sage (1979) has summarized research on the most commonly identified "functions" of sport from a variety of social science disciplines. Sage sees this research classifying answers to the question of "why" people play sports into seven categories: instinct, developmental-cognitive, mastery, social integration, socialization, social control, and personal-expressive.

Instinct. Some instinct functions of sport were stated early on, and perhaps best summarized, by Spencer's (1855, 1872) "surplus energy" theory of play. Here play was seen as becoming more important as basic needs were met. With time on their hands, people had "restless energy" that was dissipated by play activities. However, as one thinks about the comparatively passive state of the "armchair quarterback" watching a sporting event on television, it suggests that another type of instinctual "energy" may be present. Perhaps the "lethargic energy" level of the television sports fan who is viewing from a comfortable easy chair signals an instinct to regenerate the energy expended by participation in modern life. Spencer's larger point—that in a technological society one's environment and one's instincts about it change—holds true. But the functionality of instinctual responses is not a simple matter. They change with the world, and as one progresses through the world.

Developmental/cognitive. The focus on the developmental and cognitive functions of sport originates in the work of Piaget (1962), Mead (1934), Bruner, Joly, and Sylva (1976), and others. The concern here has largely been with children, and the role that play fills in their development. Game playing (of which sports activities are a part) is seen as a way the child learns, practices, and develops a consciousness about rules that can guide creative problem solving in later life.

However, children also attend to mediated sport. And that mediated sport in large part exists to transport advertisements to adults. Both the cultural messages about the mediated contest and the surrounding advertising are not designed for children. Thus children consuming these messages may become "adultized" in a way that is completely different from what a focus on game playing would recognize. Just what children are learning from mediated sport and what cognitive abilities it tends to stimulate and retard are questions worthy of specific inquiry. How children attending to mediated adult sports "miscomprehend" because of gaps in social understanding is a central question for media inquiry.

Mastery. Freud's work *Beyond the Pleasure Principle* (1962) suggests how sports perform a mastery function. As Sage (1979) points out, from this view, "play enables the child to deal with anxiety evoking situations by allowing him to be the active master of the situation, rather than the passive victim" (p. 10). Again, when the situation is transposed to mediated sports experience, the dynamics of mastery change. The child, or adult for that matter, does not quite become passive victim, but the qualities of mastery and activity change dramatically from those characterizing participation in sporting activities.

The mastery that is involved in consumption of mediated sports is much more in line with what Roberts (Roberts, Arth, & Bush, 1959; Roberts & Sutton-Smith, 1962; Sutton-Smith & Roberts, 1970) has called "cultural mastery." In this case, the sports fan, child or adult, is mastering the culture of mediated sport and larger cultural forces that endorse its relatively height-ened placement in society.

Social integration. That sports serve a social integration function is a widely held view. Sports are seen as encouraging normative social integra-tion through group membership on teams and the shared symbolic meaning that is required in the playing of sports contests under agreed-upon rules. Individuals develop group identities through the team's common cause of winning sports contests, and loyalty to and identification with the team con-tributes to group integration.

Also, social integration comes about as the ritual and ceremony associated with sport become part of the common ground, mirroring the values of American society (Sage, 1979). Cozens and Stumpf (1953) see such commo-nality occurring in sports spectatorship as "fostering understanding across class lines, and increasing the intimacy of association with different classes," and go on to say that "spectator sports have contributed to those integrating forces which are vital and indispensable in the preservation of our demo-cratic way of life."

Once again, in the mediated version of sport, the processes of social integration are played by changed rules. In consuming mediated sports, one does not develop loyalties to the group by being part of the group playing the sport, or understandings by rubbing elbows with different kinds of fellow spectators. Here one roots for one's team from afar. The intimacy in medi-ated consumption of sports is not based on a firsthand "intimacy of associa-tion with different classes." Instead, the mediated intimacy is "parasocial" (Horton & Wohl, 1956) in nature and takes place with the sportscasters and players, who both qualify as celebrities in American life. Clearly, this is still crossing class lines, but it is comfortably restricted to a rather select, elite group that has been anointed with media fame.

Socialization. In many ways, the socialization functions of sport serve as a backdrop for the other functions that have been mentioned. Certainly, what counts as an instinctual activity, what are desirable cognitive attributes associated with decision-making skills, what things are worth mastering, and what degree of normative integration is valued in a given society are largely culturally determined. In a sense, socialization is the character of social integration. The focus is on the learning and internalization of societal values, norms, and behaviors (Dobringer, 1969). Social science inquiry has largely been restricted to looking at socialization in the context of sports team membership.

As Sage (1979) points out, the values stressed in sports socialization — courage, self-discipline, leadership, cooperation, loyalty, and honesty — are thought to "build character." As will be discussed in greater detail below, Edwards (1973) sees these and other values as constituting the "American Sports Creed." For the media researcher, the transaction of the "American *Mediated* Sports Creed" with that dispensed from traditional channels of socialization (e.g., family, teachers, coaches) should shed much light on the role of mediated sport in American culture.

Social control. The notion of sports serving as a mechanism of social control has origins in many camps. Similar to catharsis theories of mediated violence (Feshbach, 1969), sports involving vigorous exercise are seen by many to cathartically control aggression through socially sanctioned channels (Scott, 1970). In that sports activities by necessity take one away from day-to-day concerns, it has often been suggested (especially by Marxist critics) that they serve as an "opiate" that distracts the masses from problems in the polity. For example, Hoch (1972) sees contemporary sport in America as a manifestation of materialistic capitalism that "robs people of their power to make decisions and their creativity, and sets them in search of opiates in consumption and entertainment."

Whether one goes so far as to consider sport an opiate or not depends on one's critical position. However, it seems clear that the mediated version of sport is "entertaining" — it certainly is not work — and holds a two-pronged press to consume. Not only is mediated sport content designed to be pleasurably consumed, it is packaged as a vehicle that carries messages promoting the consumption of products. Whether there is control in that is in the eye of the beholder.

Personal-expressive. That engagement in sports activities can bring enjoyment in and of itself points to one of the least instrumental and most obvious functions served by sports. People play sports because they are enjoyable, satisfying, fulfilling on a very existential level. According to Ingham and Loy (1973), sport merely "provides a setting for sociability and fun" (p. 7). Mediated consumption of sport could easily be interpreted in the same way.

On the individual level, consumers of mediated sport are very obviously enjoying themselves. Televised contests are entertaining fare that may be enjoyed by a single individual or by small groups. And the aftermath of the contests and the reportage of them fuel equally enjoyable conversations with other fans.

However, isolating only the personal-expressive functions of mediated sports paints a picture rather naively seen through rose-colored glasses. It ignores the monies and motives of those involved in seeing to it that the mediated sports fan is a satisfied customer. Looking only at the personal-expressive aspects of sports consumption ignores issues of social control, socialization, integration, and cognition.

Finding Value and Ideology in American Mediated Sport

In the United States, there is a special character to both mainstream media organizations and sports organizations with teams that are featured as frequently in the media marketplace as they are on the field. Media organizations buy and sell sport much as they do any other news or entertainment commodity. The content per se is not what is being sold; rather, it is the audience for that content that is being sold to advertisers.

A sports organization directly markets a product—its team's playing abilities—to spectators who pay for the privilege of watching the team play. The organization indirectly markets this product to broadcast media organizations, who repackage and embellish the product as the lure for the audiences that advertisers seek to reach. For sports organizations participating in the media world, this holds true in varying degrees, whether sports is the sole focus of the organization (such as some professional sports teams) or a secondary focus (such as collegiate teams from universities or professional teams owned by large and highly diversified conglomerates).

The print media differ from the broadcast media mainly in that they do not pay sports organizations for the rights to a contest. Instead, the print press and the sports organizations maintain a reciprocal relationship aimed at captivating an audience. The print press sells to advertisers the readers that sports organizations want to become paying customers—both at the gate and in the broadcast media audience. This is strictly a barter deal, with the sports print press gaining an audience and the sports organization—if all goes well—gaining the public goodwill, which leads to an audience.

As the major media and sports organizations can be considered dominant institutions in American society, the values they espouse can be characterized by a central core of obligatory norms. According to Williams (1970), "institutional norms are: 1) widely known, accepted, and applied;

(2) widely enforced by strong sanctions continuously applied; (3) based upon revered sources of authority; (4) internalized in individual personalities; (5) inculcated and strongly reinforced early in life; and (6) objects of consistent and prevalent conformity" (p. 37).

Edwards (1973) has made the case that sports qualifies as an institution under these criteria. An argument can certainly be made that sports and sports organizations have had their norms institutionalized at an accelerated rate as they are bought and sold—albeit in changed form—through media organizations. With this acceleration, this neoinstitutionalized form of sport becomes even more dominant in its ideological dispersal than sport in its pre- or nonmediated forms.

To the degree that a unified mediated sports ideology, through its beliefs and values, becomes more widely known, enforced, revered, internalized, inculcated in early life, and promotes conformity, there is evidence of cultural hegemony. Because of this, questions about the content of mediated sports take on added importance (see Gramsci, 1971).

Asserting cultural hegemony is commonplace with many critical scholars, but proving it is quite another matter. Looking at the content of mediated sport to see if it indeed represents a *unified* ideology will be only a starting point. If this can be determined, then scholars will need to link intentionality on the part of media and sports organizations with the perceptions and utilities of the audience.

The values stressed in mediated sports complement and grow out of those already existing in sports. Certainly, the structures of presentation—the rules of sportswriting and the rules governing production of broadcast sports coverage—add another set of ritualistic understandings to the already familiarly structured sports contest. Even though this added layer of structures may alter the value mix, the point of departure remains largely with the sports contest and their heroes, for without them, the media commerce concerning sports would not exist. How these core values are presented, altered, and added to becomes central in mediated sports inquiry.

Williams (1970) has summed up the values of American society as achievement and success, activity and work, morality, humanitarianism, efficiency and practicality, progress, material comfort, equality, freedom, external conformity, science and secular rationality, nationalism, democracy, individual personality, and group superiority. Embracing much in Williams's inventory, Edwards's (1973) "American Sports Creed" pinpoints the values of character, discipline, competition, physical fitness, mental fitness, religiosity, and nationalism as those having special meaning in sports culture.

Edwards's work in particular, in combination with the work of Williams, Rokeach (1973), and others, should help point communications scholars toward a definition of the American *Mediated* Sports Creed. In the setting of mediated sport, the focus shifts to the values associated with the consumption of content produced by sports journalists responding to situations defined jointly by sports and media organizations. Here ideology is expressed in two main ways: (1) through the value statements expressed in the mediated sports content, and (2) through the values associated with consuming that content. Departing from Edwards's work, some brief examples of these two variants are considered below.

Value statements in content. Assessments of the character of athletes, their teams, and sports organizations come up frequently in the sports pages, in television sports reports, and as filler in the play-by-play announcing of game broadcasts. Although Edwards was thinking of such general issues as clean living, proper grooming, "red-bloodedness," loyalty, and altruism, specific character issues change with the times.

For instance, Edwards focuses on "long hair" on athletes as a character issue that influenced sports and society. Today, that issue has largely been displaced by other issues, such as drug use and violent criminal behavior (rape, murder) among athletes. How the sports press responds (or does not respond) to these off-the-field actions is important in defining mediated sport ideology.

Also, the dynamic relationship between the sports press and sports organizations may in some part be charted by following media content. "Bad" character may make a "good" story, but it is likely that it comes with a normative charge for sports organizations to "clean house." How sports organizations respond to stories of "bad" character is part of the story, and one that media researchers need attend to. It is a process through which media normalizes things, similar to "out with the bad air, in with the good." The portrayal of the "right" way to "right" an endemic problem within the system is indeed a cultural lesson.

Other character issues may have been precipitated by the media themselves, such as the focus on skyrocketing athletes' salaries, which, as initiated by "free agency" and then supported in good part by lucrative media contracts, may tend to subvert traditional values of altruism — unselfishness, self-sacrifice — so commonly associated with sports. Content issues such as these provide opportunities to study the media's role in value displacement.

Values associated with consumption. Although value statements may be easier to pick out in the media content itself, values are also placed on the activity of consuming mediated sport. These values may change over time in response to events in society. They may also differ with consumption level, and may be perceived differently by those actually doing the consuming and those affected by it.

Basic questions for media research might center on "content ruboff" onto the activity of consuming mediated sport. Perhaps a loyal fan of sports through the media perceives the activity as "All-American," requiring mental fitness, alertness, and basic knowledge, or in some other way helpful in preparing for life. If culturally embraced, such valuation says much about the character of American society.

Values associated with consumption may conflict, just as values in content may conflict. For example, the unappreciating spouse may have ongoing value conflicts with a mate who is a die-hard media sports enthusiast. And the occasional fan may value mediated sports consumption along quite different lines than the sports "addict." Such value conflict is important in understanding the cultural role of mediated sport.

A Model for Mediated Sports Inquiry

Getting an accurate view of the media and sports relationship in society will require understanding from a variety of perspectives. Answers to questions concerning the "functionalities" of why mediated sports are consumed and valued by *audiences* will provide part of the picture. Critical assessments of the *content* of mediated sports and the values that are articulated in that content will also be needed. Answers to yet other questions concerning the workings, motives, and interrelationships of organizations and professionals within the *media sports production complex* that aims to captivate audiences will give yet another part of the picture. Finally, all of these elements and how they relate to one another will need to be viewed within the context of the larger *society*.

A transactional model for such mediated sports inquiry is suggested in Figure 1.1. The model is a general one, made up of a hierarchical ordering of *transacting* systems (see Wenner, 1985a). Here four systems—society, the production complex, mediated sport content, and the audience experience with that content—transact with each other over time. The suprasystem—or containing frame—is the society that brings about a subsystem of sports media production organizations. Through sports journalists, these organizations produce the content that serves as the basis for audience experience.

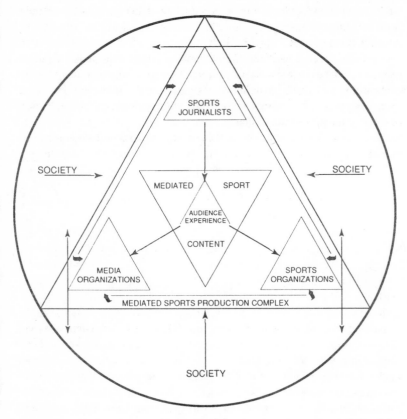

Figure 1.1.   A Transactional Model of Media, Sports, and Society Relationships

In a *sociological* approach, the point of departure is most typically with
the concept of society. The model pictured here would be approached "outside in," considering the experiences of the audience last. In a *transactional*
view of communication, theory development also entails societal — or
suprasystem — assessments. However, the point of departure is "inside out,"
studying audience experience first.

From this view, it is presumptuous to assume that there is an objective
world "outside" and to comment on how people are responding to it. Rather,
it follows Ittelson and Cantril's (1954) mandate that perception "can only be
studied in terms of the transactions in which they can be observed" because

"neither a perception nor object-as-perceived exists independently of the total life situation of which both perception and object are a part," and thus "it is meaningless to speak of either as existing apart from the situation in which it is encountered" (pp. 2–3).

In the transactional view, the audience's perceptions are as much "cultural indicators" as the content material to which they respond. Although its point of departure is audience experience, a transactional approach to mediated sport also entails assessments of content in conjunction with the forces that have led to the production of that content. Taking an "inside out" approach, the discussion that follows looks at the component parts of the communication of sport model.

The Mediated Sports Audience

Remarkably few studies have systematically examined the special qualities associated with the consumption of mediated sport, although ground was broken on this line of inquiry some time ago. Hastorf and Cantril's (1954) classic study reports Princeton and Dartmouth students "seeing" a markedly different contest played by their football teams when viewing an "objectified" film version of it. The differences in perception were traceable both to the preexisting mediated context for the game—the student newspaper game coverage that subjects read prior to the film viewing—and to the magnified view of the contest that the film version presented. Hastorf and Cantril conclude that "there is no such 'thing' as a 'game' existing 'out there' in its own right which people merely 'observe.' The 'game' 'exists' for a person and is experienced by him only in so far as certain happenings have significances in terms of his purpose" (p. 133).

Just as a mediated sports contest may be "seen" differently by members of the audience who bring their own perceptions to that coverage, the appeal of that coverage may differ greatly among members of the audience. Gantz's (1981) study of the motives and behaviors associated with the viewing of television sports stands out as one of the few empirical studies that has examined a wide range of "gratifications" that people may receive from mediated sports.

Using a student sample, Gantz looked at the motives for viewing football, baseball, hockey, and tennis on television. While the sample was motivated most strongly to watch team sports, there was surprising consensus across sports in the motivation structures related to viewing. The strongest motivation revolved around the desire to "thrill in victory." Viewers were curious about who would win, moved to root for favorite players and teams, and felt better by their winning. Next in importance was the motivation "to let loose." Here sports viewing gave one the excuse to drink alcohol, let off steam, and "get psyched" by the event. These motives were particularly evident when viewing took place in the company of friends. Of lesser importance were motives to learn about the game and players, and to pass time. Gantz suggests that most television sports fans have advanced knowledge about the sport and players, and attend to the televised contest for reasons other than having "nothing else to do."

Although an exploratory study, Gantz's research also makes inroads by linking motives to affective "feelings" (nervousness, excitement, anger, happiness) during sports viewing and to behaviors (talking, reading, drinking, applauding) both during and prior to the watching of televised sports. Viewers who "thrilled in victory" or "let loose" reported strong feelings and behaviors during the game, and also prepared for the televised contest with a most discernible set of behaviors. Two-thirds frequently talked to friends about the upcoming game, half frequently read in advance about the contest to be televised, and one-third often "fortified themselves" with a drink or two in preparation for the contest. Especially when viewing with others, these "sports fans" were the most likely to engage in communication behaviors — yelling in anger, disputing an official's calls or coach's tactics, or just talking about the action.

These findings and others from Gantz's (1981) study point to ways that a "gratifications" approach can serve as a starting point in understanding audience experiences with mediated sports. Other approaches will need to address the consequences of audience experience with mediated sport. These "effects" inquiries will nonetheless need to consider the ways audience gratifications transact with mediated sport content. The variants and degree of gratification experienced by the audience member will play a modifying role in the effects mediated sport can have (see Palmgreen, Wenner, & Rosengren, 1985).

Just as Gantz's results show that gratifications may differ when viewing takes place with friends, the context of exposure may also influence perceptions about the sporting event. Sapolsky and Zillmann (1978) found elements of social control guiding perception when a group of friends viewed a basketball game between American and Yugoslavian teams. The "friends" exerted social control so that the plays leading to Yugolav baskets were not enjoyed. When viewing of the same event took place in a larger group where friends were in the minority, the lessened social control allowed for the appreciation of good plays by the Yugoslavian team.

The earlier discussion of Edwards's (1973) American Sports Creed suggests that one promising avenue for other effects inquiries will be in the area of impact of mediated sport on values and ideology. Prisuta (1979) has taken a step in this direction by examining the socializing effects of televised sports on political values. In a study of high school students, Prisuta presents evidence that frequent television sports viewing is associated with a variety of conservative political values, and particularly promotes authoritarian and nationalistic values.

Another line of inquiry that seems obvious when looking at the nature of team sports such as football and hockey is the effect that viewing of "violent" sports programming may have on aggression. Looking at this question, an experimental study by Celozzi, Kazelskis, and Gutsch (1981) finds support for the basic premises in the work of Bandura (1973) and Berkowitz (1969) that suggest that exposure to violent programming tends to make one more aggressive. Celozzi et al. found that aggression levels increased in already aggressive male high school seniors upon viewing televised violence in ice hockey.

One element of mediated sports coverage that makes audience experience with it differ from observing a game in a stadium situation is the presence of the sports announcer. Some studies have begun to look at the influence of such "commentary" on television viewers' perceptions about sporting events. For example, Comisky, Bryant, and Zillmann (1977) found that commentary for a televised hockey game that stressed "roughness" in "normal action" play made it seem rougher than "rough" play, while commentary that did not emphasize roughness in "rough" play made it seem less rough. Higher entertainment value was also placed on televised action when commentary stressed the "roughness" that was not actually taking place in "normal" play.

Commentary may affect enjoyment of televised sports in other ways. Bryant, Brown, Comisky, and Zillmann (1982) have found that commentary contributes most to the enjoyment of a televised sports event when "opponents are perceived as hated foes, rather than as good friends or as neutral opponents" (p. 109). Such commentary that paints a picture of great animosity between opposing players or teams tends also to make the televised sporting event more exciting, involving, and interesting for the audience.

Mediated Sport Content

Just as assessing the impact of sports commentary is basic to audience inquiry, assessing the actual substance of commentary is basic to the study of mediated content. By revealing structure and content characteristics that may not be obvious, the intense examination of such "mediated sport language" can both influence audience study and illuminate the signposts of cultural significance.

Commentary in the form of "play-by-play" announcing is only one form of mediated sport language. Other variants are evident in game reporting and feature articles in newspaper sports pages and in popular sports magazines, in the sports reports within regularly scheduled news broadcasts, and in the specialized sports feature programming that leads in and out of game coverage or reviews the week's or day's sports contests.

The language of mediated sport often takes a vivid and dramatic form. It contrasts markedly with the pointedly descriptive language associated with "hard" news reporting in both the print and electronic media. Even with the expressed purpose of providing play-by-play descriptions of the game, "game" announcing provides a goodly portion of dramatic commentary.

In looking at the game commentary of television network football announcers, Bryant, Comisky, and Zillmann (1977) found that while descriptive sentences (72%) did indeed proliferate, more than a quarter of the sentences (27%) were dramatic and "intended to create the impression of conflict, intensify a struggle or emphasize something that was essentially superfluous to an account of the play as such but which could further the spectator's interest in the game" (p. 142).

Bryant et al. (1977) also found that drama was built by conflict posed in intrapersonal, rather than in team or interpersonal, terms. This was more frequently done through complimentary statements about players or teams than through derogatory remarks about them. Overall, more than half the dramatic sentences used four motifs: performance competence (ability, consistency, versatility), gamesmanship (strategy, leadership), comparison (with self or others), and the "old college try" (making up for shortcomings).

While such knowledge about dramatic commentary provides part of the cultural backdrop for mediated sport, there may be other content characteristics in game announcing that are more telling about cultural sensibilities associated with mediated sport. For example, one study found a high degree of covert racial prejudice in professional football announcers' commentary on the three major television networks. Rainville and McCormick (1977) conclude that, in describing play, "the announcer is building a positive reputation for the white player by more frequently praising him during play, more often depicting him as the aggressor, and granting him more positive status. The announcer is, at the same time, building a negative reputation for the black player by negatively comparing him to the other players, making negative references to his past achievements, and depicting him as the recipient of aggression" (pp. 24–25).

In this study the announcers were, as they remain largely today, white. As Rainville and McCormick (1977) note, this allows for commentary upon the "one sphere of social activity in which blacks have achieved success and prominence" (p. 21). Indeed, professional sports on television presents an unusual microcosm of American life. Blacks are proportionally over-represented as players and underrepresented as commentators and coaches. One of the few parallels to this in American life may be the military, where blacks are overrepresented as foot soldiers. However, unlike the world of combat, in the sporting world it is the foot soldiers (players), not the generals, who are the "stars" under media scrutiny. As it is a most unusual world that is being presented, the socialization that comes from it is most worthy of study.

Studies that examine game announcing for evidence of dramaturgical dominance or covert racial prejudice provide clues about the values that may be hidden in mediated game coverage. However, with televised game coverage, "mediated sports language" extends well beyond what the announcers say. Here, much of what the game means is expressed visually. Thus studies of visual language used to portray sports contests complement studies of game commentary.

It is fairly obvious that watching a game on television gives the spectator a completely different vantage point than watching the contest in the stadium. Both the context of viewing and the content of it are different. In viewing a televised game, the context includes the familiar surroundings of home, family, and friends, and the viewer is subject to "real-life" interventions that are not part of the stadium spectating experience (e.g., telephone calls, unexpected visitors). In the stadium, the spectator is among an unfamiliar mass of fans, but the sole reason for being there is to view the game. "Real life" does not as easily intervene.

In viewing the contest at the stadium, the fan takes in a large view—the players, the playing field, the other fans—and must decide what to focus on. In the mediated version, such "focus" is decided for the fan, by the television director who is making decisions about what is visually important. As Birrell and Loy (1979) have observed, such experience is not "integrative," and the technology has "transformed the sport spectacle, disrupting the natural rhythm of the game and synthesizing action through highlighting to enhance the excitement value" (p. 11).

This highlighting via "technological disruption" in televised sport comes about in many ways. Zoom lenses allow the view of the contest to be narrowed or widened. Isolated cameras focus on selected actions of an individual player or group of players. Split-screens allow the fan to focus on different aspects of the game at the same time, so that taking in both narrow and wide views of the action is possible. Instant replays of "isolated" aspects of action first seen in wide view allow the fan to reassess the play from multiple points of view. The instant replay also "fills time" between the plays on the field so that action seems "continuous" and "up close" even though it is neither. Time can be manipulated in other ways. Actions shown in slow motion extend time and magnify each movement so that significance unseen in real time may be apprehended. Time may also be speeded up or stopped (stop action), and events happening at different times may be juxtaposed (edited) to show relationships transcending their lack of temporaneousness.

Birrell and Loy (1979) suggest that these techniques "enhance the sport experience for the fan rather than diminish it" (p. 13). Simple observation holds this to be true. Attending the live game event at the stadium, American fans often come equipped not only with radios, but with portable television sets. This supplemental use of television is popular because it allows the fan "to see the game better." However, it is not so much the "technical enhancements" themselves, but how they are strung together to structure the event in a particular way that should be of greatest interest to the media scholar.

Williams (1977) has begun to look at this visual structure in the presentation of professional football by the three major television networks. His findings demonstrate how the televised or "medium event" imposes both its own structures and ideological viewpoints on the "stadium event." Individual shots had an average duration of 13 seconds, and by a wide margin tended to show individual players in close-ups or groups of players tightly framed by the camera. With such emphasis, the visual language reinforced commentary by casting action in terms of individual rather than team effort. In fact, only 4 per cent of the shots included a view of all 22 players on the field; a view which approximates the stadium spectating experience.

Not only were shots short and focused on individual action, but there was camera movement – panning, tilting, zooming – in over half of them. Williams (1977) found that such active camera movement, when combined with the editing strategy of breaking down action into short shots of selected players, served to generate excitement and to "focus attention on the ball and ball-carriers to the exclusion of other players as well as of the overall geometry of the game" (p. 137). In short, it seems that the visual language of televised football structures an exciting story of individual "heroes" engaged in team play, rather than teams playing each other.

Not only is there evidence that mediated sports in America places greater value on individualism than team effort, there is greater emphasis placed on the outcome – or winning – of a contest than on the process or fine points of playing it (Goldstein & Bredemeier, 1977). Leonard (1980) has remarked that "the prevailing sports ethos in America has shifted from 'It's not whether you win or lose, it's how you play the game,' to 'Winning isn't everything – it's the only thing'" (p. 244). Such values are expressed not only in game broadcasts, but also in reporting leading to and reflecting upon the game.

How the sportswriters and reporters on local television news programs portray winning and losing was the subject of Ekdom and Trujillo's (1986) study of coverage given to the Dallas Cowboys football team. Using a dramatistic approach, these authors isolated the rhetorical devices used in defining, explaining, and evaluating winning and losing. Their analysis suggests "that even though the 1985 Cowboys had a winning record (10·6), they were ultimately portrayed as failures by the Dallas sports media." Apparently, "winning" in the eyes of the media is more than merely winning games, it is a complex concept that is defined largely by media expectations of a team, both in a given game and over the course of a season.

Another study by Trujillo and Ekdom (1985) looks more broadly at the American cultural values associated with baseball sportswriting. Considered are the dominant themes guiding the *Chicago Tribune* coverage of the a 1984 Chicago Cubs baseball team, which gave the press high hopes with a winning season, but whose season ultimately came to a disappointing end in the playoffs for the National League championship. Trujillo and Ekdom show how themes posed throughout the season in oppositional pairs – winning and losing, tradition and change, teamwork and individualism, work and play, experience and youth, logic and luck – were used by the press to explain both the success and the failure of the team. Their study uses sports as a parable for American society, where similarly paradoxical themes often surround the ideologies of success.

How American political values are used in the "hyping" of the Super Bowl is the subject of Wenner's (1986) study of NBC's two-hour "pregame show" leading into their telecast of the National Football League's championship game. Looking at the fantasies surrounding the buildup of the game, Wenner found a rhetorical vision stressing nationalism, patriotism, racial and ethnic integration, rugged individualism, hard work, and other values central to the American Dream. One recurring strategy used by NBC's announcers was the painting of "Super Bowl Sunday" as an "unannounced American holiday." With the attention the announcers were giving to nationalistic values, this certainly was not an "unannounced" holiday.

Similarly, Real's (1975) cultural analysis of the Super Bowl game telecast sees this "main event" as a microcosm of American life. Real sees the televised game as replete with myth, heroic archetypes, and interlocking story lines involving lifelike issues of labor, management, territoriality, and property ownership. Real (1975) concludes:

> The structural values of the Super Bowl can be summarized succinctly: *North American professional football is an aggressive, strictly regulated team game fought between males who use both violence and technology to gain control of property for the economic gain of individuals within a nationalistic entertainment context.* The Super Bowl propagates these values by elevating one game to the level of a spectacle of American ideology collectively celebrated. (p. 42)

Real's cultural approach crosses over the line of examining content alone, and considers as well the media sports production complex in the context of American society. The component parts of the "infrastructure" Real points to are examined in the next section.

Mediated Sports Production Complex

The larger point that Real (1975) makes about the institutional organization of professional football—that "it is not *like* American business; it *is* American business" (p. 40)—can be extended to all mediated sport in America. In terms of communication transactions, the infrastructure can be broken into three component parts: sports organizations, media organizations, and sports journalists.

Most sports organizations have some involvement with the media. The results of high school baseball contests and occasional features on these teams and their star players appear in metropolitan daily newspapers. Even the results from industrial or recreational league contests may find their way into the local papers.

However, for the communication scholar, the focus is largely on those sports organizations that have ongoing "dependent" relationships with the media. There are a variety of these kinds of organizations. Obviously, professional sports teams fall into this fold, but even they are of varying character. Some professional teams are owned by large corporations with a variety of nonsports holdings (sometimes in the media industries), while other teams are the only business of the company.

Major colleges and universities playing "big time" college sports do so in the very profitable limelight of the media. Even though their sports teams are explicitly subsidiaries of their educational goals, mediated coverage of their sports teams may be the most visible products they offer to the mass marketplace, and, as such, are often a key to the institution's visibility in the educational marketplace.

Both collegiate and professional sports teams are subject to another layer of organizational control. Professional teams are franchised and governed by "leagues" such as the National Football League, Major League Baseball, and the National Basketball Association. Although occasionally competing leagues challenge these "major players" in the marketplace, the most lucrative media contracts are largely monopolized by the existing organizations and the teams that they franchise.

The character of organizational control over collegiate media contracts has changed recently. In the past, the National Collegiate Athletic Association had gained strength by being the sole agent of national broadcast rights for its member teams. In 1984, this practice was struck down by the Supreme Court as limiting competition and restraining trade in the marketplace. Individual colleges now negotiate these rights, but the NCAA still controls many aspects of intercollegiate sports that pertain to media.

Other sports organizations come into play when the media rights to the Olympic Games are put up for sale. For the 1984 Summer Games in Los Angeles, the International Olympic Committee, the U.S. Olympic Committee, and Los Angeles Olympic Organizing Committee all had a hand in distributing these rights. Not only are broadcast rights expensive for the Olympic Games — ABC paid over $316 million for rights to the 1984 Winter and Summer Games — but they come with "strings attached" about how the coverage may proceed (Miller, 1984).

Media organizations that cover sports are playing for similarly high stakes — betting that they will be able to sell the sports audience to advertisers at a hefty price. As is the case with sports organizations, these media organizations are of varied character. Playing for the highest stakes and the most visible of these media organizations are the three television networks — ABC, NBC, and CBS. Already centerpieces in well-established and highly diversified corporate entities, these networks have in recent years tended to be taken over by even larger "megacorporations." Although only a component part of the revenue-gaining strategies of these corporations, sports programming remains important in market positioning.

A "premium product"— the live coverage of major sporting events — proliferates in network programming on the weekends, and has found its way into prime time as well with *Monday Night Football* and *Monday Night Baseball* broadcasts. That its sports product is perceived as "premium" is crucial to a network's goal of maintaining dominance in the television marketplace. With decreasing market shares coming about in recent years with increased competition by cable networks and independent stations, holding the line with a "quality" sports image bolsters a network's entire programming schedule.

A second-tier, "off-network" product is offered by specialized cable networks and superstations. ESPN sends sports programming to cable viewers nearly 24 hours each day. This "live" coverage often includes "less premium" and more eclectic sporting events (e.g., pistol shooting). And, consistent with cable programming strategies (and more limited budgets), ESPN often reruns this programming in the days following the event. Most of the remainder of the ESPN schedule is filled in with non-contest-related sports programming. Some programming highlights, updates, and discusses the day's sports news (e.g., *Sportsworld*), some shows retrospective highlights (e.g., *NFL Football Highlights* from a 1963 championship game), and other programming focuses on audience interest in participating in a particular sporting activity (e.g., aerobic exercise programs or programs for fishing enthusiasts).

Cable superstations like WGN in Chicago and TBS in Atlanta are local television stations that are distributed via satellite to cable companies and then to their cable subscribers. These local stations aim to succeed in a national marketplace by offering programming of broad interest, but different from that offered by the big three television networks. Live sports programming fits that niche, drawing men away from the network prime-time programming that almost always rates higher with women. Also, superstations featuring sports frequently have a built-in supply of sports programming by way of a common ownership of both station and sports team. For example, WGN, the *Chicago Tribune*, and the Chicago Cubs are under common ownership. In Atlanta, Ted Turner owns TBS as well the town's baseball Braves and basketball Hawks.

In local markets, independent television stations and radio stations often seek to position themselves as sports stations by presenting play-by-play coverage of local teams in as many games and in as many sports as they can afford. Especially for independent television stations, the "sports station" image helps them in carving out an "island of success" against the major networks by drawing male viewers (Aiken, 1985). The identifiable "quality" image of a sports station gives radio stations a "hook" to position themselves in a large market, where they may be competing with as many as 70 other stations.

Local broadcast stations also feature sports reports within their news broadcasts. Depending on the demographics of the audience it is trying to attract and on whether or not it is trying to reinforce a sports image, the time a station devotes to sports reporting can be substantial, often rivaling that devoted to hard news. On Sundays, typically a slow hard-news day, one Los Angeles television station follows a 15-minute 11 p.m. news report with one of equal length reporting on the "busy" sports weekend. By doing so, the station succeeds in keeping some of the desired men up a little bit longer for their advertisers.

In the print marketplace, mediated sport plays a role similar to that in the local television newscast. For the major metropolitan daily, the sports section is largely a way for advertisers to reach men in an atmosphere they enjoy. A paper with a reputation for strong sports coverage will have little trouble selling advertising space to advertisers with an eye on men. The sports pages also help sell newspapers. Malette (1971) presents findings that "about 30 per cent of the people who buy their papers do it primarily for the sports news" (p. 109).

The sports section in daily metropolitan newspapers largely offers timely reporting about sports contests to its readers. Many of those readers may have seen the games in person or seen or heard play-by-play broadcasts. Fans can compare their perceptions of the events with those of "expert" reporters.

One of the main virtues of sports news as a commodity is its infinitely expandable middle. Feature coverage of major sports can be beefed up and reportage can be broadened in scope to include more obscure sports or to cover major sports at a more obscure level (e.g., covering high school contests). The sports section also offers the insights of columnists who comment on larger, less timely trends and often profile individuals involved with athletics. Feature material often precedes events that are to take place in the near future. These features may focus on teams, but most often isolate on individual players or coaches.

Sports magazines also concentrate on feature material of interest to the sports enthusiast. The features in these weekly or monthly magazines are less time bound, and tend to look backward at individuals or teams that have already played in a contest, rather than forward to an event about to happen. These magazines aim to subdivide the sports enthusiast market even further. Some magazines are of general interest, such as *Sports Illustrated* or *Sport*, while others are sport specific. Some stress rather general feature material and others, such as *Sporting News*, cater to the subset of fans with an apparently insatiable appetite for sports "statistics."

The symbiotic economic relationship between sports organizations and media organizations has created a large marketplace for mediated sport. However, the product for that market depends on the subculture and work of the sports journalist. The sports journalist is servant to many. Professional ethics call on the sports journalist to report the news accurately and fairly to the audience. At same time, the sports journalist often reports for a media organization that may make stylistic or substantive demands on that reporting. And finally, the sports journalist must remain on good terms with sports organizations, their teams, players, coaches, and other personnel, for without access to these sources, there is no access to the "inside story" that is so valued by the mediated sports audience.

As a result, the sports journalist must respond to a variety of countervailing pressures. The question of who is paying the bills resolves some of the dilemma. Often, local broadcast announcers are paid by the professional teams they are "reporting" on. This leads to the sports "journalist" becoming a "rooter" rather than "reporter." Sports organizations negotiate with broadcast organizations for the right to hire their own game announcers because they may fear that "negative reporting" about the home team could jeopardize ticket sales. However, even for the sports journalist being paid by a media organization, there are many pressures to prevent "calling it as they see it."

Smith's (1976) study of the sports journalism social system isolates myriad problems confronting the sports journalist. Many of these result from the persuasive influence of the sports promoter (in sports organizations) in doling out direct and indirect gratuities to the journalist. According to Smith (1976), the system is plagued by journalists faced with role conflict and misplaced priorities:

> The resultant of the interlocking between the sports journalist and the sport promoter is often a schizoid sports journalist. The sports journalist has dichotomous responsibilities. If he performs one of his functions, he automatically neglects the other. On the one hand he is supposed to be objectively reporting sports news to the public; on the other hand, he is expected to glorify a particular sport for the benefit of a promoter. Usually these two functions are in direct opposition to each other. (p. 13)

When he adds to these problems the often-noted problems associated with bringing in the "ex-jock" as substantive expert but amateur journalist, Smith

(1976) concludes that "sports journalism is not really a profession" (p. 21). It remains merely one cog in the wheel of the media sports production complex, and, as Real (1975) suggests, "American business."

Smith's study is unusual in that it looks intently at one element in the triad—sports journalist, sports organization, media organization—defining the media sports production complex. Most of the studies of the production complex have focused more broadly on the interrelationships among these component parts and the significance of them to larger society. For example, Parente (1977) looks at how the interdependence of sports and television has affected the sports product. He details how mandatory time-outs, foreshortened halftime intermissions, and even changes to playing fields have been instigated to make a "television sports product" come into line with other entertainment products on television.

While Parente (1977) sees an interdependent business relationship, he concludes that television is clearly the controlling stockholder: "Once a sport, league, or team has had its 'product' bought by television for use as programming, that entity can seldom exist thereafter, at least in the same style or manner, without the financial support of television" (p. 128). This seems a consensus view, even within the television industry. As ABC Sports' Roone Arledge has admitted: "So many sports organizations have built their entire budgets around network TV that if we ever withdrew the money, the whole structure would collapse" (Altheide & Snow, 1979, p. 217).

Altheide and Snow (1979) see this as changing not just selected rules governing the playing of sports, but the whole character of sports: "Not content with just broadcasting the game, television creates a game through the entertainment perspective" (p. 218). For them, this "entertainmentization" of sports has paralleled the rise of the "celebrity" sportscaster. A quick dose of celebrity is found in importation of the "ex-jock" with marquee value into the broadcast booth. Some sports organizations go overboard with this strategy; a case in point is the seven former players on the nine-man New York Yankees broadcast "team" (Newhan, 1986).

In the broadcast booth, a play-by-play announcer plays the lead role as "master of ceremonies," and the supporting cast is largely made up of ex-jocks who serve as "color" announcers. The color announcer fills in "dead spots" with insider's information. This insider's information can be technical background about the rules or statistical information with a bearing on strategy, but just as often may be a humorous "historical" story about the participants. Retold many times, these stories become part of the mythic structure of mediated sports culture.

These myths become part of the marketable commodity mix "sold" from the broadcast booth. In that "seasons" can be remarkably long in professional sports—162 games in Major League Baseball and 82 games in NBA basketball (not counting preseason and postseason playoff games)—much ritualism is involved in the regular consumption of game broadcasts. Also, over the course of these long seasons many lopsided contests occur. During these "runaway" games, something other than the action on the field has to be provided to "entertain" the fans at home. Without such "diversionary tactics" the broadcaster has not only a runaway game, but a runaway audience that is not there for commercials running late in the game broadcast.

The seeming success that "celebrity" and "entertainment" have had as commodities in the broadcast booth has led to the packaging of an overtly variant form on the playing field as well. Contrived spectacles of "celebritysport," where network "personalities" and/or ex-jocks "compete" in athletic events, have crept into the network schedules in recent years. Often, these "sporting" events are slapstick alterations of real sports, more typically associated with events scheduled for laughs at a company picnic (such as two-person "three-legged" potato sack races).

This rather ludicrous "entertainmentization" of sport ties back into the basic need to package an attractive product for the market. Marxist critics such as Hoch (1972) and Jhally (1984) would have a field day with sport so vigorously transformed for the market. "Celebritysport" would be seen as a case study in how value is created by the sports/media complex. Here, as Jhally (1984) has argued concerning all mediated sport, the "spectacle" is not so much a spectacle of sports as a "spectacle of accumulation."

However, as Jhally (1984) points out, the economic role of the mediated sports production complex is worked out within a cultural context: "Relationships between the media and audiences are characterized by negotiation and struggle rather than domination" (p. 48). It may be argued as well that relationships among the components of the media sports production complex are of a similar character.

The mediated sports product that ends up in the marketplace is not, in the strict sense, foisted upon an unknowing public. That public tends to embrace and reflect the values celebrated in mediated sport. As was pointed out earlier, these values are fairly conservative, authoritarian, nationalistic, and rather clearly in line with those embraced by the American Dream, Edwards's (1973) American Sports Creed, and Williams's (1970) assessment of American cultural values. Like many others, Jhally (1984) has observed:

> Sports are an explicit celebration of the *idealized* structures of reality—a form
> of capitalist realism. They mediate a vital social dialectic, providing both an

escape from the alienated conditions of everyday life and a *socialization* into these very same structures. (p. 51)

This celebration has been transformed and made a bit more public as sport has become a more well-entrenched media product. However, it is the dialectic that largely defines the product for the marketplace and necessarily fuels the relationships among the components parts of the mediated sports production complex as the product is readied for market.

Closing Remarks

In reviewing and analyzing the research about the communicative import of American mediated sport, this essay illustrates some of the possibilities in a transactional approach to the communication of sport. It is a first attempt at charting the substantive terrain that defines an area surprisingly overlooked by communication scholars. Also, in basic terms, the model suggests groundwork for a transactional theory of the communication of sport.

The analysis is informed by many of the generalizations that have come out of social science inquiry into sport. Direct parallels between the roles, functions, values, and ideologies of sport in American society and those in mediated sport have not been drawn. Instead, bridges have been built in an attempt to illustrate how the issues are transformed when analysis takes place in a communicative context.

The model takes an "inside out" look at the transacting parts of the social system that produce and consume mediated sports content. *Audience experience* is seen as active, but taking place within a cultural context. As such, audience experience may be thought of as a cultural indicator, rather than as proof of hegemonic control.

The research concerning audience experience with mediated sport has to this point raised many more questions than it has answered. Thus far there has been only exploratory inquiry into the motives for and gratifications derived from mediated sports. In the future, research of this type will need to look more closely at how the stadium audience experience differs from viewing a game at home. We also need to ask about the unique aspects of gratifications derived from televised sport compared to consumption of other forms of television content.

That certain kinds of television game commentary bring more "enjoyment" to sports fans points to other avenues of inquiry outside the game context. A good portion of mediated sports consumption has little to do with the information about who is winning or losing a game that is broadcast live. In that much mediated sports consumption is ritualized activity of minimal instrumental value, we might ask about what influences enjoyment of the sports pages or a radio talk show devoted to discussion of sports "issues."

Similarly basic questions remain to be asked about the effects of mediated sport on the audience. Preliminary evidence suggests that mediated sport has socializing effects, and in certain cases promotes conservative values and aggression. Although much is asserted by the critics, we know little about the range of ways mediated sport may contribute to socialization. Given that a good many of the athletic stars in the United States come from a minority group, we might ask how communication about sports influences our perceptions about racial and ethnic groups. Similarly, with more women participating in sports and partaking of mediated sports fare, questions need to be asked about the role the media's gender stereotyping plays in the socialization process. The effects of gender portrayals are not limited to females. How the stereotyped "macho" male athlete in the media affects the development of male adolescents seems an equally important question.

Mediated sports content serves as a cultural signpost for American society. It is a signpost built by many forces and written in many languages. Even within mediated sports content, there may be "competing" events being reported in different languages. As Bryant et al. (1977) suggest, commentary on a televised game may be quite at odds with the game that is being visually presented. Thus beginning a "deep reading" of mediated sports content requires some very basic decisions. Should the analysis deal extensively with the spoken or written forms of mediated sport, the visual aspects of it, or the interaction between spoken/written forms and the visual?

The ideological stance of the spoken and written forms of mediated sports language is relatively easy to discern. "Text" either appears on the written page or may easily be translated to it. As the preliminary research has suggested, value "motifs" may be found in a wide variety of settings, ranging from the pregame "festivities" leading into a televised sporting event to the game commentary itself, and extending into the sportswriting and televised reporting about a team over the course of a season. The dominant values of American culture – nationalism, patriotism, individualism, teamwork, and the like – are readily evident in the text of mediated sport.

Although not as easily deciphered, the visual languages of mediated sports also impose structures and ideological viewpoints on game coverage and other forms of sports "reporting." While research is still largely at the stage of defining the visual "vocabulary" of mediated sport, there is some indication that the visual language is biased toward individualistic values and the promotion of the "hero" over team effort. Much remains to be known about how the visual language of televised sport signifies meaning.

Regardless of the language structures they focus on, studies of mediated sports content may fuel inquiries concerning the audience experience. While the most basic of American values may perpetuate ethnocentrism, some values — such as covert racism in football game commentary — tend to subvert America's image of itself as a "melting pot" of ethnic integration. Other covert values in mediated sport lend themselves to further content and audience study. The covert gender valuation in the mediated sport marketplace may be one of the strongholds of traditional sexism in a society where such values are losing utility as social roles can less often be equated with gender.

The more overt values associated with mediated sport may be studied in the form of the advertising that surrounds it in the marketplace. Advertising is part of the mediated sport "message," and in many ways forms a contextual base from which the sporting event is understood. Especially in the American model, there would be no mediated sport without its commercial value, and thus it is surprising that no research has examined the content of the advertising messages being placed in a sporting context.

The dynamics in the *mediated sports production complex* create a "negotiated" and transformed sports product and bring it to market for the audience to sample. Mediated sports product is produced by the transaction of two types of organizations — sports and media — that bring pressures to bear on the sports journalist. Both sport teams and individual media outlets are subject to a higher level of organizational control. Teams that compete in the mediated marketplace are "owned" by organizations of widely varying character and priorities. Similarly, the individual media outlet — whether it be individual station, network, newspaper, or magazine — can find its sports marketing goals influenced by corporate pressures from above.

Surprisingly little scholarly inquiry has been aimed at understanding the organizational pressures that pertain to the production of mediated sports. Much about the economic transactions between sports and media organizations is reported in the trade press. Similarly, glimpses of internal decision making at both types of organizations have been provided by the popular press. Since this information provides only "snapshots," there remains a strong need for systematic research programs aimed at understanding the organizational situations in which mediated sports product is produced.

Similarly, apart from Smith's (1976) now somewhat dated study of the newspaper sports reporter, scholarly analysis of the occupational norms of the sports journalism social system has slipped through the cracks. Perhaps this has stemmed from the common perception that sports reporting is the "toy store" of the journalism world. Certainly, there are more "serious issues" out there in the world of journalistic watchdogging, but these "important" things may have no greater import in terms of understanding a culture.

The mediated sports complex is more often approached as a whole. Scholars have taken critical stances by piecing together fragments of knowledge about the component parts. In particular, Jhally's (1984) analysis suggests that there is much promise in historical critical analysis. Too often, however, critical scholars have jumped aboard the cultural hegemony bandwagon without taking a close look at the variety of mediated sports content in the marketplace and the varied uses to which that content is put.

The transactional approach to the study of mediated sport does not negate a critical perspective. In fact, it might be considered hypercritical, in that it demands thorough analysis of all of the subparts in the mediated sport social system before any judgment call is made. Looking for hegemony is one matter, but finding it prematurely without having surveyed the terrain of the audience is quite another. Unfortunately, this has been a glaring weakness in much critical scholarship.

A transactional view of mediated sport in culture requires many different kinds of assessments. Clearly, if we are to understand the communicative import of mediated sport, we cannot forget to ask the audience what they make of it. However, very often, the audience may not have a cogent idea of why they are using media in a certain way, or they may not be able to express it. To depend exclusively on audience assessments is to err in another direction. Such structural-functional assessments of the audience have largely drawn conclusions about system maintenance in a static system.

From a transactional perspective, communications systems are always in a state of flux; the dynamics of the communications process is what is being studied. Applied to the communication of sport, this transactional view can be both "neofunctionalist" and "neohegemonic." No doubt a critical stance is needed to formulate and test assumptions. And, equally, there is no doubt that the media sports system is an ever-evolving one. The system that is here today may not be there to be maintained tomorrow.

References

Aiken, E. G. (1985). Independent station programming. In S. T. Eastman, S. W. Head, & L. Klein (Eds.), *Broadcast/cable programming* (2nd ed., pp. 186–204). Belmont, CA: Wadsworth.

Alexander, J. C. (Ed.). (1985). *Neofunctionalism*. Beverly Hills, CA: Sage.

Altheide, D. L., & Snow, R. P. (1977). Sports versus the mass media. *Urban Life, 7,* 189–204.

Altheide, D. L., & Snow, R. P. (1979). *Media logic*. Beverly Hills, CA: Sage.

Balbus, I. (1975). Politics as sports: The political ascendancy of the sports metaphor in America. *Monthly Review, 26,* 26–39.

Bandura, A. (1973). Social learning theory of aggression. In J. F. Knutson (Ed.), *The control of aggression: Implications from basic research*. Chicago: Aldine.

Baseball bags almost $370 million in rights. (1988, March 7). *Broadcasting*, pp. 54–63.

Berkowitz, L. (1969). *The roots of aggression*. New York: Atherton.

Birrell, S., & Loy, J. W. (1979). Media sport: Hot and cool. *International Review of Sport Sociology, 14,* 5–19.

Broadcasters to spend $536 million on football. (1983, August 8). *Broadcasting*, pp. 40–42, 47, 52–53.

Bruner, J., Joly, A., & Sylva, K. (Eds.). (1976). *Play: Its role in evolution and development*. New York: Penguin.

Bryant, J., Brown, D., Comisky, P. W., & Zillmann, D. (1982). Sports and spectators: Commentary and appreciation. *Journal of Communication, 32,* 109–119.

Bryant, J., Comisky, P., & Zillmann, D. (1977). Drama in sports commentary. *Journal of Communication, 27,* 140–149.

Buell, J. (1980). Superhype. *Progressive, 44,* 66.

Buscombe, E. (1975). *Football on television*. London: British Film Institute.

Celozzi, M. J., Kazelskis, R., & Gutsch, K. U. (1981). The relationship between viewing televised violence in ice hockey and subsequent levels of personal aggression. *Journal of Sport Behavior, 4,* 157–162.

Comisky, P., Bryant, J., & Zillmann, D. (1977). Commentary as a substitute for action. *Journal of Communication, 27,* 150–153.

Cozens, F., & Stumpf, F. (1953). *Sports in American life*. Chicago: University of Chicago Press.

Dewey, J., & Bentley, A. F. (1949). *Knowing and the known*. Boston: Beacon.

Dobringer, W. M. (1969). *Social structures and systems*. Pacific Palisades, CA: Goodyear.

Edwards, H. (1973). *Sociology of sport*. Homewood, IL: Dorsey.

Eitzen, S., & Sage, G. H. (1978). *Sociology of American sport*. Dubuque, IA: Wm. C. Brown.

Ekdom, L. R., & Trujillo, N. (1986, February). *The rhetoric of winning and losing*. Paper presented at the annual meeting of the Western Speech Communication Association, Tucson, AZ.

Feshbach, S. (1969). The catharsis effect: Research and another view. In R. K. Baker & S. J. Ball (Eds.), *Violence and the media*. Washington, DC: Government Printing Office.

Fierman, J. (1984, November). Advertisers show signs of football fatigue. *Fortune, 110,* 141.

Freud, S. (1962). *Beyond the pleasure principle*. New York: Bantam.

Gantz, W. (1981). An exploration of viewing motives and behaviors associated with television sports. *Journal of Broadcasting, 25,* 263-275.

Goldstein, J. H., & Bredemeier, B. J. (1977). Socialization: Some basic issues. *Journal of Communication, 27,* 154-159.

Gramsci, A. (1971). *Selections from the prison notebooks* (Q. Hoare & G. Nowell-Smith, Eds.). New York: International.

Hastorf, A. H., & Cantril, H. (1954). They saw a game: A case study. *Journal of Abnormal and Social Psychology, 2,* 129-134.

Hoch, P. (1972). *Rip off the big game.* Garden City, NY: Doubleday.

Horton, D., & Wohl, R. (1956). Mass communication and para-social interaction. *Psychiatry, 19,* 215-229.

Ingham, A. G., & Loy, J. W. (1973). The social system of sport: A humanistic perspective. *Quest Monograph, 19.*

Ittelson, W. H., & Cantril, H. (1954). *Perception: A transactional approach.* Garden City, NY: Doubleday.

Jhally, S. (1984). The spectacle of accumulation: Material and cultural factors in the evolution of the sports/media complex. *Insurgent Sociologist, 3,* 41-57.

Leonard, W. M., II. (1980). *A sociological perspective of sport.* Minneapolis: Burgess.

Loy, J. W. (1978). The cultural system of sport. *Quest Monograph, 29.*

Loy, J. W., McPherson, B., & Kenyon, G. S. (1978). *Sport and social systems.* Reading, MA: Addison-Wesley.

McQuail, D. (1985). Gratifications research or media theory: Many models or one? In K. E. Rosengren, L. A. Wenner, & P. Palmgreen (Eds.), *Media gratifications research* (pp. 149-167). Beverly Hills, CA: Sage.

Mead, G. H. (1934). *Mind, self, and society.* Chicago: University of Chicago Press.

Melnick, M. J. (1979). A critical look at sociology of sport. In S. Eitzen (Ed.), *Sport in contemporary society* (pp. 19-35). New York: St. Martin's.

Mermigas, D. (1988, February 1). Olympics are major risk for networks. *Electronic Media,* pp. 36, 81.

Miller, S. (1984, November). Television and sports: The ties that bind. *USA Today, 113,* 81-83.

Morse, M. (1983). Sport on television: Replay and display. In E. A. Kaplan (Ed.), *Regarding television: Critical approaches—an anthology* (pp. 44-66). Frederick, MD: University Publications of America.

Newhan, R. (1986, April 20). In broadcast booth, Yankee nine talks it up. *Los Angeles Times,* part III, p. 3.

Nimmo, D., & Combs, J. E. (1983). *Mediated political realities.* New York: Longman.

Nixon, H. L. (1982). Idealized functions of sport: Religious and political socialization through sport. *Journal of Sport and Social Issues, 6,* 1-11.

Nowell-Smith, G. (1981). Television-football-the world. In T. Bennett (Ed.), *Popular television and film* (pp. 159-170). London: British Film Institute.

Palmgreen, P., Wenner, L. A., & Rosengren, K. E. (1985). Uses and gratifications research: The past ten years. In K. E. Rosengren, L. A. Wenner, & P. Palmgreen (Eds.), *Media gratifications research* (pp. 11-37). Beverly Hills, CA: Sage.

Panelists see sports saturation on television. (1985, April 22). *Broadcasting,* pp. 80-81.

Parente, D. E. (1977). The interdependence of sports and television. *Journal of Communication, 29,* 94-102.

Piaget, J. (1962). *Play, dreams and imitation in childhood.* New York: Norton.

Pooley, J. C., & Webster, A. V. (1976). The interdependence of sports, politics and economics. In A. Yiannakis, T. McIntyre, M. Melnick, & D. Hart (Eds.), *Sport sociology: Contemporary themes* (pp. 35–42). Dubuque, IA: Kendall-Hunt.

Prisuta, R. H. (1979). Televised sports and political values. *Journal of Communication, 29,* 94–102.

Rainville, R. E., & McCormick, E. (1977). Extent of covert racial prejudice in pro football announcers' speech. *Journalism Quarterly, 54,* 20–26.

Real, M. R. (1975, Winter). Super Bowl: Mythic spectacle. *Journal of Communication, 25,* 31–43.

Roberts, J., Arth, M. J., & Bush, R. R. (1959). Games in culture. *American Anthropologist, 61,* 597–605.

Roberts, J., & Sutton-Smith, B. (1962). Child training and game involvement. *Ethnology, 1,* 166–185.

Rokeach, M. (1973). *The nature of human values.* New York: Free Press.

Rose, D. (1982). A critique of non-normative sport sociology in the United States. *International Review of Sport Sociology, 17*(4), 73–89.

Rothenbuhler, E. W. (1987). Neofunctionalism for mass communication theory. In M. Gurevitch & M. Levy (Eds.), *Mass communication review yearbook* (Vol. 6, pp. 67–85). Newbury Park, CA: Sage.

Sage, G. H. (1979, September). Sport and the social sciences. *Annals of the American Academy of Political and Social Science, 445,* 1–14.

Sapolsky B. S., & Zillmann, D. (1978). Enjoyment of a televised sport contest under different conditions of viewing. *Perceptual and Motor Skills, 46,* 29–30.

Sciulli, D. (1985). The practical groundwork of critical theory: Bringing Parsons to Habermas (and Vice Versa). In J. Alexander (Ed.), *Neofunctionalism* (pp. 21–50). Newbury Park, CA: Sage.

Scott, J. (1970). *The athletic revolution.* New York: Free Press.

Smith, G. J. (1976). A study of a sports journalist. *International Review of Sport Sociology, 11*(3), 5–26.

Snyder, E. E., & Spreitzer, E. (1978). *Social aspects of sport.* Englewood Cliffs, NJ: Prentice-Hall.

Sobel, R. (1984, February 20). Webs pay hefty TV rights; regional cable expands. *Television/Radio Age, 31,* 35–37, 92–96.

Spencer, H. (1855, 1872). *Principles of psychology* (2 vols.).

Sutton-Smith, B., & Roberts, J. M. (1970). The cross-cultural and psychological study of games. In G. Lushhchen (Ed.), *The cross cultural analysis of sport and games* (pp. 100–108). Champaign, IL: Stipes.

Taaffe, W. (1985, February 11). He spent a lot to save a lot more. *Sports Illustrated, 62,* 168.

Tedesco, R. (1987a, March 23). Networks and ESPN satisfied with NFL deal. *Electronic Media,* pp. 4, 57.

Tedesco, R. (1987b, September 21). On the rebound: Sports regain viewers, advertisers. *Electronic Media,* pp. S1-S8.

Tedesco, R. (1988, January 25). ABC expects windfall from Super Bowl ads. *Broadcasting,* p. 16.

Trujillo, N., & Ekdom, L. R. (1985). Sportswriting and American cultural values: The 1984 Chicago Cubs. *Critical Studies in Mass Communication, 2,* 262–281.

Wenner, L. A. (1985a). Transaction and media gratifications research. In K. E. Rosengren, L. A. Wenner, & P. Palmgreen (Eds.), *Media gratifications research* (pp. 73-94). Beverly Hills, CA: Sage.

Wenner, L. A. (1985b). The nature of news gratifications. In K. E. Rosengren, L. A. Wenner, & P. Palmgreen (Eds.), *Media gratifications research* (pp. 171-193). Beverly Hills, CA: Sage.

Wenner, L. A. (1986, February). *The Super Bowl pre-game show: Fantasy becomes theme.* Paper presented at the annual meeting of the Western Speech Communication Association, Tucson, AZ.

Williams, B. R. (1977). The structure of televised football. *Journal of Communication, 27,* 133-139.

Williams, R. (1970). *American society: A sociological interpretation* (3rd ed.). New York: Alfred A. Knopf.

2

Media Made Sport:
A History of Sports Coverage in the United States

Robert W. McChesney

Sport and the mass media enjoy a very symbiotic relationship in American society. On one hand, the staggering popularity of sport is due, to no small extent, to the enormous amount of attention provided it by the mass media. On the other, the media are able to generate enormous sales in both circulation and advertising based upon their extensive treatment of sport. Media attention fans the flames of interest in sport and increased interest in sport warrants further media attention. This notion of symbiosis also provides a fruitful manner of approaching the history of the sport-mass media relationship in the United States. Virtually every surge in the popularity of sport has been accompanied by a dramatic increase in the coverage provided sport by the media. Furthermore, each surge in the coverage of sport has taken place during a period in which the mass media have sharply increased their penetration into the nooks and crannies of American social life.

Yet, the nature of this symbiotic relationship extends far beyond some sort of "you scratch my back and I'll scratch yours" phenomenon. The nature of the sport-mass media relationship has been distinctly shaped by the emerging contours of American capitalism since the 1830s. On one hand, much of sport and virtually all of the mass media have been organized as commercial enterprises throughout this history. Many of the specific developments in the sport-mass media relationship can be fathomed only through the continual recognition that each of these institutions has been constituted of individual units first and foremost striving for economic profit in some level of competition with each other. On the other hand, sport emerges as an institution especially well suited culturally and ideologically, first, to the emerging industrial capitalism of the century, and, second — and indeed far more so — to the mature corporate capitalist society of the twentieth century.

This chapter will review some of the critical developments in the sport-mass media relationship and the nature of sports journalism over the past 160 years. This is an ambitious goal, particularly for such a brief essay, and hence two provisos must be offered at the outset. First, some very important material must be either ignored or dealt with only in a most cursory fashion. The focus of the narrative will be to develop the notion of the symbiotic relationship as characterized above and, therefore, will draw upon material that best helps to illuminate this theme. Second, this chapter will make no attempt to explain the spectacular rise in the popularity of sport. This is a tremendously complicated issue that has rightly attracted attention from a host of disciplines. While this chapter posits mass media coverage as a sine qua non to the rise of sport to its position as a cornerstone of modern American culture, this is not meant to imply that media coverage alone caused the emergence of sport. Indeed, the mass media have largely capitalized upon other currents in American society and used them to their own advantage.

Prior to the 1830s, the preponderance of newspapers and magazines were directed at a relatively small and well-to-do portion of American society. Nonetheless, between the American Revolution and the era of Jacksonian democracy, the literacy rate gradually increased. The first three decades of the nineteenth century witnessed a sharp increase in magazine publishing, with several hundred magazines commencing operations during this period. These magazines were quite unlike those found in the periodical industry that would emerge later in the century. In a manner similar to the newspaper industry of the period, magazine publishing was not especially profitable and, indeed, most publishers linked their magazines to other professions and interests, frequently of a political nature. There was nothing remotely resembling a profession of journalism at this time; in general the editor-publisher was the sole owner, manager, and primary author for his or her particular magazine.

The first American magazine dedicated to sport made its debut in the late 1820s. Seven sport magazines appeared between then and 1835, but only two would survive more than three years. These magazines, and the American reading public, were strongly influenced by the well-established sporting magazine industry of Great Britain, which had emerged by the 1790s. The dominant American sport magazines of this period were John Stuart Skinner's *American Farmer* and *American Turf Register* and William Trotter Por-

ter's *Spirit of the Times*. Sport was generally considered vulgar and dis-
reputable among a large portion of the American reading public at the time.
Hence these magazines tended toward the coverage of more respectable
endeavors, like horse racing, and tread gently in their treatment of sports
such as boxing, which tended to appeal to the lower classes. Magazines like
Spirit of the Times published columns of schedules and results from race
courses all over the country (Stevens, 1987). Many of those who wrote for
the sporting press at this time did so under pseudonyms, to protect their real
identities (Berryman, 1979).

American society entered a period of dramatic social change in the 1830s
and 1840s. The first great wave of industrialization swept the Northeast, and
the populations of the major cities swelled with immigrants from abroad and
from the countryside. There was a tremendous expansion in the size of the
reading public as well as a growing interest in sport. In addition, it became
clear that magazine publishing could be a very profitable enterprise. Porter's
Spirit of the Times became the dominant sport periodical and saw its circulation expand to 100,000 by the 1850s. Porter expanded coverage to boxing,
and he made a concerted effort to establish cricket as the national game in
the 1840s (Nugent, 1929). By the 1850s Porter decided to emphasize the
emerging sport of baseball as the American national game, and he did much
to popularize the rules and terminology of the sport. This process was
accentuated by Frank Queen's *New York Clipper*, which was founded in 1853
and quickly replaced the *Spirit of the Times* as the premier sporting weekly.
The *Clipper* employed Henry Chadwick, the first full-fledged American
sportswriter, whose efforts to popularize baseball earned him the nickname
of "The Father of the Game" (Betts, 1953a; Stevens, 1987).

The 1830s and 1840s also witnessed the birth of the modern newspaper
industry, which would generate profit as much from the sale of advertising
space as from circulation. With decreasing printing costs and an expanding
market, there emerged the "penny press," aimed at a working-class and
middle-class urban readership (Schiller, 1981). While coverage was modest
by later standards, sport began to receive regular attention from newspapers
vying for a large readership. James Gordon Bennett's *New York Herald* was
in many respects the pacesetter, with its coverage of prizefighting, thorough-
bred racing, and trotting matches. Bennett was one of the first exponents of
"sensationalism" as a means of generating circulation, and sport fit comfortably within this rubric. Yet sport was far from acceptable as a topic for newspaper coverage at this time; Bennett's *Herald* occasionally expressed regret
at the role of sport in society but continued to cover it nonetheless. Horace
Greeley's *New York Tribune* also covered major sporting events, as did

Henry Raymond's very respectable *New York Times*, albeit with considerable regret. By the Civil War, major prizefights and horse races received coverage in most daily newspapers, but there was still nothing along the lines of a regular sports page or sports department. Coverage was sporadic, seasonal, and highly regional (Betts, 1974).

During the middle third of the nineteenth century, sport became increasingly organized and commercialized. The Civil War introduced baseball to an entire generation of Americans, as the troops on both sides played the game when time permitted. Indeed, baseball emerged as the preeminent national team sport during this period. By 1869 the first publicly proclaimed professional baseball team was established, and an organized league of professional teams, the National League, followed shortly thereafter. A number of sportswriters, particularly Henry Chadwick, actively encouraged the creation of the professional league and helped to standardize the game's rules (Stevens, 1987). Chadwick and a handful of other metropolitan sportswriters were responsible for the development of box scores and the extensive statistical analysis of baseball (Voigt, 1966, p. 94). The development of organized professional play, with standardized rules and statistics, would permit vastly expanded coverage of baseball in the future.

The sporting press of the middle nineteenth century also performed a crucial function by actively working to legitimate sport as a cultural institution. The Puritan legacy of general hostility toward sport was greatly undermined by the developments of the nineteenth century. The newspapers of the major cities and the sport magazines became increasingly assertive by midcentury concerning the health benefits of athletics to urban dwellers. Indeed, the tone gradually shifted from a mild defense of athletics to the promotion of sport as the ideal mechanism to train men to compete in the battle of life, particularly in the unnatural urban environment (Adelman, 1986). By the end of the century, there would be an extensive "Muscular Christian" movement that would extol the virtues of sport for society (Mrozek, 1983). While the general acceptance of professional sports would take considerably longer, this was a necessary first step.

The 1880s and 1890s were another period in which there was a surge of interest in, as well as media coverage of, sport. In addition, this was a period of intense industrialization, immigration, and urbanization; in many respects this was the period of America's transformation into a modern, industrial world power. Professional baseball became entrenched as the national spectator sport and by the beginning of the twentieth century two national leagues fielded professional teams in most of the major cities of the

Northeast and Midwest. Boxing moved from the saloon brawls of the 1830s and 1840s to organized bouts held in large buildings. Recreational activities such as golf and bicycling came to play a prominent role in the lives of countless middle- and upper-class Americans.

This was the period in which newspapers began the process of supplanting weekly magazines as the primary medium covering sport. Sport magazines did not suffer during this period by any means. There were 48 sport periodicals in the 1890s, compared to only 9 in the 1860s and 3 in the 1840s (Betts, 1974, p. 377). Indeed, the *National Police Gazette*, which was transformed into a sporting magazine by Richard Kyle Fox, surged to a nationwide circulation of 150,000 by the 1880s. Some issues sold as many as 400,000 copies. With a large readership among the "masses," the *National Police Gazette* emphasized boxing and baseball and was generally regarded as the "arbiter of sports news" (Betts, 1953a, p. 51). In many respects Fox showed newspaper publishers the potential for attracting a mass readership through sport coverage.

Newspaper circulations soared to previously unimagined heights in the 1880s and 1890s as technological innovations reduced the cost of printing while the swelling cities provided an enormous market. American capitalism was continuing to evolve and commercial advertising was becoming a primary competitive sales weapon for retail businesses. Newspaper publishing was becoming a big business and publishers were beginning to accrue nearly one-half of their revenues from advertising. Sport, with its proven capacity to attract readers, became a logical area of emphasis in this era of "yellow journalism," a period in which the journalistic conventions of earlier times were shredded in the competitive fight for profit. To some extent the sensationalism of the late nineteenth century was but a much larger version of the emergence of the penny press in the 1830s.

New York, Chicago, and a handful of other major cities were the forerunners in sport journalism during this period; other cities would follow suit gradually over the following generation, depending upon their level of development of sport and sport journalism. James Gordon Bennett's *Herald* continued to provide ample coverage of sport but was passed by in the 1880s by Charles Dana's *New York Sun* and Joseph Pulitzer's *New York World*. In 1883, Pulitzer established the first sport department, and prominent fights or races received front-page coverage. Most major newspapers had their own sports editors and staffs by the end of the century. In 1895, William Randolph Hearst, in the midst of his circulation war with Pulitzer, introduced the first distinct sports section in his *New York Journal*. This innovation caught on gradually in the major cities before becoming a staple item for a major daily newspaper in the 1920s (Betts, 1953a). And with the emergence of the telegraph, newspapers were capable of providing timely sports information from anywhere in the nation.

This was the period that witnessed the emergence of sports journalism as a distinct genre. As David Voigt (1966) has observed, baseball writers in particular "enjoyed greater literary freedom" than other newspaper writers and they tended to develop an "exaggerated, colorful descriptive style" (p. 93). Sportswriters became celebrities in their own right. The prose was often very colorful and entertaining. Newspaper publishers bid for the services of the most popular sportswriters. Indeed, the development of the newspaper sports department and the regular sports section clearly enhanced interest in sport during this period; one no longer needed to attend games or be an athlete to enjoy sports. The newspapers did everything they could to encourage this development, even going so far as to publish the rules of various games to educate the uninitiated.

The last two decades of the nineteenth century truly marked the crystallization of the modern sport-media symbiotic relationship. Professional baseball teams were becoming recognized as a source of civic pride, and newspapers found it incumbent upon themselves to support their cities' franchises. In Kansas City, for example, the *lack* of a developed sports journalism probably prevented the success of Major League Baseball there in the late nineteenth century (James, 1985). Sportswriters such as Henry Chadwick served as advisers to the baseball owners on the most weighty of issues. When the baseball writers formed a national association in 1887 to standardize scoring and promote the game, they noted that, as for the relationship of the owners and the baseball writers: "All sides now recognize that their interests are identical. The reporters have found in the game a thing of beauty and a source of actual employment. The game has found in the reporters its best ally and most powerful supporter. Hence the good feeling all along the line" (Seymour, 1960, p. 351).

From the turn of the century until the end of World War I, sport consolidated its position in American society and increasingly became a national phenomenon. Whereas many newspapers outside of the major cities had very little coverage of sport in the 1880s and 1890s, by 1910 virtually every paper gave prominent play to major sporting events, like championship prizefights and horse races, and the World Series in baseball, which had been established in 1903. This "nationalization" of sport was greatly encouraged by improvements in transportation, communication, and social mobility. In addition, World War I, in a manner far more extensive than the Civil War, encouraged the nationalization of sport by popularizing and promoting sport among soldiers from all regions of the nation (Lewis, 1973).

The 1920s was the decade in which sport assumed its modern position as a cornerstone of American culture. The decade is commonly referred to as the "Golden Age of Sports" in both common and academic parlance. Noted sport historian John Rickard Betts (1952) has observed that "sport swept over the nation in the 1920s and, at times, seemed to be the most engrossing of public interests" (pp. 422–423). Warren Susman (1975) has written that

it was in the '20s that the American infatuation with professional athletics began, giving a virtual coup de grace to religion as the non-economic and non-sexual preoccupation of millions of middle-class Americans. (pp. 191–192)

In the 1920s sport emerged as a prime source of entertainment and communal bonding for Americans in a society that had been revolutionized over the preceding two generations (Lipsky, 1981). This was also the decade when sports moved to its position as an indispensable section of the daily newspaper — Robert Lipsyte (1975) has argued that the Golden Age of Sports was really the Golden Age of Sportswriting (p. 170). In the 1920s, tendencies that had been hinted at for 40 years crystallized, and the basic dynamic that has propelled the sport-newspaper relationship to the present day came into play; hence that era merits a relatively close exposition.

To understand why newspapers would turn over such a substantial portion of their pages to sport, it may be helpful to turn to a broader political economic view of American society. The 1920s was the decade that marked the complete establishment of oligopolistic, corporate capitalism as America's political economic system. As Alfred DuPont Chandler (1977) has noted, by the end of World War I,

the shakedown period following the merger movement was over. The successful mergers were established and the unsuccessful ones had failed. Modern business enterprise dominated American industries, and most of these same firms continued to dominate their industries for decades. (p. 345)

Chandler's schema was certainly present in the newspaper industry of the 1920s (Covert, 1975). As Alfred McClung Lee (1937) notes, after World War I, "the major units in the industry have become huge, relatively stable, monopolistic ventures" (p. 173). The total number of newspapers declined, while circulation increased by 25%. Major newspaper chains came to dominate the industry, and by 1933 fully 40 cities with populations over 100,000 were one-newspaper towns (Weinfeld, 1936, p. 368).

Another basic aspect of corporate capitalism also had a serious impact upon the newspaper industry. Advertising, which had been on the periphery of the economy in the nineteenth century, became a primary form of competition for large corporations in oligopolistic industries where explicit price warfare had become generally recognized as unhealthy (Baran & Sweezy, 1966; Pope, 1983). Advertising accounted for only 50% of newspaper revenues in 1890; by 1929 the portion had risen to 75% (Lee, 1937, p. 749). The growth in advertising sales largely fueled the newspaper boom of the 1920s, and, indeed, it has accounted for the growth not only in the newspaper industry but in the broadcast media as well ever since. In short, profitability in newspaper publishing was now based on the capacity of the newspaper to attract a large readership that could then be "sold" to commercial advertisers.

In this context, the three dominant editorial trends of American newspapers in the 1920s become understandable, and coverage of sport fit quite comfortably within each of them. First, newspapers tended to decrease their coverage of "hard news" and politics and instead emphasized escapist and sensational fare that would attract the largest possible readership (Villard, 1944). Sport fit perfectly within this conception of the press. A 1930s survey revealed that fully 80% of all male newspaper readers read some portion of the sports page on a frequent basis (Slusser, 1952, p. 4). One survey of circulation managers in the 1940s indicated their belief that fully 25% of all newspapers were sold on the basis of their sports sections (Woodward, 1949, p. 35).

Second, newspapers tended to standardize and rationalize the editorial process to reduce costs. In an oligopolistic market, these cost reductions could be passed along almost directly to the bottom line. This led to what Villard (1944) has termed the "mass production of dailies" (p. 6). The wire services enjoyed a period of great expansion after World War I, as syndicated material was far less expensive than staff-generated material (Lee, 1937, p. 526). In addition, one survey has shown that as much as 50–60% of all news articles appearing in the metropolitan press of the 1920s — including the "prestige" papers — were generated by press agents for specific interests (Schudson, 1979, p. 144).

Coverage of sport fit perfectly within this rubric. Much of the copy was generated by wire services; in the 1920s the Associated Press established a separate sports department, with a full-time staff of twelve (Nugent, 1929, p. 338). Furthermore, sport promoters and organizations were often willing to underwrite newspapers' expenses to gain coverage; indeed, this was the standard practice in professional baseball (Voigt, 1970, 1976). And, finally, outright payoffs to sports editors and reporters for coverage were not uncommon, particularly with regard to boxing (Lipsyte, 1975; Shecter, 1969; Tunis, 1928).

Third, newspapers of the 1920s began to deemphasize the strident political partisanship that had been expected of publishers in the nineteenth century (Link & Catton, 1967, p. 296). As Silas Bent noted in 1927: "The deplorable fact is that mass production demands a product which will offend as few as possible among hundreds of thousands of readers" (p. 264). Yet, while professing nonpartisanship on the surface, newspapers, as huge corporations supported largely through advertising from other businesses, became what John Tebbel (1963) has termed "by and large a conservative defender of the status quo" (p. 228).

Sport was very well suited to the editorial needs of the emerging giant newspaper corporations. Sport was "safe" ideologically and did not antagonize any element of the desired readership. It did not even offend those who were put off by the sex and sensationalism of the front page. Sport also lent itself to all sorts of civic boosterism on the part of the newspaper. As sport gave cohesiveness and identity to a community, a newspaper's coverage and promotion of sport could be considered a significant contribution to its metropolis. Finally, coverage of sport never called into question the dominant social relations. It offered the spirit and excitement of conflict and struggle in a politically trivial area.

Whereas one survey showed that the average newspaper devoted .04% of its editorial coverage to sport in 1880 and 4.0% in 1900, by the 1920s the proportion of editorial space ranged from 12% to 20% for virtually every daily newspaper (Schlesinger, 1933, p. 199). Sport historian Benjamin Rader (1983) has observed that "nothing before or since—not even the cool waves of television—created quite the same hot romance between sport and the public as the newspapers in the 1920s" (p. 199). The typical sports section, which was commonplace by the 1920s, was filled with color and excitement. It would have been difficult *not* to be a sports fan if one read a newspaper and had the slightest inclination in that direction. Sportswriters were major figures; at best, styles ranged from the colorful verse of Grantland Rice to the literary stylishness of Paul Gallico, Damon Runyon, and Westbrook Pegler. At worst, there was a pervasive cliché-ridden mediocrity. All sportswriters tended to glorify sport heroes and present them as larger-than-life figures (Rader, 1984, p. 21; Stevens, 1987, pp. 7–8).

As sport and sports coverage flourished in the 1920s, so did their symbiotic relationship. The close interaction between sports promoters and sportswriters was at times so corrupt that it led more than one sportswriter to quit (Tunis, 1928). Newspapers even became promoters themselves on occasion; Captain Joseph Medill Patterson, publisher of the *Chicago Tribune* and the *New York Daily News*, helped introduce the amateur boxing Golden Gloves competitions in both Chicago and New York. Arch Ward, sports editor of the *Chicago Tribune*, was responsible for devising both the baseball All-Star Game and the College All-Star Football Game (Rader, 1984, p. 20). Newspapers across the country became active in promoting participant and spectator sport activities in their communities.

Baseball, boxing, and college football were the prime beneficiaries of the sport boom in the 1920s. Major League Baseball was still the premier spectator sport and had the strongest standing relationship between management and the press. Its attendance doubled in the 1920s, and Babe Ruth of the New York Yankees became a national hero. Boxing was able to shed its reputation for sleaziness and become a national institution of sorts; heavyweight champion Jack Dempsey even had an audience with an "unusually talkative" President Coolidge. This would have been unthinkable a generation earlier (Roberts, 1979, p. 195). No small part of boxing's surge was due to the extraordinarily skillful promotional work of Tex Rickard, who managed both Madison Square Garden's boxing cards and heavyweight champion Jack Dempsey. Rickard was especially adept at cultivating the press, and it was not uncommon for him to use payoffs to assure favorable publicity (Shecter, 1969, pp. 21–22).

Perhaps the most dramatic success story of the 1920s was the emergence of college football. Prior to the 1920s, college football was generally a sport played by well-to-do college boys for their fellow students, family, and alumni. In the 1920s the sport became a mass attraction; revenues for 65 leading football schools more than tripled during the decade. Colleges built enormous stadiums to accommodate the spectators, often with generous assistance from local businesses and alumni, and 55 new concrete stadiums were constructed as seating capacity nearly tripled during the decade (Lasch, 1978, pp. 118–120; Steiner, 1933, pp. 88–89). The intense pressure to field a winning team brought scandal and corruption to this "amateur" sport. Many academics were dismayed by the emphasis on football played by students who often were little more than professionals (Gallico, 1938).

The controversy over the huge role of intercollegiate football dominated American campuses through the 1920s. Indeed, an extensive study of the subject funded by the Carnegie Foundation placed a large part of the blame on newspapers for "distorting" the importance of football in college life. The study examined several major urban newspapers and discovered that the space allocated to college sports, mostly football, had more than tripled between 1913 and 1927 (Savage, 1929, chap. 11). Like baseball and boxing, college football lent itself especially well to newspaper coverage. There were several conferences with set schedules and championships, breeding the sort of statistics, scores, and heroics that the sporting press coveted. There was scarcely any remorse expressed by publishers or sports editors for their extensive coverage and promotion of the college game. One social critic commented that the press treated college football like a "heroic god that the American masses are supposed to worship" (Engdahl, 1925).

The 1920s was also a watershed decade for the sport-mass media relationship because of the emergence of radio broadcasting. In 1922, radio was found in only 1 of every 400 homes, but by 1929 fully one-third of American homes had radios (Spalding, 1963–64, p. 35). During the early and mid-1920s, sport was capitalized upon by broadcasters to promote the acceptance of this new medium (Jhally, 1984, p. 45). Sports were not yet broadcast on a regular basis, but ad hoc networks were established for major prizefights, football games, and the World Series. When the Dempsey-Tunney championship bout was broadcast in 1927, it was estimated that it generated sales of over $90,000 worth of radio receivers in one New York department store alone (Betts, 1952, p. 471).

Yet as much as sport contributed to popularizing radio, radio contributed even more to the popularity of sport; it opened up new vistas for millions who had never had access to a major sporting event in the past. The emergence of broadcasting continued the nationalization of sport and helped to entrench it even more as a fundamental social institution. The dominant sports broadcaster of the 1920s was Graham McNamee, who had little understanding of sports and frequently made errors while broadcasting sports events. Nonetheless, McNamee had a soothing voice and a tremendous flair for the dramatic. According to *Radio Digest*, 127 fight fans dropped dead listening to McNamee's tense description of the second Tunney-Dempsey heavyweight fight (Rader, 1984, p. 25). McNamee was the first instance of a sports broadcaster who was a celebrity and, for career purposes, an entertainer above all else (Parente, 1974, p. 34).

By the early 1930s, radio broadcasting had become dominated by two major networks, the National Broadcasting Company (NBC) and the Columbia Broadcasting System (CBS), which were finding it very profitable to sell time on the network stations to advertisers. Advertisers soon began to purchase the right to broadcast major sports events. In 1934, for example, the Ford Motor Company paid $100,000 for the privilege of sponsoring the

World Series on both major networks (Rader, 1984, p. 25). Yet many in baseball were convinced that radio broadcasting of baseball games would hurt attendance, and in 1932 the owners came very close to forbidding teams to let their games be broadcast (Parente, 1974, p. 38). By the 1940s this fear had subsided, and all the major league teams had contracts with broadcasters and advertisers to broadcast all of their home games. The New York Yankees, for example, received $100,000 per year from three advertisers in the late 1930s. Most teams had their own broadcasters, who would be on the payroll of either the advertisers or, more likely, the teams themselves. This set the pattern for the "unobjective" or "homer" baseball announcing that still exists today.

Radio broadcasting of sports events reached its mature stage in the late 1940s and early 1950s. The networks broadcast all major national sports events and, furthermore, most professional baseball and major college football teams had contracts either with broadcasters or, more likely at this point in time, directly with advertisers who would then negotiate their own deals with commercial stations to broadcast the games. Most baseball teams could not sell the rights to broadcast their "away" games; rather, stations would "re-create" the games in their studios, with announcers improvising the action off of the Western Union ticker. When the courts ruled in 1955 that broadcasters had to pay teams for the right to "re-create" their games, the practice came to a virtual halt (Rader, 1984, pp. 27–28).

Radio sports broadcasting held its own quite well, in a competitive sense, during the first decade of televised sport and well into the late 1950s. While sport did play a prominent role during television's early years, it did so in a manner that would not anticipate the sports-television "revolution" of the late 1960s and early 1970s. The nature of the technology made it difficult to telecast team sports effectively at the time. Indeed, two of the leading sports on television were professional wrestling and Roller Derby. They were often broadcast during prime time, since they were ideally suited for low-budget television; a single camera could focus on one or two people at a time. Both sports consisted of staged violence, and the promoters were so eager for publicity that they frequently would not even charge stations for broadcast rights (Powers, 1984, pp. 48–49; Rader, 1984, pp. 37–39). At its high point, wrestling was broadcast by over 200 stations on a weekly basis, but it was quickly relegated to the fringes of television, along with Roller Derby, as television turned to baseball and football and more expensive nonsports prime-time fare by the mid-1950s.

The one traditional American sport that was permanently altered by television in the late 1940s and 1950s was boxing. Like wrestling, it was ideally suited to the technology of the period. Rader (1984) has noted that during this period "the passionate affair between television and professional fighting turned into an orgy" (p. 41). Fight nights were commonplace on television during this period over both the networks and independent stations and, indeed, some local broadcasters even staged their own fight cards. The saturation of boxing over the air led to the demise of local fight clubs, as fight fans now stayed home to watch the fights on TV; there were but 50 fight clubs in 1960, compared to 300 in 1952, and the number of professional boxers declined by more than 50%. Furthermore, sluggers came across on television far more effectively than finesse fighters, and promoters and producers gave brawlers the highest priority. Finally, there was an incessant need not only for fighters to fill out the television cards, but for fighters with winning records who would make desirable match-ups. Since both of these criteria were impossible to fill, the result was a wave of corruption and scandal unusual even by boxing's own standards. The sport entered the 1960s a shell of its former self; the first effect of television on organized sport was a knockout punch (Rader, 1984, pp. 40–46).

Both Major League Baseball and college football were apprehensive about telecasting their regular season games during the early 1950s. Both were suffering from severe attendance slumps after World War II, while minor league baseball, like boxing clubs, had been decimated. Many felt that television was to blame. The National Collegiate Athletic Association (NCAA) even placed severe restrictions on the ability of broadcasters to televise college football games; these restrictions began to be lifted only when colleges began to sense the amount of money that could be made by doing so (Rader, 1984, pp. 67–75). Furthermore, those who managed the major networks were far from convinced that sports programming was especially profitable; it was deemed to have little appeal for affluent viewers and women (Powers, 1984, pp. 52–53).

Everything began to change by the late 1950s and early 1960s. First, television came to penetrate the overwhelming majority of American homes; it was now clearly a mass medium. Second, the technology for sports broadcasting radically improved with the advent of color television, videotape (with its slow-motion and instant-replay capacities), satellites, and portable cameras. Third, Congress passed the Sports Broadcasting Act of 1961, which permitted professional sports teams in a league to negotiate as one unit with broadcasters. This had previously been considered an infringement of antitrust laws. Fourth, the networks and stations began to purchase broadcast rights directly from the teams and leagues and then sold time on those telecasts to advertisers. These two developments made sports broadcasting potentially a far more lucrative operation for sport owners and broadcasters alike. But the most critical factor was simply that certain advertisers discovered that sports provided access to a very desirable market – not only for "blue-collar" products like beer and razor blades, but for big-ticket items like automobiles and business equipment.

The first sport to ride the wave of all these factors was professional football through the National Football League (NFL). In the early 1950s, pro football was a minor attraction, relative to baseball and the college game, with a fairly small but devoted following. With national exposure in the late 1950s and early 1960s, the sport, which seemed ideal for video transmission, captured the national imagination. Within a decade it became America's leading spectator sport. The commissioners, Bert Bell in the late 1950s and later Pete Rozelle, understood fully the importance of television to the league's success. In 1958, Bell permitted "television time-outs" to increase the amount of advertising revenue each game could generate (Powers, 1984, p. 84). Rozelle's function was basically to negotiate television contracts, something at which he proved rather adept. In 1962, CBS agreed to pay the NFL $4.5 million per year for broadcast rights; just two years later, as Nielsen ratings climbed by 50%, Rozelle negotiated a pact with CBS that called for $14 million per year (Rader, 1984, pp. 89–92). Broadcast revenues had become the independent growth variable in the future of the NFL.

The tremendous success of the NFL on CBS drew the envy of entrepreneurs in major cities without NFL franchises as well as of the other major television networks, NBC and ABC. In 1960, the American Football League (AFL) was established and had a contract with ABC prior to its first kickoff. This was a major development in the sport-mass media relationship: The networks, with an eye on anticipated advertising sales, essentially created or encouraged the creation of new sports products with the hope that audiences would develop. And when new sport products were not created to satisfy advertisers, existing sport enterprises were radically altered to maximize potential broadcast rights payments (Sugar, 1978, pp. 54–60).

The AFL survived strictly on the basis of its ABC contract in the early 60s. Then, in 1965, after NBC lost its bidding war with CBS for NFL rights, NBC agreed with the AFL to a rights contract worth $42 million over five years. This was an astronomical sum that nearly approached the NFL contract with CBS. The aim of NBC with this contract, quite clearly, was to provide the new league with the wherewithal to field a major-league product. In effect, the network had become a copromoter of the AFL. The plan worked. The AFL began to sign top NFL players and the NFL, once it realized that the NBC contract guaranteed the AFL's existence, agreed to a merger. As part of the deal, NBC was permitted to telecast half of the merged league's games along with CBS.

The 1960s witnessed the first wave of the TV sports explosion. ABC, the weakest of the three networks, was the most aggressive; it launched *Wide World of Sports* in 1961. This was a weekly program that covered a variety of sports events and was another example of a network becoming essentially a sports promoter. ABC also pioneered coverage of the Olympic Games, taking them from relative anonymity to the premier sporting event telecast every four years. Rights payments for Summer Olympics broadcasts jumped from a then astronomical $5 million in 1968 to several hundred million dollars by the 1980s. ABC also pioneered prime-time sport on a regular basis with its highly successful *Monday Night Football* in 1970. *Monday Night Football* was predicated on the notion that prime-time success for sports depended upon making it an entertaining production first and foremost. Furthermore, ABC was at the forefront of the movement to incorporate new technologies and techniques into its sports coverage, from instant replay to slow motion. To no small extent, ABC rode its success with sports programming from third place to the top of the heap among the networks by the mid-1970s. The director of ABC's sports division, Roone Arledge, was rewarded with a promotion to head of the network's news division (Patton, 1984, pp. 59–75).

During the 1960s, Major League Baseball, professional basketball, professional hockey, college football, and college basketball all enjoyed network broadcast contracts. By the 1970s, both NBC and CBS began to appreciate fully the immense profitability that sports programming offered. During the 1970s, the annual number of network hours of sports programming increased from 787 to 1,356; by 1984 the annual hours of sports programming was 1,700, double the figure for 1974. Advertisers were increasingly delirious with the sports market. A Simmons market research survey conducted in 1981 found that six times as many affluent males aged 18–49 watched pro football as watched *Dallas*. By the mid-1980s the three networks were selling over $1 billion in advertising for their sports programming, which was not much less than the gross revenues of the various professional sports leagues (Powers, 1984, pp. 11–22; Rader, 1984, pp. 118–137). In addition, countless hours of sports programming were televised on a local basis. Sports broadcasters had little relation to their counterparts in the sports departments of newspapers. They were celebrities and entertainers in their own right whose presence on the air could sway ratings (and advertising revenues) significantly. Hence the leading sportscasters by the 1980s earned seven-figure incomes, and even local sportscasters frequently earned incomes in six figures.

The major professional leagues and college "amateur" sports of football and basketball all profited mightily from the advertising dollars eager to sponsor their broadcasts. By 1982 the NFL had a five-year contract with the three networks worth $2 billion. Some business analysts estimated that a few NFL teams might be able to cover their expenses before they even sold any tickets. Major League Baseball's network contract was worth $1.1 billion for six years in the 1980s, and this was for only the World Series and a handful of regular season games telecast on a national basis. Most teams made considerably more money through the sale of the rights to their regular-season games to local stations.

The networks became desperate for sports programming to occupy their weekend daytime hours. By the late 1970s a number of "trashsports" were created by the networks—for instance, celebrity tennis matches, battles of network "superstars"—but most of them failed to deliver high enough ratings. Creating sport that the public would accept as legitimate has proven to be a tricky business. Numerous professional leagues have been formed, all in hopes of emulating the AFL and cashing in on the television money. The World Football League, World Team Tennis, World Hockey League, and American Basketball Association all failed to get precious network contracts and had to disband. Lack of a TV contract has simply made it impossible for a sports league to survive in any form of direct competition (Rader, 1984, pp. 117–137). In the 1980s the United States Football League was established. So clearly was this an effort to seize advertising dollars through rights payments that the league's first commissioner was Chet Simmons, a career sports executive for ABC and, later, the Entertainment and Sports Network (ESPN). The USFL disbanded in 1986, after it received only a token dollar from its antitrust suit against the NFL, in which the USFL claimed that the NFL had a monopoly on network broadcast rights payments. Thus the explosion in sports revenues due to television has had several losers in addition to its winners.

More than a few analysts have looked at these casualties and predicted that sports, in general, were being overexposed on television and that eventually public sentiment would turn against them. That has yet to happen, at least in the minds of the all-important advertisers who have subsidized the boom. Not that revenues and profits have increased without upheaval; as with any industry, there have been ups and downs for specific firms and general excesses caused by speculative frenzy. Nevertheless, the general pattern has been upward. In the 1980s several cable networks have been established that have given sports coverage prominence; indeed, they rank among the few cable operations that have had any success. Specifically, ESPN was established to broadcast sports 24 hours a day. Upon its creation, one ESPN executive remarked that "we believe the appetite for sports in this country is insatiable" (Rader, 1984, p. 136). Aimed at a smaller and more sophisticated market than that targeted by network sports coverage, ESPN has raised the level of sports broadcasting significantly.

The importance of TV has never been greater for sport. By the 1970s it had become axiomatic that successful management of professional sports leagues and franchises is based on the capacity to best exploit rights payments. To a certain extent commercial sport has been colonized by the advertising community. Sport's insatiable hunger for these ad dollars accounts for many of the recent major developments in American sport: new leagues; vast increases in "championship" events, such as college football bowl games; new forms of sports, such as indoor soccer; enormous salaries, as players attempt to capture some of the booty; changes in rules meant to increase "excitement," to appeal to the less sophisticated fan and to allow for more commercial interruptions; and lengthened schedules. Many purists feel that this commercialization has degraded and cheapened sport. In any case, the shapes of both sport *and* the mass media have been permanently changed.

It has not been television alone that has exploited sport (and vice versa) over the past 30 years. Radio, which was forced to find a new role after television replaced it as the centerpiece of the American living room, was still a superior and, for advertisers, relatively inexpensive means of transmitting games. Virtually every professional or major collegiate sports team receives some radio broadcast rights payments, including many lower-level college teams that are unable to generate large enough audiences to attract TV contracts.

Magazines, which had developed into an immensely profitable and highly concentrated industry on the basis of the emergence of national advertising, have also become an increasingly important medium for sports since the 1950s (Peterson, 1956). While there was a dramatic increase in the coverage of sport in general-circulation magazines in the first half of the century, the only sport-specific magazines were those like *Ring* and the *Sporting News*, which were essentially the trade publications for boxing and baseball (McChesney, 1986). With the emergence of television in the 1950s, general-interest magazines began to struggle for survival, as they could no longer compete on a cost-per-thousand basis with the networks for national advertising. The magazine industry began to focus more on specific subjects that would attract readerships with distinct interests and more sharply defined demographic characteristics. These more select readerships would then impress important groups of advertisers and justify the relatively high cost of the advertising. Sports—especially the major team sports plus golf, tennis, and Olympic sports—tended to attract the types of educated, affluent, and consumption-oriented audiences that many major advertisers fantasize about. A host of major sports publications have been launched since the 1950s. *Sports Illustrated*, which was first published by Time-Life in 1954, has been the most successful, with a circulation of several million copies per week. It is generally regarded as the best sports magazine in terms of the quality of writing and production.

Newspapers have also adjusted to the advent of television, with its implications for sports, and the two media have found that they can enjoy a very complementary relationship. The level of sports coverage remained in the 12–20% of editorial content range that had been established in the 1920s until the 1970s, when it tended to move upward for the very reasons it was so high in the first place: Sports coverage was very popular, relatively inexpensive, and noncontroversial. *USA Today*, the state-of-the-art national newspaper launched by Gannett in the early 1980s, devoted fully 25% of its editorial space to sports. To many it seemed that sports was responsible for the preponderance of the newspaper's circulation; Frank Deford described it as "a daily *Sporting News* wrapped in color weather maps." Newspapers were also increasingly narrowing their focus to middle-class readers over less affluent inner-city and blue-collar residents who held minimal interest for major advertisers. Thus sports with a decidedly non-middle-class following—bowling, stock car racing, tractor pulls—received scant attention in the nation's sports sections (Stevens, 1987). Furthermore, sports with limited commercial exploitation were generally accorded minimal attention. Hence the extraordinary explosion in women's athletics over the past generation has been relatively underreported.

The nature of newspaper sports journalism changed as well. With the emergence of extensive sports telecasting, far less energy was expended recounting the story of the game, which most readers would have seen for themselves. Rather, newspapers began to provide more analysis, background information, and statistical data that the other media found it difficult to provide. At sportswriting's very best, some exceptional writers like Red Smith of the *New York Times* began to combine a critical intelligence with a great love of sport. Furthermore, reporters began to center their game stories on quotes from players and coaches; the postgame trip to the locker room became standard operating procedure for the sportswriter. At its worst, this approach has produced a mindless formulated genre of reporting that essentially entails the stringing together of a series of cliché-ridden and superficial quotations.

In addition, sportswriting became more serious, particularly with the spectacular increase in sports revenues brought on by television rights payments and all the attendant changes that increase brought for the world of sport. The "real world" had invaded the sports page. Some have even attempted to extend the "adversarial" stance of the newsroom toward politicians, government officials, and criminals to the relationship between sportswriters and athletes and sports promoters. However, while this has had some impact, it contradicts the fundamental symbiotic nature of the sport-newspaper relationship. Most sports sections eagerly promote professional and commercial sports in their communities, if for no other reason than to assure employment for sportswriters.

Sports has risen to staggering and unprecedented levels of importance in American society in the 1980s. During the Shiite kidnaping crisis of June 1985, the kidnapers were quoted as saying, "Americans don't care about politics, they are only interested in sports" (*ABC Evening News*, June 21, 1985). Sports have come to dominate American life in a manner that only a few observers have paused to recognize (Lipsky, 1981; Michener, 1976). This chapter has endeavored to reveal how integral the commercial mass media have been to the development of this cultural edifice that Lipsyte (1975) has aptly termed "SportsWorld." Whether it can make further inroads remains to be seen; however, there is no reason to anticipate any step backward. Insofar as advertising is fundamental to modern capitalist political economy — indeed, it has outpaced the balance of the economy over the past decade and many experts anticipate continued relative rapid growth through the 1990s — then the economic foundation for the modern sport-media boom will remain intact until advertisers find some source of programming radically superior to sport. Hence every indication is that the sport-media marriage will continue to evolve in its present pattern, with all the implications that entails, for some time to come.

References

Adelman, M. A. (1986). *A sporting time: New York City and the rise of modern athletics, 1820–70.* Urbana: University of Illinois Press.

Baran, P. A., & Sweezy, P. M. (1966). *Monopoly capital.* New York: Monthly Review Press.

Bent, S. (1927). *Ballyhoo.* New York: Boni & Liveright.

Berryman, J. W. (1979, May). The tenuous attempts of Americans to "catch-up with John Bull": Specialty magazines and sporting journalism, 1800–1835. *Canadian Journal of History and Physical Education, 10,* 33–61.

Betts, J. R. (1952). *Organized sport in industrialized America.* Unpublished doctoral dissertation, Columbia University.

Betts, J. R. (1953a, Spring). Sporting journalism in nineteenth-century America. *American Quarterly, 5,* 39–46.

Betts, J. R. (1953b, September). The technological revolution and the rise of sport, 1850–1900. *Mississippi Valley Historical Review, 40,* 231–256.

Betts, J. R. (1974). *America's sporting heritage: 1850–1950.* Reading, MA: Addison-Wesley.

Chandler, A. D., Jr. (1977). *The visible hand.* Cambridge, MA: Belknap.

Covert, C. (1975, Autumn). A view of the press in the twenties. *Journalism History, 2,* 66–67, 92–96.

Engdahl, J. L. (1925, November 14). Commentary. *The Daily Worker.*

Gallico, P. (1938). *Farewell to sports.* New York: Alfred A. Knopf.

Guttmann, A. (1979, September). Who's on first? Or books on the history of American sport. *Journal of American History, 66,* 348–354.

James, B. (1985). *The Bill James baseball abstract 1985.* New York: Ballantine.

Jhally, S. (1984, Summer). The spectacle of accumulation: Material and cultural factors in the evolution of the sport/media complex. *Insurgent Sociologist, 3,* 41–57.

Lasch, C. (1978). *The culture of narcissism.* New York: W. W. Norton.

Lee, A. M. (1937). *The daily newspaper in America.* New York: Macmillan.

Lewis, G. (1973, Fall). World War I and the emergence of sport for the masses. *Maryland Historian, 4,* 109–122.

Link, A. S., & Catton, W. B. (1967). *American epoch.* New York: Alfred A. Knopf.

Lipsky, R. (1981). *How we play the game.* Boston: Beacon.

Lipsyte, R. (1975). *SportsWorld.* New York: Quadrangle.

McChesney, R. (1986). *Sport, mass media and monopoly capital: Toward a reinterpretation of the 1920s and beyond.* Unpublished master's thesis, University of Washington.

Michener, J. (1976). *Sports in America.* New York: Random House.

Mrozek, D. J. (1983). *Sport and American mentality, 1880–1910.* Knoxville: University of Tennessee Press.

Novak, M. (1976). *The joy of sports.* New York: Basic Books.

Nugent, W. H. (1929, March). The sports section. *American Mercury, 16,* 329–338.

Parente, D. E. (1974). *A history of television and sports.* Unpublished doctoral dissertation, University of Illinois.

Patton, P. (1984). *Razzle dazzle: The curious marriage of television and professional football.* Garden City, NY: Dial.

Peterson, T. (1956). *Magazines in the twentieth century.* Urbana: University of Illinois Press.

Pope, D. (1983). *The making of modern advertising.* New York: Basic Books.

Powers, R. (1984). *Supertube: The rise of television sports.* New York: Coward-McCann.

Rader, B. (1983). *American sports.* Englewood Cliffs, NJ: Prentice-Hall.

Rader, B. (1984). *In its own image: How television has transformed sports.* New York: Free Press.

Reidenbaugh, L. (1985). *The Sporting News first hundred years, 1886–1986.* St. Louis: Sporting News.

Roberts, R. (1979). *Jack Dempsey: The Manassa Mauler.* Baton Rouge: Louisiana State University Press.

Savage, H. J. (1929). *American college athletics.* New York: Carnegie Foundation for the Advancement of Teaching.

Schiller, D. (1981). *Objectivity and the news: The public and the rise of commercial journalism.* Philadelphia: University of Pennsylvania Press.

Schlesinger, A. M. (1933). *The rise of the city.* New York: Macmillan.

Schudson, M. (1979). *Discovering the news: A social history of American newspapers.* New York: Basic Books.

Seymour, H. (1960). *Baseball, the early years.* New York: Oxford University Press.

Shecter, L. (1969). *The jocks.* New York: Warner.

Slusser, J. H. (1952). *The sports page in American life in the nineteen-twenties.* Unpublished master's thesis, University of California, Berkeley.

Spalding, J. W. (1963-64, Winter). 1928: Radio becomes a mass advertising medium. *Journal of Broadcasting, 8,* 31-44.

Steiner, J. F. (1933). *Americans at play.* New York: McGraw-Hill.

Stevens, J. (1987, Fall). The rise of the sports page. *Gannett Center Journal, 1,* 1-11.

Sugar, B. R. (1978). *"The thrill of victory": The inside story of ABC Sports.* New York: Hawthorn.

Susman, W. (1975). Piety, profits and play: The 1920's. In H. H. Quint & M. Cantor (Eds.), *Men, women, and issues in American history.* Homewood, IL: Dorsey.

Tebbel, J. (1963). *The compact history of the American newspaper.* New York: Hawthorn.

Tunis, J. R. (1928). *Sports, heroics and hysterics.* New York: John Day.

Villard, O. G. (1944). *The disappearing daily.* New York: Alfred A. Knopf.

Voigt, D. Q. (1966). *American baseball.* Norman: University of Oklahoma Press.

Voigt, D. Q. (1970). *American baseball* (Vol. 2). Norman: University of Oklahoma Press.

Voigt, D. Q. (1976). *America through baseball.* Chicago: Nelson-Hall.

Weinfeld, W. (1936, December). The growth of newspaper chains in the United States: 1923, 1926-35. *Journalism Quarterly, 13,* 357-380.

Woodward, S. (1949). *Sports page.* New York: Simon & Schuster.

3

Cultural Studies and the Sports/Media Complex

Sut Jhally

> Men make their own history, but not in conditions of their own choosing.
> — Marx

The Critical Legacy: Circuses, Opiates, and Ideology

On September 26, 1987, *The Nation* magazine, one of the leading voices on the American Left, editorialized against the decisions by both the *New York Times* and CBS to give priority to sports coverage over the coverage of "real" (political, economic, and social) events. While recognizing that the coverage of politics by these organizations leaves a great deal to be desired, the editors nonetheless reflected what has been the Left's attitude toward sports in noting that sports has come to usurp the role that politics had occupied in American public life and noted, disapprovingly, that "it's more important for a paper of record to report ball scores than to analyze the week's events." Sports spectating is a deflection, an activity that channels potentially critical political activity into a safe and neutral realm. Sports have taken over the function in advanced capitalist societies that Marx believed religion fulfilled in the nineteenth century — an "opiate of the masses," providing the basis for spectacular shows and "circuses" that narcotize large segments of the population. An unimportant area of life obscures a more fundamental and important one.

Gary Whannel (1983) notes, however, that at the same time socialists decry the importance sports has achieved in social life, they are also attracted to the possibilities it opens up, of what could happen if that energy were directed to political activity instead. But that vision is a fantasy. The challenge for a cultural studies approach to sport is to use the fantasy creatively, to understand the context within which sports spectating, as a cultural activity, takes place so that the domain of sport becomes not merely something to be deplored, but a site on which to fight for definitions of the social world. Such a project involves moving beyond the predominant "circuses and opiates" position. It also means moving beyond much of the work that has tended to characterize and define critical approaches to sport. Although simplifying an increasingly complex field, it is possible to identify two major themes in this literature: sports spectating as (1) ritual/ideology and (2) compensatory fulfillment.

Much of the tacit background to critical work on sport as ideology and ritual is based upon a search for those factors that have prevented the economic contradictions of capitalism from being expressed in revolutionary movements. The orthodox argument runs that the ideological sphere of capitalism has prevented workers from seeing the reality of their exploitation and has convinced them to identify with the system that dominates them. Sport is a key institution in this process. Sports function as a form of celebration of the dominant order. Other writers have extended the analysis beyond the notion of ideology to that of ritual. Noting that all societies require ritualistic celebration of their central value systems, these writers focus on the role of sports in these processes. Michael Real (1975) labels sport a form of mythic spectacle and argues that "in the classical manner of mythical beliefs and ritual activities, the Super Bowl is a communal celebration of and indoctrination into specific socially dominant emotions, life styles, values . . . all functional to the larger society. . . . Rather than mere diversionary entertainment, it can be seen to function as a 'propaganda' vehicle strengthening and developing the larger social structure" (pp. 36, 42). Richard Lipsky (1981) argues that the ability of sports to function as a socializer of dominant values as well as providing a form of refuge is derived from its existence as a "dramatic life-world" where the values of the larger society are highlighted and celebrated by being inserted into a different (human) context.

In a different vein, John Alt (1983) argues that while traditionally Western sport has functioned as a ritual of liberal values, recent changes in the productive sphere of a corporate and bureaucratic society have led to a new role for spectator sports: that of compensatory fulfillment. Arguing that liberalism and its attendant ideologies of fair play and moral order have broken down in the face of the increasing bureaucratization of social life and its ends-oriented organization, sports now have to cater to the "new cultural-emotional needs of the masses." In short, as one part of the social world robs people of meaning and emotional gratification, another part offers it to them in the form of commodified spectacles. Sport offers excitement and emotional gratification denied to the citizens of a corporate society. We are back once again in the world of opiates.

This, then, is the legacy of a critical approach to sport. I do not want to deny the utility of such analyses or their many considerable insights into the role that sport plays in advanced capitalist societies. Indeed, later in this chapter I hope to fill out in more detail the specifics of this ritualistic, escapist ideology. I do, however, want to insist that terms such as *ideology* are necessary but ultimately insufficient for a full understanding of the role that sports play in modern society and that the task now is to build on this base while at the same time overcoming the obstacles that it throws up.

The New Direction: Cultural Studies

One of the problems with the approaches outlined above is that they have a tendency to treat the people involved in these ideological and ritualistic processes as largely passive, internalizing and accepting the definitions of the situations presented to them. They also tend to be static and functionalist in their modes of explanation. While terms such as *power* (and even *manipulation*) are vital to a proper understanding of sport, we must treat them as dialectical notions, rather than as unidirectional and one-dimensional concepts.

The most ambitious attempt at this kind of reworking of the ideological/cultural sphere has been connected with English cultural studies, specifically with the writers associated with the Center for Contemporary Cultural Studies (CCCS) at the University of Birmingham in England (especially under the directorships of Stuart Hall and Richard Johnson). It is part of an attempt to shift the focus of debate from a concentration on ideology to one on *culture* and to focus on power from the viewpoint of contestation. Richard Johnson (1986–87) stresses the following three premises as the minimum basis of critical cultural studies: (1) "Cultural processes are intimately connected with social relations, especially with class relations and class formations, with sexual divisions, with the racial structuring of social relations and with age oppressions as a form of dependency"; (2) "culture involves power and helps to produce asymmetries in the abilities of individuals and social groups to define and realise their needs"; (3) "culture is neither an autonomous nor an externally determined field, but a site of social differences and struggles" (p. 39).

Now certainly *culture* as a term cannot be used unproblematically in the sense that there is wide agreement as to what it means—there is not. Raymond Williams (1976) argues that it is one of the two or three most complicated words in the English language. Johnson recognizes this and suggests instead that cultural studies should focus on the terms *consciousness* and *subjectivity*, "with the key problems now lying somewhere in the relation between the two. . . . cultural studies is about the historical forms of consciousness or subjectivity, or the subjective forms we live by, or, in a rather perilous compression, perhaps a reduction, the subjective side of social relations" (p. 43).

For the study of sport, these are highly pertinent and relevant organizing terms. First, *consciousness* refers to the way in which we cognitively make sense of the world, the knowledge we have of it, of how it works, and of our place in it. It is largely a conscious, known process. *Subjectivity*, on the other hand, refers to the absences in consciousness, or to the possibility that some things that move us (such as aesthetic or emotional life) remain consciously unknown to us. For Johnson, subjectivity "focuses on the 'who I am' or, as important, the 'who we are' of culture, on individual and collective identities" (p. 44). Sports certainly offer a mapping of the world, a way of understanding the social relations within which we live our lives, but, unlike other media messages (e.g., the news), sports also involve us in other ways. There are passions involved, emotional entanglements with the events that we witness that cannot simply be explained under terms such as *consciousness* and *ideology*. They are a part (for many people, heretofore largely male) of how social identity is formed.

Raymond Williams has coined two key terms ("way of life" and "structure of feeling") that can describe this tension between consciousness and subjectivity. Williams (1961) stresses that a simple description of cultural phenomena will not be sufficient to understand those forms:

> Cultural history must be more than the sum of the particular histories, for it is with the relations between them, the particular forms of the whole organization, that it is especially concerned. I would then define the theory of culture as the study of relationships between elements in a whole way of life. . . . A keyword, in such analysis, is pattern: it is with the discovery of patterns of a characteristic kind that any useful cultural analysis begins, and it is with the relationships between these patterns, which sometimes reveal unexpected identities and correspondences in hitherto separately considered activities, sometimes again reveal discontinuities of an unexpected kind, that general cultural analysis is concerned. (pp. 46–47)

Connected with this "way of life" is a "structure of feeling" that refers to the "felt sense of the quality of life at a particular place and time: a sense of the ways in which particular activities combined into a way of thinking and living. . . . It is as firm and definite as 'structure' suggests, yet it operates in the most delicate and least tangible parts of our activity" (p. 48). Sports, perhaps more than any other cultural phenomenon, lies at this tension between consciousness and subjectivity, between "way of life" and "structure of feeling."

While Williams has made an immense contribution to the development of cultural studies, I think it is fair to say that the very fierce critique of his work by E. P. Thompson has yielded just as valid contributions. In his now classic review of Williams's *The Long Revolution*, Thompson (1961) stresses (at least) three things in opposition. The first is with a concern to break with the literary tradition when talking of culture and to include within a "whole way of life" the terrain of everyday, concrete, practical cultural processes that are cut through and through with power. Second, while Williams coined the term "way of life," Thompson insists on a corrective to a "whole way of conflict . . . a way of struggle." Third, uniting the first two, Thompson wants to substitute for Williams's abstract historical forces the idea that it is people who make history, rather than vice versa. As Marx has noted: "History does nothing, it possesses no immense wealth, fights no battles. It is rather *man*, real living *man* who does everything, who possesses and fights."

However, while Thompson is undoubtedly a key figure in the development of cultural studies, the inclusion of his concerns into an evolving theoretical framework depended in part on the appropriation by critical scholars of the newly translated work of the Italian Marxist Antonio Gramsci. Gramsci's key contribution to Western Marxism has undoubtedly been the notion of "hegemony." In many appropriations this has simply been taken as a slightly more complex form of ideological domination. In contrast, Gramsci insisted that power and domination are always exercised in a combination of force and consent, that the two never operate in isolation. Hegemony consists in part of a class asserting intellectual and moral leadership in a particular period. This is not done in a way that simply *imposes* ideology on a passive and accepting subordinate class; instead, the hegemonic process is one of negotiation, compromise, and struggle in which the ruling class, or more precisely the ruling bloc, gives concessions in one area so that it may receive them in another.

Similar to Thompson, Gramsci (1971) also insists that if and when hegemony is won, it operates not solely at the level of coherent philosophies but at the level of everyday consciousness or common sense. To the extent that hegemony operates at this level it becomes far easier to *naturalize* a particular way of defining things because common sense is not coherent and does not have to be. It has been "inherited from the past and uncritically absorbed" (p. 333). It is the "way things are." Raymond Williams (1977) notes that, for Gramsci, hegemony "is a lived system of meanings and values—constitutive and constituting—which as they are experienced as practices appear as reciprocally confirming. It thus constitutes a sense of reality for most people in society, a sense of absolute because experienced reality" (p. 110). Similarly, John Hargreaves (1982b) argues: "It is easy to see how, from this point of view, popular culture, and specifically sport, could be given their proper share of attention alongside other cultural constituents of civil society, like language usage, formal and informal education, the media, habits and customs, etc., as resources out of which a class fashions its hegemony" (p. 115).

It was undoubtedly Gramsci's discussion of these issues that led Louis Althusser to his seminal redefinitions of the field of Marxist ideology studies and his reworking of the base/superstructure metaphor. Although, for many different reasons, Althusser's work has in recent years been much criticized and sometimes simply ignored, there is much of value that can be drawn from his writings. For example, Stuart Hall (1985) paraphrases Althusser's formulation of ideology in *For Marx* in the following way: as "systems of representation—composed of concepts, ideas, myths or images—in which men and women . . . live their imaginary relations to the real conditions of existence" (p. 103). Althusser (1977) argues that *all* societies (even socialist ones) require ideology because the understanding of real conditions does not occur in any simple or direct way—there is no one understanding or experience of social existence that imposes itself in our minds in a direct, unmediated way: "It [ideology] is a structure essential to the historical life of societies" (p. 232). Our understanding of our conditions is always socially constructed. This does not mean that social relations are not real, that they do not exist separate from our understanding of them. As Hall (1985) says: "Social relations do exist. We are born into them. They exist independent of our will. They are real in their structure and tendency. . . . Social relations exist, independent of mind, independent of thought. And yet, they can only be conceptualized in thought, in the head" (p. 105). These real relations, however, do not declare their meanings directly and unambiguously. That is why Althusser calls ideology an "imaginary relation." Ideology is *the way* that people live the relation between themselves and their conditions of existence. Moreover, this is not simply "false consciousness" as in the traditional Marxist sense of ideology because people have to *live* these imaginary relations, they have to survive and operate practically in the material world according to these imaginary relations. Ideology must then bear some relationship to real conditions, otherwise it could not work, it would fall apart as obviously false. This is the sense in which Althusser (1971) is able to talk about ideology not simply as abstract representations but as having a *material* existence in that ideas are lived out in practices: "The 'ideas' of a human subject exist in his actions. . . . I shall talk of actions inserted into *practices*. *And* I shall point out that these practices are governed by the *rituals* in which these practices are inscribed, within the *material existence of an ideological apparatus*, be it only a small part of that apparatus: a small mass in a small church, a funeral, a minor match at a sports' club, a school day, a political party meeting, etc." (p. 158).

From this context, it becomes easier now to make sense of Althusser's central claim that "ideology interpellates individuals as subjects." It is through ideology defined in this way that we recognize ourselves as socially constituted individuals in our own particular culture. We are again back to our starting terms of *consciousness* and *subjectivity*. Althusser (1977) writes:

> In truth, ideology has very little to do with 'consciousness', even supposing this term to have an unambiguous meaning. It is profoundly *unconscious*. . . . Ideology is indeed a system of representations, but in the majority of cases these representations have nothing to do with 'consciousness': they are usually images and occasionally concepts, but it is above all as *structures* that they impose on the vast majority of men, not via their 'consciousness'. They are perceived-accepted-suffered cultural objects and they act functionally on men via a process that escapes them. (p. 233)

This formulation again has a great deal of relevance for the study of sport precisely because it is viewed as separate from the rest of social life, as neutral when it comes to issues of power and politics, and it works at multiple levels of social existence in a very powerful and profound way.

While Althusser tends to collapse the distinction between ideology and culture, other writers who have been influenced by his work insist on the analytic separation. For example, Clarke et al. (1976) define culture as "that level at which social groups develop distinct patterns of life and give *expressive form* to their social and material life-experience" (p. 10), distinguishing among the dominant culture, the class culture, and the youth subculture. It is the *relation* among them that is important to investigate. There is no straightforward passage from culture to ideology in this perspective. Paul Willis (1977) argues that the cultural level is a mediation through which wider structural determinants (class, gender, race, and so on) need to pass to reproduce themselves in distinct social ways. Moreover, the cultural level is not determined but is open for contestation. In relation to the key terms I have been working with here, perhaps the best formulation of this relation is to say that *ideology* is the form that *culture* takes in conditions of *hegemony*.

I have spent a good deal of time and space elaborating on some of the main features of cultural studies because I believe that critical scholars of sport *must* address these issues, which have redefined the field. It is a framework that insists upon the cultural level as a place where people actively seek to understand the conditions of their existence, where social groups battle and struggle over the definitions given to social life, and where unequal access to the resources to accomplish this lead to the privileging of some groups' views over those of others. The production of culture (or "cultural production") is an active process with no predetermined result that can be read from its relation to other levels of the social formation.

While insisting on the analytic necessity of terms such as *struggle* and *contestation*, we should take care not to privilege them in situations where they are not to be found. Sports may be one of those arenas that is relatively free from real contestation. As Chas Critcher (1986) says: "Sport is no longer, if it ever was, a major area of cultural contestation. . . . Change and tension are always evident but these are principally within rather than over sport. Understanding how and why this has happened remains an important question to those interested in understanding how capitalist culture works" (p. 343). The vital question then becomes, In what ways are some cultural forms taken out of the play of overt struggle?

Cultural Studies, the Media, and Cultural Commodities

These issues have specific reference to the study of sports. In the remainder of this chapter I address the task of cultural studies in understanding sport, paying special attention to the role of the media.

I have not dealt specifically with the sports/media relation as yet because I was concerned to establish the proper theoretical background that is necessary with regard to the broader field of cultural studies. However, as soon as we concentrate specifically on the subject of sports in capitalism it becomes apparent that we can talk *only* about a *sports/media complex* (see Jhally, 1984). This can be (briefly) justified in two fundamental ways: (1) Most people do the vast majority of their sports spectating via the media (largely through television), so that the cultural experience of sports is hugely mediated; and (2) from a financial point of view, professional, and increasingly college, sports are dependent upon media money for their very survival and their present organizational structure.

Within the tradition of cultural studies that I have been examining, there are a couple of "models" of media analysis that can be readily adapted for the study of mediated sport and that I will use in the following sections. Stuart Hall (1980) lays out what has become a very influential approach to media studies with his "encoding/decoding" model. Drawing upon Marx's model of the circuit of capital (production, circulation, distribution/consumption, reproduction) and criticizing traditional mass communication sender/ message/receiver models, Hall encourages us to think of the different moments of the communication process as "a 'complex structure in dominance', sustained through the articulation of connected practices, each of which, however, retains its distinctiveness and has its own specific modality, its own forms and conditions of existence" (p. 128).

Richard Johnson (1986–87) also draws upon Marx's model of the circuit of capital to suggest his own "circuit of culture" model, which bears many resemblances to Hall's, as well as exhibiting important differences (such as being able to be applied to cultural products in general and not simply media forms). The model "represent[s] a circuit of the production, circulation and consumption of cultural products. Each box represents a moment in this circuit. Each moment or aspect depends upon the others and is indispensable to the whole. Each, however, is distinct and involves characteristic changes of form. It follows that if we are placed at one point of the circuit, we do not necessarily see what is happening at others. The forms that have most significance for us at one point may be very different from those at another. Processes disappear in results" (p. 46). There are four moments of the process: (1) a focus on the production of cultural products, (2) a focus on the texts that are produced, (3) a focus on how these texts are read by ordinary people, and (4) a focus on "lived cultures" and "social relations" that relate to the "uses" made of the readings of texts, as well as being materials that new forms of cultural production can draw upon. It is with these types of understanding about the nature of this circuit of culture and the relations among the different moments that I shall proceed with the specific discussion of mediated sports.

Production: The Commodity Context

The cultural and ideological role of sport in advanced capitalism (especially in the United States) is impossible to understand without locating the centrality of commodity relations to the framework of which it is a part. If we follow through the political economy of professional and college sports, we will see that each stage is dominated by a concern with commodities. The overall *logic* is provided by the processes concerned with the circulation of commodities in general.

Corporations directly sponsor teams and events in the hope of attaching their names to the meaning of the particular activities. The auctioning off of the Los Angeles Olympics was perhaps the most spectacular example to date of this linking of the spheres of commerce and sports. (Its blatancy led some commentators to describe them as the "hamburger Olympics.") Indeed, given the prevalence of brand names in the athletic events themselves and the use made of sporting themes in the advertisements that appeared between the events, the blurring of the line between the two realms was so complete that, at times, it was difficult to tell exactly what one was watching.

In addition to the direct sponsorship of events, corporations also buy advertising time on broadcast media during sports programming. This is connected to the very elusive and "concentrated" audience that sports programming is able to capture. Sports constitute a very important part of the schedule of the major television networks, who sell the time of particular audience segments to corporations who wish to reach those people with advertising messages. The material importance of this relationship between sports and the media will vary from society to society, depending in large part on the extent of private versus public control of the broadcasting sphere. Where there is private control (with revenues being drawn largely from advertising), it will be very difficult to separate media from sports. Where there is public control of broadcasting (through the state), the relationship will be less important, because the media are not governed by the same criterion of programming *having* to create audience segments that advertisers want. There is thus at present a major difference between the United States and Western Europe when it comes to defining this relationship, although as broadcasting in the latter increasingly falls into private hands we can expect that difference to decrease (see Seifart, 1984). In the United

States not only does sports programming generate a great deal of revenue for the media, but the media can advertise their own upcoming programs during sports events, and thus increase ratings and advertising revenues for non-sports programming. This is what ABC was able to accomplish through its coverage of the 1984 Olympics.

Following from this, there is an argument that because media revenues are so important to their functioning, professional sports have been *transformed* and changed, that something pure has been lost in their commercialization (Altheide & Snow, 1978). Such an argument detracts from the fact that sports have *always* been based on commercial relations. Professional sports depend on two kinds of commodity sales, the relative importance of which has shifted historically. First, they sell tickets to fans who come to see the live event. For the first 30 years of this century, the role of the media was basically to act as publicity agents for sports, to get people into the stadiums. (This is still largely the role of newspapers today.) Second, professional sports sell the rights to broadcast events to the media. Historically, this has become far more important (contracts can now run into the billions of dollars) and is the basis of the claim that the broadcast media have transformed sports. While this is undoubtedly a valid observation, it seems to imply that before the influence of the media there was something that was pure sports. But sports have always been tied into a commodity sphere of one kind or another, their shape and organization always dependent upon their level of profitability. In the latter period the major commodity that sports sell has changed; it is not that sports have suddenly been inserted into a commercial realm. The question is to what extent these historical transformations constitute a qualitatively new stage for the domain of professional sports. This is a very interesting question that we have not yet really begun to answer. The field awaits a detailed historical study of the political economy of professional sports as well as data on the extent of cross-ownership among the spheres of sports, media, and commerce.

While the commodity structure is an indispensable way of understanding the interlocking of sports, media, and commerce, it is also a useful way of looking at the role of individual players within this framework. The advertising revenues that manufacturers provide to media, who in turn buy broadcasting rights, is at the root of the sizable increases in player salaries over the last 30 years. The players then are able, like other workers, to sell their specialized labor power to employers for its market value. In addition to this, however, players are also trying to create a commodity that they can in turn sell—celebrity. In this way players can obtain revenues directly from manufacturers who are interested in having famous players endorse their products. For many players this may be of even greater value than higher sports salaries, in that they can trade in their celebrity for many years after they have finished playing.

The last major actor that needs to be understood in this commodity structure is the state. Although the state itself, in the United States, is not involved in the production and sale of commodities, it performs a vital function for the whole structure – it defines the *conditions* within which the other activities take place. With specific regard to the media and sport we can identify three important areas. First, the state provides an exemption from antitrust legislation for sports leagues in their negotiations with television networks. This leads to far higher prices that networks have to pay, although they are guaranteed a nonfractioned audience (see Horowitz, 1978). Second, advertising expenditures by manufacturers are tax deductible as business expenses. If they were not, the whole structure of the sports/media complex would be altered, as the proportion of advertising revenues directed toward broadcast media would be much smaller. Third, the state can impose (or lift) restrictions on the types of products that can be advertised, and the media they can be advertised on, and thus again can affect the amount of advertising dollars the sports/media complex can attract.

There has been a great deal written about the effects that this commodity structure has had on the organization and nature of professional sports. It has led to sports leagues changing the rules of the game to provide a better television package; clubs moving from one city to another based not upon stadium support but upon the television audience; the flow and momentum of the game being interrupted as the game is stopped for time-outs that are called so that television can show commercials; the creation and destruction of entire sports leagues based upon whether or not television support could be found; and the ability (or inability) of teams to sign players, depending on the size of the television market a team controls.

A corresponding view treats the process of the increasing commercialization of sport (largely through the media) as leading to a "massification" of sports, as the search now is for new mass audiences for advertisers, rather than the appeal to the "cultivated" minority who really understand what sports are about. John Alt (1983) writes:

> The form of the spectacle – commodity rationalization – comes to envelop the structure of sports performances, shaping, changing, and altering the game to meet market and technical criteria. . . . Packaging the game, altering the rules and action, is undertaken to create special effects, usually in the form of visual-audial images. . . . In the extreme, the spectacle form reduces sport to its most

banal and sensational elements as standards of excellence are repressed by commercial norms. (p. 98)

Additionally, the increasing commercialization of professional sports has led to players' paying more and more attention to individual rather than team accomplishments and has changed the way that sports are played. Community and team loyalty are jettisoned in favor of self-identification in the building of celebrity.

Production: Encoding the Message

The last section looked at the wider constraints that are produced by the commodity-logic of the market setting on the way that sports "appear" to us in this society. In this section I wish to focus on the more immediate and practical factors that affect the nature of the mediated sports message on television. The first point that needs to be made is simple but vital: Television does not present us with a sports event but with a sports event (already highly structured by the commodity-logic) that is *mediated* by television. A sports event is live and unscripted, and television is forced to provide its own structures and ideological viewpoints in a unique way. Directors, producers, camera operators, editors, and commentators are inserted between the live event and the home audience. As Stuart Hall (1980) notes: "The production process is not without its 'discursive' aspect: it, too, is framed throughout by meanings and ideas: knowledge-in-use concerning the routines of production, historically defined technical skills, professional ideologies, institutional knowledge, definitions and assumptions, assumptions about the audience frame the constitution of the programme through this production structure" (p. 129).

Gary Whannel (1984) provides an illuminating example from the coverage of the 1980 Moscow Olympics of what happens when this hidden production process loses its internal unity. Soviet television provided the video pictures of the events, to which British television could add its own commentary. The agendas of these two institutions, however, were very different. While Soviet television wanted to present the games as being unaffected by the U.S.-led boycott, British television wished to emphasize their abnormal character. This led to an "enthralling television battle—a struggle between Soviet television and the British channels to define the meaning of the Games" (p. 36).

As this example illustrates, the mediating production process is not a closed system. "They draw topics, treatments, agendas, events, personnel, images of the audience, 'definitions of the situation' from other sources and other discursive formations within the wider socio-cultural and political structure of which they are a differentiated part" (Hall, 1980, p. 129). In this sense, the encoding process involves precisely what it says—using *codes* (technical, organizational, social, cultural and political) to produce a *meaningful discourse*. Wren-Lewis and Clarke (1983) offer a reading of the television coverage of the 1982 soccer World Cup from the perspective of the surrounding political context (the Malvinas/Falklands war). From the perspective of the Johnson model mentioned earlier, this wider context from which materials are drawn would constitute the moment of "lived cultures" and social relations.

The existing research on this production moment of the circuit of culture is very sparse. The few studies that do exist tend to work back from the encoded messages to a reading of motives and practice. Peters (1976), Buscombe (1974), and Williams (1977) have conducted these kinds of studies. Whannel also works backward from the message to come up with four important aspects of television sports production: "First, hierarchization, the process of signalling that some things are more important than others. Second, personalization, the presentation of events from an individualized perspective. Third, narrative, the telling of events in the form of stories. Fourth, the placing of events in the context of frames of reference" (as cited in Cantelon & Gruneau, 1988).

In Canada, Rick Gruneau and Hart Cantelon are attempting at the present time the most ambitious and thorough analysis of TV sports from the viewpoint of production that I am aware of. This involves, among other things, a focus on the organizational structures of the sports commentators' booth through both ethnographic and interview research methods (in addition to content analysis of the actual encoded messages). Such a project is urgently required for the American situation also. Todd Gitlin (1983) has shown how this can be accomplished for the understanding of prime-time television. The time is ripe for an *Inside Sports Time* companion to his work.

The Texts of Mediated Sport

Within critical analyses of sports, the reading of sports (through the media or directly) for their ideological meanings has been very prominent, and these readings are very important follow-ups to the focus on production and encoding – a shift from process to product. As we have seen, there is no natural meaning of sport. The meaning of mediated sport is the outcome of a complex articulation of technical, organizational, economic, cultural, political, and social factors. There is nothing accidental about this process, and we should not forget, for all the stress on complexity, negotiation, and struggle, that this cultural production takes place within a *capitalist* context, where access to resources is differentially distributed. As Whannel (1983) notes: "Sport offers a way of seeing the world. It is part of the system of ideas that supports, sustains and reproduces capitalism. It offers a way of seeing the world that makes our very specific form of social organization seem natural, correct and inevitable" (p. 27).

Many writers have focused on this general ability that sports discourses have, because of the seeming separation of sport from other areas of life, to *naturalize* forms of organization that have a social and political basis. Despite increasing evidence to the contrary (boycotts, kidnappings, player strikes, and so on) the refrain to keep politics out of sport is still constantly heard. In the remainder of this section I wish to highlight briefly some of the major tenets of this naturalized and ideological version of the world.

Militarism and Nationalism

Many major sports telecasts are saturated with militaristic values that start with the presentation of the colors, or the flying overhead of fighter airplanes as the "Star Spangled Banner" is sung. Again, I need to stress that this is simply not "showing" what is going on at the game: The television presentation of these events is normally *highly* technically mediated, with elaborate camera angles, overlapping pictures of players, flags, and weapons, and careful use of juxtaposition and dissolves. The Super Bowl especially seems to be inextricably tied up with this militaristic ideology. Writers have also noted the manner in which the very language of sports commentators embodies the vocabulary that one would actually expect of a society that houses the military/industrial complex at its heart. For example, in football, phrases such as "the bomb," "the aerial attack," "advancing into enemy territory," "the bullet pass," and "the offensive arsenal" are common ways of describing and interpreting the ostensibly sporting action (see Hoch, 1971).

A theme accompanying the militaristic one is, of course, the nationalistic one. This takes place in two related movements. First, "we" are separated from "them," the foreigners, through the use of stereotypical representations. "They" are different from us culturally and psychologically. Second, "we" who are separated from them are drawn together under the mythical sign of the "nation." This itself involves a two-step procedure. In the initial step our real differences (of class, ethnicity, religion, and so on) are dissolved to create a false unity of "nation" (Americanness, Englishness, and so on). As Clarke and Clarke (1982) write of the English situation regarding this, the unity is not simply a sum of the different parts, but

> is structured in a particular direction. It draws its conceptions of Englishness from a specific set of social images and practices — those of the dominant social groups. Nationalism as an ideology works in two directions. One is to mark us off from the 'others'— foreigners, strangers, aliens — it identifies and values what is unique to us. The other is to draw us together, to unite us in the celebration, maintenance and furtherance of 'our' way of life. (p. 80)

Competition and the Rules of the Game

At the heart of all sports is competition. The definition given to the form of the competition found in sports is thus an important dimension to their understanding. As for most factors involved in the analysis of cultural products, there is no single definition that holds cross-culturally. Joan Chandler (1983) argues that there are important differences between the United States and Britain in terms of the relationship between competition and social mobility and that these are reflected in the structures of competition found in their respective sports and the meanings given to them by the media.

In the United States, competition in sport is viewed as essentially competition between equals without differential access to resources playing an important role. Moreover, the rules of the game are clear and neutral, so that the basis of the competition is unobscured. It is essentially *fair* competition, with the individual being the prime unit of action so that failures become individual rather than social or class failures. The relationship of this kind of definition of competition to the way in which dominant groups would like to define competition in the wider economic, social, and cultural world is an important issue to discuss (see Jhally, 1988).

Labor, the Team, and Authority

One of the major themes in the critical analysis of sport is that sports reflect and celebrate the basic features of the capitalist labor process by presenting them in an idealized form. John Hargreaves (1982a) summarizes this approach in the following terms:

> In their organization and functioning the major popular sports are seen as replicating all the fundamental features of modern rationalized industrial production: a high degree of specialization and standardization, bureaucratized and hierarchical administration, long-term planning, increased reliance on science and technology, a drive for maximum productivity, a quantification of performance and, above all, an alienation of both the producer and consumer. (p. 41)

The media, with the constant stress on quantification of specialized performance and the focus on the coaches and managers as being the place where decisions are made, ritually celebrate the most alienating features of the capitalist labor process. This is accomplished by a stress on the sports world as above all a *human* realm rather than a technical one. The media transform authority structures that are hierarchical and exploitative into ones that become identified by the personal and the human (see Lipsky, 1981). An abstract alienated authority is personally mediated by very visible owners and coaches who are not an impersonal corporate elite but concerned leaders who *care* along with the ordinary fans.

Gender

All societies differentiate along lines of sex. It is a universal marker of human identity. These biological divisions, however, do not have the same meaning cross-culturally. The social understanding of biological difference is what many writers have termed the domain of "gender." This refers to the specific cultural and social meanings surrounding what it means to be male or female in any society. This is obviously a huge subject, and I do not want to do more here than give the briefest indication of the role that mediated sports play in the complex processes that produce this meaning. There are, I think, three analytical dimensions to the issues: (1) How do mediated sports define notions of masculinity? (2) How do mediated sports deal with the relation between male and female athletic performance? (3) How do mediated sports define notions of femininity? (For discussions of these issues, see Hargreaves, 1986; Sabo & Runfola, 1980; Willis, 1982.) Much important work remains to be done in this area.

Race

Mediated sports present perhaps the most visible arena for racial minorities. While in many other cultural forms minorities have a token role, in contemporary sports they play an absolutely fundamental role. As such, black players act as powerful role models for black youngsters. However, just as for gender, race in sport is defined within a hugely ideological field. In 1987, a major controversy was created by the insensitive (although entirely reflective of the group of which they are a part) remarks by Al Campanis and Jimmy "the Greek" Snyder on blacks not having the intellectual capabilities needed for managerial positions in sports. The absence of blacks from managerial posts and even from playing positions that stress decision making and thinking provides powerful definitions of the kinds of activities that particular groups of people are capable of performing. Again in the 1987 basketball season the accurate (although perhaps ill-timed) remarks of Dennis Rodman and Isiah Thomas that white players (such as Larry Bird) are given credit for working hard to achieve what they have done, while black players (such as Magic Johnson) are credited with natural ability that did not have to be cultivated or worked upon, showed how sensitive minority groups are to media definitions. Again, much work remains to be done in this area.

Sports Culture and the Culture of Consumption

While the stress in this section has been on the meaning of the mediated sports text, we should not forget that one very important part of these texts is that of messages that principally concern commodities, rather than sports – the advertisements. There needs to be a focus on the manner in which the world of consumption articulates with the ideology of sports that we have been discussing (see Jhally, 1987). Especially important in this regard is the manner in which the essentially naturalizing form of sports ideology is attached to other (equally) political domains so as to render them natural as well. Rick Gruneau (1988), writing of the 1984 Olympic Games, notes that

> the combination of the location in Los Angeles, the organization of the Games by a private corporation, the advertising strategies employed by Olympic and other sponsors, the style of the Reagan Presidency, and the frequent speculation on Olympic programs about the future financial careers of victorious athletes,

all became elements in a common discourse. Within this discourse, the themes of athletic success, healthy lifestyles, community, and Olympic ideals were continually circuited back to the success of corporate capitalism and the values prominent in American consumer culture. . . . Sport, like art itself, has become drawn into the discourses of modern publicity—a vehicle for expressing the common sense of modern consumer culture. (pp. 22–23, 26)

Readers and Decoding

The study of texts is important, but only to a point. It is very useful to know what a formal analysis can tell us about the structure and content of the message, but we cannot simply infer *audience* readings from *our* readings. As Fred Fejes (1984) has pointed out, however, the field of critical media studies has been very reluctant to take this step toward audience research (for good historical reasons). I think this step is now imperative, especially as regards the cultural understanding of sport. An ethnography of sports viewing and the manner in which media messages are a *part* of the process through which meaning is constituted have to be included in the future of critical cultural studies. If we take Althusser's formulations on ideology as an imaginary lived relation seriously, then we have to investigate the way in which sports discourses fit into the web of social practices of different groups. For instance, Althusser points out that the ruling classes do not propagate their ideology as a false myth but as the way they experience their real relations. They have to believe their own myths of freedom before they can convince others of them. Thus in relation to sports, it is possible that, for example, images of competition are appropriated differently by groups in different social and class locations—the bourgeoisie see it as a reflection of existing relations, while others look to it as a realm of escape, where justice actually appears to prevail, unlike "real life."

Moreover, there needs to be a recognition that sports is a realm of *popular pleasure*. People like sports. We need to focus on why some cultural forms become popular, become "principles of living." Further, "what are the *different* ways in which subjective forms are inhabited—playfully or in deep seriousness, in fantasy or by rational agreement, because it is the thing to do or the thing *not* to do" (Johnson, 1986–87, p. 72)? There are real dangers associated with this move. A focus on the audience has the potential to elevate and privilege the audience's own understanding of its situation in a way that divorces the analysis from the wider contextual conditions of power. Tania

Modleski (1986) has warned of this recent trend in which ostensibly critical cultural studies come close to winding up as studies of "uses and gratifications."

To avoid these obvious temptations, we have to keep in mind two important analytical points. The first has to do with the nature of the texts that audiences decode. Although in abstract theory the meanings associated with these are open-ended, in concrete practice social constraints act to close the range of possible meanings. Recognizing that texts are open to more than one interpretation, Stuart Hall (1980) warns: "Polysemy must not, however, be confused with pluralism. Connotative codes are *not* equal among themselves. Any society/culture tends, with varying degrees of closure, to impose its classifications of the social and cultural political world. These constitute a *dominant cultural order*, though it is neither univocal nor uncontested. This question of the 'structure of discourses in dominance' is a crucial point" (p. 135).

The second analytical point flows from the first: Audience readings take place in particular *conditions*, and the identification of these becomes vital. For instance, sports on television is a certain type of "watching," where one's time is being sold to advertisers. What effect do the surrounding conditions have on the nature of our watching? Why are we watching rather than doing other activities? How have cultural patterns changed with the introduction of television? The answer to these questions (and many others that could be posed here) emphasizes that "reading" takes place in certain social conditions that are connected to the way people live their everyday lives, and that we cannot ask questions about audience decodings divorced from these wider questions. In general, we need to remember Richard Lipsky's (1981) insight that sports can both provide an escape from particular social conditions and be a powerful form of socialization back into those same conditions.

Lived Cultures / Social Relations

In a 'determinate' moment the structure employs a code and yields a 'message': at another determinate moment the 'message,' via its decodings, issues into the structure of social practices. We are now fully aware that this reentry into the practices of audience reception and 'use' cannot be understood in simple behavioral terms. The typical processes identified in positivistic research on isolated elements—effects, uses, 'gratifications'—are themselves framed by structures of understanding, as well as being produced by social and economic relations, which shape their 'realization' at the reception end of the chain and

which permit the meanings signified in the discourse to be transposed into practice or consciousness (to acquire social use value or political effectivity). (Hall,
1980, p. 130)

Stuart Hall here has given us the challenge that a critical cultural approach
must meet. Ultimately all the analyses of production, texts, and audiences
must be integrated and contextualized within the broader frame of how people live their lives and the constraints and possibilities imposed by wider
social, cultural, political, and economic movements. I wish here to mention
briefly *some* of the factors that a critical approach to mediated sports must
consider in attempting this wider framing (in addition to all the ones previously mentioned).

The first issues are historical ones. Nicholas Garnham (1983) has noted
that there is a *class* basis to cultural consumption. These issues need to be
analyzed and linked to the distribution of what Pierre Bourdieu has called
"cultural capital." Additionally, we need to analyze the manner in which the
arena of cultural consumption has shifted and changed through this century,
and especially since the introduction of television. Obviously, this will be
linked to the process that has been labeled "the industrialization of culture,"
in which cultural products are increasingly provided directly by the market,
rather than by nonmarket areas of social life. This again is related to the
declining importance of cultural institutions such as the family, religion, and
traditional working-class community. In the latter regard, Stanley
Aronowitz (1988) has noted that as the objective basis for working-class cultural life was eroded by economic movements in the 1950s, the locus of the
new forms of community shifted to the emerging medium of television, and
that, although a coherent working-class no longer exists, the residual images
of that culture are still present on TV in the guise of cop shows and the cama-
raderie associated with beer commercials. The relation of sports (especially
its mediated, commercial form) to this disappearing cultural realm is a vital
axis around which relevant research questions can be posed.

Questions need also to be posed in terms of the relations between the
meanings of commercial sports and the shifting field of gender relations.
Many writers have suggested that sports has become a refuge for males who
are increasingly threatened by the appearance of new gender roles and relations. Whatever the merits of this kind of argument, we need answers to the
question of why sports has become defined in the almost exclusively male
manner that it appears in our culture and exploration of the historical shifts
in the nature of this identity.

In more general terms, there needs to be an analysis of the relation between the predominant forms of mediated sports (the relative importance of baseball and football within popular culture in different historical periods) and the shifting nature of the surrounding social and economic relations. For instance, some writers such as McLuhan have argued that the emergence of football as the most popular sport in the past 30 years is connected to it being much more suited to television ("the medium is the message") than other sports. Others have suggested that there is a close correlation between cultural forms and the wider economic system and that the emergence of football is strongly related to the shift from a competitive capitalism to its contemporary corporate and administered form. Again, we need to devote more thought to these issues.

There are also other, more contemporary issues. For example, why is sports so important as a form of nationalism, and what is its ideological and cultural link to the military/industrial complex? Also, in addition to the linking of sports discourses to the naturalizing of the commodity-form, the language of sports has also been used in other spheres, especially the political. Why has sports language become an important way to describe the activities of the state (see Balbus, 1975)? Similarly, issues connected to the arms race are often couched in sporting terms. In all these spheres, the key factor to be conceptualized is the nature of *competition* in these realms (which becomes increasingly more obscure) and the ability of sports to provide an illumination to the darkness (see Jhally, 1988). Again, the field awaits a close historical analysis of the changing nature of competition in many domains and the relation of this to the discourse of mediated sports competition.

Conclusion

Richard Johnson (1986–87) has argued that cultural studies in general need to focus on two sets of questions. The first group has to do with the *use-values* of cultural forms and the issues of pleasure and popularity. The second concerns the *outcomes* of these cultural forms. Do they lead to repression or freedom? How do they define social ambitions? Do they encourage a questioning of the existing social realm? Do they point to alternatives? Answers to these questions cannot be found by focusing on production or on texts or audiences alone: "They can best be answered once we have traced a social form right through the circuit of its transformations and some attempt to place it within the whole context of relations of hegemony within the society" (p. 72). Ultimately, of course, for our purposes here, what is called for is a thorough, nonreductive analysis of the articulation of mediated sports to social, cultural, political, sexual, racial, and economic factors — in short, a totalistic theory of sport and society and sport *in* society. The basic analytical research framework outlined in this chapter should enable us to get started on this important work.

References

Alt, J. (1983). Sport and cultural reification: From ritual to mass consumption. *Theory, Culture and Society, 1*(3).

Altheide, D., & Snow, R. (1978). Sports versus the mass media. *Urban Life, 7*(2).

Althusser, L. (1971). Ideology and ideological state apparatuses. In L. Althusser, *Lenin and philosophy*. London: New Left.

Althusser, L. (1977). *For Marx*. London: New Left.

Aronowitz, S. (1988). Working class culture in the electronic age. In. I. Angus & S. Jhally (Eds.), *Cultural politics in contemporary America*. New York: Routledge.

Balbus, I. (1975, March). Politics as sports. *Monthly Review*.

Buscombe, E. (Ed.). (1974). *Football on television*. London: British Film Institute.

Cantelon, H., & Gruneau, R. (1988). The production of sport for television. In J. Harvey & H. Cantelon (Eds.), *Not just a game*. Toronto: University of Toronto Press.

Chandler, J. (1983). Televised sport: Britain and the U.S. *Arena Review, 7*(2).

Clarke, A., & Clarke, J. (1982). "Highlights and action replays": Ideology, sport and the media. In J. Hargreaves (Ed.), *Sport culture and ideology*. London: Routledge & Kegan Paul.

Clarke, A., et al. (1976). Subcultures, cultures and class. In S. Hall & T. Jefferson (Eds.), *Resistance through rituals*. London: Hutchinson.

Critcher, C. (1986). Radical theorists of sport: The state of play. *Sociology of Sport Journal, 3*(4).

Fejes, F. (1984). Critical mass communications research and media effects: The problem of the disappearing audience. *Media, Culture and Society, 6*(3).

Garnham, N. (1983). Public service vs. the market. *Screen, 24*(1).

Gitlin, T. (1983). *Inside prime time*. New York: Pantheon.

Gramsci, A. (1971). *Selections from the prison notebooks*. London: Lawrence & Wishart.

Gruneau, R. (1988). Television, the Olympics, and the question of ideology. In R. Jackson & T. McPhail (Eds.), *The Olympic movement and the mass media*. Calgary, Alberta: Olympic Organizing Committee and University of Calgary.

Hall, S. (1980). Encoding/decoding. In S. Hall et al. (Eds.), *Culture, media, language*. London: Hutchinson.

Hall, S. (1985). Signification, representation, ideology: Althusser and the post-structuralist debates. *Critical Studies in Mass Communication, 2*(2).

Hargreaves, John. (1982a). Sport, culture and ideology. In J. Hargreaves (Ed.), *Sport culture and ideology*. London: Routledge & Kegan Paul.

Hargreaves, John. (1982b). Sport and hegemony: Some theoretical problems. In H. Cantelon & R. Gruneau (Eds.), *Sport, culture and the modern state*. Toronto: University of Toronto Press.

Hargreaves, Jennifer. (1986). Where's the virtue? Where's the grace? A discussion of the social production of gender relations in and through sport. *Theory, Culture and Society, 3*(1).

Hoch, P. (1971). *Rip off the big game.* Garden City, NY: Doubleday.

Horowitz, I. (1978). Market entrenchment and the Sports Broadcasting Act. *American Behavioral Scientist, 21*(3).

Johnson, R. (1986–87). What is cultural studies anyway? *Social Text, 16.*

Jhally, S. (1984). The spectacle of accumulation: Material and cultural factors in the evolution of the sports/media complex. *Insurgent Sociologist, 12*(3).

Jhally, S. (1987). *The codes of advertising.* New York: St. Martin's.

Jhally, S. (1988). *Competition, sports and the commercialized media.* Paper presented at the annual meeting of the International Association for Mass Communication Research, Barcelona, Spain.

Lipsky, R. (1981). *How we play the game.* Boston: Beacon.

Modleski, T. (Ed.). (1986). *Studies in entertainment.* Bloomington: Indiana University Press.

Peters, R. (1976). *Television coverage of sport.* Unpublished manuscript, Center for Contemporary Cultural Studies, Birmingham, AL.

Real, M. (1975). Super Bowl: Mythic spectacle. *Journal of Communication, 25*(1).

Sabo, D., & Runfola, R. (Eds.). (1980). *Jock: Sports and male identity.* Englewood Cliffs, NJ: Prentice-Hall.

Seifart, H. (1984). Sport and economy: The commercialization of Olympic sport by the media. *International Review of Sport Sociology, 3–4.*

Thompson, E. P. (1961). The long revolution [Book review]. *New Left Review, 9–10.*

Thompson, E. P. (1963). *The making of the English working class.* New York: Vintage.

Whannel, G. (1983). *Blowing the whistle.* London: Pluto.

Whannel, G. (1984). The television spectacular. In A. Tomlinson & G. Whannel (Eds.), *Five-ring circus: Money, power and politics at the Olympic Games.* London: Pluto.

Williams, B. (1977). The structure of televised football. *Journal of Communication, 27*(3).

Williams, R. (1961). *The long revolution.* New York: Columbia University Press.

Williams, R. (1976). *Keywords.* New York: Oxford University Press.

Williams, R. (1977). *Marxism and literature.* New York: Oxford University Press.

Willis, P. (1977). *Learning to labour.* Farnworth: Saxon House.

Willis, P. (1982). Women in sport in ideology. In J. Hargreaves (Ed.), *Sport, culture and ideology.* London: Routledge & Kegan Paul.

Wren-Lewis, J., & Clarke, A. (1983). The World Cup: A political football. *Theory, Culture and Society, 1*(3).

II

The Media Sports Production Complex

4

Sports Programming:
Scheduling, Costs, and Competition

Susan Tyler Eastman
Timothy P. Meyer

Sports, as a form of television programming, will change so radically in the next decade that many inside the industry will barely recognize the business. Most changes will result from cable channels' competition for telecasting rights and major advertisers' reluctance to pay ever-higher rates for network commercial time when smaller but more targeted audiences are available at much lower advertising rates than the networks command. These changes result from cable's penetration into more than half of U.S. television households, and they will make sports programming options more complex than at present and create new problems for programming researchers.

Viewers receive televised sports one of four ways: broadcast, cable, TVRO, or closed-circuit. Games or events can be delivered by broadcasters such as the network-affiliate stations that relay programs originated by the three major broadcast networks or the local independent stations that televise local games or carry a regional sports-only network. Broadcast stations can be received directly over the air or relayed by a cable operator. In the United States, about 89 million homes receive one or more broadcast stations, and the three major networks reach most homes simultaneously with the same programs, whereas independent ("nonnetwork") stations carry different programs in every market.

Sports delivered by cable operators come from three satellite-distributed sources. The most widely available are the basic cable networks, such as ESPN and USA Network, and the superstations—TBS, WGN, and WWOR—reaching over half of U.S. television homes. Basic cable subscribers (over 46 million homes) pay a lump monthly fee for a bundle of a dozen or more basic services, viewing as much or as little as they choose; nearly all cable operators supply ESPN and at least one superstation. All cable operators also distribute national pay cable services such as HBO, and many also carry regional pay cable sports channels, such as SportsChannel and SportsVision, for which cable subscribers pay an extra monthly fee; over one-fourth of television households (about 24 million) subscribe to— and presumably watch—a national pay service; most of the programming is movies, however, not sports, but boxing and wrestling have been very popular on national pay channels. Regional pay sports networks (there are 14 currently operating) usually carry the games of a single team to a geographic area, although SportsChannel recently captured the rights to National Hockey League (NHL) championship games (away from ESPN—basic cable). Operating several services along the East Coast, SportsChannel reaches about 10 million homes. In addition, some cable operators offer pay-per-view services such as Request Television or Viewer's Choice, which charge a per-event fee to those who choose to watch. Less than 12% of homes (just under 10 million), however, now have the addressable equipment needed to receive pay-per-view services. (An addressable home can be programmed by a cable system's computer to descramble a channel for a predetermined amount of time.) The number of pay-per-view households will double by the mid-1990s, as cable operators upgrade their systems (Reiss, 1989).

Private owners of backyard satellite dishes (numbering about 2 million) also can subscribe to satellite-delivered services called TVRO packages (for "television receive only"), which require a descrambler (often supplied by the local cable operator). Home dishes pick up the same satellite services that cable systems carry (ESPN, TBS, HBO, Viewer's Choice, and so on) and, like cable subscribers, TVRO subscribers pay a lump monthly charge for a bundle of channels and may pay extra for pay services. Most TVRO households have the equipment to receive pay-per-view programs when nationally distributed by satellite.

Finally, sports fans can see special events through closed-circuit television, a distribution means technically similar to pay-per-view and TVRO (usually requiring a satellite dish and addressable equipment) but available only to public viewing sites such as bars, arenas, and theaters. Event organizers charge fees for local closed-circuit rights to unique sports events.

The Trends

The three broadcast networks dominated television sports programming until the mid-1980s. They carried all the choice events, and the increasing amounts they paid for rights in turn fueled the National Football League (NFL), Major League Baseball (MLB), the National Basketball Association (NBA), the National Collegiate Athletic Association (NCAA), and the Olympic Games (Bellamy, 1988; Halberstam, 1981; Harris, 1987; Ohlmeyer, 1979; Rader, 1984; Spence, 1988). By the late 1980s, however, it had become evident that sports rights would have to be spread among several services—broadcast, basic cable, and pay cable—to continue raising the large amounts of money on which the major sports industries had come to depend (Harris, 1987; Spence, 1988). The shift of NFL games to ESPN broke the barriers; then professional hockey moved to pay-per-view cable, a further step away from the broadcast networks' control. By the late 1980s, cable television was actively bidding for Major League Baseball and NFL games.

Changes in the availability of televised sports to viewers were also apparent. Where once the broadcast networks had restricted sports programming to weekends and a few prime-time hours, the basic cable networks and superstations could supply 24-hour schedules of sports-related programming. And the content was shifting from a limited schedule of mass-appeal events to a wide stream of sporting events, sports scores and highlights, and sports talk on cable services (Eastman, 1989b). At the same time, the broadcast networks have continued to suffer from a shortage of live sports events with sufficient mass appeal to attract audiences comparable to other entertainment programs. And slowly, as addressable technology penetrates, unless Congress intervenes, economic pressure will force the biggest events away from broadcasting to pay-per-view television (Craig, 1988; Eastman, 1989a; Spence, 1988; Taaffe, 1988).

Network Television Sports Schedules

Sports accounted for over 1,800 hours of broadcast network television in 1988 (see Table 4.1), about 5,000 hours of cable television, and countless thousands of hours of radio and local broadcast television on independent television stations (Blair Television Programming, 1988). In the 1980s, the collective cost for sports programming rights exceeded $1.5 billion

Table 4.1
Network Sports Programming by Daypart, 1988

	Weekdays/Nights[a]	Saturdays	Sundays	Hours/Year	Hours/Week
ABC					
sports	121.5	155.0	134.5	411.0	10.8
Olympics	35.0	36.5	42.5	114.0	
anthologies[b]	–	32.5	6.0	38.5	
CBS					
sports	60.0	230.5	281.5	572.0	11.5
anthologies[b]	–	15.0	10.5	25.5	
NBC					
sports	37.5	201.5	184.0	423.0	12.4
Olympics	114.0	30.5	33.0	177.5	
anthologies[b]	–	6.5	38.5	45.0	
Total (hours)	368	708	730.5	1,806.5	11.6[c]

a. Mostly in prime time (Mondays).
b. ABC's *Wide World of Sports*; CBS's *Sports Saturday* and *Sports Sunday*; and NBC's *Sportsworld*.
c. Average hours per week per network.
SOURCE: Blair Television (1988).

annually—in the United States alone. And though the ratings for most sports on television are far lower than for prime-time series and movies, the most popular sports events command a 60% share of television households and enormous revenues.

Sporting events were a dependable profit center for broadcast television networks in the 1970s, but became marginal in the early 1980s as the cost of sports rights escalated, and plummeted in 1985 as the advertising market faded while rights costs continued to grow. In 1983 television ratings for professional football—the mainstay of network sports—declined for the first time, attributed to factors such as a glut of televised sports, the rise of competing sports options (e.g., cable, VCRs, and the fitness fad), and tarnished images of sports athletes. As a result, ratings declined, and advertisers refused to pay the network freight the following year. In 1985, CBS earned only $10 million on sports, NBC earned nothing, and ABC lost about $50 million (Goodwin, 1986). In 1986 and 1987, NBC also lost money on sports, and CBS about broke even. According to the head of ABC Sports, ABC is expected to continue losing money on sports until 1989 or 1990 ("Keeping Tabs," 1987).

Analysis of 1988 network sports programming (based on the daily schedules supplied to station representatives, affiliates, and advertisers) shows that the three broadcast networks each aired over 11 hours a week of sports in 1988 (see Table 4.1). They carried three-fourths of their sporting events on weekends, with one-fourth (26%) on weekdays (other than Olympics coverage, this was mostly Monday prime time on ABC). Examination of past schedules shows that this pattern remained steady throughout the 1980s, in both Olympics and non-Olympics years. Cable television and local independent stations (and radio), on the other hand, carried hundreds of collective hours of live and taped sports in any and all dayparts and days of the week by the late 1980s, but always the events and games the broadcast networks did not want (or were not willing to pay enough for).

Prime time is the most lucrative portion of network programming, attracting the largest audiences (of both sexes) and the largest advertising revenues. To avoid interrupting prime time while still providing the sports programs that strongly appeal to men (and to most network and advertising executives themselves), the broadcast networks generally have restricted sports programming to weekend days. Sports get sizable audience shares on weekends (collectively, more than half the available audience), but total audience size remains small (ratings on the order of 4% of television households per station). The introduction of "peoplemeters" was expected to boost the ratings of televised sports by recording the actual number of people watching an event (larger groups than for other programs, it was thought), but Nielsen and AGB results to date (fall 1987 and spring 1988) have failed to support that view. Peoplemeters have, in fact, revealed smaller audiences than were previously estimated.

On the other hand, for the national cable networks, sports in prime time drew bigger audiences than other programming in the 1980s. The early and late rounds of the NBA playoffs on WTBS (now TBS), for example, set all-time cable ratings records — not only for sports but for all nonsports ratings as well. On the broadcast networks, sports scheduling patterns are likely to become more varied as program executives feel increasing pressure to compete effectively with cable and VCRs. Tracking these changes in sports programming will involve weighing the factors that affect the selection, scheduling, and evaluation of all entertainment programming.

Selection, Scheduling, and Evaluation Factors

Program executives have traditionally been concerned with access to content, exclusivity, control, and the (largely) economic measures of program success or failure in comparison to other programming options. They must choose among the various types of programs (genres) to fill national broadcast network (and national cable) schedules according to the same priorities that apply to other types of programming. Programmers are concerned with a program's time window, its cost, potential ratings, and potential revenue, and how well it creates differentiation.

The first programming priority is the *rights window*—when a program is available. Network executives must be concerned with whether that window dovetails with prior network commitments and whether audiences (and advertisers) are available. Broadcast networks want to fill large amounts of time without locking in the prime-time hours so rigidly that a single failure has a huge impact on ratings. Thus prime-time entertainment is not stripped daily, and sporting events are relegated to weekend days. Network executives are leery of a sports block injuring prime-time schedules. In 1987, for example, CBS declined to seek rights to an eight-game NFL package (later obtained by ESPN), and NBC has repeatedly refused to preempt its potent Thursday- and Friday-night lineups as it bids for sporting events.

When being considered for carriage, as a class of programming, sporting events (and related pregame and postgame shows) face the same economic selection criteria as other programs: above all, a concern for the comparative costs of license fees (rights) and/or production costs. One difference between sports and most other entertainment programming is that sports events usually involve both *rights costs* and *production costs*, whereas other program genres either come complete for a license fee (movies, most prime-time series) or are produced by the network itself (news, talk shows). For networks, competitively bid sports rights account for 75% to 80% of sports programming costs (Spence, 1988).

Under corporate pressure to remove financial risk, the broadcast networks have begun to (1) contract for production of sports events by local producers or (2) require guaranteed sponsorship of events. Until the 1980s, most network sporting events were produced and hosted (announced) by the networks. By the late 1980s, however, the networks were increasingly contracting with outside producers for the actual production of games, bringing only their own announcers and on-air staffs. Except for pro football and the Olympics, nonnetwork agencies (syndicators/distributors, local production houses) can produce live and taped sporting events of equivalent technical quality at much lower cost than networks tied to restrictive union contracts. In cable, many events such as college basketball are commonly sold as complete packages, fully produced and including bartered advertising. The other change in sports is full sponsorship. Called "entitlement," it means that the advertiser gets its name included in the event's name and purchases enough commercial time for the network to break even. High cost is driving the networks increasingly into such risk-free arrangements for sports programming.

Cost, however, is always relative: It must be interpreted in relation to potential *ratings* and, ultimately, the availability of advertisers. Unfortunately for programmers, ratings are not always predictable, and although speculation about the variables affecting the ratings of superevents blankets the press, few scholars have looked at sports ratings. The basic programming practice is to choose the most popular program (higher share of audience) among those with the same hourly cost since the potential profit from advertising sales will be greater (the number of advertising minutes per hour being more or less constant). Not all audiences are equal, however. Generally, today, women aged 25–54 are the most desired network audience, with adults 25–54 and men 18–49 and 25–54 demanded by specific advertisers. Most sports target the male audience – though women are watching in greater numbers, especially events such as gymnastics and figure skating. Televised women's golf and women's basketball have recently shown strength in attracting women viewers. Perhaps surprisingly, bowling gets higher ratings on network television than most college basketball and all golf and tennis, while having two advantages: Bowling has very low production costs and attracts a blue-collar demographic group distinct from golf and tennis audiences. Boxing has the special advantage of drawing difficult-to-attract young black and Hispanic males.

Another aspect of ratings is a program's function as a lead-in to subsequent programs. Thus certain highly rated sports events drawing broad audiences are important vehicles for promotion of and flow to other programming. Viewers of the World Series and the Super Bowl, for example, are inundated with promotion for subsequent network entertainment programs.

Finally, "owning a sport" or certain sport superevents – the World Series, the NCAA basketball tournament, the Super Bowl, the Masters golf tournament, the Kentucky Derby – can provide *differentiation*, separation from competing networks and cable services in audiences' and advertisers' minds. This has positive results for the network in public image, promotability, and advertiser identification with a particular program. Because so much of prime-time programming is similar, sports play a strong role in providing network differentiation. CBS has historically "owned" basketball, for example, and until 1988, ABC "owned" the Olympics. Televising football games on Monday nights successfully provided differentiation for

ABC during the 1970s. This also explains why the networks compete for superevents such as the Olympics—although they often expect to lose money carrying them.

Golf is an exception to the usual cost and differentiation priorities. All three broadcast television networks carry large amounts of golf (60 to 70 hours each in 1988) for two reasons: Some advertisers are willing to pay to reach the upscale executive who watches golf on television, and advertisers themselves want "to rub shoulders with the golf greats at the major golf events" (Ohlmeyer, 1979; Spence, 1988). More than other sports, golf helps merchandise network television by encouraging contact between advertising executives and golf stars. Other superevents—such as the Super Bowl and Kentucky Derby—may be excessively expensive or inappropriate as advertising vehicles, but demand remains high because advertisers gain access to otherwise impossible-to-get tickets.

Sports as Programming

In the popular press, much is made of the role of network tradition (incumbency as the rights holder). Moreover, the male 25–54 audience has special value to some advertisers, such as breweries and car manufacturers. Increasingly, however, women decide about car purchases and even beer, and men in large numbers have joined the audiences for other entertainment programming. As of the late 1980s, many traditional sports advertisers began seeking their target demographic groups in entertainment programs as well as sports, reducing the demand for advertising time in network sports programs.

Once a program or sports event is known to be available for an appropriate time period, a program executive's foremost concern becomes its potential to generate revenue and profit. The networks bounce their cameras and most popular announcers to the games most likely to have the biggest national audiences, ignoring claims of loyalty to teams, fans, or geographic regions. The most desired rights—to playoffs and championship games commanding higher ratings—come with obligations to carry lower-rated regular-season games. World Series ratings, for example, are typically 33–39% of television homes (32.6/50 in 1987), and the Super Bowl continues to be the highest-rated television event each year (Super Bowl '87 captured a rating of 45.8 and a share of 66). But the national audience for sports on television is smaller than some fans admit: The 1987 NCAA Division I Basketball Tournament Championship game rated lower (19.6/28) than the concurrent Barbara Walters special (23.3/33) and the Academy Awards (27.5/43). Several NCAA tournament games even took a ratings beating from regular episodes of *Alf*.

In minor sports, even championship events may not rate highly enough to compete with network entertainment programs. To last more than a year in network prime time, a situation comedy or drama usually needs to attract 15% or more of television households (in other words, a rating of 15). In 1987, the highest-rated network boxing event, for example, rated only 6.8/14 (Spinks-Cooney and Tyson-Thomas heavyweight matches). The highest-rated golf—the Masters—reached only 9.9/24 in 1987 and was even lower in preceding years. The highest-rated horse racing—the Kentucky Derby—captured only 10.5/30 in 1987. The highest-rated tennis—one night of Wimbledon—was only 8.3/22. Wrestling, however, on Saturday nights on NBC achieved 11.6/33 for one night in 1987, generating fresh excitement at the networks. Wrestling and boxing have been especially successful for HBO and pay-per-view services. Even the most popular sport on television, professional football, averages only about 16% of homes during the regular season, though the AFC Championship, for example, reached 28.4/56.

Minor sports events are usually negotiated per event by the networks. The single-day superevents—the Super Bowl, the Kentucky Derby, the Indianapolis 500, the Rose Bowl—also are negotiated or bid as individual programs. Major team sports rights (football, basketball, baseball) are negotiated in packages of games for specific days of the week and times (prime time, early afternoon, late afternoon). Excepting the Olympics, the multiday superevents—the World Series, the NBA finals, and the NCAA Basketball Championship—are negotiated or bid as part of packages with regular-season events. The networks generally agree to air increasing numbers of regular-season games toward the end of a season as competition for top place tightens. In addition to conference, division, or league playoffs and championships, the specials—all-star games, the NBA's Slam Dunk Championship, the Pro Bowl—are negotiated item by item, beyond the regular-season packages.

Because programmers assume that winners attract ratings, even during the regular season, the television networks usually air only the games of the highest-ranked teams in a conference, division, or league, just as in individual events such as golf and tennis, the cameras focus on the leaders. Acquired rights often encompass many more events than actually reach the air. For example, ABC Sports purchased the rights to twice as many evening Major League Baseball games as it aired in the late 1980s (because of low prime-time ratings). In addition, during the regular season, the networks feed different baseball, football, and basketball games to different regions of the country, thus multiplying production and talent costs while generating only two to four hours (depending on the sport) of programming. On the other hand, local television and radio stations and some cable networks (especially the superstations), are tied to the games of specific teams or a league/conference, and their ratings vary with the team's win/loss record.

Table 4.2 shows the number of hours of each sport carried by each of the three broadcast television networks in 1988 (based on projected 1988 schedules). These hours include pregame shows and specials when devoted to a single sport. Anthologies covering highlights of many events and the Olympics are listed separately but appear within the total hours.

The relationships among the various sports as types of programming— for comparison to each other and to other programming options—have not been much explored by scholars for a number of reasons. First, the bulk of trade information about sports is about particular games and events rather than collectively examining sports as a type of program; sports journalism as investigative reporting and critical commentary is underdeveloped. Second, most articles about sports programming focus on how much the leagues, teams, conferences, and schools get from television contracts, often to speculate about the impact of TV rights on players' salaries (whereas the programmer wants to know what the network/station pays). Third, when trade publications do report the huge sums for lengthy multigame contracts, they rarely relate rights to production and talent costs.

Programming researchers need factual descriptive information on comparative total costs per hour, scheduling patterns, and ratings for each sport (for each season by daypart) to investigate hypotheses about sports as programming. However, this information is normally proprietary. Rep firms maintain computerized records of national sports ratings going back to the 1970s (Blair Television, for example, reports sports ratings for sports specials from 1976 to the present). Such records include many events/games, their network/day/time/hours broadcast, and their NTI rating/share. This information, however, is incomplete regarding regularly scheduled sports (*Monday Night Football*, regular-season NFL or MLB games, college games, and so on). To begin filling some gaps in knowledge, we next look at the available information about football, baseball, and basketball as network programming options, estimate and compare programming costs and ratings results for the three major televised team

Table 4.2
Network Sports Programming by Hours per Sport, 1988

	ABC	*CBS*	*NBC*	*Total Hours/Sport*
Baseball	75.5	3.0	108.0	186.5
Basketball	27.5	189.0	52.5	269.0
Bowling	28.5	–	7.5	36.0
Boxing	7.5	–	4.5	12.0
Football	140.0	230.0	138.5	508.5
Golf	68.0	71.5	61.5	201.0
Olympics	114.0	–	177.5	291.5
Racing	40.0	12.0	12.0	64.0
Tennis	22.0	59.5	37.0	118.5
Anthologies	38.5	25.5	45.0	118.5
Other	2.0	7.0	1.5	10.5
Total Hours/ Network/Year	563.5	597.5	645.5	1,806.5

sports in 1987, and compare these to costs for other types of network programs.

Football

Professional football is the most popular sport on television and commands the highest ratings. Relatively few professional football games are played (compared to professional baseball and basketball), so individual games take on greater importance as programming; in the programmer's terminology, each is a "special." As of the late 1980s, professional football means the National Football League (NFL) to broadcasters. Semiprofessional arena football (played indoors on smaller "fields") has, as yet, minimal popularity (ratings of 1 to 2 on ESPN, lower even than hockey).

Scheduling

After swallowing various competitors (USFL and AFL), the National Football League divided into two national conferences. The American Football Conference (AFC) and the National Football Conference (NFC) each has 14 teams playing 16 regular-season games, plus 4 or 5 preseason exhibition games each, the postseason playoffs and AFC and NFC championships, and the Super Bowl. Altogether, then, there are about 280 NFL games—of which one-fourth (about 75) are nationally televised annually on the broadcast networks (although many others are regionally telecast). Until 1987, NFL games did not appear on national cable. Professional (and college) football games have been scheduled for 3½ hours of airtime since 1986, allowing for more advertising time than the 3-hour scheduling used prior to 1986. Before important games, the networks also add a half-hour pregame show (low-budget talk, tape, and graphics). The networks produce all pro football games they carry—one each on CBS and NBC most Sunday afternoons during the season.

Professional Football Rights and Costs

The broadcast television networks purchased NFL football rights from 1978 to 1981 for a combined cost of $646 million. The next contract, a 5-year $2.1 billion deal starting in 1982, consisted of 20 weeks of games annually (dropping to just 9 weeks in 1982 because of the 57-day players' strike). In 1987, a 3-year deal was negotiated. It was a 1987–1989 package costing $1.42 billion, and for the first time, ESPN became a participating national network along with ABC, CBS, and NBC. In the 1982–86 contract, CBS and NBC each aired one NFC game for 16 Sundays (not head-to-head, but sequentially), and ABC aired the AFC on 16 Monday nights and occasional Thursdays and Sundays (from 25 to 29 pro games per year total, including preseason and postseason). Under the 1987–89 contract, ABC continues to air a package of 16 games on Monday nights; CBS airs an NFC game on 16 Sunday afternoons; and NBC airs an AFC game on 16 Sunday afternoons (making 48 regular-season pro games per year). Exhibition games (preseason) and special events—Thanksgiving Day games, wild-card games, the Super Bowl and Pro Bowl—are negotiated within the total price for each year of the combined contract. When ESPN joined the package, it bought the right to telecast annually 8 regular-season games in Sunday prime time, 4 exhibition games, and the Pro Bowl from 1987 to 1989. The Super Bowl is negotiated separately from the rest of the NFL package, running $17 million a year in the late 1980s and rotated among the three networks.

College Football

Until 1984 the National Collegiate Athletic Association negotiated television rights for all 509 member schools that had intercollegiate teams; annually, 16 games (includes bowls) appeared on the broadcast networks. Since 1984, each of the 104 Division I-A schools (and some smaller programs) has negotiated its own rights or assigned those rights (usually for a percentage fee) to a network, syndicator, or representative conference organization (Big 10 Network, College Football Association, Pac 10 TV Association, and others). The syndicator usually produces the games and sells the rights to national television networks (who produce their own games for the national network), national cable networks, and local television stations.

Each I-A team plays 11 to 14 Saturday games plus conference bowls, making a total of about 750 games that could be televised. The number actually appearing on national broadcast television (including bowl games) was 16 in 1983–84, 13 in 1984–85, 14 in 1985–86, 13 in 1986–87, and 15 in 1987–88. CBS and ABC negotiated about 32 games per year (CFA and Big 10/Pac 10/ACC packages) for about $31 million for 1988 to 1990. National Nielsen ratings averaged 6.9 in 1986 and 6.6 in 1987 for Saturday-afternoon college football.

Start Times

From a ratings standpoint, Saturday college football does best on national television between 3:30 p.m. and 7 p.m. In contract negotiations, ABC and CBS attempt to avoid 12:30 start times (which conferences prefer) because television viewer levels rise after 2 p.m. EST. ESPN and TBS schedule their college games on Saturday nights. In 1986–87 WTBS moved its start time to 7:05, a half hour ahead of ESPN, to gain an audience advantage (WTBS had lost money on college football in 1985 and 1986). This strategy had pitfalls because ABC and CBS games did not end until 7:30 p.m., and ratings for games on WTBS in 1986–87 were only somewhat higher than the 2.6 they earned in 1985–86 (ESPN averaged 3.6 that year).

Baseball

For broadcast television, baseball means professional Major League Baseball, although cable and some independent stations carry some minor-league and college games. Network and regional/local television/cable/radio account for more than half of MLB revenues, and national rights are negotiated by representatives of the league owners for all 26 teams. Local and regional rights are negotiated by each team's owner. For the five years from 1984 to 1989, collectively, Major League Baseball received over $1.1 billion for national television rights, about $650 million for local broadcast and regional cable rights, and about $35 million for radio rights. NBC and ABC negotiated exclusive national television rights; national cable (or superstation) contracts were not permitted so as to preserve broadcast network exclusivity. However, five superstations carry most games of at least one team, greatly increasing the number of professional baseball games available to viewers in cabled (or TVRO) homes.

Major League Baseball

Major League Baseball consists of two leagues—the American and National—each with East and West divisions. Each American League division has 7 teams; the National League divisions have 6 teams. Altogether, the 26 MLB teams play more than 2,200 games each year (162 regular-season games for each team plus exhibition games and playoffs). In the late 1980s, about 1,800 games were televised annually. Of these, only about 75 games (just over 3% of all games) appeared on the broadcast networks, although rights to a much larger percentage of games were held by the broadcast networks. The March to October professional baseball television season consists of preseason exhibition games (March), the regular season (April to early October), and postseason playoffs, including the World Series (October).

Schedules and Ratings

One difficulty in studying baseball contracts and ratings (purely as programming) is that the networks air different games in different parts of the country (at least two games most Saturdays). Moreover, nearly all baseball teams have local or regional television contracts supplying away games to the home market. Many also have pay cable contracts supplying games only to subscribers to regional pay sports or pay-per-view services. As many as half a dozen different baseball games may be simultaneously available in a large market, but the home team can be participating in only one of those games.

Network Strategies

In 1987, NBC purchased exclusive rights to 37 *Game of the Week* Saturday-afternoon telecasts (including 4 double-headers, 2 prime-time games, and the All-Star Game, but not including the 7–14 league playoffs it also carried). NBC negotiated complete exclusivity for Saturday afternoons; no other MLB games could be televised at that time (on cable or any broadcast station), and NBC achieved an average 6 rating (considered very successful for weekend daytime programming; weekday soap operas and game shows also strive for a 6 rating). This was consistent with previous Saturday-afternoon ratings in 1985 and 1986.

ABC's prime-time ratings for 11 regular-season games, however, ranged from 9.5 to 8.7 in the late 1980s, far lower than most prime-time entertainment shows achieve (a 15 rating minimum to avoid cancellation in 1987–88). Consequently, ABC reduced the number of prime-time baseball games carried over the years, dropping from 18 in 1982 to only 8 in 1988 (plus the All-Star Game and league playoffs). For 11 years, ABC broadcast Major League Baseball games on Sunday afternoons, ending that practice in 1987 because exclusive Sunday rights could not be obtained (ratings were in the 2s and 3s).

League playoffs and the World Series are the pot of gold for network baseball, but they become profitable only when sixth and seventh games are played; shares for the World Series are then on the order of 40–50% of homes using television, and advertising spots sell for $275,000 for 30 seconds. And of course, each game represents 3 hours or more of television, meaning that other programs do not have to be purchased to fill the time. In addition, pregame and postgame shows are generally low in production costs (although low in ratings) and provide a promotable package (bolstering differentiation).

Basketball

In the 1980s, basketball regained the wide popularity it lost in the point-shaving scandals of the 1950s, becoming one of the most profitable sports to program on broadcast and cable television. In the 1987–88 season, about 450 professional and college games appeared on television—about 100 on the three broadcast networks and about 350 on basic cable, pay and pay-per-view cable, and local broadcast television. Unlike the case with baseball, networks, stations, and teams make money regularly from basketball.

Professional Basketball

As of 1988, professional basketball means the National Basketball Association in the United States. Other leagues—such as the Continental Basketball Association and International Basketball Association—feature players of little interest to television programmers. The NBA consists of two conferences with two divisions each. As of 1988, the Eastern Conference had 11 teams, separated into the Atlantic Division with 5 teams and the Central Division with 6 teams. The Western Conference had 12 teams, separated into the Midwest Division with 6 teams and the Pacific Division with 6 teams. The awarding of four new franchises in 1988 will increase the NBA from 23 to 27 teams (and slightly increase the number of games played by each team).

Through 1988–89, each NBA team played 82 regular-season games, plus a few preseason exhibitions and, when possible, postseason playoffs (up to 45 games) and championship games (a best-of-7 series). Altogether, there are about 1,040 games (plus 5 NBA event specials) that could appear on television. In the late 1980s, however, barely 12% of games and events appeared on national television.

Rights and Contracts

The television rights to professional basketball are sold five ways. First, there are national broadcast television packages and national cable packages. In the early 1980s, national television rights were divided among CBS, ESPN, WTBS, and USA Network. Then, in the mid-1980s the NBA decided to restrict its games to one broadcast network and one cable network, seeking to maintain the value of the individual games. Since the 1984–85 season, CBS has had primary rights. It next negotiated a four-year contract running from 1986 to 1990 for $173 million ($43.25 million/year) for 15 regular-season games and the pick of playoff action (up to 26 games) and the championship (a best-of-7 series). For 1986–88, WTBS purchased the national cable rights for $25 million, covering 50 regular-season and up to 25 playoff games each year. For the next two years, WTBS doubled its rights payment in a $50 million pact for 75 games (50 regular season, 25 playoff) plus 5 special events annually: the NBA Draft, the Slam Dunk Championship, the Legends of Basketball Classic, the Long-Distance Shootout, and the NBA Awards show. NBA ratings on the broadcast networks averaged about a 7 for the 1988 playoffs, down from 10 or higher in previous seasons, but the championship games averaged about 16 in 1987. On TBS, NBA games average about a 3 rating, though one 1988 all-star game on TBS captured 7.5% of the cable audience.

On the local level, professional basketball clubs use three different cost approaches to sports production and rights (Aiken, 1989). A club can sell all rights to a syndicator or station for a flat fee or a share of revenue (safe); it can retain the rights in-house and produce its own games (most risky); or it can form a partnership with a local broadcaster, sharing costs and revenues (somewhat risky). Local television rights can run as high as $1 million dollars for a package of about 36 away games. Pay cable and pay-per-view rights are another source of revenue, operating successfully nowadays for about a dozen regional pay sports services. The trends are toward exclusive broadcast and cable contracts and retention of rights by the club, a pattern copied from the successes of the Portland Trail Blazers (Butler, 1988).

College Basketball

Selected NCAA basketball games and the NCAA tournament appear on national network television; otherwise, most college games appear on cable and local television. In its 1988–90 contract with the NCAA, CBS agreed to supply major markets with varied semifinal games at 7:30 p.m. EST, followed by a nationwide game (pushing back the start time of the national game). After the national network contract (traditionally CBS) for selected games has been negotiated, colleges and universities with Division I basketball teams (291 as of 1988) generally sell the rights to their games to a syndicator or form a conferencewide television company to produce and syndicate the games (and sell part of the advertising time). Typically, national and regional networks televise between 30 and 50 games in the most popular conferences, and the top five conferences make large amounts of money for participating schools. As few as a dozen or so games may be televised for less popular conferences.

Increasingly, CBS seeks exclusivity in televised college games within a given time period. For example, in its contract with the Big East Conference, CBS has exclusive national rights to Big East games; no other Big East games can be televised in the country before 7 p.m. EST and only local broadcasts (of Big East games) can occur after 7 p.m. (with two exemptions). In its 1988-90 contract, CBS paid an annual premium of $4 million for exclusive rights to the NCAA Final Four basketball tournament. In 1987, the final NCAA championship game captured a 19.6 rating. Other trends are toward shorter network contract lengths (fewer years) for college basketball and more commercial time (the NCAA permitted CBS to increase from 18 to 20 minutes of commercials in a tournament game in the most recent contract). Over the years, televised games (in all sports) have slowly become longer, occupying more airtime and therefore stretching the amount of television programming for a given rights fee.

Comparative Network Program Costs

Programming football and baseball is much more expensive to the networks than basketball, which accounts for part of basketball's profitability (the other part is its popularity). Table 4.3 shows 1987 sports rights costs (combined for the three broadcast networks but separated by daypart when available), estimated production and talent costs per game, the calculated cost per hour for network programming, and average 1987 ratings.

The broadcast network estimates in Table 4.3 do not approximate the actual cost to each network. In practice, sports rights costs are not divided equally among the three networks because advertising spots within prime-time games sell for a higher rate than weekend spots, and some games are "specials" and others less valued. Therefore Table 4.3 shows only the average cost per hour for each sport for the networks (in the same way that averages for other entertainment genres are calculated in programming).

Actual production costs vary somewhat depending on the location and who produces and how extensively (number of cameras, special effects, and so on) and is more costly for the highly produced superevents, but costs remain relatively consistent for the three networks because all use union crews (although CBS's union contract is less restrictive—mostly affecting

Table 4.3
Estimated Hourly Programming Costs, 1987

	$ Rights	Estimated Total Cost: Rights/Production/ Talent per Game[a] ($)	Cost per Hour ($)	Average Ratings 1987
Professional sports				
NFL football (81 regular-season games)				17.2 prime time[b]
	430 million	7,078,000	2,020,000	10.7 Sunday
Major League Baseball (32 weekend day and 11 prime-time, regular-season games, plus World Series, playoffs, All-Star Game)				8.7 prime time
	177 million	4,452,830	1,480,000	6.1 Saturday
NBA basketball (45 regular-season games and playoffs)				
	43.2 million	1,280,000	512,000	6.2 prime time
Prime-time entertainment				
Situation comedies (two 30-minute episodes)			800,000	15.0 prime time[c]
Dramatic series (one 60-minute episode)			900,000	15.0 prime time[c]
Action-adventure series (one 60-minute episode)			1,000,000	15.0 prime time[c]
Movies (hourly cost)			800,000	12.0 prime time

a. Production and talent costs calculated at 25% over rights cost.
b. 1987 ratings depressed over 1986 because of early season scab games.
c. Usual minimum for renewal of prime-time programs by 1987.

production of sports other than football). Until 1987, all football games were produced by the networks themselves, though the amount of equipment (and therefore costs) varied. ABC typically used the most equipment (eight to ten cameras, four or five tape machines), but NBC had similar costs with less equipment because of its bookkeeping methods (Ohlmeyer, 1979). CBS averages about five cameras and three tape machines per game. Trade reports claim that the three broadcast networks combined lost $45-$50 million on NFL football in 1985 and even more in 1986, but that profits rebounded in 1987 ("Football Rights," 1987; Goodwin, 1986; Taaffe, 1986).

In Table 4.3, production and talent costs are calculated at 25% above rights costs (Spence, 1988). Talent alone can run $100,000 a game ($28,500/hour), since salaries for the network announcing superstars escalated in the mid-1980s (less prior to 1986). Production costs for ESPN (and other cable services) are about half the average broadcast network cost, largely because of nonunion cable crews (Fabrikant, 1987). Cable's talent costs also are less than half those of the broadcast networks. The figures in Table 4.3, then, provide a way of comparing hourly network programming costs for major sports with the cost of other types of programs. Advertising rates each year can be tracked in relation to these costs to estimate the profitability of sports to the networks.

One further point affecting the calculations in Table 4.3 is the value of pregame shows. On Sundays (though not usually in prime time), the networks produce inexpensive half-hour pregame shows, add low-cost talk and scores between games, and fill out any remaining time with talk and interviews after games, bringing the entire Sunday afternoon to 6½ or 7 hours of football during the season. Pregame shows were not figured in the calculations in Table 4.3, but they would effectively reduce football sports costs per hour somewhat from the $2 million shown. (For comparison, the total cost for football per hour in the late 1970s ran about $1 million; Ohlmeyer, 1979.) Pregame and postgame shows play much less of a role in regular-season games and playoffs in baseball and basketball, contributing to the unprofitability of network baseball. Of course, "surround shows" become more important in these sports during the championship games and World Series.

In comparison to the typical cost of less than $800,000 for two half-hour situation comedies or about $900,000 for a 60-minute prime-time drama, the networks' hourly expenses for professional football and baseball appear excessively high. Comparatively, basketball is a bargain. On the other hand, high ratings normally lead to high advertising rates, successfully recouping the cost of football for the networks and also making basketball highly profitable. Baseball, on the other hand, is not likely to last long on the broadcast networks.

Issues for Programming Research

The emergence of cable as a major sports distribution medium raises many economic and policy questions. For example, who—the broadcast networks, cable networks, or a combination—can program which sports most cost-effectively? Concerns here include efficiency, entitlement, incumbency, and windows of availability, along with scheduling matters such as the impact of stretched seasons, sports runovers, and varying start times. Another important economic question, raised by declining network ratings for many events, is the value of exclusivity. Is it the key to higher ratings or an expensive promotional gimmick? What is the role of access to postseason play, the number of games that will maximize ratings for a network? In sum, what factors most influence the success of sports programming? Systematic programming research that will objectively evaluate the performance of televised sports is needed.

The trade press abounds with informal theories on the effects of (1) the intensity of interest in the home team in a local market; (2) the intensity of interest in the team in the surrounding region (the "shadow of the stadium" theory); (3) the impact of controversies such as doctored baseballs and bats, drugs, strikes, and exorbitant player salaries; (4) the previous success of a given team; and (5) the number and appeal of competing "outside" games (what else is broadcast or on basic cable or pay channels). The FCC's reinstatement of syndicated exclusivity creates further pressure for "exclusive" sports programs on superstations. Moreover, the emergence of Ted Turner's new basic cable network TNT (Turner Network Television) provides yet another national competitor for sports rights, and the possibility of a baseball-only basic cable channel in the 1990s has been suggested (Clarke, 1988) and has been considered seriously by the baseball commissioner's office. These events are shaking the established sports world and, in consequence, are rattling television programmers.

Another set of economic questions raised by declining network sports ratings concerns television audiences and their attractiveness to advertisers. Perhaps more clearly than any other type of program, sports represents the predicted movement of television generally from a state of "broad"-casting to "narrow"-casting, referring to the shift from large, fairly heterogeneous audiences to smaller, more homogeneous audiences. The criteria used to constitute an audience are undergoing significant changes. No longer is it efficient for advertisers to use standard demographics groupings alone to make the best audience buys. Programmers' knowledge of which factors— other than interest in viewing a particular sport or event—draw broadcast and cable audiences is becoming essential.

Another area of interest focuses directly on public policy issues. Government officials have traditionally assumed that sports programming is not essential to the operation of a democracy and an informed electorate (unlike news and public affairs programming). Congress and the Federal Communications Commission, therefore, have not acted to assert a public right of access to major sporting events, choosing instead to allow economic and marketplace forces to drive the television sports market. Since many people live in geographic areas impractical to wire for cable television and lack the resources to expend on home satellite receivers (TVRO), they will find themselves cut off from sporting events that shift from over-the-air broadcasts to cable. And even within cabled areas, households without the means to pay for premium channels or pay-per-view will lose access to some sporting events. Major boxing, wrestling, and hockey events have already jumped to pay-per-view. It is widely predicted that the major racing events (Kentucky Derby and Indianapolis 500), tennis (Wimbledon and U.S. Open), and playoff games in the NFL, NBA, and MLB, as well as parts of the Olympics, will soon move almost exclusively to cable, probably even pay-per-view. Who decides what programming is essential and what rights the public has are policy questions that need to be debated in advance of their realization.

This chapter provides a starting place for research into sports programming. The analysis points to several trends, most prominently the expanded roles of pay-per-view and basic cable in the coming decade. But the complex array of economic and policy questions posed but as yet unanswered shows much work ahead for programming scholars. Sports programming will be the crucible for programming research in the 1990s.

References

Aiken, E. (1989). Independent television station programming. In S. T. Eastman, S. W. Head, & L. Klein (Eds.), *Broadcast/cable programming: Strategies and practices* (3rd ed., pp. 229–248). Belmont, CA: Wadsworth.

Baseball bags almost $370 million in rights. (1988, March 7). *Broadcasting*, pp. 54–64.

Baseball rights approach $350 million. (1987, March 2). *Broadcasting*, pp. 47–55.

Basketball '87. (1987, October 19). *Broadcasting*, pp. 43–55.

Bellamy, R. V., Jr. (1988). Impact of the television marketplace on the structure of major league baseball. *Journal of Broadcasting and Electronic Media, 32*, 73–87.

Blair Television Programming. (1988). *Network sports calendar, 1st, 2nd, 3rd, and 4th quarters, 1988.* New York: Author.

Butler, C. (1988, January 18). Sports page: Winning on the home screen. *View*, p. 35.

Clarke, N. (1988, May 22). 24-hour cable channel idea grand slam. *Sunday Herald-Times*, p. 88.

Costas, B. (1987, November). The rules of the game. *Channels*, pp. 61–62.

Craig, J. (1988, July 11). Boxing bust is food for pay-per-view thought. *Sporting News*, p. 8.

Eastman, S. T. (1989a). Cable system programming. In S. T. Eastman, S. W. Head, & L. Klein (Eds.), *Broadcast/cable programming: Strategies and practices* (3rd ed., pp. 252–281). Belmont, CA: Wadsworth.

Eastman, S. T. (1989b). Basic cable programming. In S. T. Eastman, S. W. Head, & L. Klein (Eds.), *Broadcast/cable programming: Strategies and practices* (3rd ed., pp. 282–318). Belmont, CA: Wadsworth.

Fabrikant, G. (1987, June 9). It's first and goal for ESPN. *New York Times*, pp. 27–31.

Football rights hold line at $570 million. (1987, August 3). *Broadcasting*, pp. 39–58.

Goodwin, M. (1986, February 4). At ABC, the reaper's season arrives. *New York Times*, p. 29.

Halberstam, D. (1981). *The breaks of the game.* New York: Ballentine.

Harris, D. (1987). *The league: Inside the NFL* (rev. ed.). New York: Bantam.

It's a whole new ball game. (1988, March 7). *Broadcasting*, pp. 27–28.

Keeping tabs on ABC's variety of sports. (1987, April 6). *Broadcasting*, p. 127.

Ohlmeyer, D. (1979). Sports. In S. Morgenstern (Ed.), *Inside the TV business.* New York: Sterling.

Rader, B. G. (1984). *In its own image: How television has transformed sports.* New York: Free Press.

Reiss, J. (1989). Premium programming. In S. T. Eastman, S. W. Head, & L. Klein (Eds.), *Broadcast/cable programming: Strategies and practices* (3rd ed., pp. 319–346). Belmont, CA: Wadsworth.

Simon, E. (1986, September). Regional sports webs take on growing importance. *Cable Marketing*, pp. 34–47.

Spence, J. (1988). *Up close and personal: The inside story of network television sports.* New York: Atheneum.

Taaffe, W. (1986, February 24). TV to sports: The bucks stop here. *Sports Illustrated*, pp. 20–27.

Taaffe, W. (1988, July 11). Get out your checkbook. *Sports Illustrated*, p. 67.

Tedesco, R. (1987, September 21). Sports: Special report. *Electronic Media*, pp. S1–S8.

Up front. (1986, February 24). *Sports Industry News*, pp. 385–387.

5

Professional Sports Organizations: Media Strategies

Robert V. Bellamy, Jr.

The relationship between the television industry and professional sports leagues is one of mutual convenience and need. Sports leagues provide television with a source of successful programming, and television provides sports leagues with revenue essential to their operation. The relationship revolves around both mutual interest and the economic primacy of television. Television could survive without professional sports, but professional sports could not exist in their present form without television monies.

This essay details the relationship between professional sports organizations and the television industry in order to explain how professional sports organizations prosper and maintain a level of autonomy in an economic environment in which they are clearly subservient. The focus will be on the "Big 3" national sports leagues (Major League Baseball, National Football League, National Basketball Association), which provide television with some of its most popular programs.

The Economic Structure of Professional Sports Leagues

Competition is the primary product that sports organizations offer television. Without competition between teams, there would be no leagues and no product for television. As such, the sports industry has adopted measures that seek to ensure competitive equilibrium among league members. For example, player drafts force athletes to bargain with only one team, teams with poor records are given priority in player drafts, various restrictions limit the movement of players among teams, and national television revenues are shared equally (Closius, 1985; Davis, 1974; Sobel, 1977).

The leagues' ability to produce and maintain competitive equilibrium is related to the market structure of the professional sports industry (Bain, 1968; Caves, 1972; Greer, 1980; Scherer, 1970). The most salient point of the market structure is that professional sports leagues are oligopolies in which a small number of team owners control major sports. In addition, the owners strictly control the number of teams in the leagues, which increases the value of the existing teams. Another barrier to entry involves the formation of competitive leagues. The success of the Big 3 in promoting themselves as the *only* source of major league action in their respective sports has either precluded the creation of other leagues (in baseball) or led to the failure of competing leagues (in football and basketball).

The professional sports league oligopolies exhibit shared monopoly behavior in terms of admitting new members, colluding to obtain national television revenue and control of the player's market. This behavior is reflective of a cartel, where firms attempt to effect "a collusive (monopolistic) set of price output decisions" (Davis, 1974, p. 351). The Sports Broadcasting Act of 1961 (P.L. 87–331) gave legal sanction to the professional sports cartel by allowing leagues to negotiate joint broadcasting agreements. Major League Baseball (MLB) also has an explicit judicial exemption from antitrust laws in dealing with rival leagues (*Federal Baseball Club v. National League*, 1922). This is a major reason that there have been no new baseball leagues since the advent of television.

Even though various attempts to expand the federal precedent to the other league sports have failed (e.g., U.S. Congress, 1958), the other major leagues have been able to act as cartels in essentially the same manner as MLB. This is the result of the "leniency" of government institutions (e.g., courts, Congress), which have regarded sports as different (i.e., "purer") than other businesses and promulgated protections such as the Sports Broadcasting Act.

The collective bargaining process between leagues and players also provides certain legal exemptions from antitrust activity (Closius, 1985). For example, the National Football League (NFL) used its cartel and political power to absorb the rival American Football League (AFL) and implement an even share of television revenues among all member clubs through congressional dispensation (15 U.S.C., section 1291, 1966). Similarly, the

National Basketball Association (NBA) has been able to monopolize professional major-league basketball in North America by consolidation with a rival league (American Basketball Association). The cartel power of the leagues impairs the ability of competing leagues to attract financial backing, television money, and fan support.

The Economic Relationship of Television and Professional Sports Leagues

Mutual dependence does not imply equality between the television and professional sports industries. A simple comparison of the financial status of the industries demonstrates that television has the upper hand in the relationship. For television, organized sports are a source of programming, with the same status as any other form of successful programming (i.e., that attracts a viewership that can be sold at a premium price). For professional sports, however, television is the lifeline that has allowed them to prosper and influence the leisure-time activity of a large segment of the population. This dependence on media has been cited as the major factor that influences the structure of sports (Jhally, 1984; Loy, McPherson, & Kenyon, 1978; Rader, 1984).

To assert that television has changed sports is to state the obvious. More important is how and why such changes are implemented. This question relates to a consideration of the economic power of the television industry, which, not unlike sports, traditionally has operated as a government-sanctioned oligopoly of three major networks.

While television is clearly the dominant partner, professional league sports are not powerless in the relationship. Sports organizations have developed a constituency of fans and policymakers that tends to check the power of the television industry to implement changes in the relationship. Television acts *with* rather than *against* other institutions to support the political economic status quo of which it is a part and on which it depends for its very existence (Curran, Gurevitch, & Woollacott, 1982; Mosco, 1979; Turow, 1984).

An overview of the three major professional sports leagues and a review of their relationship with the television industry will answer questions about the economic relationship between the television and sports industries. The focus will be on the strategies that the sports leagues have adopted as means of exerting power and maintaining their position with the economically more powerful institution of television.

Television and the Big 3 Sports Leagues

Major League Baseball

Professional league sports began with the establishment of the National League of Professional Base Ball Clubs (NL) in 1876. The NL was set up with a strong organization to control the behavior of franchise owners, to bring uniformity to scheduling and rules, and, most important, to subjugate the players to the power of the franchise owners through such devices as the reserve clause of 1879, which removed the players' ability to sell their services to the highest bidder (U.S. Congress, 1976, p. 79). In 1903 the NL signed an agreement with the new (i.e., established in 1901) American League (AL) in which all clubs agreed not to sign each others' players, and for their respective pennant winners to engage in an annual "World Series" (Schlossberg, 1980). This event and the 1920 hiring of a commissioner with broadly defined powers to operate in "the best interests of baseball" welded the NL and AL into an institution known as Major League Baseball (U.S. Congress, 1958, p. 146).

As the only professional league sport that had a fully developed structure at the advent of commercial radio in the 1920s, MLB's relationship with the broadcast industry developed somewhat differently from those of the other major sports. The key factor in the relationship is the emphasis on local and regional broadcast rights fees as a major source of income for the individual teams. Even with the highly developed national television industry of today, MLB still receives approximately half of its television money from local and regional rights fees ("Baseball Bags," 1988). A corollary to this emphasis on local and regional television is that teams receive varying amounts of money for their rights. This is a major financial bonus for the teams in the largest media markets (e.g., New York, Los Angeles, Chicago), where teams can expect to generate much more revenue than teams located in smaller media markets. In 1988, for example, the New York Mets received approximately $17 million for local broadcast rights, while the Cleveland Indians received $3 million ("Baseball Bags," 1988, p. 56). This revenue disparity, combined with a policy that ensures the home team will keep approximately 90% of gate proceeds (David Alworth, director, Baseball Administration, MLB, personal communication, March 5, 1987), leads to a situation where the major market teams have the clear potential to be differentiated from the "have-nots" in terms of playing field success, a situation that clearly is not conducive to the production of competition. The television money disparity is further complicated by the fact that the "haves" also are the primary beneficiaries of pay television services (Bellamy, 1988).

Although the concept of revenue sharing is a "constant concern" of MLB, the idea of sharing television revenues equally has always been opposed by many owners. While they share some revenue from pay television operations and have forced the teams with superstation cable outlets to share a portion of their revenue, there is little possibility of an equal sharing of all broadcasting revenues (Bryan Burns, senior vice president, MLB, personal communication, February 4, 1988).

As in the other major sports leagues, MLB teams split all national television revenue equally. Under the terms of the six-year contracts with ABC and NBC that began in 1984, each team receives approximately $8 million a year (Nightingale, 1987). From 1990–93, CBS will have network exclusivity for MLB due to a bid of $1.1 billion, which equals approximately $11 million per team per year (Martzke, 1988). Although criticized for paying too much, CBS justified the deal by explaining that it provides the network with exclusive coverage of most of the major sporting events (e.g., World Series, NCAA Basketball Tournament, NBA Championship, and several Super Bowls), and that the World Series will provide momentum and promotional opportunities for its third-place prime-time schedule (Buckman, 1988).

MLB has adopted several strategies to hold down costs and generate new sources of income. First, the owners have cut back the number of expensive long-term player contracts that were prevalent in the first few years of free agency (i.e., where veteran players can sell their services to the highest bidder) in the late 1970s and early 1980s (Chass, 1988). Second, MLB now scrambles all satellite feeds of games to "protect baseball's copyrighted material" and to set in motion a plan to charge dish owners for game reception ("Baseball to Scramble," 1987; Bryan Burns, personal communication, February 4, 1988). Third, baseball officials have discussed the formation of an all-baseball basic cable channel (Craig, 1988). Fourth, and as a possible forerunner of a cable channel, MLB will air 175 games a year on ESPN (the majority owner of which is Capital Cities/ABC) for four seasons at $100 million per year beginning in 1990 (Warner, 1989). This deal excludes all but 12 regular-season games a year from network coverage (Martzke, 1988). Finally, outgoing Commissioner Peter Ueberroth has suggested structural changes aimed at generating more fan interest and television income.

Among the suggestions are expansion of the leagues' memberships, a new tier of playoffs involving "wild-card" teams, and a limited schedule of inter-league games that could be scheduled as "event" television (Nightingale, 1987). Although the unexpectedly large bid from CBS seemingly precludes such changes in the next few seasons, the search for ever-higher television revenues is likely to keep such ideas on the agenda of baseball officials.

In sum, MLB's television strategy consists of several components. First, individual teams continue to expand their offerings on such alternative outlets as basic and pay cable. Second, MLB is developing the rudiments of a direct broadcast satellite (DBS) system to generate a new source of income. Finally, and most instructive of the power of television, MLB is considering structural changes to enhance its television appeal.

National Football League

The other major professional sports leagues resemble MLB in their evolution from loose confederation into strongly centralized leagues. The National Football League, organized in 1920 with several small city franchises, evolved by the late 1930s into a league with a small group of teams located in the largest metropolitan areas of the eastern and central United States (Patton, 1984).

The strong relationship between the NFL and television has been the subject of various books (Durso, 1971; Johnson, 1971; Patton, 1984). As the only sport league with all regular-season games telecast, the highest ratings, and where approximately 60% of its revenues come from television (Val Pinchbeck, director of broadcasting, NFL, personal communication, December 15, 1987), the evidence for the NFL being a television-made sport is strong.

The relationship between the NFL and the television industry is the result of several factors that converged in the early 1960s. First, the Sports Broadcasting Act of 1961 (P.L. 87–331) gave all professional sports leagues an antitrust exemption to sign leaguewide television contracts. This allowed the NFL to set in place a steady stream of equally split revenue for each team to complement the 60/40 home/visitor gate receipt split that had long been in effect (Patton, 1984, pp. 54–55). Second, the network television industry had by the 1960s begun making extensive use of demographic audience data to sell advertising time. With the numbers suggesting the strongly male and reasonably affluent characteristics of the NFL audience, the networks began to compete to gain these rights (Patton, 1984, p. 54). As an example, the value of the network contract for each NFL team increased from approximately $200,000 in 1960 to $1 million in 1965 to $17 million in 1987 (Craig, 1987a; Parente, 1974, p. 77). Finally, the formation of the American Football League in 1960 not only increased the public interest in professional football, but allowed the networks that could not gain NFL rights (ABC, NBC) to air pro football games. The AFL gained legitimacy through television coverage to the degree that the NFL was compelled to reach an accommodation. The result was a government-sanctioned absorption of the AFL into the NFL and the subsequent establishment of a common player draft and postseason championship game called the Super Bowl (15 U.S.C., section 1291, 1966).

The role of the major television networks in the "merger" of the AFL and NFL is indicative of the ability of television to effect change in professional sports in several ways. First, the networks that covered the NFL (CBS) and AFL (NBC) remain the networks that cover the reorganized NFC ("old" NFL) and AFC (AFL). Second, the only network that was not covering professional football at the time of the merger (ABC) became the outlet for prime-time games when CBS and NBC were unwilling to broadcast prime-time games in 1970, although a higher bid was reportedly made by the syndicated Hughes network (Johnson, 1971, p. 142). Third, the three networks rotate coverage of the Super Bowl, which is always one of the highest-rated telecasts of the season. In essence, the oligopoly of the three major networks has formulated an accommodation with the shared monopoly that is the NFL. Fourth, the two leagues that have attempted to challenge the NFL since the 1970 merger (WFL, 1974–75; USFL, 1983–85) were unable to obtain network contracts to compete directly with the NFL (although the USFL had a contract with ABC for spring games). In addition, in a repeat of the Monday night/Hughes/ABC situation of 1970, ABC kept the *Monday Night Football* contract for 1987 even though the fledgling Fox Network reportedly offered more money (Craig, 1987b). Finally, the NFL's first cable contract was with ABC's ESPN service.

According to the NFL, the 1987 move to ESPN was an experiment implemented because the league was the last major sport without a cable contract (Val Pinchbeck, personal communication, December 15, 1987). A more likely scenario is that by spreading its games over four television services, the league was able to increase the amount of money flowing from television to approximately $17 million per team per year from $13.6 million (Craig, 1987a). The basic television strategy of the NFL is to maintain its position as the most widely covered and lucrative of the major sports. While the key is network television coverage, the league has demonstrated that it will move games to other outlets (at least those controlled by the networks) if that will maintain or increase its revenue.

Besides using television, the individual clubs have been able to increase their financial position by threatening to move or actually moving to new cities. The nearly insatiable desire of cities to be associated with "big-time" sports has led many cities to offer generous lease terms and new or remodeled playing facilities (Axthelm with Murr, 1987; "Perks Line," 1988). Failure on the part of a city to match or exceed these offers can result in the loss of a team, as was the case in Baltimore, Oakland, and St. Louis. "Abandoned cities" are characterized by either stagnant economies or overlapping media markets, while the new league cities (Los Angeles, Indianapolis, Phoenix) are all growing television markets.

In addition, the NFL, more than the other major sports, has been able to control player costs by holding its ground against the league players' union. This can be seen in the decision by all three networks to run regular-season games with "replacement" players during the 1987 players' strike. Even with the rebates that the NFL had to pay to the networks due to the lower ratings of such games (Tedesco, 1987a), the fact that they were carried gave the owners a stream of revenue and the appearance of legitimacy that was vital in forcing an end to the strike. The NFL, more than any other sports league, has reached a comfortable accommodation with the television oligopoly.

National Basketball Association

The NBA was created in 1949 from the merger of the Basketball Association of America and the National Basketball League (U.S. Congress, 1958, p. 563). As recently as 1957, the league had only 8 franchises, including such cities as Fort Wayne, Indiana; Minneapolis, Minnesota; Rochester, New York; and Syracuse, New York. Except for Minneapolis, none of these was or is a major television market as measured by Arbitron and Nielsen. By 1963, these cities had been replaced by the major markets of Detroit, Los Angeles, Cincinnati, and Philadelphia, respectively. Subsequent expansion and the absorption of teams from the failed ABA have resulted in a league of 25 clubs (with 2 more to begin play in 1989–90), in most of the nation's major cities.

The two major reasons for locating franchises in large cities are to increase attendance and to make the sport more attractive to television networks, which are obviously interested in gaining affiliate clearance in the largest media markets. Indeed, the expansion of the NBA was crucial in gaining it a national television contract, first with ABC and since 1973 with CBS (Parente, 1974, p. 89). However, the NBA has certain attributes that make its relationships with television and with its fans different from the other major sports. First, unlike the NFL, the home team in the NBA keeps all of the gate revenue. The impact of this has been an emphasis on placing teams in cities where there is a core of basketball fans who will turn out in substantial numbers regardless of the performance of the team. Thus traditionally "non-major-league" cities such as Charlotte, Portland, Sacramento, and Salt Lake City have NBA franchises. In this "big fish in a small pond" scenario, these franchises are successful because they are the only major-league sport in town (Ed Desser, director of broadcasting, NBA, personal communication, October 20, 1987). The problem is that such cities are not highly valued by the networks. Second, the imbalance in league revenues resulting from the home/away gate split and the fact that one or two players can turn around the fortunes of a team have led to a situation in which a small number of teams dominate the league.

With television revenues equal to or exceeding the box office for several NBA teams (Ed Desser, personal communication, October 20, 1987), the league has moved into cable and pay television distribution on both the national and local/regional levels. Currently, the league has national deals with CBS and the TBS cable superstation worth $173 million over 4 years and $50 million over two years, respectively (Tedesco, 1987b). In addition, some clubs (e.g., New York Knicks) have successfully implemented pay services (Ed Desser, personal communication, October 20, 1987).

Unlike MLB and the NFL, with their strong institutional ties to the conventional television networks, the NBA's television strategy is based more on maintaining a network presence while increasing both cable and local/regional coverage. Cable is of particular importance to the league, as it provides an outlet for many regular-season games that the networks are no longer interested in telecasting. However, this is not to imply that the league is unconcerned with network coverage. In fact, the league adjusted its playoff schedule to ensure that the games in the final series would occur after the May ratings sweeps and be carried in network prime time (Ed Desser, personal communication, October 20, 1987).

In addition to the search for increased television revenues, the NBA has taken other steps to enhance its financial situation and promote intraleague competition. Player costs are controlled through such devices as a salary cap that limits the amount of money each team can spend on player salaries. Competitive equilibrium is bolstered through a right of first refusal rule that allows a team to retain the services of a free-agent player (with less than seven years of service) by matching another team's offer (Hubbard, 1988).

Sports Leagues and the Evolving Television Environment

With multiple channels to fill, cable television has a voracious appetite for programming. In order to fill their schedules, cable services have scheduled such tried-and-true programming as off-network reruns, news, weather, and, especially, sports. The effectiveness of this strategy is reflected in the fact that 10 of the 20 highest-rated cable programs in the fourth quarter of 1987 were sports oriented (Stilson, 1988). In addition to such major sports as professional football and hockey (ESPN), college football (ESPN, TBS), professional basketball (TBS), and college basketball (ESPN, TBS, USA), such sports as professional wrestling, Australian rules football, and arena football have received extensive cable exposure. In fact, the now extinct United States Football League was supported by and partially owned by cable interests (Patton, 1984, pp. 220–221). Besides national cable, regional and even local cable operations have provided new outlets for sports coverage.

The mutually beneficial relationship of the cable and sports institutions sees that cable receives a source of popular programming and sports organizations acquire new presentational outlets while "weaning" themselves from dependence on the networks. However, a closer look suggests more limited benefits. First, cable is more a replacement than a new outlet for the major professional sports leagues. The three major sports leagues moved games to cable because the major networks were no longer willing to carry their games, either in the quantity or for the price that they once were. Second, with the present exception of the NFL, sports leagues receive less money from cable than from network sources. The NBA, for example, receives $173 million for four years from CBS and $50 million over two years from TBS (Tedesco, 1987b) although many more games are aired over cable. Third, local and regional cable services are increasing the revenue disparity between teams in MLB and the NBA. This has the potential to weaken league structures by decreasing intraleague competition. Fourth, the revenue potential from cable and, more specifically, pay television is likely to be restrained by government bodies that seek to preserve major events for advertiser-supported television. After several years of dormancy, such discussions are again on legislative agendas (Isle, 1987).

Finally, Jhally (1984) suggests that the growth in cable and related distribution systems may weaken the traditional television industry (as exemplified by the three networks) and subsequently may change the dynamics of the sports/television relationship. However, cable's subscriber growth and ability to pay more for programming makes it more of a power within the structure of the television industry, a fact recognized by ABC's and NBC's involvement in cable sports services (ESPN, SportsChannel America).

The present strategy of professional sports leagues is to use cable to supplement broadcast television. This strategy has benefited sports organizations as they combat the broadcast networks' threats to reduce rights fees for sports telecasts. However, emerging patterns of control in the cable industry make it likely that the power advantage will remain with television and not the sports leagues.

Conclusions

Television's dominant position frames the mutual dependence of the television and professional sports industries. While the money that flows from television is necessary to the maintenance of sports leagues, it also creates problems that can have a negative impact on the level of intraleague competition that is also necessary for the survival of the leagues. For example, the availability of more television money tends to increase the demand for higher player salaries. Larger-city franchises have a greater base of potential fans and possibility to exploit media rights payments that make it easier for them to absorb increases in salaries and other operational costs. Four primary coping strategies are employed by professional sports leagues: the use of cable and related outlets as a supplement to traditional broadcasting outlets, structural changes, increased marketing efforts, and the stabilization or lowering of player costs.

All of the major professional sports leagues have agreements for cable coverage, varying from purely local or regional coverage to high-priced national deals. The problem is that cable coverage is in many respects replacing rather than supplementing traditional national network coverage and paying considerably fewer dollars for the right to do so. On the local level, large-market franchises are able to generate cable revenue that is unavailable to the other teams. At present, only the NFL has been able to use cable as an actual supplement to network coverage. For the other major sports, cable appears to contribute to a decrease in the production of competition.

In order to increase their attractiveness to the television industry, all of the major sports leagues have implemented changes in both structure and the conduct of operations. Expansion, franchise shifts, and increased playoffs are the most common examples. Since 1946 (the approximate beginning of the television era), MLB has grown from 16 to 26 teams, the NFL from 10 to 28, and the NBA from 11 to 25. The movement of franchises to more lucrative television markets has been a continuing trend (with the possible exception of the NBA), as has the continual increase in the number of teams that qualify for the playoffs.

Beyond the search for new sources of media money, all of the major sports leagues have increased their marketing efforts in order to increase attendance. The record attendance figures in MLB and the NBA attest to the success of such efforts. However, the strategy has limited utility for the NFL, where many teams have traditionally had sellouts for every home game.

After a period of rapid salary increases for professional team athletes that began with the advent of free agency (the system varies by league), sports owners have recently adopted measures to control or even reduce salary costs. The NBA limits the amount that teams can spend on salaries. The NFL "broke" the 1987 players' strike. However, this strategy has proven limited in the case of MLB, where an arbitrator ruled that the owners illegally colluded to prevent the movement of free agents (Chass, 1988). Ultimately, the success of a salary stabilization strategy depends on whether or not sports owners can avoid the legal ramifications of such actions.

In addition to specific strategies, professional sports leagues exert influence in their relations to the television industry through their political power. Special government treatment of sports leagues has exempted the Big 3 from several areas of antitrust law. The dilemma for sports leagues is that certain strategic steps that may be taken to increase their financial position (e.g., shifting franchises, moving more games to pay television) have the potential to erode the "goodwill" and political clout that sports traditionally have had with policymakers.

With problems in every strategy available to them, the professional sports industry faces continuing domination by the television industry. However, two major factors offer hope. First, the television industry is entering a shakeout phase brought about by the success of cable and the possibility of other program distribution mechanisms. Although the traditional powers of the broadcast industry are likely to remain influential, institutional flux gives sports organizations a window to exploit new opportunities. An instructive example is the recent CBS/MLB deal, where the network's desire to compete with its rivals in prime time and in prestige as the network of sports exclusives led it to bid far more than most had expected.

Second, television's power over sports is so complete and accepted by both parties that the two industries are not antagonists. Rather, their joint ability to break an NFL players' strike or to eliminate competing leagues is evidence of a partnership of oligopolies. The parallel growth of professional sports and broadcasting industries established the parameters of the relationship years ago. The joint formula for success that characterizes the marriage of television and professional sports leagues is not likely to be altered substantially in the near future.

References

Axthelm, P., with Murr, A. (1987, December 28). Rx for cities: Build a dome. *Newsweek*, p. 21.

Bain, J. S. (1968). *Industrial organization* (2nd ed.). New York: John Wiley.

Baseball bags almost $370 million in rights. (1988, March 7). *Broadcasting*, pp. 54–63.

Baseball to scramble satellite backhauls in 1988. (1987, November 2). *Broadcasting*, p. 37

Bellamy, R. V., Jr. (1988). Impact of the television marketplace on the structure of Major League Baseball. *Journal of Broadcasting and Electronic Media, 32*, 73–87.

Buckman, A. (1988, December 19). CBS stations cheer baseball buy. *Electronic Media*, pp. 1, 60.

Caves, R. (1972). *American industry: Structure, conduct, performance* (3rd ed.). Englewood Cliffs, NJ: Prentice-Hall.

Chass, M. (1988, February 1). Gibson, six others are free-look free agents. *Sporting News*, pp. 32, 36.

Closius, P. J. (1985). The ground rules of immunity, exemption, and liability. In A. T. Johnson & J. H. Frey (Eds.), *Government and sport: The public policy issues* (pp. 140–161). Totowa, NJ: Rowman & Allanheld.

Craig, J. (1987a, July 13). FTC probing what kept Fox from NFL door. *Sporting News*, p. 7.

Craig, J. (1987b, September 21). A primer on the NFL's marriage to television. *Sporting News*, p. 8.

Craig, J. (1988, May 9). All-baseball cable channel on drawing board. *Sporting News*, p. 8.

Curran, J., Gurevitch, M., & Woollacott, J. (1982). The study of the media: Theoretical approaches. In M. Gurevitch, T. Bennett, J. Curran, & J. Woollacott (Eds.), *Culture, society and the media* (pp. 11–29). London: Methuen.

Davis, L. E. (1974). Self regulation in baseball, 1909–71. In R. G. Noll (Ed.), *Government and the sports business* (pp. 349–386). Washington, DC: Brookings Institution.

Durso, J. (1971). *The all-American dollar*. Boston: Houghton Mifflin.

Federal Baseball Club v. National League (1922). 259 U.S. 200.

Greer, D. F. (1980). *Industrial organization and public policy*. New York: Macmillan.

Hubbard, J. (1988, May 9). NBA again sets proper example. *Sporting News*, p. 41.

Isle, S. (1987, June 15). Yankee TV bill. *Sporting News*, p. 21.

Jhally, S. (1984). The spectacle of accumulation: Material and cultural factors in the evolution of the sports/media complex. *Insurgent Sociologist, 12*, 41–57.

Johnson, W. O., Jr. (1971). *Super spectator and the electric Lilliputians*. Boston: Little, Brown.

Loy, J. W., McPherson, B. D., & Kenyon, G. (1978). *Sport and social systems*. Reading, MA: Addison-Wesley.

Martzke, R. (1988, December 15). Baseball scores big at the bank. *USA Today*, pp. 1C-2C.

Mosco, V. (1979). *Broadcasting in the United States*. Norwood, NJ: Ablex.

Nightingale, D. (1987, December 21). Looking down expansion road: 15-team leagues. *Sporting News*, p. 44.

Parente, D. E. (1974). *A history of television and sports*. Unpublished doctoral dissertation, University of Illinois, Champaign-Urbana.

Patton, P. (1984). *Razzle-dazzle*. Garden City, NY: Dial.

Perks line a new nest. (1988, January 25). *Sporting News*, p. 24.

Rader, B. G. (1984). *In its own image: How television has transformed sports*. New York: Free Press.

Scherer, F. M. (1970). *Industrial market structure and economic performance*. Chicago: Rand McNally.

Schlossberg, D. (1980). *The baseball catalog*. Middle Village, NY: Jonathan David.

Sobel, L. S. (1977). *Professional sports and the law*. New York: Law-Arts.

Sports Broadcasting Act. (1961). P.L. 87-331, 75 Stat. 732.

Stilson, J. (1988, January 25). NFL games top ratings for cable. *Electronic Media*, pp. 3, 70.

Tedesco, R. (1987a, November 16). NFL sets rebates to networks. *Electronic Media*, p. 6.

Tedesco, R. (1987b, November 30). Turner can run NBA games on TNT. *Electronic Media*, p. 66.

Turow, J. (1984). Pressure groups and television entertainment: A framework for analysis. In W. D. Rowland, Jr., & B. Watkins (Eds.), *Interpreting television: Current research perspectives* (pp. 142–162). Beverly Hills, CA: Sage.

U.S. Congress, House of Representatives, Select Committee on Professional Sports. (1976). *Inquiry into professional sports* (94th Congress, 2nd session). Washington, DC: Government Printing Office.

U.S. Congress, Senate, Committee on the Judiciary. (1958). *Organized professional team sports* (85th Congress, 2nd session). Washington, DC: Government Printing Office.

Warner, R. (1989, January 6). ESPN wins TV rights to baseball. *Arkansas Democrat* (Little Rock), pp. 1D, 4D.

6

Making Spectacle:
A Case Study in Television Sports Production

Richard Gruneau

> This is the immanent structure of television as a communicative praxis. It is
> embedded in socio-economic structures and institutions, and these in turn
> within political and ideological configurations which establish outer limits and
> determinations, but which bear back upon the screen and the image itself—its
> production, distribution and reception—through the internal practices. (Hall,
> 1975)

The language of television sports is dominated by a sense of immediacy and
actuality. Announcers talk incessantly about "event coverage," "showing us
the game live," or "taking us to the stadium." However, many analysts of
sport and the media have emphasized that television's realist claims to
immediacy and actuality are mythical (see Buscombe, 1975; Clarke &
Clarke, 1982; Whannel, 1984). What is "shown" on television is always the
result of a complex process of selection: what items to report, what to leave
out, what to replay, and what to downplay. Television sports production also

Author's Note: So many people have helped with this chapter that it will be impossible to thank
them all. Special thanks should go to Bob Moir at CBC sports, Jim Marshall, Ken Read, Brian
Williams, and all the members of the Whistler production crew. Everyone gracefully indulged
the questions of a nosy academic who did nothing but get in the way. I also want to thank Michel
Beaudry, Steve Podborski, and Dave Skinner for help with additional background material.
Thanks also go to Hart Cantelon and the rest of the people associated with the Queen's Television Sport Project. Most of all, I want to thank Shelley Bentley for her patience and editorial
advice.

involves a wide range of processes of visual and narrative representation—choices regarding the images, language, camera positioning, and story line required to translate "what happened" into a program that makes "good television."

What factors influence these processes of selection and representation? Morris and Nydahl (1985) emphasize the creative choices made by individual directors, "auteurs" who employ television's technical magic to create unique and dramatic spectacles. By contrast, Hargreaves (1986) argues that media sports production personnel employ a set of "media sport news values" constituted within the determining pressures and limits of a capitalist consumer culture. These production "values" tend to express dominant ideological tendencies in capitalist societies. Somewhat similar arguments have been made by Gitlin (1979), McKay and Rowe (1987), and Clarke and Clarke (1982). The processes of selection and representation involved in the production of sport for television have been viewed as manifestations of such (allegedly) "dominant values" as hero worship, instrumental rationality, obedience to authority, possessive individualism, meritocracy, competitiveness, and patriarchal authority.

In many instances, these latter arguments have been made primarily on the basis of qualitative analyses of the visual "text" of sports television programs. The apparent realism of television sports, or the analysis of selective emphases in the sports/television discourse, have become standard points of departure for broader discussions about the production of ideology in Western capitalist societies. Yet, this "textual" perspective has tended to downplay analysis of the political and economic limits and pressures that operate as context for television sports production, and it has all but ignored analysis of the actual technical and professional practices—the labor process—involved in producing sports for television. In the absence of detailed case studies in these areas, assessments of relationships between television sports "texts" and their "contexts" of production have been speculative at best.

In this chapter, a modest case study of television sports production is presented, to begin to fill the gap in the literature noted above. More specifically, the chapter reports on fieldwork undertaken during Canadian Broadcasting Corporation (CBC) "coverage" of a World Cup downhill ski race held at Whistler Mountain, British Columbia, in March 1986. The Whistler Downhill was produced for the CBC's showcase Saturday sports program, *Sportsweekend*, a three-hour sports variety show roughly similar to *Wide World of Sports* in the United States.

There are two related sites for production on *Sportsweekend*: studio production and "remote" or "location" production at the event being covered. The discussion here is limited to the analysis of production on location. With the support of the executive producer of CBC sports, I was able to join the Whistler World Cup production crew for several days leading up to and including the event. During this time I was given access to production facilities, meetings, and personnel.

The first part of the chapter examines political-economic, organizational, and technical pressures and limits that operated as a context for producing the Whistler Downhill on the CBC. The second part of the chapter shifts to a discussion of production values and representational practices employed in televising the event. The concluding section briefly assesses some ideological implications of these values and practices.

The Social Context of Production

Political-Economic Pressures and Limits: World Cup Skiing and the Canadian Sports/Media Complex

The men's World Cup downhill ski tour is sometimes called "The White Circus." Each race on the circuit is an elaborate and expensive spectacle. Like the Olympics, although on a smaller scale, the combination of high costs and promotional possibilities has created powerful alliances of interest between the media and advertising industries, sports organizations, and governments.[1] At Whistler it was often difficult to differentiate between the respective partners in these alliances. Sport, television, and advertising all seemed to have fused into a single promotional entity.

Sut Jhally (1984) has drawn attention to the centrality of television in what he calls the "sports/media complex." Throughout the 1950s and 1960s, sport provided television with a relatively inexpensive way to reach large audiences of males in their peak earning years. Network competition for the sale of these audiences to advertisers increased the value of "television rights" to various sports and provided commercial sports organizations with a massive infusion of capital. As this occurred, everything from event scheduling to the location of franchises was reevaluated with television markets in mind. Additionally, there was growing pressure for cross-ownership among sports, media, and business sponsors.

Competition for audience viewing time since the early 1960s also led to significant innovations in styles of televisual representation and narration. Rather than simply attempt to "cover the event," television's technical capacities were employed to create increasingly dramatic and entertaining forms of sporting spectacle. Gary Whannel (1986) has argued that this trend reflects a concern evident in all forms of capitalist entrepreneurship and rationalized production for reducing uncertainty in the production of commodities:

> The increased penetration of sport by capital and resultant infusion of spectacular, internationalized and glamourized forms of entertainment can be seen as an attempt to reduce the uncertainty of the sporting commodity, at least as far as its entertainment value is concerned. Hence, television's tendency to try and ensure that even if the event is dull, by judicious highlights, action replays, interviews, etc., the program itself can be entertaining. But television's conventions as to what constitutes good entertainment have become a determining factor upon sporting cultures themselves.

In a consumer society fascinated by celebrities and glamorous life-styles, it is not surprising that part of television's definition of good sporting entertainment has centered upon individual performers and the personalities of athletes. This emphasis complements the overall promotional thrust of most sports programming and links the economic interests of individual athletes directly to the broader constellation of interests that define the modern sports/media complex.

These interests have come to include national, regional, and local governments because of the high visibility and apparent promotional qualities of modern media sports for tourism and regional economic development. Economic development initiatives became a dominant rationale for public investment in sport during the 1980s throughout Western capitalist societies. This rationale resonates well with the marketing emphasis generated elsewhere in the sports/media complex and it has directed state subsidies into the construction of stadiums and elaborate facilities, grants for staging major international events, and the "production" of high-performance athletes.

What were the most significant allied interests associated with the Whistler World Cup in 1986? In order to address this question properly it is useful to begin with some historical background. For most of the 1960s and early 1970s, the Canadian media paid little attention to ski racing outside of the Winter Olympics. However, in the mid-1970s Canadian downhill racers made an unprecedented breakthrough into the front ranks of the European-dominated World Cup circuit. Dubbed "the Crazy Canucks" for their daredevil style, the Canadians rapidly became a media sensation throughout Europe, but remained relatively unknown in their own country. Canadian press reporting of the team's successes was sketchy and television coverage was sporadic and limited in scale and expenditure.

By the end of the 1970s, the performances of Canadian downhill racers began to receive much more media attention in Canada, and ski racing became a more attractive promotional vehicle for businesses outside the ski industry. This was especially true when skiing was shown on television. The CBC began regular coverage of World Cup downhill skiing in 1980 after the addition of an annual Canadian men's downhill to the World Cup tour. The International Ski Federation (FIS) had long insisted on a major sponsor as a prerequisite for regular scheduling of a Canadian race. This condition was finally met in 1979, when Molson Brewery agreed to assume the role of major sponsor.

The existence of a Canadian World Cup downhill was a key factor in negotiation of a more formal 5-year television package between the CSA and the CBC in 1983. The CBC agreed to purchase broadcast "feeds" of World Cup downhill races from the European Broadcast Union and to work up their own production based on these feeds. The network also agreed to finance and produce coverage of Canadian World Cup downhill races and to pay an event fee to the CSA of between $5,000 and $8,000 for each race. In return, the CBC received rights to distribute the show throughout Canada. The CSA retained rights to the sale of the production in markets outside of Canada.[2]

The 1986 CBC production of the Whistler World Cup Downhill was conducted under the terms of the 1983 agreement. The most striking features of the production were its technical complexity (more about this in a moment) and immense cost. The CBC's direct cost of producing the Whistler Downhill was in excess of $250,000.

The CBC is government funded, but it is not a fully public broadcasting service and is heavily dependent on revenues generated through advertising. World Cup ski racing has received respectable ratings in Canada, but high costs for elaborate productions tend to make it a break-even proposition at best. Nonetheless, the CBC has felt obligated to cover the sport because of widespread public interest and the history of Canadian successes.

It is possible to provide coverage of skiing without mounting an outrageously expensive production. One can limit the number of cameras, televise only part of the course, forgo expensive technical effects (e.g., computerized graphics, instant replays, and slow motion), and omit prerace production extras (e.g., personality profiles of the athletes or technical information about the sport). However, in the highly competitive media markets of the 1980s, both media professionals and audiences have come to identify maximum visual coverage, special effects, and extras as another measure of good television.

Large-scale CBC productions of skiing have been possible only through the commitment of major sponsors. *Sportsweekend* sells its advertising in bulk for the season rather than on a per-event basis, and the CBC relies on major sponsors to purchase large chunks of this bulk advertising. Necessary extra money is also generated through the sale of televisual extras such as "billboards" that announce a forthcoming event and highlight the sponsor's name. One "billboard" on an edition of *Sportsweekend* prior to the 1986 Whistler race consisted of a single high camera shot of an alpine background (inserted after a commercial) accompanied by a graphic containing the words: "Coming to *Sportsweekend* next Saturday, March 15: THE MOLSON WORLD DOWNHILL!"

There has been a trend in sport toward "signature" sponsorship, in which a major sponsor attaches its name to the event in question. For instance, in the United States, the Sugar Bowl college football game is now the USF&G Sugar Bowl. By the same token, the Whistler World Cup Downhill ski race was formally called the Molson World Downhill. Molson is one of Canada's largest beer companies and, like most beer companies in North America, it has invested heavily in sport. As the signature sponsoring organization, Molson was involved in hosting and promoting the Whistler race at every level.

Molson's involvement in Canadian sport extends far beyond skiing. The company is one of the most notable corporate structures in the Canadian sports/media complex. At the time of the Whistler Downhill, Molson owned the Montreal Canadiens hockey team in the National Hockey League (NHL) and the Vancouver Canadians baseball team in the AAA Pacific Coast League. The company was also connected with promotional rights and television sponsorship of five other Canadian NHL teams (Winnipeg Jets, Calgary Flames, Edmonton Oilers, Vancouver Canucks, and Toronto Maple Leafs) and had been a decade-long sponsor of the CBC's *Hockey Night in Canada*. In football, Molson held promotional rights to the Hamilton Tiger-Cats and Saskatchewan Rough Riders. Elsewhere, the company contributed to eleven Canadian national teams, including the Canadian Men's National Alpine Ski Team. In addition to this involvement, Molson sponsored and organized a recreational racing program at ski resorts in Alberta, British Columbia, and Ontario.[3]

Race organizers in Canada depend upon volunteer help, public subsidies, and a variety of private sponsors. Depending on weather and snow conditions, direct costs for hosting a World Cup downhill can easily run as high as $300,000. However, it is expected that a large part of the financial burden will be undertaken by the signature sponsor. At Whistler in 1986, Molson paid over $250,000 for sponsorship rights to the race (these rights were in addition to what Molson paid to advertise on *Sportsweekend*) and provided additional hospitality services. Other sponsors included a mix of private and public agencies: Bose Ltd., Canadian Pacific Airlines, Omega, Pepsi-Cola Canada, Xerox, Whistler Mountain Ski Corporation, Andres Wines, BASF, Canon Video Systems, Descente Ski Wear, Expo '86, the government of British Columbia (which had already invested heavily in the Whistler resort development), Lindt's Chocolate, Melitta Canada, Perrier, and 7-Eleven.[4]

The CSA's commitment to high performance on the World Cup tour has combined with inflation to create previously unimagined costs for alpine competitive programs. For example, in 1982–83 the alpine budget was approximately $1.2 million, with 50% paid for through government grants. By 1988 the alpine budget had swollen to approximately $5.6 million, with only 20% paid for by government grants. As a result, the bulk of the budget now has to be financed through private sector sponsorship, public donations, and CSA fund-raising activities.[5]

Changes in the balance of public and private funding for the CSA alpine budget during the 1980s do not reflect government disapproval of the "investment in performance" philosophy of the CSA. Rather, they express a conscious policy decision made by the federal government to force Canadian "amateur" sport organizations to be more reliant upon private rather than public sponsorship.[6] These pressures in sport are manifestations of a broader philosophy of "privatization" that crept into Canadian government policies in the 1980s—a philosophy that also affected the CBC and pushed it even further in the direction of a greater reliance upon commercial advertising revenues. In Canada, the progressive commodification of sport and privatization of broadcasting have been parallel and partially reinforcing processes.

The CSA's 1983 television contract with the CBC did not directly contribute much to the alpine budget. However, it played an important role indirectly in the CSA's abilities to negotiate sponsorship agreements for support of the national team. Regular television coverage is a lure to equipment manufacturers and other sponsors, both for the team and for individual racers. In 1984–85, equipment manufacturers contributed $400,000 to the Canadian alpine budget plus another $300,000 in skis, bindings, clothing, and accessories. By the same token, manufacturers also made base payments and paid premiums to individual racers. In 1985 these premiums ranged between $10,000 and $25,000 for each win on the tour.[7]

The amount of sponsorship money available for racers varies from season to season in accordance with television ratings (especially in Europe) and the overall level of economic activity in the ski industry. During the mid-1980s it was not uncommon for a top downhiller to make anywhere from $100,000 to $500,000 a year. Canadian racers had most of this deposited into trust accounts, and the CSA typically claimed between 5% and 15% of these earnings. The size of the CSA share of individual racers' earnings has been an ongoing and controversial issue in the negotiations of racers and their agents with the CSA—especially in recent years, as rules governing "amateurism" in skiing have all but disappeared (see Fisher, 1984).

Technical and Organizational Pressures and Limits on Production

The CBC production crew for the Whistler Downhill was composed of 52 people plus additional part-time casual workers to assist with cable installation. Many of the European downhill sites are permanently cabled for television and employ five or six camera placements. The Whistler course has no permanent cable placements and requires miles of cable to be freshly installed for each race production. The CBC also employed enough cameras—twelve stationary, two mobile, and a Beta-Cam—to allow for "coverage" of the complete race course and finish area. Overall, the amount of equipment associated with the production was staggering. In addition to cameras and miles of cable, the crew set up three portable trailers containing machines for editing, image and graphic storage and retrieval, and computer links with the studio in Toronto. The equipment inventory also included a portable Telsat dish and a variety of microwave transmitters, videotape recorders, monitors, switchers, microphones, and other technical accessories.

Early television productions of skiing were greatly subject to the limitations of television technology and tended to be plagued with problems. The CBC technical producer at Whistler had been involved in sports production for over 15 years and noted that ski racing was "probably . . . the most technically and physically demanding" sports on television. He pointed out the difficulties of covering skiing in the early years with cameras whose lens capabilities could never provide much more than a small grainy figure. He also recounted stories of spectators walking in front of microwave transmitters and disrupting the signal, old 3-12 power cable heating up and disappearing under the snow, and unreliable portable transformers (not designed for alpine use) needed to offset signal deterioration because of the great lengths of triaxial cable involved.

Many of these problems have been solved by the use of fiber-optic cable and other technical innovations in visual image capture, transmission, and special effects. New technologies allow downhill ski racing to be produced for television in a far more complete and dramatic fashion than in the past. Nonetheless, television productions of skiing remain limited by problems of weather and distance. Even such fundamental decisions as camera placement must still be made with technical constraints in mind (e.g., positioning cameras so that they do not shoot into the sun, or where the skier will be outside optimum lens capacity).

The production crew at Whistler was "hand picked" (with the exception of the commentators) from overall network staff by the six producers and directors involved with the telecast. I was told that "experience," "flexibility," and "ability to work well under pressure on a live broadcast" were key factors in selection of the crew. Furthermore, all of the producers and directors noted that they had selected people with whom they had worked well in the past. The intention was to create a crew in which most of the production personnel "knew what was expected of them."

Approximately two weeks before the race, a small crew under the direction of the event's technical producer began to install fiber-optic cable on the mountain. The remainder of the production crew arrived a week later to set up the "remote" studio facilities, install cameras, compile research profiles on individual skiers, work out narrative themes for the production, and compile a taped prerace package setting the scene for the big event. Once installed, the main production crew operated under remarkable pressures associated with time, technology, expense, and weather. For example, official training runs were used as trials for checking camera installation, shot transitions, and the overall effectiveness of the initial production plan. But these runs were often canceled, or delayed, due to changing weather conditions, with the result that the production crew had to be continually "on call." The need to produce a great deal of taped background material quickly in a run-down mobile facility, inadequate preparation time due to bad weather, and regular minor equipment breakdowns all created pressures that promoted reliance on previously established conventions and practices in ski coverage.

The program director told me that CBC had more money to spend on this kind of production than a comparable Canadian private broadcaster. For that reason, he felt additional pressure to "do a good job." When asked to clarify, he went on to add that doing a good job meant "higher production values," more features, and fewer technical mistakes.

> You can tell a bad sports production when you notice the production itself. . . . the trick is, for me, when you don't notice the show . . . you feel like you're there . . . your interest is kept up all the time . . . [and] you're not aware of any of the production values. You're just glued to the set.

The director was the undisputed voice of authority on the production, and he continually pushed the production crew through a combination of good-natured ribbing and mildly grumpy complaints. The exception was one production meeting when he gave a rather aggressive locker-room-style speech complaining about falling behind schedule in prerace preparations. The use of a sports analogy here is deliberate. Like a team with coaches and players, the production crew at Whistler was extremely hierarchical in organization. The lines of authority ran from the six producers — the managerial staff — down to workers, ranked through a complex set of formal and informal statuses tied to job type, experience, and the traditions of the craft.

The crew's attitudes toward their work and the interactional style that prevailed on the job site were even more notable. The sense of teamwork generated from having to perform collectively under pressure, the closeness that comes from being on the road away from home, and the bantering, male-oriented atmosphere (there were only three women involved with the production) seemed to correspond in many ways to the occupational culture of high-performance sport. This correspondence was further signified through the widespread use of blue-and-white CBC "team" jackets and an apparent commitment to a "work together, play together" occupational culture. As one of the associate producers noted, "Our people have to be able to party as well as work."

"Team" jackets were very much in evidence all over the race site. Molson had their own "team" of representatives wearing skier-like outdoor uniforms, and I met a jacketed representative from "Team Xerox" in a bar who regaled me with propaganda about his "team's" commitment "to winning." What struck me most about all this was the way it illustrated the elective affinity between the racers and the race organizers, sponsors, and television production personnel. By "elective affinity," I mean the way in which particular beliefs and material interests seek each other out.[8] At Whistler, the sense of common purpose among various interest groups was very high. In this context, it would have been unusual for the CBC production team to make choices and selections in the production that were incompatible with the interests of those with whom they shared an affinity.

Production Values and Representational Practices

Production Values for the Whistler Downhill

I asked the director to talk about his "philosophy" for televising sports and he began with a point about the "necessity" of high entertainment values:

> In most sports, sports are boring. There are only a few moments that are really exciting, and the trick, I guess, is to bridge from one exciting moment to another with something that is entertaining . . . so we keep the interest by doing the features, doing the extras.

He went on to point out how sports programming has changed in Canada in ways that go far beyond mere technical innovation, and elaborated on some of the values that guided his production practices:

Director: [Sport on television] . . . has changed quite a bit. Ah, used to be that it was just cover the event, now it's make a story, that's what it is.

R.G.: When you do story, do you feel bound in any way by the same kinds of conventions about balance and objectivity that are supposedly part of the culture of news broadcasting?

Director: Ah . . . not really, because we're not out telling lies, were not falsifying information, we let the viewer decide, we . . . try very hard not to make it one-sided.

R.G.: But let's use an example . . . in today's show, you talked about . . . Aspen [where there had been a skiers' boycott of a race the previous week], right? And there was a sense on your part where you said, "Okay, we've got to make sure we get. . . . "

Director: [interrupts] . . . a fair balance.

R.G.: A fair balance?

Director: Yeah, because I said none of us were there except Ken [former "Crazy Canuck," Ken Read, now a *Sportsweekend* skiing color commentator] . . . and I don't want . . . to put a black mark on my show. . . . I don't want people to remember my show because of the boycott story, first of all . . . but we have to do something about it, its our responsibility, we're the only skiing show in this country.

The exchange noted above is significant in two respects. First, it demonstrates the importance of narrative for the director of the Whistler Downhill. There is little self-delusion here about television as a neutral transmitter of events. With the exception of the reference to "falsifying information" (which implies an absolute standard of truth), television sports production is acknowledged to be a self-conscious exercise in storytelling. This point has been made repeatedly by recent analysts of sports/television discourse. For example, Gary Whannel (1984) discusses narrative in television sport in language remarkably similar to that used by the Whistler director. Whannel points out that

> the insistence that television does not simply cover events, but transforms them into stories—is to raise questions about the polarity between actuality and fiction. Television sport can clearly be seen in terms of dramatic presentation and analysed as a form of narrative construction. (p. 102)

Chas Critcher (1987) has argued that the concentration on narrative construction in television sport provides a point of convergence for two dominant "models" of coverage—"news actuality and dramatic entertainment." Television sport brings these elements together in a unique manner. On the one hand, it is steeped in a commitment to actuality coverage—"covering the big game" as it happens and bringing us up to date on various bits of "sporting news," team and individual performances, or statistics. Yet, these tacit claims to represent "reality" are combined almost magically with a celebration of high levels of mediation. The real "trick" in sports telecasting is to combine all the features, extras, and special effects—effects that often involve wildly altered perceptions of time and space—into an entertaining narrative that retains its claims to actuality.

This raises the second point I want to make in regard to the interview material presented above. I have always felt uncomfortable talking about "news values" in television sports, particularly when these are contrasted to "entertainment values" as if "news" was something more "true" or noble than "spectacle." In fact, historically, the line between news as "information" and news as "entertainment" has been notoriously difficult to draw. Modern television news programs geared to mass entertainment carry on a tradition that goes back to the earliest commercial mass media, the penny papers of the early nineteenth century (Hallin, 1986, p. 11). Certainly, television news today seems as much a teller of stories as television sports. ABC's appointment of Roone Arledge, the founder of *Wide World of Sports*, to head its news division in 1977 merely moved a great storyteller from one division of the network to another.

Nonetheless, television news reportage has retained trace elements of professional ideals from print journalism about "objectivity" and "balanced coverage." These ideals are particularly evident at the CBC, which has a strong documentary tradition. In the interview under discussion, the director acknowledges the primacy of "dramatic entertainment" but denies feeling bound by journalistic conventions often associated (at least ideally) with "news actuality" coverage. Yet, in the same breath, he talks about not wanting to be "one-sided" and goes on to say how he felt a "responsibility" to pay at least some attention to a skiers' boycott of the race that had occurred the previous week.

The most revealing passage, however, is the statement about "coverage" of the boycott leaving "a black mark" on the show. He senses a danger that "coverage" of such a self-consciously "political" act will deflect attention from the positive atmosphere of the race itself. Herbert Gans (1980) has noted how "news values" in North America often involve conflict and highlight problems or "negative events." But, to the extent that we can use the category at all, sports "news" is cast in a markedly different tradition. Critcher (1987) concludes:

> The very occurrence of the event is good news, a reassuring sign of normality (making its interruption by politics, hooliganism, or even the weather especially hard to bear). . . . sport provides a positive image of the world, in counterpoint to the negativity which is evident in most other kinds of news. (p. 135)

From Production Values to Production Practices

Production values are only general objectives that must be realized through actual practices of production. These practices draw on a broad stock of knowledge — a set of informal rules and conventions — shared by various members of the production crew. Rules and conventions of production operate like an underlying grammar that structures the selective construction of images and narrative. Audiences become familiar with this grammar without really noticing its presence. It is even difficult to get people in television sports production to say much about it. Few of us "know," or can articulate, the formal rules of grammar we use to structure our speech. People in television sports production are no different when it comes to an examination of their own professional practices.

This was particularly evident in a conversation with one of the camera operators at Whistler. During the race, each of the fixed-installation camera operators focused upon the skier as soon as the skier came into range. All of the camera shots were displayed on monitors in the studio truck and the director made editing cuts among the cameras' "coverage" at his discretion. However, each camera operator had a degree of discretion about how lens changes could be employed to enhance the coverage. If the director did not like the shot, he simply told the camera operator to change it. After the skier passed any given camera installation, the camera operator put up shots of crowds, scenery, and so on, to give the director transition material between racers or between "live" coverage and a commercial. I asked a camera operator (C.O.) if he could tell me how he knows what to shoot:

C.O.: Well, you always have to listen to what's being said on air. That's very important. Program sound . . . we call that program sound . . . we always have that on so you can always know if they say "Peter Mueller's hand" . . . well, you zoom in on his hand if you can.

R.G.: So . . . if we see a crowd shot . . . is it because the director says, "Gimme a crowd shot now"?

C.O.: That's right, but going back to program sound, if you hear the crowd cheering and you're not on the air [with a racer] you automatically go to it . . . and [if the director likes the shot] he'll say take camera 4 or 5 or whatever. . . . after working for a director for a while you learn his style . . . but sometimes you just have to follow your impulse.

R.G.: But about those impulses . . . how do you determine what makes a good shot?

C.O.: Well . . . jeez . . . I don't know . . . I ah . . . it just feels right to me . . . it just feels right. I can't really explain it . . . something just goes "click" and inside me it says "go"!

This camera operator went on to tell me that you have to be "born" with the ability to "know" those good shots — that it cannot be learned. But I think we can safely assume that the knowledge of "good" shots is learned behavior, part of the unconscious conventions that are picked up on the job. The director was able to articulate how some of these conventions work in a conversation we had about editing. I had observed that at certain points in the telecast he used a "straight cut" between two shots, whereas in other instances he employed a "dissolve" or a "wipe," and I inquired about the rationale for these various shot transitions.

Director: Well, the effect is to show a transition in time, that was why it was invented. . . . it's just an effect . . . and the dissolve . . . is just to relay to the viewer . . . other than the fact that we've changed the picture and there is a new face . . . that, okay, we're gonna show you a new racer now.

R.G.: So a straight cut implies continuity and the other stuff . . .

Director: [interrupts] . . . implies a transition in time. And the wipe is to show that you're on the same guy but you're down the course . . . you've cut something out. . . . Its simple, but after a while the viewer catches on to what you're doing . . . subconsciously, I guess, I'm sure if you asked someone they wouldn't know . . . [the rationale for] what they were seeing.

These conversations begin to suggest the complexity of representational practices employed in the Whistler production. However, space here does not allow a detailed exploration of the wide range of practices associated with different job tasks or a discussion of the conventions underlying all of these practices. It is possible only to highlight some of the most notable elements employed to make the program entertaining.

Most important is narrative construction. The key structuring elements in the CBC narrative at Whistler were spectacle, individual performance, human interest, competitive drama, uncertainty, and risk. These elements were specific manifestations of the director's broader commitment to entertainment values.

The director strove to achieve a sense of immediacy and excitement that built to a dramatic climax. In downhill skiing, risk and speed are central to the drama and are viewed as elements that audiences want to see. For this reason, camera positioning was of vital importance to the Whistler production. Cameras do not simply "show" us sporting action; they position us as viewers by placing us in a particular spatial relationship to the action being viewed. A camera shot taken from a scaffold, with the skier going away from the camera, positions the viewer much differently from a shot taken at ground level with the skier approaching the camera. The director for the 1986 race had also produced the race in 1984, and he told me he moved the camera positions this time in an effort to "make the course look faster." He elaborated by noting that

> two years ago we had a lot of following asses. The skier was very short seeing him front on, then a lot of seeing the back of him ski away from you. And that's slow. It's always slow when you look at something going away. When they're coming to you it's always faster.

The director went on to say that his number one "rule" of production was to pose a question or problem to be resolved in the program and then "don't give away the story until it's time." In order to accomplish this, and combine it with a sense of immediacy and mounting excitement, he adopted a loosely structured approach to scripting the race. The "scene was set" in a half-hour prerace show before "live" transmission. But the live transmission was not really "live" at all. *Sportsweekend* did not go on the air until an hour after the race was over, and the one and a half hours of scheduled skiing were not on until the second half of a three-hour time block. The race itself was "shot" and taped without the final verbal commentary and the "on-air" show was assembled at the last minute. With the exception of the prerace package, the announcers did a "live to tape" telecast on the air. Yet everything about their commentary was geared to create the illusion that they were seeing the action for the first time. The use of active verb tenses, emotion, and even prediction ("He should do well here!") was all staged—it was pure show business.

From the producer's point of view, the "buildup" to the "live to tape" telecast was every bit as important as the race itself. The prerace package took up a third of the on-air time and was scripted well prior to the race. The actual script was written by one of the announcers, but the plot line was created by the director. Before the race, a great deal of energy was devoted to preparation of short video packages that could be drawn upon for both the prerace show and the race itself. Every skier's head was shot and placed in a blue "frame" that featured the flag of the skier's home country, the Whistler mountain resort logo, and the Molson World Downhill logo. In addition, researchers attempted to compile two or three basic "hero notes" on each skier. These stills and accompanying information were then stored in computers and could be called up at a moment's notice by the director. On race day, short taped packages based on the week's work were assembled "live" on the air prefaced by taped footage of the commentators taken the morning of the race. Again, the desired effect was to surround the prerace material with a sense of immediacy and actuality.

The top story in the prerace package was the "season-long battle" for first place on the World Cup tour between Peter Mueller and Peter Wirnsberger. The package was cued from the Toronto *Sportsweekend* studio by the studio announcer's brief introduction noting how Wirnsberger and Mueller were only 5 points apart in World Cup standings. The audience was then "taken" to Whistler and to the remote announcer, who, the audience was told, would "tell us how they [Mueller and Wirnsberger] got there." The remote announcer's introduction blended into fast-paced music with a voice overlay on a still head shot of Wirnsberger. This was wiped to videotape of his wins during the season. The audience was then told, "But we all overlooked that old Swiss veteran Peter Mueller," and a similar visual and narrative progression of Mueller's performances unfolded.

This dramatic buildup was followed by a high mountain shot overlaid with a CBC graphic and the announcement that the Molson World Downhill was coming "Today from Whistler." Following this, the visuals cut back to the remote announcer and color commentator. The announcers noted that "the scene is all set" and "a Hollywood scriptwriter could not have set it up any better." The prerace show went on to discuss Mueller's come-from-behind "story" in detail, including interviews and a spectacular replay of a recent fall in which Mueller broke his hand.

After a transition in and out of a Molson commercial, the show moved on to lighter topics and played taped footage of "the return of the original 'Crazy Canucks'" to Whistler for a celebrity ski race. Then, "on a more serious note," the announcer introduced a short package on the Aspen boycott. This was followed by a report about the "young Canadian team," featuring rising star Rob Boyd. Afterward, color commentator Ken Read introduced his weekly "Read Report" on the "news" of the World Cup tour, and then breathlessly described the race course, alerting the audience to the challenges posed in different sections. A final discussion of weather conditions led into a preview of "heads" of the first seed and of the Canadian team. At this point, a high alpine shot was used as a transition to the first skier in the starting gate.

The director controlled the pace of the "live to tape" telecast by regulating the length of transition shots between racers and through the use of replays that were employed to use or to buy time. Timing was particularly important, because there were always two racers on the course simultaneously. In order to show a complete race for each contestant, the director had to tape the beginning of each run and then pick up the same skier "live" further down the course.

This constant back-and-forth among several tape machines and live "real time" camera work was extremely complicated and created occasions when time needed to be made up. For example, there was a high priority given in the telecast to spectacular falls, but in one instance the director felt he was getting behind the rhythm of the race and elected not to insert a replay of a fall at the finish line. He instructed the announcer to say (about the fallen skier), "It's okay, he's all right," as the cameras moved on to the next racer. On the other hand, when British racer Martin Bell fell, the director screamed to the iso-director, "Jesus, I've got to get a replay of this . . . get me a replay." The replay was a desirable hospitality gesture because the BBC had purchased the "feed" and was doing its own commentary.

One closing note about production practices. The quest for spectacular shots was not the only thing that excited the director. In taping the award ceremony, the mobile Beta-Cam operator had the winner's head blocking a large Molson logo on the stand behind the podium. The director responded in a way that underlines my earlier point about elective affinities. He screamed into the camera operator's headphones: "Frame the Molson! Frame the Molson! . . . You're blocking the Molson. . . . Jesus, how long have you been doing this?"

Concluding Comments

The processes of selection and representation in CBC coverage of the 1986 Whistler Downhill cannot simply be reduced to any one set of pressures and limits. While there are fundamental economic and ideological pressures and limits in operation, they do not determine everything that we see on the screen. Yet, neither can we argue that the production is constructed freely, without any determining limits and pressures at all. The Whistler director may appear to have acted as an "auteur," but his production values and practices cannot be completely disentangled from the political-economic, organizational, and technical contexts within which he operated.

The Whistler production was a series of stories told from a particular point of view. It would be a rationalist illusion to suggest that television could somehow "cover the event" without mediating it in substantial ways. The meanings that human beings give to events are *never* naturally contained within the events themselves. To paraphrase Stuart Hall (1982, p. 67), real life does not contain or propose its own integral, single, and intrinsic meaning, which is then neutrally transmitted to us through language or other systems of communication. On the contrary, meaning is a social production, something created through a set of rule-governed practices. At one level, the CBC production might simply be understood as a set of practices—a labor process—that transformed raw material (the race) into a television show designed to attract audiences that could be sold to advertisers. But this process involved the material production of a symbolic product as well.

It has become fashionable to argue that the symbolic meanings produced in television productions are interpreted in very open-ended ways by audiences. Newcomb and Hirsch (1987) note, for example, that television functions as a forum "in which important cultural topics may be considered" (p. 460). They argue that television does not present firm ideological conclusions "so much as it *comments on* ideological problems." John MacAloon (1984) has made somewhat similar arguments about the meanings associated with Olympic spectacle.

But it is important to remember that in assessing the significance of different "accounts" of the world, some accounts *count* much more than others. It is precisely because images are polysemic—subject to a variety of interpretations—and because stories can be differentially interpreted that television producers must work so hard to position viewers in particular ways and gain credibility for their own preferred viewpoints. This involves an active process of marginalizing, downgrading, or delegitimating potentially alternative explanations.[9] This is not done through some finely tuned process of political socialization on the part of the production crew; rather, it simply reflects the routine acceptance of discursive practices in production (e.g., the ways cameras are positioned to make the course look fast, shots composed to emphasize the individual, the language and form of questions used in interviews, the thematic organization of narrative, rhythm of the production) viewed as necessary to the making of good television.

Undoubtedly, the Whistler production put contradictory images on the screen and the storytelling that went on had a potentially open-ended character. But the underlying codes defining good television and the elective affinity among producers, advertisers, and race organizers led to coverage that treated the existing structures and competitive promotional culture of the modern sports/media complex as natural—an example of "common sense." Television sports programs like the one at Whistler contribute directly to capital accumulation in the sports/media complex. But they also figure indirectly in winning consent for a dominant social definition of sport ideally suited to a capitalist consumer culture. It is a definition in which sport is widely understood as a naturally open, achievement-based activity, conducted to further individual sports careers and to generate investment. Equally important are the notions that specialization is the modern definition of excellence, that enjoyment is tied to skill acquisition, and that economic reward is an integral and necessary component of sporting entertainment.[10] Whether this modern "common sense" about sport is "good sense" is a question that falls well outside the inferential frame of reference typically employed in any television sport production.

Notes

1. For a discussion of these alliances surrounding the 1984 Olympics, see Gruneau (1988).

2. These data come from interviews with Dave Skinner, managing director of the CSA alpine program, and Jim Marshall, the producer/director of the 1986 Whistler Downhill.

3. This information comes from a special advertising supplement included by Molson in the *Vancouver Sun* (June 17, 1986).

4. This information was compiled from official press releases put out during the Whistler Downhill.

5. These figures were provided by Dave Skinner, managing director of the CSA alpine program.

6. Background information on Canadian government policies in sport during the 1970s and early 1980s can be found in Macintosh et al. (1987).

7. Some of this information was supplied by Dave Skinner; the rest comes from Beamish (1985).

8. The concept of "elective affinity" comes from Max Weber (1946, p. 280), although Weber uses it in a fundamentally different context.

9. I have discussed the broader ideological dimensions of this process in other work (Gruneau, 1983, 1988), and in a subsequent paper I plan to examine the Whistler coverage of the Aspen boycott to demonstrate this process in more detail. The director claimed he presented the boycott "fairly," but my research suggests a form of storytelling "framed" in a way that clearly favors the interests of the FIS and the ski industry.

10. See Gruneau (1983, 1988) for a critical discussion of this current dominant social definition of sport.

References

Beamish, M. (1985, February 23). Crazy Canucks preach patience. *Vancouver Sun*.

Buscombe, E. (1975). *Football on television*. London: British Film Institute.

Clarke, A., & Clarke, J. (1982). Highlights and action replays. In J. Hargreaves (Ed.), *Sport, culture and ideology*. London: Routledge.

Critcher, C. (1987). Media spectacles: Sport and mass communication. In A. Cashdan & M. Jordin (Eds.), *Studies in communication*. Oxford: Basil Blackwell.

Fisher, M. (1984, April 6). Podborski won't spell it out but he's probably a millionaire. [Toronto] *Globe and Mail*.

Gans, H. (1980). *Deciding what's news*. New York: Vintage.

Gitlin, T. (1979). Prime time ideology: The hegemonic process in television entertainment. *Social Problems, 26*(3).

Gruneau, R. (1983). *Class, sports and social development*. Amherst: University of Massachusetts Press.

Gruneau, R. (1988). Modernization or hegemony? Two views on sport and social development. In J. Harvey & H. Cantelon (Eds.), *Not just a game*. Ottawa: University of Ottawa Press.

Gruneau, R., & Cantelon, H. (1988). Capitalism, commercialism and the Olympics. In J. Seagrave (Ed.), *The Olympic Games in transition*. Urbana, IL: Human Kinetics.

Hall, S. (1975, July). *Television as a medium and its relation to culture*. Unpublished manuscript, Centre for Contemporary Cultural Studies.

Hall, S. (1982). The rediscovery of "ideology": Return of the repressed in media studies. In M. Gurevitch, T. Bennett, J. Curran, & J. Woollacott (Eds.), *Culture, society and the media*. London: Methuen.

Hallin, D. (1986). We keep America on top of the world. In T. Gitlin (Ed.), *Watching television*. New York: Pantheon.

Hargreaves, J. (1986). *Sport, power and culture*. New York: St. Martin's.

Jhally, S. (1984). The spectacle of accumulation: Material and cultural factors in the evolution of the sports/media complex. *Insurgent Sociologist, 12*(3).

MacAloon, J. (1984). Olympic Games and the theory of spectacle in modern societies. In J. MacAloon (Ed.), *Rite, drama, festival, and spectacle*. Philadelphia: ISHI.

Macintosh, D., et al. (1987). *Sport and politics in Canada*. Montreal: Queen's-McGill University Press.

McKay, J., & Rowe, D. (1987). Ideology, the media and Australian sport. *Sociology of Sport Journal, 4*.

Morris, B., & Nydahl, J. (1985). Sports spectacle as drama: Image, language and technology. *Journal of Popular Culture, 18*(4).

Newcomb, H., & Hirsch, P. (1987). Television as a cultural forum. In H. Newcomb (Ed.), *Television: The critical view* (4th ed.). New York: Oxford University Press.

Weber, M. (1946). *From Max Weber* (H. Gerth & C. W. Mills, Eds.). New York: Oxford University Press.

Whannel, G. (1984). Fields in vision: Sport and representation. *Screen, 25*(3).

Whannel, G. (1986). The unholy alliance: Notes on television and the remaking of British sport. *Leisure Studies, 5*.

III

Media Sports Content

7

The Super Bowl Pregame Show: Cultural Fantasies and Political Subtext

Lawrence A. Wenner

In the United States, when the Super Bowl comes on television, the world stops. The highways empty of traffic and the shopping malls become barren of customers. Year in and year out, the Super Bowl — more descriptively, the championship game of American professional football — is one of the highest rated of all television programs. This phenomenon has been going on for some time. The Super Bowl has passed out of childhood and adolescence, and in human form would be a number of years past voting age. And this young adult is a professional, well compensated for services rendered. The "million-dollar minute" is now a bargain rate for advertising not found in buying advertising time during the Super Bowl (Goodwin, 1986).

Fittingly, then, the most frequently cited study of mediated sports has been Real's (1975) study of a Super Bowl telecast. Using a cultural approach, Real looks at the Super Bowl telecast as a microcosm of American life, replete with myth, ritual, heroic archetypes, and interlocking story lines involving lifelike issues of labor, management, territoriality, and property ownership. Real concludes:

> The structural values of the Super Bowl can be summarized succinctly: *North American professional football is an aggressive, strictly regulated team game fought between males who use both violence and technology to gain control of property for the economic gain of individuals within nationalistic entertainment context.* The Super Bowl propagates these values by elevating one game to the level of a spectacle of American ideology collectively celebrated. (p. 42)

157

A football game, of course, starts with a kickoff. However, as a media event, the Super Bowl starts with a "pregame show," typically two hours in length. The pregame show is the culmination of two weeks of what Buell (1980) and others have called "superhype." As Buell has remarked: "The hyping of televised football seems to have no limits" (p. 66). All of the mediated scenarios, fantasies, rumors, couched predictions, psychological profiling, and the like have seemingly reached their saturation point by the time of the pregame show. This study looks at the "outer limits" of media hype – the saga of the pregame show that frames the Super Bowl broadcast with a set of values intricately developed in over two hours of fantasy theme chaining (Bormann, 1972). More specifically, the focus here is on NBC's pregame show for Super Bowl XX – a contest that featured the Chicago Bears playing the New England Patriots on January 26, 1986.

An Approach to Superhype: Fantasy Theme Analysis

Bormann's (1972) fantasy theme analysis is a seemingly appropriate method to apply to the hodgepodge of themes that were bandied about during NBC's coverage of the preevent nonevent that the Super Bowl pregame show clearly is.[1] As a genre, the pregame show is notable in that it is very different from most sports programming on television. Commenting on the role of mediated sports in socialization, Goldstein and Bredemeier (1977) have noted that "one effect of the prevalence of sports on television has been an emphasis on outcome rather than process" (p. 155). One of the most distinguishing features of the pregame show is that it is exclusively composed of process. In a sense, it is the communication equivalent of being pregnant. It is a process in and of itself, and while there may be expert conjecture as to whether the pregnancy will be difficult or easy, the labor long or short, the child male or female, or the delivery simple or full of complications, a good many of the details of both the pregnancy and its outcome remain unknown. However, unlike pregnancy, the process of the Super Bowl pregame show is one of pure fantasy.

Bormann's approach hits at the heart of both process and fantasy. Derived from Bales's (1950) work in group interaction process analysis, Bormann's method uncovers the rhetorical visions that come out of group interactions. He goes about this by focusing on "how dramatizing communication creates social reality for groups of people" (p. 396). By "dramatizing communication," Bormann means the specific dramatic or story elements that appear as members of the group communicate with each other. For Bormann, as group communication progresses, the participants become less self-conscious and the tone of interaction becomes more lively, to a point where dramatizing accelerates into the building of a group fantasy or alternate reality. The content of the group fantasy "consists of characters, real or fictitious, playing out a dramatic situation in a setting removed in time and space from the here-and-now transactions of the group" (p. 397).

Bormann is interested in the fantasy themes that develop out of the dramatic elements in a group's fantasy because they tend to constitute the "reality" of a group posed with a problematic task. As Nimmo and Combs (1983) have put it, "for those who share them, the fantasies are real, the fantasy reality" (p. 13). The symbolic reality that results Bormann calls a "rhetorical vision" that is "constructed from fantasy themes that chain out in face-to-face interacting groups, in speaker-audience transactions, in viewers of television broadcasts, in listeners to radio programs, and in all diverse settings for public and intimate communication in a given society" (p. 398).

Thus the rhetorical vision of a sports program such as NBC's Super Bowl pregame show can be understood in terms of the fantasies chained by the group participants — sports announcers, commentators, coaches, athletes, and the like — and embraced by the audience that has chosen to enter the fantastic reality by becoming members of a larger fantasy group. In the case of the yearly Super Bowl event the fantasy group becomes so large that, in a sense, it defines a recurring fantasy that is at one with American culture.

Looking Through a Chain Link Fence: The Political Fantasy Type

The political implications of sport in a culture have been commented upon frequently in the sociology of sport (Eitzen & Sage, 1978; Jhally, 1984; Pooley & Webster, 1976; Snyder & Spreitzer, 1978). The relationship between politics and sport takes place on a two-way street. Sports contests are played within the political context of a given culture (Pooley & Webster, 1976), political values (e.g., conservatism, nationalism) are seen to abound in the playing of sports (Goldstein & Bredemeier, 1977; Nimmo & Combs, 1983; Prisuta, 1979; Real, 1975), and sports themes are commonly used metaphorical devices in both the rhetoric of politics (Balbus, 1975) and the reporting of politics (Carey, 1976).

In short, the symbiotic relationship between politics and sports has yielded both recurring sports themes in politics and recurring political themes in sports. In Bormann's framework, such recurring themes in a body of discourse are "fantasy types" (Bormann, 1977; Bormann, Koester, & Bennett, 1978). Thus the political themes that make up part of the fantasy of mediated sports discourse constitute one such fantasy type. This study focuses on the web of political fantasies woven about the Super Bowl pregame show, setting the stage for the game itself. One may see the web of political fantasy as spun in the form of fantasy chains, linked together, surrounding the body of discourse and the public event to which it refers (in this case the Super Bowl game) as a fantasy "chain link fence."[2] To the degree to which the fantasy type is dominant in the body of discourse, the chain link fence becomes a somewhat distinct variant of a "frame" through which the event, and the body of discourse about it, is interpreted by the audience.

The chain link fence is a constructed entity, built by the participants in the discourse. So constituted, it inherits many of Goffman's (1974) notions about frame analysis, and Tuchman's (1978) application of it to the construction of reality in news. The difference here is the overt focus on fantasy. Frames, as they are used in news and everyday life, aim to "get things right," to construct reality accurately. Especially with regard to sports, fences constructed of fantasy chains are unlikely to have such a goal. More likely, the aim is to construct an altered reality that has intrinsic, but not necessarily practical, value. As such, chain link fences exist in the world of ritual, of which commentary on and spectatorship of sports play a part. As Stephenson (1967) might sum it up, frames have to do with work, and fantasy chains have to do with play.

Such fantasy construction is not without linkages to the real world. Nixon (1982) has noted that the "metaphorical interpretation of sport as an American 'fantasyland' of character, virtue, and the romanticized pursuit of the American Dream and embodiment of the Protestant ethic stands in striking contrast to the somewhat tarnished picture of the 'real world' outside the sports arena" (p. 2).

In noting this contrast, some critics have suggested studying sports and politics as a social dialectic. For instance, in looking at American sports, Jhally (1984) has observed:

> Sports are an explicit celebration of the *idealized* structures of reality — a form of capitalist realism. They mediate a vital social dialectic, providing both an escape from the alienated conditions of everyday life and a *socialization* into these very same structures. (p. 51)

This dialectic is at the heart of much cultural criticism in communication that attempts to understand the phenomenon of hegemony. Such inquiry is also basic to the sociology of sport. Sociologists such as Loy (1978) see the legitimation of sport in a society tied to such dialectically opposed functions:

> Sport fulfils the first and characteristically cultural function by mirroring the hegemony of the American success ideology; and . . . sport fulfils the second and characteristically expressive cultural function by providing a medium and a context for ecstatic experience in everyday life. (p. 79)

In short, the issue of looking at the political fantasies of mediated sport can be seen as central to understanding sport in culture.

Structure of the Pregame Fantasy

One need not wield a fine-tooth comb between the lines of subtext to find political connections in the sports fantasy offered to the Super Bowl viewers who tuned into the pregame "festivities." From its opening seconds at 3 p.m. EST, NBC's pregame show was cast as "An American Celebration." The "celebration" began with the slick graphics and video effects that we have come to associate with American news and sports coverage. Just what "we" were "celebrating" was not so clear at the outset, but by the close of the two-hour lead-in to the game, it was clear "we Americans" were "celebrating America." The general idea seemed to be to bring the spirit of the Fourth of July to the middle of January. However, nowhere to be seen were Washington, Jefferson, Madison, and their contemporaries. This was a celebration of the American present. The only times a historical perspective intervened, we "learned" of the history of the Super Bowl spectacle in terms of the "great men" who fought the good fight in years gone by.

An overview of the pregame show is presented in Table 7.1. Using the beginning of the program as time zero, this table pinpoints the starting time of each segment in the show in terms of hours, minutes, and seconds into the program. The program had 14 segments, each ending with a commercial break of varying duration. Commercial announcements filled slightly more than 30 minutes, over a quarter of the total running time of the program.

The typical program segment ran 4–7 minutes before a commercial interruption. The shortest segments (13 and 14) contained under a minute of

Table 7.1
Overview of the Super Bowl Pregame Show

---

1   00:00:00   Opening segment: An American Celebration
   1.1   00:00:00   Field: announcer Dick Enberg introduces theme
   1.2   00:00:49   Feature rock video: "United Nation"
   1.3   00:07:26   Field: Enberg segue to studio anchor
   1.4   00:07:26   Studio: anchor Bob Costas with game introduction
   1.5   00:09:13   Bears Feature: reporter Ahmad Rashad
   1.6   00:11:54   Studio: Costas/Rashad ponder Bears "overconfidence"
   1.7   00:13:13   Commercial break 1
2   00:15:30   Pondering the Patriots
   2.1   00:15:30   Studio: Costas segue to Patriots feature
   2.2   00:15:56   Patriots feature: reporter Bill Macatee
   2.3   00:18:02   Costas/Macatee ponder Patriots strategy
   2.4   00:19:09   Commercial break 2
3   00:21:29   The Team That Time Forgot
   3.1   00:21:29   Studio: Costas segue to "yesteryear" feature
   3.2   00:22:16   1966 KC Chiefs feature: reporter Charley Scott
   3.3   00:28:57   Studio: Costas segue to commercial
   3.4   00:29:38   Commercial break 3
4   00:31:33   Game Announcers Ponder Key Elements
   4.1   00:31:33   Studio: Costas segue to game announcers
   4.2   00:31:59   Field: announcers Enberg/Merlin Olsen
   4.3   00:33:58   Studio: Costas-Enberg/Olsen Q&A interaction
   4.4   00:34:54   Commercial break 4
5   00:37:16   Quarterbacks and Bill Cosby's Refrigerator
   5.1   00:37:16   Studio: Costas segue to quarterback feature
   5.2   00:37:37   Quarterback feature: Pete Axthelm reports
   5.3   00:39:51   Studio: Costas/Axthelm ponder quarterbacks
   5.4   00:40:53   Studio: Costas segue to Bill Cosby feature
   5.5   00:41:10   Cosby feature: comedy relief
   5.6   00:44:09   Commercial break 5
6   00:46:13   The Coaches
   6.1   00:46:13   Studio: Costas segue to coaches feature
   6.2   00:46:35   Coaches feature: Larry King reports
   6.3   00:51:16   Studio: Costas/King ponder coaching style
   6.4   00:52:35   Commercial break 6
7   00:54:53   Strategy and the Family Business
   7.1   00:54:53   Studio: Costas segue to Bob Griese/Olsen
   7.2   00:55:04   Field feature: Griese/Olsen ponder strategy
   7.3   00:59:27   Studio: Costas segue to "intermission"
   7.4   01:00:29   Intermission: movie theater cartoon ad for snack bar
   7.5   01:01:19   Intermission: countdown minute with Muzak
   7.6   01:02:30   Studio: Costas segue to family feature
   7.7   01:03:35   Family feature: Macatee reports on Sullivan family
   7.8   01:07:48   Commercial break 7

Table 7.1 (continued)

8	01:09:08	The Bear Defense
8.1	01:09:08	Studio: Costas segue to Bear defense feature
8.2	01:09:59	Defense feature: Rashad reports on Buddy Ryan
8.3	01:13:19	Studio: Costas/Rashad ponder Bear defense
8.4	01:15:17	Commercial break 8
9	01:17:27	Rodney Dangerfield as Everyman
9.1	01:17:27	Studio: Costas segue to Dangerfield feature
9.2	01:18:10	Dangerfield feature: comedy relief
9.3	01:21:11	Studio: Costas/Axthelm segue to commercial
9.4	01:21:45	Commercial break 9
10	01:24:06	"Ain't That America"
10.1	01:24:06	Studio: Costas segue to Americana music video
10.2	01:24:38	"Ain't That America" music video
10.3	01:27:49	Studio: Costas segue to commercial
10.4	01:28:20	Commercial break 10
11	01:30:15	The Great General
11.1	01:30:15	Studio: Costas segue to Vince Lombardi feature
11.2	01:30:48	Lombardi feature: Great man/more than football theme
11.3	01:37:59	Commercial break 11
12	01:40:59	Presidential Themes
12.1	01:40:59	Studio: Costas segue to President Reagan feature
12.2	01:41:23	Reagan interview: Tom Brokaw reports
12.3	01:49:29	Studio: Costas segue to commercial
12.4	01:49:50	Commercial break 12
13	01:51:51	Insider's Predictions
13.1	01:51:51	Studio: Costas with Axthelm game prediction
13.2	01:52:29	Commercial break 13
14	01:54:53	Closing Remarks and Credits
14.1	01:54:53	Studio: Costas with voice over credits
14.2	01:55:43	Commercial break 14
15	01:57:49	Game Show Begins: kickoff still 20 minutes off

program material. The longest segments (1 and 7) ran approximately 13 minutes before hitting a commercial. These segments served as the "kickoff" and "halftime show" in the structure of the pregame program.

The telecast was composed of three types of program elements. Of the first variety were the *studio reports*, which were anchored by announcer Bob Costas and featured live appearances by other reporters/commentators. The studio reports provided segues that held the rest of the program elements together. A second essential program element was the *field report*. Field reports featured "live commentary" from game announcers Dick Enberg and Merlin Olsen and color commentator Bob Griese. The third type of program element was the *feature segment*. Features were prerecorded (and edited) segments that focused on one of two things: (1) the upcoming game or (2) other things. These other things usually featured some aspect of professional football's history, football's role in American society, or both.

While all of the program elements have fantasy components that may be construed to have a political bent, the feature segments, especially those focusing away from the game, contained the most political fantasy. The six features that contained the richest and most clearly defined political fantasies were singled out for analysis.

"Forever Young" in the "United Nation"

The pregame show begins with the full-screen graphic "NBC SPORTS PRESENTS" and dissolves to inspirational music and a second graphic showing an American flag and silver football trophy. Over this second graphic is superimposed: "SUPER SUNDAY: AN AMERICAN CELE-BRATION." Announcer Dick Enberg begins speaking as a montage begins with an aerial shot of the stadium superimposed over crowds on city streets and fans in football stadiums. Enberg tells us:

> New Orleans, Louisiana. Super Bowl Sunday. Tens of thousands will watch in the Superdome as Chicago plays New England. A hundred million others will share the experience on television. Rich and poor, young and old, joining together on a day when a game makes our differences less important. While men play a boys' game, we stand and take sides.

Enberg's voice segues us into another set of visuals. We get a clue that this is a music video as the voice of Bob Dylan singing "Forever Young" is mixed in with Enberg's. The video (actually a short film by Bob Giraldi) superimposes the title "United Nation" as Dylan sings, and Enberg reads his last line of introduction: "Today we unite in an American celebration."

Dylan's song is interwoven throughout "United Nation," and provides the thematic base for the visuals. In this context, "Forever Young" is at once a symbol of a young nation, a celebration of strength and youth, and a call for a fountain of youth for those no longer young. Dylan amplifies the myth of America as a God-blessed country, a place where children may fulfill dreams of success through a climb to the top, and where righteousness, truth, courage, and strength win out. In short, the song paraphrases the

American dream, and along with it the values that are at the heart of American existence.

"Forever Young" ties together three intercut stories in "United Nation." All of the stories take place on Super Sunday and all involve elements of American myth and ritual. The main story line finds a middle-aged Minnesotan father irked at two problems: (1) a broken television antenna, and (2) a daughter getting married. Both interfere with the father's watching the Super Bowl game, something he values highly. The groom comes to the rescue, grounding the television set's antenna to receive the game. The net result is twofold: (1) The father is happy that he can watch the game, and (2) the father now appreciates his future son-in-law. On the surface, this story line celebrates the tradition of marriage and its role in welcoming (integrating) new members into the fold of the family. However, what is different here is the relative devaluation of the marriage celebration in contrast to the Super Bowl celebration. There also seems to be a secondary theme of accepting outsiders into the family only if it helps one become further engrossed in a shared sports culture. As well, women are seen as peripheral in this story, as brides or mothers. It is clearly a male-oriented world we have entered.

The second story line in "United Nation" involves a more straightforward theme of integration. Here we see a New York businessman hurriedly getting into a cab to get to the airport so that he can meet his family in Hawaii. Again, we see the goal of bringing together the family. The businessman and his black cab driver get stuck in traffic. The "problem" is solved as the cabbie heads to Brooklyn, with the businessman in tow, to watch the Super Bowl game that is about to start. The white businessman looks unsure of himself as he enters the house and confronts a group of black friends and family members, but he then relaxes and calls his family, and the racially integrated group "unites" in watching the Super Bowl on television. The fantasy makes integration in America a simple matter.

The third story in "United Nation" is set in a veterans' hospital where the male patients are getting ready for the "biggest game of the year." The diverse mix of patients, apart from being male, symbolizes America as a "melting pot." An apparently greedy attendant named Julius is selling tickets so that the patients can see the game on television. The "problem" is that the television set is too small, and no one can see very well. The patients turn on Julius, who shrugs off their complaints because he "has work to do." The surprise ending has Julius taking the money he has collected to buy a large color set so that all can see the game. Julius becomes a hero, and the united patients watch the game. Here, as well, the fantasy theme involves integration. What may be most unfortunate is the stereotypical casting of Julius as the "Jewish businessman" who is the subject of group hate, even though the stereotype is broken later in the story. Apart from this, the fantasy of a "United Nation" under football is upheld.

In case viewers did not get such a thorough "reading" of the music video in viewing the program, announcer Dick Enberg tells them what they have seen:

> That's a symbolic tribute to the millions of you who share in the Super Bowl experience today. It's kind of unlike what you would expect at the start of a Super Bowl telecast where normally there would be flying footballs and crashing padded bodies and touchdown celebrations. . . . We're going to pay tribute to what this day represents—an unannounced American holiday. For there is no time all year long where so many of us gather together around one event.

One doesn't need a magnifying glass to read the "meaning" of all this. Not only was NBC intermixing its vision of the American Dream with themes of integration, it was appealing to our sense of nationalism, and calling for a national holiday. And "unannounced" it certainly was not. The media hype had been building for two weeks at this point, and the Super Bowl pregame show had just begun.

Quarterbacks in the Judicial System

Approximately 35 minutes into the pregame show, reporter Pete Axthelm chooses to use an extended "legalistic" analogy in looking at different quarterbacks as lawyers with different styles. Axthelm's fantasy starts with the premise that "the Super Bowl can be a courtroom for quarterbacks, a chance to offer strong arguments and then deliver the proof." Axthelm has New York Jets quarterback Joe Namath overturning "the Supreme Courts of football." Pittsburgh Steeler quarterback "Terry Bradshaw was a country lawyer, supposedly too dumb; he won his super case four times." Chicago Bears quarterback Jim McMahon is cast as "a young F. Lee Bailey, willing to flaunt tradition to win." In this fantasy, National Football League commissioner Pete Rozelle becomes the "NFL Chief Judge," and is seen on screen replete with gavel penciled in. According to Axthelm, Judge Rozelle "fined" the maverick McMahon "for wearing an advertising headband in court."

Thus the manifest fantasy that Axthelm presents takes note of differences in style, but values authority in the form of the judge (in this case, Pete

Rozelle) even more. This is very much a traditional law-and-order scenario. What is most interesting about Axthelm's presentation is that it includes a latent fantasy that is almost directly in opposition to the normative values that the judicial system is there to enforce.

The oppositional fantasy is posed by the Jimmy Buffett song "Changes in Attitudes, Changes in Latitudes," which is used as a musical theme underneath Axthelm's narration. Buffett's song celebrates an alternative "partying" life-style that has little to do with following traditional rules, let alone laws. In Buffett's song, attitude changes are linked to alcohol use, and perhaps even abuse. One particular passage of the song that celebrates "craziness" is juxtaposed over Bears quarterback Jim McMahon. In the scene, McMahon is dressed in a football jersey, a head stocking, yellow gloves, and punk-style sunglasses—hardly traditional attire no matter how one looks at it. McMahon is jumping up and down, pointing, seemingly in a taunting manner, and the relative proximity of this shot to the one of "Judge Rozelle" suggests that McMahon is taunting Rozelle. As such, the oppositional fantasy celebrates yet another kind of American mythical hero—the maverick. With this added touch, Axthelm has made McMahon both more and less than a "young F. Lee Bailey." McMahon has become the crazy man defending himself in court—perhaps without a law degree—and winning the case. As well as celebrating the traditional values of the American criminal justice system, Axthelm seems to be celebrating its equally strong counterpart, the American maverick spirit.

An Immigrant Family and the American Dream

America did not become a melting pot by chance. The notion that a family can come to America, work hard, and succeed is a basic component of the American Dream. The most basic of American political values concern equality, fairness, nondiscrimination, and the like. These values are heard in the retelling of rags-to-riches stories of immigrant families. These stories have became part of American myth, as has the continued valuation of the family business in the age of multinational corporations. The modern-day continuation of that myth concerns the family that struggles to stay together and keep the family business alive.

Football mirrors these values, and in the past professional football teams were often family businesses. This has fallen by the wayside in a trend toward corporate ownership of professional sports teams. In today's world, evidence of the existence of a family-owned professional football team symbolizes that some part of that American Dream still lives.

The Super Bowl match-up between the Chicago Bears and the New England Patriots made the best of the myth that was left. It pitted two teams with histories of family ownership. The Bears family history is legendary in football circles. The team was coached and owned for 60 years by "Papa" George Halas, and the team continues to be owned by his descendants. The Patriots are the family business of the Sullivan family. NBC decided to lead the second hour of its pregame show with a profile of the Sullivan family.

Reporter Bill MacAtee's feature on the "colorful and controversial" Sullivans typecasts the family as "an indomitable strain of Irish Catholics" with "fierce loyalty to one another." In MacAtee's fantasy, they are a family "battling for respect." This is graphically illustrated with film of a postgame "scuffle" that took place because of "bad blood" between Pat Sullivan, "the youngest of the Sullivan clan," and an opposing team's owner. After fisticuffs with a player on that opposing team, a bandaged and tough-talking Pat Sullivan says:

> Let me tell you something. We're just getting back for Jack Tatum and all the other crap that this football team has put on our football team for twelve years.

The way the family story is posed, Pat Sullivan is defending his family's honor and, specifically, the honor of the 70-year-old Billy Sullivan, who is cast as the "patriarch of the Sullivan family." In fact, in this fantasy of protecting the family name, the patriarch later blames himself for provoking Pat's actions, because before that game he had said that he was tired of his family "being used as a punching bag."

As fantasy, the Sullivan family story serves as an analogy for the relatively recent turnabout in American nationalistic values. The fiefdom of Sullivan had been violated, and the young soldier in the clan had succeeded in restoring luster to the family crest. Like the Sullivans, many Americans have recently perceived their country as being the "punching bag" for the world. This feeling has stemmed from perceptions of a "no-win" war in Vietnam and national disgrace in Watergate, to Jimmy Carter's sense of political "malaise," and was brought to a head by the Iranian hostage crisis. To many observers, the "stand tall" image and resultant policies of the Reagan administration have replaced the symbol of "America as punching bag." The new image reflects the cinematic fantasies of Sylvester Stallone's Rocky and Rambo, and, like Pat Sullivan, restores the honor of the American "family." President Reagan's hopes for America seemingly parallel the Sullivans' hopes for the Super Bowl.

"Ain't That America"

A John Cougar Mellencamp song focusing on the American Dream serves as the centerpiece for segment 10 of the pregame show. Coming at a point nearly an hour and a half into the program, Mellencamp's rock song is juxtaposed with NBC's two-pronged fantasy asking the audience to appreciate (1) America in a football context, and (2) football in an American context. The song is unabashedly introduced by studio anchor announcer Bob Costas:

> Super Sunday, an American celebration. As we said, it's almost like an undeclared national holiday and certainly our fascination with football in general and the Super Bowl in particular is a wonderful and sometimes curious piece of Americana—set now to the music of John Cougar Mellencamp.

The music video piece that follows is indeed a "curious" mixture of football images from stock footage intercut with NBC's visions of America.

The image we first see is a full-screen stylized American flag with equally stylized three-dimensional silver stars becoming larger as they move toward the viewer via special effects. Next to follow in this pattern of American stars zooming at us over red and white stripes is a larger, but equally silvered, logo for the National Football League. The logo comes at us until it fills the screen and is dissolved away as more silver stars continue to come at us. Next, the stars are interspersed with images of football "greats" that continue in a pattern of moving toward us over the backdrop of the flag's stripes. The net result is the equation of both the NFL and its "stars" with the stars and stripes that symbolize nationalistic values for all Americans. In doing this, NBC's fantasy has made professional football's heroes into American heroes. In the tautological reasoning of this fantasy, the NFL, as the organization responsible for bringing these heroes to us, is imbued with nationalistic sentiment in much the same way that the military's role is heightened at a time of celebrating war heroes.

The bulk of the visuals in the remainder of the video follow in the pattern of linking the flag to the playing of professional football. A frequent transitional device is a full-screen flag with sixteen dancing stars filling the frame. From this base, transitions are made to the some of the more notable football players and coaches. In NBC's sense of football history, these are notable coaches and players because, for the most part, they have participated in a Super Bowl game. History "in the making" is shown by juxtaposing the players and coaches of the upcoming contest with their counterparts in the most significant of these games in the past. Thus, by participating in the construction of a hero-based history, the fantasy group is also allowed to participate in the making of history.

With John Cougar Mellencamp's lyrics relying on a chorus that is based on the "Star Spangled Banner" axiom of America as "home of the free," nationalistic values seem to dominate this song. However, this is still rock and roll, and there are some oppositional themes being posed as well. Beginning with the title of the song, "Pink Houses," Mellencamp provides a counterpoint to the idealized visions of Americana through football that NBC apparently seeks to emphasize. NBC avoids revealing the song's title, which Mellencamp uses in a secondary refrain as shorthand for the parceled-down dream that America leaves for its working class.

When such oppositional references come up in the song, NBC presents imagery that symbolically says these little houses are a thing of the past. We see short glimpses of stylized "color-tinted" houses that look like hand-painted postcards from an era predating color photography. We see romanticized country clapboard houses, log cabins, trailers, and even row houses and other small dwellings quickly mixed in with an occasional mansion. Mellencamp, however, is not talking about the past. For him, the problems that exist today call into question the myth of American Dream.

Debunking other American myths in the song, Mellencamp poses as absurd the common wisdom that anyone can grow up to be president. NBC wrestles with Mellencamp's assertions in an interesting fashion. When Mellencamp sings of a boy who is going to grow up to be president, NBC shows us the smiling Republican congressman from Buffalo, Jack Kemp, who just happened to be a former NFL quarterback. At the point of this telecast, Kemp was widely regarded in the press as a "presidential hopeful" of some promise. However, because of lines that follow in Mellencamp's song, it is ambiguous as to whether NBC is "endorsing" Kemp for the presidency. But clearly the association of Kemp with the main story line of football heroes in the land of the free did not injure his chances for the presidential nomination.

It is interesting to note that almost all of the nonfootball images accompanying Mellencamp's song look as though they were produced by artificial means, most likely by a sophisticated computer graphics machine. Only three scenes contain nonfootball people doing something in America. One is a two-shot sequence of bikini-clad young women—one shot showing a frontal view of two women "hanging out" at the beach and the other shot showing two women dancing together at what appears to be a party. Bikini-clad women may not be such an alarming novelty, but this is the first time we have focused on any women in this program since the "bride" in the "United Nation" video that opened the program. Thus it has taken an hour and a half to get from bride to bikini. Even on this "super" day dedicated to celebrating some of the strongest of male athletes, this is less than "super," especially if one is to take seriously NBC's themes concerning integration, family cohesiveness, and a system of American justice that stresses fairness and equality.

The Great Man Theory of Coaching

In closing out the last half hour of the pregame program, NBC continues to weave its nationalistic fantasy with two segments focusing on leadership. In recent presidential elections, "leadership" has become a political issue, one that is central to the success of a candidate. In developing themes about leadership, NBC first profiles Vince Lombardi, the late coach of the Green Bay Packers, and follows this segment with an "exclusive" interview with President Reagan.

Leading into the commercial break after which the Lombardi segment will appear, anchor announcer Bob Costas's "promo" sets a stage for "understanding" the Packer coach:

> When we come back an affectionate remembrance of the man for whom the Super Bowl trophy is named, the legendary and sometimes misunderstood figure—Vince Lombardi—of the Green Bay Packers.

After the commercial break, and as the segment nears, Costas continues:

> The Lombardi Trophy, that's what these Bears and Patriots are vying for. And the man whose name is inscribed on that trophy led the Packers to victory in the first two Super Bowls. The late Vince Lombardi, regarded by most as the finest coach of his era. Regarded by his players as something more than that.

As it turns out in this fantasy, that "something more" than a coach that Lombardi turned out to be was a "great leader" or "great man." As historian Daniel Boorstin (1961) has alluded to in his book, *The Image*, "great man" theories are a common, but uncomplex, way to explain history. In the fantasy here, great leaders are great leaders in more than one sphere. For NBC, Lombardi, the great coach, becomes one of the great philosophers of life.

The feature segment is structured as a testimonial in which Lombardi's better-known players attest to the twofold "greatness" that their former coach possessed.

The clear-cut, or manifest, "greatness" in Lombardi was in his being a tough coach who demanded respect from his players. His coaching philosophy is summed up by the often-quoted Lombardi-ism: "Winning is not everything, it is the only thing." This "win at all costs" coaching philosophy is seen many times over in the course of the segment on Lombardi. However, in this Lombardi fantasy, winning comes about as a result of pride. Pride is stressed in a sequence where Lombardi introduces himself and his philosophy to the team. Shot from a low angle that emphasizes Lombardi as an authority figure, the strict "disciplinarian" tone of Lombardi's voice is embellished by a green tinge to the color film. Lombardi emerges as a symbolic Marine Corps sergeant speaking to his recruits:

> My name is Vince Lombardi. I want to welcome you to the Green Bay Packers. If you have the dedication, the total commitment, and the pride necessary to become part of this team that has been built around pride, you will stay here.

The less clear-cut, or latent, "greatness" in Lombardi is brought about largely through the hindsight of his former players. The extension of Lombardi's greatness beyond football and into life is best summed up by Bart Starr, a longtime quarterback on Lombardi's teams:

> The quality of coach Lombardi that enabled us to transcend the football field and be successful in other fields as well was the fact that he never talked in terms of football, he talked in terms of life.

In the fantasy that is passed along here, Lombardi's greatness in passing along the values for a successful life was "loved" by his players. As former player Fuzzy Thurston put it, "I sure loved him and I still miss him today as much as I ever missed anybody in my life."

Even though the major fantasy theme poses Lombardi as a multifaceted and loved leader, it can be seen that NBC's fantasy about Lombardi's "greatness" is based on a perception of him as a "common man." As the very beginning of the segment, we hear an inspirational musical theme as we see the silver Lombardi Trophy glimmering with light on a black background. It is the music that adds meaning to the trophy and carries the visual transition to an extreme close-up of Lombardi, who is about to speak. By no mere happenstance, the music that plays in the background is American composer

Aaron Copland's "Fanfare for the Common Man." In this setting, we eagerly await Lombardi's first words:

> Unless a man believes in himself and makes a total commitment to his career and puts everything he has into it — his mind, his body, and his heart — what's life worth to him?

In total, the fantasy about Lombardi takes on mythlike proportions in the world of professional football. NBC's presentation of it chains the fantasy to the world outside. It is a world where a "great leader" or a "great man" is hard to find.

The President as the President

A mythlike act like the Vince Lombardi segment is undoubtedly a difficult act to follow. In keeping with the overall theme of Super Bowl XX as "An American Celebration," NBC presents, as a closing act for the Super Bowl pregame show, a headliner whose mere presence on stage signifies the legitimacy of such a thematic choice. Symbolically riding on the coattails of the Lombardi myth, President Ronald Reagan appears on stage. The appearance of the president of the United States attaches national importance to any event. In this case, NBC presents a live interview with President Reagan at the White House. The appearance of the president on this program tautologically reifies the nationalistic themes that NBC has worked so hard to develop over the duration of the pregame program. Here is a living, breathing symbol of all that is American, and he is on this program "celebrating" America and the Super Bowl. In one fell swoop the rhetorical vision that has been constructed out of fantasy becomes reality.

Studio anchor announcer Bob Costas provides the background for the president's appearance:

> Like most of the rest of us, President Ronald Reagan is a football fan and he's got a varied background in the sport. The chief executive played some college football, was later a sportscaster in Iowa, and of course he had the role of the Gipper in the film biography of Notre Dame Coach Knute Rockne.

After this introduction, we see reporter Tom Brokaw and the president sitting in comfortable chairs in the library of the White House. The tone of the interview is set by the benign nature of the opening series of questions. Brokaw inquires as to which team the president favors in the Super Bowl game. Amplifying the themes of fairness and equality posed in earlier segments, the president declines to pick a favorite. Shortly thereafter, a question about the national holiday status of Super Bowl Sunday is posed by Brokaw:

> Super Bowl Sunday has become a kind of undeclared national holiday. Do you think occasions like this help to shape our national character or are they just kind of entertaining diversions from things like the deficit and terrorism and Kadafi?

The president responds:

> Well I think it's typically American that we can have or be diverted by things like this from the serious problems. I think it's part of the American personality and I know that other countries take athletics seriously too, but there is something different about it in America. It's so much a part of American life that I think it's part of our personality.

In essence here, the president has endorsed the national holiday fantasy by giving the presidential seal of approval to being "diverted" from "serious problems" by the Super Bowl game. The president has extended the fantasy being chained here to some degree. Not only is such diversion officially endorsed with a stamp of nationalistic value, but such an official endorsement may raise questions about the patriotism of those Americans who choose not to participate in the Super Bowl fantasy. In total, the president had taken one more step in the direction of putting the Super Bowl fantasy at one with American culture.

Brokaw's interview with the president rambles on for over eight minutes, making it the longest feature segment in the pregame program. The bulk of the interview concerns Reagan's football playing days, his role playing the part of the Gipper and some related privy knowledge of Notre Dame coach Knute Rockne, and his days as a sports announcer. At only one time during the interview does Brokaw press the president with an overt political question. In this instance, Brokaw does so in such a creatively round-about fashion that he may succeed in further accelerating the fantasies being chained about football and politics:

> Mr. President, football is a metaphor for so many things in American life, including politics. Now at the end of this game today one team is going to be

at a deficit situation and all those players are going to face a very taxing year in 1986. You're about to deliver the State of the Union Address. Are you going to put the American people through the same experience in 1986 — a taxing year?

Brokaw's question so fully integrates football and political fantasies that it is nearly impossible to decipher what is football and what is politics. The president, however, easily distinguishes between the two and knows that this is a "holiday" and no time to answer questions about either the State of the Union Address or taxes. The heretofore blurred line between politics and sports is clearly redrawn by the president.

Other evidence of the president's "political" control over this pregame "sports" program can be seen in Brokaw's attempt to finish the interview. Brokaw poses to the president: "Final chance, do you want to pick a score or a team?" The president replies, "No, but do I have a second so I can tell you a little incident in my memories of football?" Brokaw responds, "Sure, absolutely," much as a person would respond to the proverbial 800 pound gorilla asking to sit in one's favorite easy chair. The president then launches into a story about his audition as a sports announcer that lasts approximately two more minutes.

This incident clarifies some of the more realistic aspects of the sports and politics fantasy. A president who knows the rules of broadcasting as well as the rules of politics can control the fantasy-building conduit, at least for a limited time. Also, any country having a president who has as one of his more visible attributes the fact that he is a former sportscaster, cannot help being fenced in by a fantasy chain link fence that surrounds politics with sports and sports with politics. The president is merely demonstrating which of the two elements in the fantasy hold the key to the reality gate. In this fantasy, as reality approaches, politics holds that key.

Closing the Gate

The political fantasy type that pertains to sports programming has been chained out to a large degree in this limited analysis of six segments that appeared on NBC's 1986 Super Bowl pregame show. The nationalistic fantasy that was developed in the course of this program was based on themes central to the American Dream. Among the more prevalent of these were themes concerning racial and ethnic integration, national and family unity, due process of law, rugged individualism in the form of the maverick, hard work, family businesses, patriotism, heroism, simplicity in the form of the common man, equality, the multifaceted character of great leaders, commitment and pride, and last, but not least, the relationship of sports to American character. Taken together, this conglomeration of fantasy themes builds a chain link fence through which professional football, and perhaps all mediated portrayals of sports in America, may be better understood.

If this political chain link fence can be seen as formed by the program elements, NBC added a gate to that fence in the form of nationalistic promotional announcements for the network's sports programming. Peppered throughout the two hours of the program, these announcements were of varying lengths, but all shared a rapid-fire visual style highlighting well-known American athletes (especially Olympic athletes) to a bouncy tune proclaiming NBC as the American choice in sports programming. Through this, NBC was attempting to stake a claim on the political fantasies that were woven during the program itself. This rather parasitic relationship between the general network goals and the specific program was striking. If the fantasy chain link fence that was constructed in the program material was in any sense successful in containing our perceptions of the Super Bowl game in a nationalistic pen, then NBC wanted to close the gate and contain us within that fantasy for the long haul.

The only program element that could tamper with the political fantasy being constructed here was political reality in the form of the president. Symbolically holding the key to the gate, the president seized control over the pattern of fantastical discourse being fashioned by the media reporters and commentators. President Reagan opened the gate and walked in, adding his story to the political fantasy as the gate closed behind him. What lingered, however, was the knowledge that the president, and political reality generally, can intervene at any point in the political fantasies that mediated sports may conjure up.

The analyses here have shown the wide range of political fantasies embodied in the Super Bowl pregame show. These fantasies were sandwiched in at either end of the show by fantasies of youth, albeit slightly different ones. The show opened to the theme of Bob Dylan's "Forever Young," and essentially closed with a youthful-looking but nearly 75-year-old president one-upping NBC's senior news anchorperson in an interview setting.

The youthful "bread" holding together the political fantasy in this "sports" program helps to remind us that America is a young country, as well as a country that values and frequently celebrates youth. Professional sports are played by comparatively young people. Collegiate and Olympic sports typically feature even younger athletes. The new health and exercise conscious-ness is propelled, to some degree, by the desire to stay youthful looking and by fears of getting old. One of the major concerns about the presidential candidacy of Ronald Reagan was his age. However, as his youthful appearance belied stereotypes of old age, the issue seemingly disappeared into a fountain of youth.

Similarly, it is clear that the fantasy themes that grew with the participants of the Super Bowl pregame show had little to do with reality. This point was not lost on *Los Angeles Times* television critic Howard Rosenberg (1986), who bemoaned NBC's packaging of the Super Bowl with a double scoop helping of Americana:

> The Super Bowl? That's no American celebration. That's a marketing phenom, an incredibly successful sales job on Americans to convince us that there is something symbolically patriotic about a game between two professional foot-ball teams that have played previously and are playing again so that they, the National Football League, TV and sponsors can score a big payday. (p. 1)

In Rosenberg's cautioning against confusing the game with "America, the Beautiful" there is recognition that fantasy themes, chains, and the chain link fences that they yield may be full of contradictions. Also, they may fly in the face of reason or observable fact. The aim is to construct an altered reality that has intrinsic, but not necessarily practical, value. As Jhally (1984) has suggested, because sports celebrate idealized structures of reality in a ritualistic manner, they bridge an essential social dialectic of fantasy and reality. Mediated sport may accelerate the workings of such a dialectic by providing somewhat uniform fantasies. This study is merely suggestive of how the merger of political and sports fantasies breeds uniform interpretations about the significance of both elements in American culture.

Notes

1. It is not my intention to fall into the great crevasse of disagreement about Bormann's (1972) fantasy theme analysis. Although it is admittedly applied in a playful way here, my reading of Bormann's approach is based on his seminal statement about it, not on the controversy that followed.

2. While the notion of a "fantasy chain link fence" is playfully inspired by Bormann's (1972) use of ambiguously overlapping terms, he is no way responsible for striking such a phrase.

References

Balbus, I. (1975). Politics as sports: The political ascendancy of the sports metaphor in America. *Monthly Review, 26,* 26–39.

Bales, R. F. (1950). *Interaction process analysis: A method for the study of small groups.* Cambridge, MA: Addison-Wesley.

Boorstin, D. J. (1961) *The image: A guide to pseudo-events in America.* New York: Atheneum.

Bormann, E. G. (1972). Fantasy and rhetorical vision: The rhetorical criticism of social reality. *Quarterly Journal of Speech, 58,* 396–407.

Bormann, E. G. (1977). Fetching good out of evil: A rhetorical use of calamity. *Quarterly Journal of Speech, 63,* 130–139

Bormann, E. G., Koester, J., & Bennett, J. (1978). Political cartoons and salient rhetorical fantasies: An empirical analysis of the '76 presidential campaign. *Communication Monographs, 45,* 317–329.

Bryant, J., Brown, D., Comisky, P. W., & Zillmann, D. (1982). Sports and spectators: Commentary and appreciation. *Journal of Communication, 32,* 109–119.

Bryant, J., Comisky, P., & Zillmann, D. (1977). Drama in sports commentary. *Journal of Communication, 27,* 140–149.

Buell, J. (1980). Superhype. *Progressive, 44,* 66.

Buscombe, E. (1975). *Football on television.* London: British Film Institute.

Carey, J. (1976). How media shape campaigns. *Journal of Communication, 26,* 50–57.

Comisky, P., Bryant, J., & Zillmann, D. (1977). Commentary as a substitute for action. *Journal of Communication, 27,* 150–153.

Eitzen, S., & Sage, G. H. (1978). *Sociology of American sport.* Dubuque, IA: Wm. C. Brown.

Gantz, W. (1981). An explorations of viewing motives and behaviors associated with television sports. *Journal of Broadcasting, 25,* 263–275.

Goffman, E. (1974). *Frame analysis.* Philadelphia: University of Pennsylvania Press

Goldstein, J. H., & Bredemeier, B. J. (1977). Socialization: Some basic issues. *Journal of Communication, 27,* 154–159.

Goodwin, M. (1986, January 20). NBC's game plan is most extensive. *New York Times,* p. C15.

Jhally, S. (1984). The spectacle of accumulation: Material and cultural factors in the evolution of the sports/media complex. *Insurgent Sociologist, 3,* 41–57.

Loy, J. W. (1978). The cultural system of sport. *Quest Monograph, 29.*

Morse, M. (1983). Sport on television: Replay and display. In E. A. Kaplan (Ed.), *Regarding television: Critical approaches—an anthology* (pp. 44–66). Frederick, MD: University Publications of America.

Nimmo, D. & Combs, J. E. (1983). *Mediated political realities.* New York: Longman.

Nixon, H. L. (1982). Idealized functions of sport: Religious and political socialization through sport. *Journal of Sport and Social Issues, 6,* 1–11.

Nowell-Smith, G. (1981). Television-football-the world. In T. Bennett (Ed.), *Popular television and film* (pp. 159–170). London: British Film Institute.

Parente, P. (1979). The interdependence of sports and television. *Journal of Communication, 29,* 94–102.

Pooley, J. C., & Webster, A. V. (1976). The interdependence of sports, politics and economics. In A. Yiannakis, T. McIntyre, M. Melnick, & D. Hart (Eds.), *Sport sociology: Contemporary themes* (pp. 35–42). Dubuque, IA: Kendall-Hunt.

Prisuta, R. H. (1979). Televised sports and political values. *Journal of Communication, 29*, 94–102.

Real, M. R. (1975, Winter). Super Bowl: Mythic spectacle. *Journal of Communication, 25*, 31–43.

Rosenberg, H. (1986, January 28). NBC's Super Bowl runneth over 'n' over 'n' . . . *Los Angeles Times*, part VI, pp. 1, 8.

Sapolsky, B. S., & Zillmann, D. (1978). Enjoyment of a televised sport contest under different conditions of viewing. *Perceptual and Motor Skills, 46*, 29–30.

Snyder, E. E., & Spreitzer, E. (1978). *Social aspects of sport*. Englewood Cliffs, NJ: Prentice-Hall.

Stephenson, W. (1967). *The play theory of mass communication*. Chicago: University of Chicago Press.

Trujillo, N., & Ekdom, L. R. (1985). Sportswriting and American cultural values: The 1984 Chicago Cubs. *Critical Studies in Mass Communication, 2*, 262–281.

Tuchman, G. (1978). *Making news: A study in the construction of reality*. New York: Free Press.

Vescey, G. (1986, January 20). Fans' moment of truth. *New York Times*, p. C15.

Williams, B. R. (1977). The structure of televised football. *Journal of Communication, 27*, 133–139.

8

Super Bowl Football Versus World Cup Soccer:
A Cultural-Structural Comparison

Michael R. Real

It is an intriguing coincidence that the number one rated sports events on television inside the United States and outside it are both called "football" but are significantly different as sports and events. The championship game of American professional football, the Super Bowl, consistently attracts some 120 million American viewers, the largest annual audience of the television year, and advertising time during the game is the most expensive of the year, now exceeding $500,000 per 30-second spot. The international soccer championship every four years, known to most of the world as the "football World Cup" (the Copa Mundial de Futbol), attracts the largest audience for any single television event, by the 1990s directly reaching an estimated 600 million to 2 billion viewers (international audience figures being extremely imprecise). The only event with a comparable appeal is also a sporting event, the Olympics, but as that comprises many different sports, it is excluded from this comparison.

Making the contrast between the two "futbol" events even more intriguing, neither one is particularly popular in the arena of the other. That is, on one side, North American-style football and the Super Bowl are virtually unheard of outside the United States and Canada except among expatriate Americans, despite the game's recent carriage on dozens of foreign television services and token exhibition games played annually in Great Britain and Japan. American football is a uniquely North American game, and the Super Bowl is a provocatively U.S. spectacle. On the other side, the Copa

Mundial de Futbol and international soccer competition are earthshaking events throughout most of the world but are nearly unheard of within the United States. While everyday human life stops on a large part of the earth's surface during the finals of the World Cup, the event is not even assured major network coverage in the United States. When the 1994 World Cup playoffs were awarded to the United States to host, due to the superior commitment of stadiums and financial support, it was a shock to many inside and outside the United States. The United States has never developed powerful teams to enter in international soccer competition, and the sport's growth in America in recent decades through youth soccer leagues, interscholastic teams, and precarious professional teams still leaves the United States behind much of the world.

The contrasting appeal of the World Cup and the Super Bowl raise the challenging question: Why? In addition to the divergent histories of the two "futbol" sports, what are structural and cultural differences between them that make each appropriate to the geopolitical arena in which it is popular and that make each inappropriate to the opposite arena? Such a question raises fundamental issues in the sociology of sport, the comparative study of cultures, and the role of media in consumer culture. Issues of ideology and hegemony move to the forefront with such a question. The significance of popular culture both as a theoretical challenge and as a human experience can be brought into sharp focus by a phenomenological and structural examination of these two most popular sociological events.

Trends in Theory, Research, and Popular Writings on Sports and Media

The importance of such questions of sport as a social force is evident in daily life, but not equally evident in research and scholarly work. Like folk art or religious cults, sports inspire more devotion than self-reflexivity. Following the prominent German social theorist Norbert Elias, Eric Dunning (1986) argues for the general significance of sport:

> The development of modern sport has taken—and is taking—place within the long-term, unplanned social process that led to the emergence of urban-industrial-nation-states. Sport occupies an increasingly important place within the structure of such societies and in the relationships between them. As such, the sociological study of sport ought to form an important part of the discipline as a whole.

One of the few modern theorists to take up this challenge is John Hargreaves in his ground-breaking book *Sport, Power and Culture: A Social and Historical Analysis of Popular Sports in Britain* (1986). Previously, Hargreaves (1982) noted the neglect of sport as a subject of intellectual analysis:

> The neglect of sport is by no means confined to sociology: nowhere in the social sciences and related fields is there more than a small minority of people prepared to take sports seriously as an analytical problem. The most obvious result of neglect is that an underdeveloped continent largely remains to be explored, of which there is as yet a relatively shallow understanding. (p. 32)

This neglect results from several causes, according to Hargreaves. First, "culture" has been academically defined with a bias toward high culture and an exclusion of popular mass "amusements" from attention. Second, when considered, sport has been assumed to be unproblematically enjoyable and unserious, or even unquestionably good. From such stances, therefore, sport presents no real analytical problems and is accorded low academic status. Third, to many observers, including academics, sport represents an idealized version of the social order, with an aura of the sacred, and any attempt to analyze it is resisted as "intrinsically subversive" to conventional wisdom about the social order and its legitimacy and meaning.

Thoughtful analyses of sports, and sports media, are becoming available, but only gradually so and from widely divergent directions, as the collection of studies in this volume illustrates. In previous work, the relationship between sports events and the larger society has been formulated in conflicting ways.

On a general level, sociologists have provided standard structural-functionalist analyses of sport in society, usually within a Parsonian framework (see Hargreaves, 1982, p. 35). Sport in this analysis is an adaptive response to the demands of stability and change, a response that connects individuals with the social order and integrates institutions such as schools into society. In the functionalist view, the expansion of mass spectator sports and media is a desirable development, paralleling the extension of democracy. Hargreaves charges that this approach uncritically assumes that "the existing structure of society is the 'normal' way modern societies function" (p. 37). Against functionalism, Hargreaves finds that an unsophisticated Marxist analysis has tended to oversimplify in the opposite direction. In this critique, modern commercialized and spectacularized sport is a captive servant of corporate capitalism, propagandizing the public into its value structure and providing escape from resulting frustrations and contradictions as an opiate for alienation. Hargreaves rightly points out that this critique provides a "pathological model of human behavior" and is "completely deterministic" (p. 41). But Hargreaves also finds a positive value here, one relevant to comparisons of the World Cup and Super Bowl: "The superiority of the Marxist tradition as a whole, as opposed to any particular version of it, has been its sensitivity to the association of culture with power, and specifically to the class basis of hegemony" (p. 42).

Popular American books on sports and media have tended to evoke the depth of sports as a social force but lack an equivalent depth in analysis, whether the proposed judgments of mediated sports are positive (Michener, 1976; Novak, 1976) or negative (Gardner, 1975; Guttmann, 1978; Hoch, 1972; Rader, 1984). Michael Novak's neoconservative celebration of sport, *The Joy of Sports* (1976), illustrates this. He sings the praises of the institutions of sport for generating a "natural religion." The ceremonies of sports overlap those of the state and of the churches, in Novak's view: "Going to a stadium is half like going to a political rally, half like going to church. . . . The Olympics are not barebones athletic events, but religion and politics as well" (p. 19). Citizens honor their country, go to church, and enjoy sports, without separating them in their minds. Sportswriters indulge in religious metaphors, and motivational sports slogans become parareligious: "You gotta believe!" and "life and death" and "sacrifice."

In his pop functionalism, Novak argues for an even deeper "religious" role for sports. He rhapsodizes that "sports flow outward into action from a deep natural impulse that is radically religious: an impulse of freedom, respect for ritual limits, a zest for symbolic meaning, and a longing for perfection." Furthermore, for Novak, sports "are organized and dramatized in a religious way" (p. 19). He finds sports "teach religious qualities of heart and soul" (p. 21) and claims, "Among the godward signs in contemporary life, sports may be the single most powerful manifestation" (p. 20). Novak then proceeds to use sports subtly as a vehicle to attack liberalism. For example, he canonizes violence in American football by observing, "One of the game's greatest satisfactions, indeed, is that it violates the illusion of the enlightened, educated person that violence has been, is, or will be exorcised from human life" (p. 78). Novak's political agenda, to which we shall return, perhaps reflects too much the mentality of sports competition—you align yourself with one side and work toward unambiguous victory—rather than dealing with the ambiguous complexities of the subject matter.

What even the weaker critiques highlight, however, is the provocative relationship between a sports event and the cultural whole, especially in the structural organization of the event and the culture. The issue of women's sports and the media has been subjected to increasingly substantive debate as, for example, in the special issue of the *Gannett Center Journal* (1987) titled "Sports and the Mass Media." But overall in the United States, sports have not provided a playing field on which the best sociocultural theorists have performed their best work. How is the Super Bowl, or the World Cup, a positive or negative force in society? Even when asked, either directly or indirectly, such questions have previously generated more heat than light. Can the structural interpretations of "cultural studies" improve this situation?

Cultural-Structural Analysis

The intriguing aspects of the Super Bowl versus the World Cup center around the *cultural* configurations with which each is associated. Cultural studies has emerged in the past decade as a "meta-discipline" (Real, 1989) concerned with key words of text, context, meaning, interpretation, ideology, and hegemony. This chapter is concerned precisely with these culturally conditioned dimensions of the Super Bowl text and World Cup text. These two events somehow resonate with the differences of the cultures with which they are associated, and cultural studies provides a vehicle for examining particular texts and their dominant interpretations in relation to the more generalized "structure of feeling" (Hall, 1980; Williams, 1961) of an entire culture. Clifford Geertz (1973) provides the prototype of applying this form of analysis to a sporting event in his classic study, "Deep Play: Notes on a Balinese Cockfight."

The differences between these events appear most clearly in their respective *structural* arrangements of space, time, action, and other materials. Vladimir Propp's (1968) structural analysis of the fairy tale provides the pattern for a syntagmatic examination of the sequential structure of football and soccer. Claude Lvi-Strauss (1963) takes us beyond this manifest meaning to the latent meaning of the texts with his paradigmatic analysis of the fundamental binary oppositions present in any social text, from ancient rituals to modern psychiatry.

The cultural-structural focus then is this: How do World Cup soccer and Super Bowl football "structure" their interactive competitions within the context of a given "culture"?

Similarities Between World Cup Soccer and Super Bowl Football

The two sports that reach their apex in the World Cup and the Super Bowl have far more in common than the shared label of "football." They share many structural and contextual features: (1) Both games are played by relatively large teams, with eleven players fielded by each side during play action. Uruguay won the first World Cup in 1930 with an eleven-man team, and Green Bay won the First Super Bowl in 1967 with the same number. (2) Teams in each game try to move the ball down a field and into or across the other team's goal to score. Argentina won the 1986 World Cup played in Mexico by scoring more goals, just as the Chicago Bears had done earlier that year in the Super Bowl. (3) Both games include kicking the ball, though in different degrees. The Bears kicked only field goals, punts, and kickoffs, while Argentina kicked continuously on its way to victory in the World Cup. (4) Success in either game at the higher levels of competition requires extensive training, intense conditioning, coordinated teamwork, and complex, carefully developed strategies. Argentina had recruited, trained, and competed internationally for nearly two full years to reach the World Cup apex, while the Chicago Bears had survived and conquered through a grueling five-month season; both were backed by immense organizations, technical resources, and extensive preparations.

In their most elaborated forms – the World Cup and the Super Bowl – each sport has become a fantastic *mass spectacle*. (5) Each marshals the most sophisticated technology of modern communications for its presentation to the scattered millions of viewers. Television cameras, production vans, digital video effects units, instant slow-motion replay decks, satellites, electronic wire services, microwaves, phone lines – every advantage of modern technology was utilized to beam Argentina's victory from Mexico City to the world and to beam the Bears' victory from the New Orleans Superdome to all Americans. (6) Each holds the center of media attention from newspapers, magazines, radio, television, and related media for days and weeks surrounding the event. The final month-long World Cup elimination tournament from Mexico City dominated media around the world; the NFL playoffs and the final game in New Orleans generated the Super Bowl's usual unparalleled media coverage. (7) Each directly involves millions of dollars of income and expense in ticket purchases, television rights, event preparation and organization, spectator travel and accommodations, player compensation, commercial sponsorship, product endorsements, and other economic factors. And each involves even more money through widespread and large-scale betting on the events. (8) Each also provides a platform and metaphors for political posturing, religious moralizing, nationalistic fervor, regional partisanship, and other symbolic exploitation. The presidents of Argentina and the United States are careful to be prominently seen in support of "the game" and its high purposes. (9) Each event stimulates profound emotional involvement among fans. Hopes and fears about success begin many years before the qualifying competition for these finals and can dominate individual and community life, whether participation is personal (as a player) or only vicarious (as a fan). These are without question the number one spectacles of their time and place.

The two events also perform similar sociological functions. Critical scholars emphasize the "rationalizing" structure at work here in accommodating the public to the systems of organization and domination that structure social life. Hargreaves (1982) summarizes these mechanisms:

> In their organisation and functioning the major popular sports all are seen as replicating the fundamental features of modern rationalised industrial production: a high degree of specialisation and standardisation, bureaucratised and hierarchical administration, long-term planning, increased reliance on science and technology, a drive for maximum productivity, a quantification of performance, and, above all, the alienation of both the producer and consumer. Major games like European and American football and the modern Olympics are taken as exemplars of this development. (p. 41)

The charge of alienation may be debated, but the other cultural structures that Hargreaves lists are readily apparent in both the World Cup and the Super Bowl. In fact, in both "futbol" sports in their ultimate expression, the finals of the playoffs, there are present the most intensified forms of each of the above structures. For example, specialization or the reliance on science and technology may take different forms in the Super Bowl and World Cup, but they are distinctly emphasized in both. As a model of behavior, the two super media events contain the above structures and serve to "rationalize" or make into an assumed common sense the prominent features of each spectacularized event: corporate capitalism in the case of the Super Bowl or a kind of socialistic nationalism in the case of the World Cup, as we see in an analysis of structural differences.

World Cup Versus Super Bowl: Structural and Cultural Differences

Despite similarities in general structure and function, there are many reflections of an old "America against the world" stereotype in the differences between the World Cup and the Super Bowl. This occurs in six different levels or spheres of social structure present in football and soccer: (1) continuity or discontinuity of action, (2) technological support systems, (3) violence and paramilitarism in player interaction, (4) player use of body parts for ball control, (5) measures of success in winning and scoring, (6) degrees of specialization and bureaucracy, (7) degrees of masculinity, and (8) broader cultural patterns relating to the differences in the two sports events.

James Michener (1976) has summarized his interpretation of why soccer, despite its international popularity, has not caught on in America:

> In the three countries in which American-style football became established first – United States, Canada with a slightly different rules, Australia with the wildest game of all – the superiority of the American game, with its violence, its variation in action and its more frequent opportunities for scoring, became evident, and fans could show no interest in the slower, more repetitious and low-scoring soccer version. (p. 304)

Do these generalizations hold up under closer scrutiny? What are their implications? Michener, with his appreciation for soccer as well as football, provides a better starting point than many commentators, such as one successful American sports announcer who claimed, "Let's face it. Soccer is a boring game. It will never catch on with American media because it's too slow and tedious" (Leitner, 1987). Only those who, unlike Michener, have never witnessed a vivid soccer match between major teams with a deeply aroused crowd could be so naive as to make such a claim.

The Historical Separation

Soccer has a long history. Variations of the game date back at least to King Edward II's warning in 1314:

> For as much as there is great noise in the city caused by hustling over large balls . . . from which many evils might arise, which God forbid, we command and

forbid on behalf of the King, on pain of imprisonment, such game to be used
in the city in the future. (quoted in Gardner, 1975, p. 96)

In 1657 the city of Boston similarly condemned "playing at foot-ball in the
streets" and imposed a 20 shilling fine for every such offense in the "Streets,
Lanes and Inclosures of this Town" (Gardner, 1975, p. 96). This soccer-style
football was often a large and loosely regulated competition. At times a ball
would be placed between two villages and all the male residents of the villages would kick it around the countryside until it reached one of the two village greens for a score. As early as 1711 it could already be said "Shrove
Tuesday . . . was . . . the great football day in England for centuries" (*Oxford
English Dictionary*, 1971).

The birth of a distinctly American version of football is officially placed
in 1869, but most authorities agree it actually began with the game in 1874
between Harvard and McGill universities (Arens, 1975, p. 5; Gardner, 1975,
p. 98; Reisman & Denny, 1969). This game followed the rugby-style practice, which had originated in 1823, of picking up the ball in the hands and
running with it. Soon the American form developed a definite line of scrimmage and center snap, replacing the "scrum" and "heal out" of English rugby.
Slugging opponents was legal and flying wedges made the game especially
dangerous, so protective equipment was added for players. More referees
were added and, in the early years of the century, the forward pass was permitted. As a consequence of these developments, throughout the twentieth
century the American autumn has been the season of the pigskin and the
gridiron. Although professional football originated in the 1890s and became
popular with the barnstorming tours of Red Grange and the Chicago Bears
beginning in 1925, it was the college game that clearly dominated until mid-
century and beyond. The 1960s witnessed a rapid rise in popularity of
professional football, especially on television, a rise that climaxed in the
first Super Bowl in 1967 and the first truly exciting Super Bowl in 1969,
when Broadway Joe Namath and the Jets brought home the first victory for
the younger of the two competing conferences.

In the meantime, soccer emerged from local nineteenth-century competitions into an immensely popular mass sport. The reigning organization, the
Federation Internationale de Football Association (FIFA), was founded in
1904 and instituted the first World Cup in 1930, with 13 nations competing.
The World Cup final in 1950 between Brazil and Uruguay was attended by
205,000 spectators, and in the 1960s television joined radio as a major vehicle for following competitions among the 24 national teams that had survived to the playoffs. South American and Western European teams have

been most successful in the World Cup, with Italy and Brazil each winning 3 of the 13 championships prior to 1990. In those parts of the world, and many other regions, soccer becomes a mass religion and the World Cup its greatest holy day, as Janet Lever's *Soccer Madness* (1983) so well points out.

The two forms of game, football and soccer, have emerged with significantly different structures, each epitomized by its final championship.

Continuity and Discontinuity of Action

The "futbol" of the World Cup has continuous action, while the "football" of the Super Bowl has discontinuous action. In North American football, action is stopped after each 3- to 8-second-long play, and the teams regroup. In this, it is like baseball, with its discontinuous action, although the control of football by a clock adds a technological dominance absent from the more pastoral baseball. Among other sports, action in golf is completely discontinuous, and that of tennis, table tennis, or volleyball is often much like football, played in brief spurts of continuity interrupted by longer interludes of recuperation and preparation.

Soccer features long periods of continuous action, resembling in this regard hockey, basketball, or aerobic dance. The ball may go briefly out of bounds or a penalty be called or goal scored, but the play generally continues for many unbroken minutes at a time.

Differences in play-calling and strategy follow this difference between football and soccer. In the case of soccer, play-calling retains a degree of interpretive, instinctual spontaneity that responds to the varied ebb and flow of the game. Players must have a sense of overall position on the field and generate creative moves that will be anticipated and responded to by teammates, somewhat as a jazz band improvises. In contrast, in the case of football, especially on offense, play-calling has an external, formal quality that can even be performed by those not on the field and communicated to the huddled players. The play as externally called then exactly prescribes the moves of each player, allowing creativity only within relatively narrow bounds permitted by the elaborate charts of Xs and Os. The action of football then is not only more discontinuous than in soccer but also more formally prescribed, at least partially because of the relatively brief time available for achievement. This difference relates to additional differences described below, such as the differential role of technology in the two games and the different degrees of specialization and bureaucratization.

The discontinuity of football means that it is played, in the words of Novak

(1976), "as a set piece, like chess" (p. 82). Opponents alternate moves in chess; in football moves are made in sets of four. Chess and football seek strategic and sustained advance, mixed with containment and return-strike capability. This paramilitary quality resembles the classic troop, weapon, or ship movement of an earlier, simpler time, Napoleonic or medieval. The time for strategic reflection is many times longer than the time for action. Before each play, the teams again assume formal distributions. Football advances one discrete play at a time, "as inexorably as chess" (Novak, 1976, p. 82). Play-calling strategy in football adds a formalized rational, intellectual dimension to the game that is not present in the same manner in soccer.

The continuous action of soccer creates a problem for the great sugar daddy of American football, commercial television. Noncommercial television, such as the state-run systems of France, Spain, Eastern Europe, much of the Third World, the BBC, and so on, have no problem because they do not need commercial interruptions to pay their bills. But U.S. television, and the systems increasingly privatized in other countries during the Reagan-Thatcher era, do not want to provide the 20–30 minutes of uninterrupted programming required by soccer's continuous action. Michener (1976, p. 304) describes the effort in 1967 by CBS to adapt soccer to American television. Referees, either by fabricating a player injury or simply by stopping action, provided television time-outs. Michener observes: "The enforced time-out, so alien to soccer, where the continuity of play is everything, gave the worn-down team time to recuperate, and the balance of the game was destroyed" (p. 305). American network coverage of the World Cup final occasionally commits a sin unforgivable in true soccer countries: It simply leaves the continuing action and goes to a commercial while the game proceeds. In 1986, NBC resorted to a split-screen presentation of the World Cup finals, with commercial and play action sharing the screen. When it proposed the same arrangement for Olympic coverage in 1988, advertisers rebelled and rejected it. In contrast to soccer, football presents no such problem, providing abundant time for commercial announcements and plugs for upcoming programs.

The continuous flow of soccer play evokes the recurring cycles of nature, while the interrupted, staccato action of football reflects a machine culture, as we see even more clearly in considering the differences in technology in the two games.

The Technological Differences

To play proper football it is necessary to have an oddly shaped ball, elaborate padding and helmets, a large, well-marked playing field, two sets of large goal posts, a line-of-scrimmage marker and first-down chain, plus whatever other amenities one may choose. To play proper soccer, it is necessary only to have a round ball, a large open space, and two relatively simple goals. Soccer, in fact, is one of the technologically simplest and cheapest sports in history, and its minimal requirements for equipment have helped to make it a universal sport, played wherever kids care to run and kick. Football is far less simple.

Football uniforms have become marvels of modern technology. The game encourages padding and protecting virtually every part of the body, without eliminating mobility. The helmet has progressed from bare leather flaps to ergonomically sophisticated shatterproof globes lined with elaborate suspension systems fronted by bars and shields. Shoulder pads, hip pads, thigh pads, and knee pads are de rigueur. Quarterbacks have the extra option of pads for the rib cage—a flak jacket, as it is called. Interior linemen often have arms and hands so braced and taped that they operate more like baseball bats than human extremities. Shoes are tough, cleated affairs that are modified for field and weather conditions. All this protection was once quite weighty, but, thanks to space-age technology, it is now sturdy, perfectly contoured, and feather light. As might be imagined, outfitting 50 or more adolescents in such gear for a school team can wreak havoc on an academic budget.

In its sophisticated professional and college versions, football requires an additional array of modern science and technology. Telephones and headsets occupy the sidelines for play-calling from a bird's-eye view. Films and videotapes are mandatory for reviewing team and player performances, as well as for scouting upcoming opponents. Computers assist with everything from scheduling to play-calling, from player recruitment to evaluation. Gardner (1975) concludes: "In many ways, football is a dream sport for gadgeteers. Computers, telephones, mounds of player equipment—and films" (p. 110). Even the estimation of potential talent works on schemas of scientific measurement—height, weight, body fat, lateral mobility, time in the forty, bench press weight, reflexes, attitude, drug test results, and others. Elaborate training facilities, weight rooms, practice fields, nutritional programs, biomechanical consultation, medical advisers, travel arrangements, and similar resources make a successful football program, in its complexity and cost, comparable to launching astronauts into space.

Soccer at the world-class level, of course, also calls on elaborate recruitment, scouting, training, planning, travel, and facilities, but the absence of ponderous uniforms and play-calling technology symbolizes the technically simpler sphere in which competition takes place.

Violence and Paramilitarism

Football is a directly violent game: A play ends when the ballcarrier is tackled and brought to the ground. Soccer is only incidentally violent: Contact and collisions occur, but are not necessary to the conduct of the game and are more constrained than in football. Soccer is physically demanding and causes injuries. It has also occasioned many hundreds of deaths, normally among spectators rather than players. But football far surpasses soccer, as well as most other sports, except for boxing, in extent of physical violence.

In interpreting the village cockfight in Bali, Geertz (1973) remarks on the meaning of its violence:

> Balinese go to cockfights to find out what a man, usually composed, aloof, almost obsessively self-absorbed, a kind of moral autocosm, feels like when, attacked, tormented, challenged, insulted, and driven in result to the extremes of fury, he has totally triumphed or been brought totally low. (p. 450)

Usually calm and restrained Balinese express themselves through this gory competition among roosters. The cockfight is a reflection of many things Balinese, including their form of violence.

> Drawing on almost every level of Balinese experience, it brings together themes—animal savagery, male narcissism, opponent gambling, status rivalry, mass excitement, blood sacrifice—whose main connection is their involvement with rage and the fear of rage, and binding them into a set of rules which at once contains them and allows them play, builds a symbolic structure in which, over and over again, the reality of their inner affiliation can be intelligibly felt. (pp. 449-450)

The violence of football is a widely debated topic. The fact of its violence is not. Phillips (1969) suggests: "All sports serve as some kind of release but the rhythm of football is geared particularly to the violence and the peculiar combination of order and disorder of modern life." Stade (1966) echoes this:

> Football is a game, which means that it is built on communal needs, rather than

on private evasions, like mountain climbing. Among games it is a sport; it requires athletic ability, unlike checkers. And among sports, it is one whose mode is violence and whose violence is its special glory.

How can the "special glory" of football's violence be explained? Sociological historians in the tradition of Norbert Elias (see Dunning, 1986; Elias & Dunning, 1986) reason that the violence of sport is a rationalized accommodation to modern conditions. With the evolution to industrialized society, affective violence becomes unacceptable and punishable by the state. But the deep primitive sources of such violence do not disappear, and the intense competition of modern society arouses them. The violence then becomes channeled by society into instrumental, rationalized uses of violence, most noticeably in sport. In Elias's words, sport thus satisfies the quest for excitement in an unexciting society as part of the civilizing process. This theory is not quite identical to a "catharsis" theory of sport violence, in which the game violence releases pent-up violence in the spectator and contributes to a less violent society. Extensive research tends to reject the catharsis theory, as Guttmann (1978) and Pearton (1986) note. In addition, historical correlations find warring societies favored combat sports and peaceful societies favored less combative games. This correlation is consistent with American preference for more violent football against world preference for soccer. The American preference became more pronounced during America's post-World War II struggle to contain communism and maintain military superiority throughout the world.

Militarism, in fact, is a structural trait many have found embedded in American football (Arens, 1976; Gardner, 1975; Guttmann, 1978; Novak, 1976). Even comedian George Carlin toys with football's military style and terminology of field generals, bombs, blitzes, artillery, ground attacks, and more. Goldstein, in *Sports Violence* (1983), identifies the negatives in the correlation among war, violence, and sports. Others seem to revel in football's warlikeness. Phillips (1969) argues:

> It makes respectable the most primitive feelings about violence, patriotism, manhood. The similarity to war is unmistakeable: each game is a battle with its own game-plan, each season a campaign, the whole thing a series of wars. Football strategy is like military strategy. . . . There is even a general draft. And one is loyal to one's country — according to geography and the accident of birth.

Novak even uses the violence and militarism as another occasion for liberal-bashing. Many have noted the simultaneous rise to prominence of football and the Vietnam War in the 1960s. Gardner (1975), for example, refers to "the 1960s, a period when American life exhibited even more than its usual share of violence, and a period in which football swept irresistibly forward" (p. 115). Novak (1976) finds self-hatred in such comments: "The hostility of many to the war in Vietnam, to the military generally, and to capitalism led some to fix on football as the symbol of their own self-hatred as Americans" (p. 88). Novak sees football as "the immigrant myth and the corporate myth" because it captures the experiences of in-group solidarity and oppositional struggle. He finds:

> Football is a fitting insult to the illusions of an enlightened, liberal age, an age as cruel as, or crueler than, any in history, but eager to maintain a public image of reason, nonviolence, and democratic process. (pp. 84–85)

In fact, to Novak, "Football is the celebration of a not innocent and not rational and not liberal human condition" (p. 88). What draws fans? To Novak, "what they love in football is precisely what the soft part of the liberal world will not admit into consciousness: that human life, in Hegel's phrase, is a butcher's bench" (p. 89). With such an analysis of football, it was perhaps inevitable that Michael Novak would become the darling of the neoconservative Reagan-era think tanks: If a person is liberal or does not like football, or (preferably) both, he or she is rejecting reality, a reality that only tough-minded conservative militarists have the courage and honesty to face and even (in football) to celebrate! This imperialist and authoritarian mentality is precisely what liberals and others fear when football fanaticism carries over into national and international politics.

Compared to football's military set-piece structure, soccer has more the quality of guerrilla warfare. The line of scrimmage and combat is not defined, there are no gentlemanly safe times during off-hours between plays, everyone is potentially on offense and defense in each play, size and violent force are not necessarily an advantage, technologically advanced countries are not necessarily victorious, and foreign intervention through off-field play-calling and massive substitution does not work. Compared to football, soccer is a fluid game with its own internal dynamic, reminiscent of anti-imperialist resistance movements in Vietnam or Afghanistan in their stubborn refusal to "fight fair" using the agreed-upon rules of conventional warfare. On a soccer team, as in a people's army, everyone (except the goalie) needs to know all the skills of dribbling, passing, and shooting, unlike the conventional warfare of football, with its clear separation of skill players, blockers, pass rushers, defensive backs, and others.

In short, not only is America's number one sporting event, Super Bowl football, far more violent than the world's number one event, World Cup soccer, but the paramilitary structure of each is decisively different, the former being more conventional and the latter more guerrilla-like.

Body Parts and Ball Control

Although both sports have been called football, soccer's claim to that title is stronger. In soccer the foot plays a much larger part in the action. In fact, using the hands in controlling the ball is not allowed for the ten team members who cover the field. Only the lone goalie has permission to grab the ball with his hands and run or pass with his hands.

In North American football, by contrast, although the kicking game is crucial in the form of kickoffs, extra points, field goals, and punts, the principal form of ball control is with the hands. The ball is snapped with the hands by the center, the quarterback hands it off or passes it with his hands, and others receive it with their hands. In fact, deliberating kicking the ball, except in a formal kicking play, is prohibited. A loose ball cannot be kicked away from an opponent and then scooped up to gain possession. The hands and arms are the crucial limbs for ball control in Super Bowl football.

This distinction occasions a variety of speculations. Because hands and manipulation (a word derived from the Latin *manus*, and literally meaning "to control with the hands") are intrinsic to football but excluded from soccer, does this imply that North American culture is more "manipulative"? Does America celebrate a manipulative national game as it attempts to manipulate the fate of the rest of the world? Because use of legs, chest, and head for ball control makes soccer a more holistic game, does this make it more suitable for less cerebral aural and nonliterate cultures such as those of Latin America, countries that have won 7 of the first 13 World Cups? But, before too much is made of the hands/no hands distinction, what of hockey, which is structured like soccer but adds skates and a stick or club in the hands of players, or basketball, the most exacting of hand-manipulative sports? Not too much can be made of any one single distinction between football and soccer, but collectively the differentiating characteristics may add up to significant correlations with other cultural factors.

Measures of Success: Scoring, Winning, and Records

The essential measure of success in sports competition is winning. To win in either soccer or football, one must score more points than the opponent.

In football this is done in a relatively high-scoring game, with final results often reaching such scores as 35 to 10 or 24 to 14. Soccer scores are much lower—usually in the range of 5 to 2 or 3 to 1. No team has ever averaged as many as 5 goals per game in their six World Cup playoff games, and the British team allowed only 3 goals in six games in the 1966 World Cup playoffs. The infrequency of scoring in soccer is a negative to some, including Michener (1976), when compared to football, with its four different levels of scoring: touchdowns (6 points), field goals (3 points), safeties (2 points), and touchdown conversions or extra points (1 point). The mechanism for scoring in soccer is to "penetrate" the goal cage of the opponent after working the ball through his defenses. In football, scoring occurs when one "overwhelms" by carrying or passing the ball successfully beyond the goal line or kicks it between the uprights.

An additional measure of success in football occurs as one progressively occupies more and more of the field territory, as the line of scrimmage moves forward, with the intention of driving the opponent into its own value-less end zone. There is a more formalized struggle to possess or own property in football than in soccer, making football the more "capitalist" game, if you will. Territorially, football has the wider goal. Offensive success is more frequent in getting the ball across a goal line as wide as the field. Success is understandably less frequent in kicking or heading the ball into a small goal as in soccer. Because play is stopped and regrouped after every five seconds or so of action in football, the opportunity for quantitative records is increased, especially in regard to property gained. As Guttmann (1978) remarks, "Football is marked by a high level of quantification" (p. 129). The statistics of the game, often emblazoned across the bottom of the television screen or filling entire pages of newspapers, include yards gained rushing or passing, first downs gained, kicking yardage, third-down conversions, time of possession, runback yardage, and more, often recorded for individual players as well as for teams. These data are compiled in every sport into official "records" that supposedly mark the greatest achievements by players and teams: Pele is the only soccer player to have played with three World Cup-winning teams (Brazil in 1958, 1962, and 1970) and Chuck Noll is the only coach who has won four Super Bowls (Pittsburgh Steelers in 1975, 1976, 1979, and 1980).

Soccer's scoring has been loosened up in recent years with the addition of higher-scoring indoor soccer and the use of tie-breaking shoot-outs of one-to-one competition between individual kickers and the goalie. But football scoring remains more flexible and frequent, even though both sports measure ultimate success by quantitative accumulation of scores.

Specialization and Bureaucracy

Soccer is a well-defined game with many player positions – forward, half-back, fullback, sweeper, goalie – and complex playing styles and strategies. But North American football stands almost alone among sports in the modern world for the degree of specialization among playing positions and the formal complexity of strategy.

Football players are first divided into offense and defense, with very few players since mid-century playing both. Offensive players are committed to structure and order: If the system is followed successfully, we score. Defensive players, despite the complex systems and zones of defenses employed, are anarchists at heart: We must disrupt and destroy their carefully charted system. Offensive players are divided into those who cannot handle the ball, the five interior linemen for whom life in "the pit" is one long series of power drives and bench presses, and those who can handle the ball. These latter are separated into the central figure, the quarterback, one or more set backs who handle most of the ball-carrying, and a core of receivers that includes a bulky but mobile tight end, some flamboyant speedster wide receivers, perhaps an H-back, and some hybrids. The defensive alignment features a front three or four who are huge, strong, hungry, and relatively mobile. They are supported by linebackers, who may have to copy linemen by rushing and tackling powerfully or may have to copy defensive backs by dropping back quickly and blocking or intercepting passes. Behind them come cornerbacks and strong or free safeties, who must be as fast as sprinters but as tough and eager to hit as residents of Death Row. Each of these positions on offense and defense requires early specialization, so that a player will normally retain the same position from the first years of high school on.

The coaching staff for such a complex team is also divided into receivers coach, quarterback coach, runners coach, offensive line coach, defensive line coach, linebackers coach, defensive back coach, offensive coordinator, defensive coordinator, kickers coach, special teams coach, and head coach. Besides working with and evaluating different sets of players in practices, these coaches have different specialized functions during games. The offensive coordinator is generally stationed up in the press box on the side of the field to call plays by telephone down to the bench, from where they are relayed to the quarterback. The special teams coach is busy getting the correct people on and off the field for kicking plays. The defensive coordinator makes strategy and adjustments throughout the game. In fact, the head coach may appear to be the only unencumbered participant, as he is left a regal space around him and, with or without headphones, given the luxury of initiating communication but receiving information only on request.

There are many additional layers of organization behind players and coaches. There are trainers, weight trainers, equipment managers, scouts, front office staff, ticket sellers, ushers, vendors, and uncounted others who make the football game a success worth continuing. But many of these specializations are shared with world-class soccer competition as well in its use of complex organizations, huge stadiums, and vast publics.

The specialization of occupations on football teams makes the game analogous to modern industrial society, in which high degrees of occupational specialization set it off from more traditional agrarian or hunt and barter civilizations. At the same time specialization grows, of course, bureaucratization also occurs, in order to coordinate and integrate the various specialized roles into a complete and accessible range of social activities and functions. Football takes this extreme specialization, bureaucratizes it into a team, and celebrates the results in competition. Arens (1976) says of football: "The sport combines the qualities of group coordination through a complex division of labor and minute specialization more than any other that comes to mind" (p. 6).

Is America's penchant for football over soccer related to a more specialized and bureaucratic characteristic in American life and ritual?

Degrees of Masculinity

Both the World Cup and the Super Bowl are competitions exclusively among males. The players, coaches, organizations, and most of the fans are male. Females may appear as cheerleaders, halftime entertainers, or feature reporters, but the central action is a masculine preserve. In these spectacles the popular release of primitive emotions, as the sociologists describe the roots of soccer and football, seems to regress to an earlier time when public life was for males and domestic life for females. The two spectacles are reminders that, whatever progress women have made in other areas, the ritual celebrations of dominant values do not yet include women.

Football, however, adds an extra dimension of masculinity absent from soccer. It is not only that girls' soccer teams and leagues have greatly increased in popularity, with no parallel movement in football; this is probably more effect than cause of football masculinity. The more extreme indications of an exaggerated masculinity in football appear in the symbolism and style of the game itself. As an anthropologist examining the ritual of football, Arens (1976) has noted how "the equipment accents the male physique." He explains:

> The donning of the required items results in an enlarged head and shoulders and a narrowed waist, with the lower torso poured into skin-tight trousers accented only by a metal cod-piece. The result is not an expression, but an exaggeration of maleness. Dressed in this manner, the players engage in handholding, hugging, and bottom patting, which would be ludicrous and disapproved in any other context. . . . In comparison rugby players seem to manage quite well in the flimsiest of uniforms. (p. 9)

The uniform, it should be noted, only serves to increase the impression of size among players who are already extremely overdeveloped physically on scales of height, weight, muscular development, speed, and other traditionally male attributes. Arens concludes, "Football plays a part in representing this (gender) dichotomy in our society because it is a male preserve that manifests and symbolizes both the physical and cultural values of masculinity" (p. 8).

The exaggerated masculinity of football can also be seen in attributes already described above, for example, in its paramilitary violence and its technological emphasis, both traditionally male arenas. Football's symbolism seems to project this masculinity into the past and future as well. Guttmann (1978) comments that a hulking, mud-splattered football player "looks like a survivor from the Stone Age, which he is" (p. 125). The uniform evokes both the primitive and the futuristic. As Stade (1966) writes, "The football player in uniform strikes the eye in a succession of gestalt shifts: first a hooded phantom out of the paleolithic past of the species; then a premonition of a future of spacemen" (p. 175). By comparison, soccer uniforms expose the well-developed calf muscles to view but otherwise resemble everyday male attire and appear sleek and normal when set against the football uniform.

Broader Cultural Patterns

There are many areas in which Super Bowl football and World Cup soccer share similar structures and cultural implications. Debates on drug use among players, increasing commercialization and salary escalation, the use of "futbol" metaphors in political and popular speech, extremities of fan behavior, and other matters come up continuously on sports pages, talk shows, and television coverage of both soccer and football.

Betting seems to be equally widespread in the two sports. Geertz (1973, pp. 425–432) finds the curious structure of betting on Balinese cockfights to be a central expression of Balinese kinship patterns, status rivalries, and social interaction. However, betting on World Cup soccer and Super Bowl football is so widespread and varied as to prevent any in-depth observations. Michener (1968, pp. 427–429) explains in detail the traditional Spanish system of betting on soccer matches, a system complicated by the commonness of ties, which means that three rather than two outcomes must be evaluated for a match. The office football pool, common in America, is a counterpart to this. But the size and scale of Super Bowl and World Cup betting are immense, with billions of dollars changing hands over the fate of a bunch of footballers. What betting on these games most exemplifies, then, is simply the cultural significance of the two events and the willingness of millions of individuals to stake monetary value on their outcome.

Differences and Similarities in Football and Soccer

Structural differences between the soccer of the World Cup and the football of the Super Bowl can be summarized as shown in Table 8.1. There are contrasting qualities in the structures of the two sports of "football." Soccer features continuous action with simple equipment and low scores achieved by kicking into a goal; the player roles are moderately specialized and involve incidental violent contact in a moderately masculine guerrilla-style strategy for offense and defense. Football features discontinuous action with complex uniforms and equipment resulting in relatively high scores; the ball is manipulated primarily by hand in directly violent interaction that resembles conventional warfare with highly specialized roles and an exaggerated sense of masculinity. The striking differences in these two top media sports events raise but do not answer a series of interesting questions. Does the more violent, militaristic American ritual relate in some way to the American role since World War II as self-proclaimed policeman to the world, complete with massive arms buildups and sales and an expansionist foreign policy? Does the isolation of the United States from the world's number one sport, soccer, reflect a nationalistic self-preoccupation and a vacuum in internationalist sensibility? Is it mere coincidence that America's top event is aggressive, territorial, technological, bureaucratic, and "imperialistic," while Third World countries and others favor the less structured and rigid forms of soccer?

Table 8.1
Structural Differences Between Soccer and Football

	Soccer	*Football*
Action	continuous	discontinuous
Technology	low technology	high technology
Scoring	low	moderately high
Ball control	feet-no hands	hands-some feet
Interaction	indirectly violent	directly violent
Paramilitarism	guerrilla style	conventional warfare
Specialization	moderate	high
Masculinity	moderate	exaggerated

Media sports both reflect and structure society. The causality is not unidirectional but mutual between popular sport and the cultural order. Lipsky (1983) notes that spectator sports provide an "aesthetic utopian refuge" from the demands of industrial society, but they are also integrated within the mechanized and technical environment (p. 88). The para-ideology of consumption and technology are affirmed. As society becomes more organized and complex, the values of teamwork and cooperation, so prevalent in the sports ideology, are important influences. Media sports serve in a dialectic role as both a socializer and an escape. Sports, often proposed as "a world apart," are essential instruments in expressing modern society and integrating individuals and social groups into it.

Historically, Hargreaves (1986) describes the crucial role of sport in the transition from early industrial society to the present. The potential independence and unruliness of the working classes became gradually transformed by increasingly organized sports and crystallized in mass involvement in modern sports in the 1880s. In the late Victorian and Edwardian eras, the British amateur-gentleman model exerted ideological influence, and hegemony over the working class was gradually achieved. Participation in the popular culture of sports expanded after World War I and helped subsume classes within the nation. Hargreaves notes, "These developments were facilitated especially by the accelerating commercialization of sports, a process in which press and radio played key parts" (p. 207). Sports brought the working class and other subordinated groups more completely into the social order, in the words of Hargreaves, "by reconstituting them within a unified social formation under bourgeois hegemony." The state played an interventionist role in supporting sports in schools and other areas, contributing to what Althusser identifies as state ideology. But the ideological achievement is best described in a Gramscian manner: Coercion has been replaced by the engineering of consent. Sports are not necessarily a central determining factor in ideological hegemony, but they have become more important as their importance in national popular culture has increased.

The massively popular sports, with all their ideological and cultural orientations, provide important points of personal identity for the public. Today the World Cup teams provide central rallying points for national identity and pride, just as soccer and football teams feed local, regional, and national loyalties at all levels. The Super Bowl occasions a national celebration, a high holiday of American civil religion, that subsumes the competing loyalties of different fans into a single event. The event, however, stops at the national level. The World Cup moves the conflicts and the unifications to an international level, a step beyond the Super Bowl in geographical scale. But both events trigger partisan loyalties while at the same time providing an encompassing social ritual and celebration that integrates everyone still further into the dominant transnational consumer culture.

The structures of specific sports serve to express cultural patterns. They are cultural texts waiting to be read "over the shoulders of the natives," as Geertz says. They do not show us the whole of a culture but only a particular face of it at a particular time. But from the texts of World Cup soccer and Super Bowl football, we can access provocative glimpses of American and world culture as they compare and contrast. Whether these reassure or disturb us, they illustrate enticingly the potential of examining today's super media sports as a source of self-understanding and human development.

References

Arens, W. H. (1976). Professional football: An American symbol and ritual. In W. H. Arens & S. P. Montague (Eds.), *The American dimension: Cultural myths and social realities* (pp. 3–15). Port Washington, NY: Alfred.

Dunning, E. (1986). The sociology of sport in Europe and the United States: Critical observations from an "Elisian" perspective. In R. C. Rees & A. W. Miracle (Eds.), *Sport and social theory* (pp. 29–56). Champaign, IL: Human Kinetics.

Elias, N., & Dunning, E. (1986). *Quest for excitement: Sport and leisure in the civilizing process.* Oxford: Basil Blackwell.

Gardner, P. (1975). *Nice guys finish last: Sport and American life.* New York: Universe.

Geertz, C. (1973). Deep play: Notes on a Balinese cockfight. In C. Geertz, *The interpretation of cultures.* New York: Basic Books.

Goldstein, J. (Ed.). (1983). *Sports violence*. New York: Oxford University Press.

Guttmann, A. (1978). *From ritual to record: The nature of modern sports*. New York: Columbia University Press.

Hall, S. (1980). Cultural studies: Two paradigms. *Media, Culture and Society, 2*(1), 57–72.

Hargreaves, J. (1982). Sport, culture and ideology. In J. Hargreaves (Ed.), *Sport, culture and ideology* (pp. 30–61). London: Routledge & Kegan Paul.

Hargreaves, J. (1986). *Sport, power and culture: A social and historical analysis of popular sports in Britain*. Cambridge: Polity.

Hoberman, J. M. (1984). *Sport and political ideology*. Austin: University of Texas Press.

Hoch, P. (1972). *Rip off the big game: The exploitation of sports by the power elite*. Garden City, NY: Anchor.

Leitner, T. (1987). [Comments on sports talk show on KFMB-AM.]

Lever, J. (1983). *Soccer madness*. Chicago: University of Chicago Press.

Levi-Strauss, C. (1963). *Structural anthropology*. New York: Basic Books.

Lipsky, R. (1983). Toward a political theory of American sports symbolism. In J. C. Harris & R. J. Park (Eds.), *Play, games and sports in cultural contexts* (pp. 79–92). Champaign, IL: Human Kinetics.

Michener, J. A. (1968). *Iberia: Spanish travels and reflections*. Greenwich, CT: Fawcett.

Michener, J. A. (1976). *Sports in America*. New York: Random House.

Novak, M. (1976). *The joy of sports: End zones, bases, baskets, balls, and the consecration of the American spirit*. New York: Basic Books.

Pearton, R. (1986). Violence in sport and the special case of soccer hooliganism in the United Kingdom. In R. C. Rees & A. W. Miracle (Eds.), *Sport and social theory* (pp. 29–56). Champaign, IL: Human Kinetics.

Phillips, W. (1969, July). A season in the stands. *Commentary, 48,* 66.

Propp, V. (1968). *Morphology of the folktale*. Austin: University of Texas Press.

Real, M. R. (1989). *Super media: A cultural studies approach*. Newbury Park, CA: Sage.

Rader, B. (1984). *In its own image: How television has transformed sports*. New York: Free Press.

Russell, A. (Ed.). (1987). *1987 Guinness book of world records*. New York: Bantam.

Sports and mass media [Special issue]. (1987). *Gannett Center Journal, 1*(2).

Stade, G. (1966, Fall). Game theory. *Columbia Forum,* pp. 173–175.

Williams, R. (1961). *The long revolution*. New York: Columbia University Press.

9

The Rhetoric of Winning and Losing: The American Dream and America's Team

Leah R. Vande Berg
Nick Trujillo

> Sport . . . that is where I had my only lesson in ethics.
>
> —Albert Camus (quoted in Novak, 1976, p. 172)

Scholars have long argued that sport, as part of the social and economic structure of American society, reflects and reaffirms such American cultural values as achievement, youthfulness, experience, courage, individualism, cooperation, tradition, progress, and hard work (see Duncan, 1983; Edwards, 1973; Lipsky, 1975, 1981; Novak, 1976; Real, 1977; Trujillo & Ekdom, 1985). Sport sociologist Harry Edwards (1973) argues that

> sport is a social institution which has primary functions in disseminating and reinforcing the values regulating behavior and goal attainment and determining acceptable solutions to problems in the secular sphere of life. . . . This channeling affects not only perspectives on sport, but, it is commonly assumed, affects and aids in regulating perceptions of life in general. (p. 90).

By playing, watching, and reading about sport, then, children and adults alike are socialized into American culture. As Lipsky (1975) suggests, "Sport is the symbolic expression of the values of the larger political and social milieu" (p. 351).

Not surprisingly, the dominant value emphasized in American sport is success. As Nixon (1984) comments, "Sport seems to be an ideal vehicle for understanding the pursuit of the American Dream . . . because achievement and success are so openly and explicitly emphasized in sport" (p. 10). Clichés about success in sport abound. The late Vince Lombardi has been immortalized as much for his maxim, "Winning isn't everything, it's the only thing," as for his coaching records. Other celebrated aphorisms about winning include Yankee owner George Steinbrenner's "Winning is second only to breathing" (*Chicago Tribune*, June 6, 1984), former Redskins coach George Allen's "Every time you win, you're reborn; when you lose, you die a little" (Michener, 1976, p. 421), Dodger manager Leo Durocher's "Win any way you can" (Novak, 1976, p. 152), and even former President (and college football player) Gerald Ford's "It is not enough just to compete. Winning is very important. . . . In athletics and in most other worthwhile pursuits first place is the manifestation of the desire to excel, and how else can you achieve anything" (Nixon, 1984, p. 21).

Sports journalism is the primary vehicle through which these maxims about winning (and their attendant stories) are passed from generation to generation; indeed, most sportswriting consists of dramatic narratives that recount the successes and failures of sports events, participants, and organizations. These dramatic narratives, however, do not merely catalog catchy slogans; they also re-present and reconstruct sport reality, providing an interpretive frame that readers use to understand the significance of success or failure on and off the field. As Lipsky (1981) points out: "It is the reporter—in all his guises who gives the game on the field human significance. . . . The sports reporter mediates the world; he assigns responsibilities, puts the game into dramatic form, and searches for the controversies and hidden meanings" (p. 46). So, for example, a story that describes a losing team being "edged out" creates a different reality than does a story about that same losing team being "bowled over yet again."

When sportswriters characterize individuals and teams in sports as successful and unsuccessful, they define, interpret, and evaluate notions of success and failure not only for sports fans but for the larger American society as well. Accordingly, sports communication researchers need to examine how success and failure are described by sports journalists. Embedded in analyses of sportswriting about winning and losing are questions about how this discourse may constrain or liberate readers in the way these values are articulated.

In this chapter, we begin this examination. We first offer an overview of the concept of success, noting two distinct interpretations of success in American culture. We then examine sports discourse about the success and failure of the Dallas Cowboys football team, a team that has been one of the most successful teams in football history. Specifically, we analyze news stories about the Dallas Cowboys appearing in the *Dallas Times Herald* and the *Dallas Morning News* between August 1, 1960, and January 1, 1988, a period that covers their entire 28-year history as an NFL franchise, up to the 1988 season. We conclude with some observations on sportswriting as a liberating and constraining communicator of cultural values.

America's Dream: The Ideology of Success

At the center of the American value system is the value of success. Despite Cooley's (1889) early observation that success "is whatever men think it is" (p. 157), at least two distinct and opposing formulations of the value of success have been evident in American culture. In one vision, success is a terminal value, a product of individual or group performance; in the second vision, success is an instrumental value, a process enacted by individuals or groups.

Success as Product: Competitive (Occupational) Achievement

The dominant conception that success is a competitive product is variously described as the (Protestant) work ethic, the achievement principle, the Horatio Alger myth, and the American Dream myth (see Cawelti, 1965; Maccoby & Terzi, 1979; Nixon, 1984; Steele & Redding, 1962). From this view, success is the end result of competitive (occupational) achievement and it is measured by indexes of personal merit such as property and wealth or first-place ribbons and Super Bowl rings. This version of success, which Fisher (1973) identifies as part of the "materialistic" American Dream myth and Hart (1984) identifies as part of the American pragmatic tradition, is associated with such traits as initiative, aggressiveness, forcefulness, and competitiveness. In its *positive* enactments, this form of success is exemplified by individuals and organizations whose energy, inventiveness, and initiative result in benefits (including fame, status, property, wealth, and power) for themselves and for others. However, in its *negative* enactments, this form of success is exemplified by self-centered, ruthless individuals, groups, and organizations who single-mindedly pursue material ends with little concern for the well-being of others.

Success as Process: Self-Actualization

The second conception of success—which can be thought of as "human success"—is also an important part of the American value system. This alternative vision casts success as a process of self-actualization in which one develops and utilizes physical, intellectual, and creative talents to become the best that one can be. Success, from this view, does not involve "besting" others in competitive endeavors but rather bettering oneself (improving one's skills, record, performance, and so on). It is associated with such traits as self-discipline, altruism, cooperation, and sportsmanship, and focuses on moral obligations and self-actualization rather than on the acquisition of fame, fortune, or status.

Although the value of human success, which Fisher (1973) terms moralistic success and Hart (1984) calls utopianism, was not a dominant one in early Puritan America, Cawelti (1965) notes it has been a persistent value in secular American culture. Indeed, he observes that in the early eighteenth-century writings of Benjamin Franklin and Thomas Jefferson, "human success" was regarded as an important criterion for total success. Furthermore, Cawelti points out that by the mid-twentieth century many distinguished between *true success* (the socially responsible use of one's intellectual, physical, and material means) and *false success* (mere acquisition of property, money, attention, or influence).

Success and Sport: "Drop Kick Me Jesus Through the Goalposts of Life"

Both senses of success as product and as process are displayed in sport and in sportswriting. However, the dominant version has been success as the product of occupational achievement, as evinced in the emphasis on game victories and earned championships (and legendary aphorisms). This emphasis on sport success as product also reveals the view of sport as *business* and athletic performance as *work*. As Snyder and Spreitzer (1978) put it: "The primary goal, a winning tradition, is the 'product' being sold by a business organization . . . [and] an outstanding athlete is valuable 'property')" (pp. 139-140). The focus thus shifts from "how you play the game" to the "bottom line" of wins and losses.

Although sports success as product is the dominant vision, sports success as process also has been endorsed in many circles. Communication scholar Noreen Kruse (1981), for example, argues:

Ideally, "winning" means "being the best one can possibly be." . . . The consummate winning team could be one that plays with courage and grace, even though other teams consistently defeat it. In some cases, a winning team is one that betters its previous record, has a .500 season, or pulls itself out of the league cellar. (p. 273)

Popular writer James Michener (1976) agrees: "The best is when the individual assesses the capacities allocated to him by his genetic inheritance and determines to use them to the best of his ability. . . . He achieves for his own sense of accomplishment by performing up to his standard" (pp. 426–427). In fact, according to Michener, "Vince Lombardi, shortly before he died, looked back on his quote which had helped get such unbridled enthusiasm started [i.e. "Winning isn't everything, it's the only thing"]. He told Jerry Izenberg, 'I wish to hell I'd never said the damn thing. I meant the effort . . . I meant having a goal . . . I sure as hell didn't mean for people to crush human values and morality' " (p. 432).

At its best, then, sports success involves striving for self-actualization. Novak (1976) describes it as "the hunger for perfection" (p. 27) and adds that "for many Americans, as for the Greeks, athletics remain the field of experience closest attuned to human perfection, where *beauty* of formal action meets the form of the *good*, where the utmost *individual achievement* is linked to perfect *solidarity* with others, where the word for "good" means at once beautiful, true, and brotherly" (p. 86). As Snyder and Spreitzer (1978) conclude: "Sport is primarily an intrinsically rewarding form of behavior that involves satisfaction from performing within a structure of rules. . . . The core of intrinsic motivation is the person's need to feel competent and self-determining" (pp. 16–17).

In sum, both senses of success in sport have received attention in the academic and popular presses. Not surprisingly, both senses of success are also displayed in sportswriting about American professional football. We now examine how these conceptions of success are revealed in sportswriting about football in general and about the Dallas Cowboys in particular.

America's Team: Where Mamas Hope Their Babies Grow Up to Be (Dallas) Cowboys

Football, many sport scholars argue, is emblematic of modern life in America. According to Novak (1976), football is "the mythic form most illuminative of the way we live" (p. 76) because it is a *corporate* game:

> Football dramatizes, on a well-defined grid, the psychic contest in which those
> who work for corporations are engaged. . . . Football's ritualized, well-
> controlled violence is a more accurate picture of the actual experience of
> American life than the pastoral peace of baseball. Baseball may be longing;
> football is the daily reality. . . . Football obliges one to confront the daily reality
> of force, pressure and coercion. (pp. 76–78)

Moreover, Novak argues that a football team "is not only assembled in one
place, it also represents a place" (p. 143). Through reading and watching
their teams, through vicarious identification with these teams, "fans can
share the intensity of public recognition" (p. 122). And Novak adds that
professional teams, especially, represent a place because "the names of
sports teams [have] tried to crystallize the attitude of cities toward themselves, to express a certain attitude or spirit, to draw from the symbol a certain energy and force" (p. 168).

In few places is football more highly valued than in Texas. Henderson
(1987) describes the dominance of winning football in Texas:

> It's a misconception to say that Texas (like Oklahoma, the state Bud Wilkinson
> founded) is obsessed with football. It is obsessed with winning football. As long
> as they win, players and coaches are endowed with a stature normally reserved
> for war heroes and holy men . . . [and] the identities, egos, and libidos of whole
> communities go with them. . . . Coaches in kiddie leagues try to sneak "ringers"
> into their lineups. . . . And when they lose? . . . Local fans had expressed their
> ire by making anonymous death threats. (p. 90)

John Steinbeck (1962) likened football in Texas to war: "Texas is a military
nation. The armed forces of the United States are loaded with Texans. Even
the dearly loved spectator sports are run almost like military operations. . . .
Football games have the glory and despair of war, and when a Texas team
takes the field against a foreign state, it is an army with banners" (p. 202).
More recently, Michener (1984) has recalled that when he took up residence
in Texas, friends there warned him, "If you want to be happy in this state you
must support God, the Republican party and the Dallas Cowboys, not necessarily in that order" (p. ix).

According to Texas historians Chipman, Campbell, and Calvert (1969),
"The Cowboys are more than a professional team, they are a social institution" (p. 134). Through the success of the Dallas Cowboys, this nouveau
riche city with gold-plated buildings and urban cowboys redeemed itself

from the violent, negative stigma that came to be associated with Dallas through the assassination of President John F. Kennedy. As Michener (1984) summarizes:

> Outside Texas, people rarely understand the emotional value of the Cowboys to the state and especially to Dallas. In 1963 the city suffered a body blow when President John F. Kennedy was assassinated here by a drifter from out of state, and many accused Dallas of the crime. It was at this point that the Cowboys began to capture the imagination of first the city, then the state, and finally the nation. Football helped erase the stigma of the tragedy. (p. ix)

Not just football, however: *winning* football. The Cowboys, whose team name evokes the American western frontier myth of individualism, unending opportunity, and manifest destiny, are one of the most successful teams in football history. As the only NFL expansion franchise ever started without a player draft, the underdog Cowboys became the champion team everyone wanted to beat. They have had the longest winning streak and have won the most playoff victories in NFL history. In 1985 they celebrated their twentieth consecutive winning season. And their history of success contributed to their being christened "America's Team" in 1978 (Stowers, 1984, p. 153).

However, the Cowboys did not begin their franchise as winners. Indeed, in their first season of 1960, they did not win a single game. When they lost a game to the powerful Baltimore Colts in that first year, headlines read "Colt-Cowboy Game a Smiling Success" (DMN, 8/21/60, 2-1).[1] But by 1980, after five Super Bowl appearances (with two victories) in the 1970s, "records of 11-5 and 12-4 were not judged successful unless they led to the addition of another Super Bowl trophy" (Stowers, 1984, p. 50). In short, the success of the Dallas Cowboys was characterized by sportswriters in different ways during different phases of Cowboy history.

In this section, we examine five such phases of the success and failure of the Cowboys, paying special attention to the metaphors used by sportswriters to characterize the Cowboys. These phases are not exhaustive or mutually exclusive periods in the 28 seasons of Cowboys football; rather, they are representative of the different formulations of success and failure displayed by Dallas sportswriters throughout the history of this sports organization.

Phase I: "Beaten But Not Cowed"

The Dallas Cowboys joined the National Football League in 1960 as the only NFL expansion team ever started without a player draft, which meant that the first Cowboy team consisted of second- and third-string players left unprotected by other teams. Not surprisingly, with these rejects the Cowboys won no games their first season and suffered through five consecutive losing seasons from 1960 through 1964. However, despite the fact that these were losing teams, sportswriters did not characterize them as inherent failures.

"Newborns," "underdogs," and "sacrificial victims." During these early years, especially during their first season, the Cowboys were not expected to win—and they did not surprise anyone. Accordingly, the metaphors used by sportswriters to characterize the Cowboys revealed this low expectation of success on the field. The Cowboys were characterized as "newborns," (DMN, 8/25/60, 2-1), "underdogs" (DMN, 8/19/60, 2-1), and "fledglings" (DMN, 8/13/60, 2-2). While these metaphors revealed low expectations, they also invited readers to view their team's losses with compassion and even condolences. Readers were told that the Cowboys, after all, were "sacrificial victims" (DMN, 8/14/60, 2-2) whose quarterback barely "escaped with his life" (DMN, 8/14/60, S-2). Such descriptions indicate, as Novak (1976) observes, that "each time one enters a contest, one's unseen antagonist is death. Not one's visible opponent, who is only the occasion for the struggle. But the Negative Spirit, the Denier" (p. 48). Quite simply, in these early years, the Cowboys' mere survival was interpreted as success by sportswriters.

"The spirited Cowboys." During these early years, sportswriters focused not on the product-oriented failures on the scoreboard but on the process-oriented successes on the field. The Cowboys were not characterized as lowly underdogs but rather as "spirited" underdogs who played with nerve and enthusiasm (DMN, 8/26/60, 2-1). They were portrayed as "scrappy charges" (DMN, 9/12/60, 2-2) and a "stout band" (DMN, 8/21/60, 2-1). As one sportswriter put it: "Victory eluded the new-born club . . . but the spirited Cowboys held heavily favored rivals to surprisingly low point spreads" (DMN, 8/26/60, 1-1). Sportswriters affirmed this processual definition of success when they interpreted Cowboys' scoreboard failures: "Scores . . . prove that the Cowboys are competitive" (DMN, 8/15/60, 2-2). Indeed, Bill Reeves, sports editor of the *Dallas Morning News*, admonished the Cowboys in his columns, "If at first—, Try, Try Again" (8/18/60, 2-1).

"Playing better in every game." Finally, sportswriters affirmed the sense of success as process by recasting losing seasons as qualified successes. They emphasized the improvement of the team during the early seasons and reiterated that the Cowboys had not embarrassed themselves in their losses. One writer commented that "the youngsters play better in every game"

(DMN, 9/29/60, 2-3), while another described the Cowboys as "beaten but not cowed" (DMN, 8/15/60, 2-2) in their losses. The day after the Baltimore Colts defeated the Cowboys in a preseason game by a score of 14-10, headlines read: "Colt-Cowboy Game a Smiling Success" (DMN, 8/21/60, 2-1). And one month later, after the Cowboys were 1-5 in the preseason, one sportswriter noted, "Though they won only one game, a 14-3 verdict over the New York Giants, the Cowboys looked bad in only one affair" (DMN, 9/13/60, 2-1).

In summary, the sense of success as process dominated early sportswriting about the Dallas Cowboys, as revealed in the metaphors and themes used by writers who covered the exploits of this newborn team. Nonetheless, sportswriters intimated that success as competitive achievement—winning games and championships—was expected ultimately for this new team. As one writer summed it up: "Though they gave [coach] Landry, a man of astonishing understanding and patience, all they had to give right down to the last play, the Cowboys were never in the game. . . . But there's always next year" (12/13/60, DMN, 1-1). Thus, even though coaches and sports journalists alike were willing to give this new organization some time to develop a winning team, the product of success was indeed expected for the proverbial "next year."

Phase II: "The Days of Wine and Roses"

While the 1964 Cowboys played better and enjoyed some scoreboard success with a 5-8-1 record, the Cowboys had their first nonlosing season in 1965 with a 7-7 record. "That 7-7 record," as one reporter explained, "may look pretty drab to other teams who have thrilled to championships and big years, but to the Cowboys its a huge bouquet of roses" (DMN, 12/20/65, B-2). Then, in 1966, the Cowboys enjoyed their first winning season when they achieved a record of 10-3-1 and earned their first berth in the NFL championship game against the Green Bay Packers (which they lost 34-27—but more on that later). It was a period of mixed success on the field, on the scoreboard, and in the sports pages.

"Stars on the rise." As the Cowboys began to win more games, sportswriters characterized the team and forecasted the future with headlines such as "Pokes Build Contenders" (DTH, 9/4/66, C-2), "Winners on Their Way Up" (DTH, 10/29/66, A-2), and "Stars on the Rise" (DTH, 9/7/66, C-4). Sportswriters chronicled the progress of these rising stars—such as their "taming of the Giants" (DTH, 12/18/66, B-3)—and advised fans to "turn the dial to

success" (DTH, 10/2/66, B-3). "First the west, next the world," reporters predicted in reference to the NFC West and the Super Bowl titles (DTH, 9/21/66, C-1). However, these "stars on the rise" were not the "fledglings" and "sacrificial victims" from the first era; rather, they were a new cast of "understudies" who had "set the scene for the next continuing stage of the Cowboys program" (DTH, 9/4/66, C-2). By using these images, sportswriters endorsed both formulations of success: They defined the Cowboys as becoming more successful while noting that ultimate success—a football championship—had not yet been achieved.

A six-year "overnight" sensation. When the Cowboys enjoyed their first winning season in 1966, sportswriters, too, enjoyed their first season of winning rhetoric. For those theatrically inclined, this first winning season was a sensation: "Almost overnight—as in the case of the Broadway star who has spent six long years in one night stands—Tom Landry's team is the sensation of the poor-boy half of the NFL" (DTH, 9/7/66, C-4). For others, the first winning season represented just one point in a long uphill struggle: "This is the story of how to build a championship contender in the National Football League. The case history is right at hand—because its the Dallas Cowboys Football club. In this instance, you start from scratch and you have one basic theorem. . . . Rome wasn't built in a day, Cat, so stick with us while we persevere" (DTH, 9/4/66, C-2). Both explanations, however, celebrated the *process* of improvement leading to the resulting winning season.

"The end of an era." When the Cowboys did achieve their first nonlosing season and then their first winning season, one reporter proclaimed that "Dallas fans are witnessing the end of an era" (DTH, 12/4/66, B-3). This new era applied as much to sportswriting about the Cowboys as it did to Cowboy performances on the field. Increasingly during this phase of media reporting, Cowboy success was defined as outscoring the competitor rather than improving the team. One story bluntly explained: "The won-lost numbers in the NFL standings are impersonal and bare. They do not tell the whole story, but they tell the only story that matters, and they do not lie" (DTH, 9/27/66, C-3). Another column, one year later, reiterated the bottom-line message: "There's only one way to measure the success or failure of a game plan. That's the scoreboard" (DTH, 12/25/67, C-2). Indeed, from the sportswriters' newfound product-oriented perspective on success, the Cowboys' 1966 season was "The Year of Arrival" (DTH, 9/11/66, B-3). However, the arrival was marred by the Cowboys' playoff loss to Green Bay, a loss that signaled "the bitter end of a nearly successful season" (DMN, 1/11/66, B-2).

Phase III: "Always a Bridesmaid, Never a Bride"

When the Cowboys experienced their first winning season in 1966, they began the first of what would be 20 consecutive winning seasons of NFL football, a "dynasty" that will be described in the next section. However, from 1965 to 1970, the Cowboys lost in postseason action and did not win that first championship trophy.

"The business of playing." With the advent of the Cowboys' first winning season, sportswriting about success shifted decisively to the narrow vision of outscoring opponents and winning championship games. As one reporter put it: "After playing Patty Cake . . . the Cowboys must now get down to the business of playing" (DTH, 10/6/66, C-2). This was a "new era," after all, one in which sportswriters expected – even demanded – that the Cowboys win games on a regular basis. Thus when the Cowboys ended the 1967 season with a 9–5 winning record and a second NFL championship berth, sports columnists still interpreted the season as a qualified failure: "Their season, compared to last year [10–3–1] and the expectations for this year, has been a disappointment, if you dast be frank about it"; the columnist went on to buttress his critique with Coach Landry's own evaluation: "I don't think we had a very good year for us. We were good enough to win the [Eastern] division, but you can't call it a good year" (DTH, 12/18/67, E-1).

During this phase, game victories sometimes were evaluated as failing efforts. In December 1966, for example, when the Cowboys beat the St. Louis Cardinals, their chief rival for the Eastern Conference title that year, one sportswriter concurred with Cowboy players' disappointment in the 31–17 victory: "It looked great in the won-lost column, but not many players thought they had turned in an adequate performance" (DTH, 12/6/66, C-1). Another writer agreed with Cowboy Mike Gaechter, who "the same as so many others on this Cowboy team who wax impatient short of perfection, doesn't think his progress is all that much remarkable . . . [because] 'You're supposed to get better every year')" (DTH, 10/6/66, C-2).

"A new plateau of futility." Given their product-oriented view of success, sportswriters expressed disappointment in the Cowboys' postseason performances during the 1965–1970 period. In their first postseason game after their .500 season in 1965, the Cowboys were crushed in a Playoff Bowl by the Baltimore Colts, 35–3. In 1966 and 1967, the Cowboys lost consecutive NFL championship games to the Green Bay Packers, 34–27 and 21–17, respectively. The latter loss to the Packers occurred in the legendary "Ice Bowl," the coldest NFL championship game to that point (22 degrees below zero). In postseason action after the 1968 and 1969 seasons, the Cowboys

experienced defeats in Eastern Championship games at the hands of the Cleveland Browns, 31–20 and 38–14, respectively. The 1970 season culminated in the Cowboys' first Super Bowl appearance against the Baltimore Colts, which they lost 16–13. As one sportswriter suggested after the loss to the Colts: "The Dallas Cowboys reached a new plateau in futility Sunday – they blew the biggest title of all – the Super Bowl" (DTH, 1/18/71, A-1). In short, "it began to appear," as Stowers (1984) would write later, that "Dallas was destined to be the most talent-blessed bridesmaid in NFL history" (p. 26).

The shift in sportswriting during this phase from success as process to success as product becomes starkly apparent when one contrasts descriptions of the 3-point loss to Baltimore in the Super Bowl following the 1970 season with the 4-point loss to Baltimore in a 1960 preseason game. As noted earlier, the day after the 1960 Cowboys lost 10–14 to Baltimore, headlines read "Colt-Cowboy Game a Smiling Success"; the day after the 3-point loss to Baltimore in the 1971 Super Bowl, sportswriters said the Cowboys had reached "a new plateau in futility."

Phase IV: "Cowboys Look to Dynasty"

The Cowboys ended the 1971 season with an 11–3 record and, after two playoff victories, another trip to the Super Bowl, this time to face the Miami Dolphins. The Cowboys beat the Dolphins 24–3, and Dallas sportswriters had a field day. One exclaimed that the "perennial bridesmaid of professional football finally waltzed down the aisle to triumph" (DTH, 1/17/72, A-1). Another hyperbolized that "for thousands of cheering Dallasites here it was a far bigger victory than the original battle in 1814 when Andy Jackson whipped upon the British in this old city" (DTH, 1/17/72, A-1). Still another put it this way: "The ghosts are now buried and quiet; the closets have been swept clean of skeletons. The Cowboy complexion is now clear of pimples" (DTH, 1/17/72, B-1).

In the 10 years following that 1972 Super Bowl victory, the Cowboys appeared in eight NFC championship games and in four more Super Bowls, winning one (against Denver, 27–10, after the 1977 season). As noted earlier, they also enjoyed 20 consecutive winning seasons from 1966 to 1985. They indeed had developed a winning "dynasty."

"Machines," "heroes," and "Hail Marys." Sportswriters used images to characterize Cowboy success during their 1970 dynasty that were very different from the "fragile newborns," "fledglings," and "victims" metaphors

of the early years. Writers employed *machine* metaphors to depict the systematic quality of Cowboy victories in this phase. One reporter described the Super Bowl victory over the Dolphins in this way: "Dallas operated Sunday with a most emotionless efficiency. . . . It was clinical the way the Cowboys went about it" (DTH, 1/17/72, A-1). Indeed, according to another reporter, they were "so clinical, you'd expected to see them scrub up and don rubber gloves between plays" (DTH, 1/18/72, C-1). As one columnist summarized the consecutive winning seasons some 11 years later: "The preferred misconception is that the Cowboys are shipped to Dallas at night in boxes marked 'This End Up.' They aren't drafted, they're assembled. They don't bleed or bruise. When damaged they just spill oil. . . . Landry doesn't give them plays. He winds them up" (DTH, 1/22/83, A-1).

However, sportswriters juxtaposed these mechanistic visions of Cowboy success with images of Cowboy *heroes* and *miracles*. Quarterback Roger Staubach, the 1963 Heisman Trophy winner from the U.S. Naval Academy, is still the most celebrated Cowboy hero in history. Throughout the 1970s, Staubach, who sportswriters told us did not smoke, drink, or swear, led his team to "miraculous" come-from-behind victories with seconds remaining on the game clock. His now legendary "Hail Mary" pass, still featured prominently in Cowboy highlight films, is emblematic. On a fourth-and-16 situation with 44 seconds remaining on the clock, Staubach completed an underthrown "prayer" to Drew Pearson that clinched a 17–14 victory over the Minnesota Vikings in the 1975 divisional playoff and paved the way for another Super Bowl appearance.

Machines and Hail Marys? It was a strange juxtaposition indeed, one that linked the logic of game plans with magic and spiritual intercession (see Trujillo & Ekdom, 1985). Yet sportswriters used this juxtaposition to cast the Cowboys as a special and unique franchise in the history of professional football.

"The Cowboy mystique: knights in blue-starred helmets." Their amazing record of victories and championships—eight NFC championship games and five Super Bowls in 10 years—was the foundation for what sportswriters called "the Cowboy mystique." During the 1970s, Cowboy merchandise outsold every other team's merchandise by an incredible margin. So, too, the *Dallas Cowboys Weekly*, the weekly newspaper produced and distributed by the Cowboys, became second only to the *Sporting News* in weekly sports newspaper circulation. Red Auerbach, president of the Boston Celtics basketball team, proclaimed, "There are only three teams in sports that have achieved true national status—the old [New York] Yankees, the Dallas Cow-

boys, and us" (DTH, 12/13/87, A-1). As one sportswriter summed up the Cowboy mystique:

> They [the Cowboys] were the beginning of a new establishment. While the once-awesome Packers faded into mediocrity, the Cowboys gradually took their place as the class of the NFL. After they broke into the ranks of the winners, it began to seem they would stay there forever. Children were born and grew to adulthood without seeing the Cowboys have a bad year. They played twenty consecutive winning seasons—a record unmatched by any other team. . . . Players on other NFL teams swore oaths to wreak destruction upon the arrogant shining knights in blue-starred helmets. (DTH, 12/13/87, A-1)

Phase V: "Didn't This Used to Be America's Team?"

By the 1980s, the Cowboys had reached a point where sportswriters expected them to appear in the Super Bowl every year. "Records of 11–5 and 12–4," writes Stowers (1984), "were not judged successful unless they led to the addition of another Super Bowl Trophy" (p. 50). Thus the Cowboys' 1984 and 1985 winning seasons were defined and evaluated as inconsistent efforts and qualified failures. As one WFAA-TV reporter critically summed up the Cowboys' 1985 season: "With this playoff loss to the Rams, the Cowboys finish the season with a record of 10 [wins] and 7 [losses]. Now its up to *you* to determine if *that* constitutes success" (Fernandez, Channel 8, Dallas, January 4, 1986). Then in 1986, the Cowboys suffered their first losing (7–9) season since 1964. One reporter remarked on "how far the mighty are fallen" (DMN, 9/3/87, B-1), while another asked tellingly, "Didn't this used to be America's team?" (DTH, 8/30/87, D-2).

Legends die hard: "Cowboys rejoin the mortals." One columnist put the situation in the mid-1980s this way: "Oh, Your Heroes enjoyed the good life for longer than most; now they have rejoined the mortals" (DMN, 10/28/87, B-1). "Legends die hard," another sportswriter agreed, and "the problem . . . is that the Cowboys are competing with their own record" (DMN, 9/13/87, A-1). Sportswriters admitted: "We have, of course, been spoiled. My youngest son, now a college junior, last year experienced the first Cowboy losing season in his lifetime. Things like that happen to other teams, never Dallas. Never, of course, is here." The reporter went on to explain how Cowboy success and failure had changed over the years: "I can remember the early 1960s when the Cowboys were losers. That was different then. They were building and were so often exciting when they lost. Losing never seems

exciting now. Ah, perspective. You can be a big loser and win but not a big
winner and lose" (DMN, 9/17/87, A-33).

"Winner's disease" and "the late great Cowboys." When the Cowboys had
their first losing season in 21 years, sportswriters reminded fans about the
team's bottom-line performance: "America's Team was a loser in 1986.
Those are cold, hard facts" (DTH, 8/30/87, D-3). One year later, another
sportswriter described a middle-season loss to Atlanta, a loss that guaranteed the Cowboys' second losing season in 22 years, as "a day of catastrophic
significance — a sort of gridiron Waterloo or Gettysburg or even — some are
saying — Hiroshima. . . . for two years in a row, the Cowboys will rest among
the losers, an ignominy they haven't suffered within the lives of their fans"
(DTH, 12/13/87, A-1).

Sportswriters also used medical metaphors to describe Cowboy losing
seasons. Their diagnosis: The Cowboy's "winner's disease" from their first
winning season (DTH, 9/16/66, C-1) was now "out of control" (DMN,
9/9/87, B-1). The Cowboys were now "comatose"; one columnist quipped,
"There's a national rush toward their bedside. Their breathing is labored.
Their pulse rate is 5–8" (DTH, 12/15/87, C-1). Indeed, the same reporter
went so far as to eulogize "the late, great Cowboys," adding, "The demise of
the Cowboys as an NFL power — nay, an institution — is getting state funeral
treatment. Dignitaries from afar arrive daily. CBS and *Sports Illustrated*
were here last week to check receding vital signs."

"Cowboys facing test of character." Typical of sports reporters' assessments of the Cowboys' lack of achievement in the 1980s were these comments about a 1987 Dallas Cowboys-Houston Oilers contest: "They used to
play this game to see who had the better pro football team in Texas. On
Saturday night, the Cowboys and the Oilers appeared to be playing to see
who had the worst" (DMN, 9/6/87, B-22). The Cowboys were losing games
and missing playoffs and sportswriters were not happy.

Some reporters explained that the downfall of the Cowboys was due to the
self-interest that had replaced team commitment: "There has been rank
individualism in blossom for some time" (DMN, 11/11/87, B-1). In an article
headlined "Ex-Cowboys Cringe at Sight of Today's Team," one writer noted
that while "there are many reasons for the Cowboy's slide . . . former players
such as Cole and Charlie Waters say the problem is one of attitude: This
team does lack heart. . . . They do lack the dedication. . . . What is dis-
couraging is they aren't fighting to win" (DTH, 12/13/87, D-1). Another
columnist explained: "On every successful NFL club there were a few
players who formed the heart and soul, the competitive core. They
demanded the best in themselves. They commanded the best in their team-

mates." The problem with the Cowboys, the reporter concluded, was that the Cowboys no longer had such leaders (DMN, 11/10/87, B-1).

Ironically, with the losing seasons of the 1980s, sportswriters again have defined Cowboy success as process rather than as product. One headline after the Cowboys' 20–24 loss to the Redskins at the end of the 1987 season underscored this shift in terminological and ideological screens: "Cowboys' Noble Fighting Spirit Makes Up for Defeat." The reporter redefined the loss as a moral victory:

> Battered, the Cowboys still weren't knocked out. Oh, they lost the decision on points to the Redskins, 24–20. Yet defeat this time carried a different dimension. There was a noble quality to it. The Cowboys were carried off on their shield for a change. They played uphill with courage. . . . It sounds peculiar to credit a team for losing, but I think the Cowboys deserve it. (DTH, 12/14/87, C-6)

Other reporters agreed: "Even having endured their fourth consecutive loss, one that assured them of consecutive losing seasons for the first time since 1963–64, Sunday's game somehow represented to the Cowboys hope for a brighter tomorrow" (DMN, 12/14/87, B-1). And the caption under a front-page picture read "Cowboys Quarterback Danny White scrambles in Sunday's 24–20 loss to the Washington Redskins. But the game, with White involved in a brawl, may have been a moral victory for Dallas" (DTH, 12/14/87, A-1). Sportswriting about the Cowboys had indeed come full circle: from building, to contending, to winning, to losing, and back to building again.

Concluding Remarks: Evaluating Sports Discourse

Sports discourse can constrain and liberate readers by enriching or restricting interpretations of sports reality for the readers. Our analysis of discourse about the Dallas Cowboys suggests several ways in which sportswriters do both.

Metaphors to Write About Football By

First, sportswriters liberate and constrain readers by employing different *metaphors* for sporting events and participants. The use of metaphor is a pervasive strategy for orienting ourselves to various phenomena. Indeed, according to Lakoff and Johnson (1980), "Our ordinary conceptual system, in terms of which we both think and act, is fundamentally metaphorical in nature" (p. 3). Metaphors thus play a basic role in creating, maintaining, and shaping sport realities.

Although sports reporters must provide descriptive accounts of games with literal (and, one hopes, accurate) game summaries, reporters also have taken a license to "poeticize reality" (see Dowling, 1977) by using evocative metaphors of sport reality. As noted throughout this essay, sportswriters use the language of *war* ("attack," "defend," "bomb"), *disease* ("winner's disease," "comatose," "pulse 5–8"), *work and machines* ("foreman of the Cowboys," "one of the finest football machines"), *theater* (Giants "act" and Cowboys "cast," "the script"), and *religion* ("sacrificial victims," "last chance at redemption," "pro football congregations") to characterize football as a social phenomenon. These metaphors invite readers to adopt particular visions of sport reality.

When these metaphors are read as innovative interpretations of games or teams that enhance our understanding or experience of American sport, then sportswriting can be said to liberate readers. However, when repeatedly used metaphors are interpreted by readers as narrow and cliché-ridden, then sportswriting becomes constraining as well. For example, we believe that the military metaphor (football as war) has been overused by Dallas and national sportswriters alike. The military metaphor, as Weick (1979) has cautioned, "forces people to entertain a very limited set of solutions to solve problems" and will lead people "repeatedly to overlook a different kind of organization, one that values improvisation rather than forecasting, dwells on opportunities rather than constraints, invents solutions rather than borrows them, devises new actions rather than defends past actions, values argument more highly than serenity, and encourages doubt and contradiction rather than belief" (p. 50). In short, when sportswriters overuse military and other metaphors, they do not invite readers to broaden their interpretations and understandings of sport.

Using History and Tradition: Reaching Out Past Jock Jargon

Second, sportswriters liberate or constrain readers by using *history* in their stories about sporting events and participants. Each game, for example, is treated as episodic drama by sportswriters who narrate every play and performance in ceremonial detail. Each season, then, becomes a serial drama that is cast as a part of the ongoing and evolving tradition of the franchise.

Our analysis suggests that this evolving tradition has consisted of at least five distinct phases of media coverage about the Cowboys, phases characterized by different (even competing) notions of American success. In the first phase, the process-oriented "human" value of success dominated the writing. Losses were defined as moral victories and wins as progress toward self-actualization, not scoreboard dominance. By the end of the second phase, however, "winning is the only thing" had begun to displace "winning is playing with courage and grace" as the dominant formulation of success. In the third and fourth phases, sportswriting embraced a sense that the Cowboys' manifest destiny was to dominate others forever. Indeed, sportswriting during the fourth phase came to define success not only as outscoring the opposing teams but as recapturing the Super Bowl trophy. However, in the fifth phase, as the Cowboys' scoreboard dominance faded, sportswriters again returned to the process-oriented definition of success. Neither of these competing visions of success faded entirely from the sports pages during these periods; rather, in different periods, one vision dominated while the other receded into the inky shadows.

The use of history in sportswriting liberates readers when sportswriters provide a broader context for understanding players and performances. Not surprisingly, when sportswriting emphasizes the broader processes of playing more than the narrow product of winning, it enriches the meaning of sports events. Unfortunately, when sportswriters focus narrowly on one point in a club's history and use that point as an unwavering standard against which all other seasons are compared, they constrain the readers' experience. Such was the case in sportswriting about the merely mortal 1980s Cowboys, who were critiqued regularly in comparison to the machinelike Cowboys of the 1970s. In a sense, then, the Cowboys "dynasty" seduced and constrained sportswriters themselves.

The Prospects and Problems of Success as Winning

Not surprisingly, sportswriters prefer a winning home team. When the home team wins, the sportswriter becomes the leader of the rhetorical celebration, fulfilling the epideictic function of journalism. However, when sportswriters focus overwhelmingly on winning, they initially liberate but ultimately constrain readers.

The focus on winning initially liberates readers by reminding fans and players that professional sports, like any business in American capitalistic society, is judged ultimately by a measurable bottom line, and that the American Dream can be achieved only by "putting up the numbers." Unfortunately, scholars and critics often dismiss a quite legitimate concern with achievement in sport when they categorically denounce the destructive and illegitimate overconcern with winning at all costs. After all, the ideal American Dream is winning by being one's best, not winning at all costs and not losing by being one's best. Sportswriters thus teach readers that productive performances do matter in America and then celebrate with readers when the home team enacts such productivity.

However, overemphasis on winning does restrict interpretation of the success or failure of a franchise. The rules of professional football have been adapted to ensure that sportswriters will cover wins and losses rather than ties—there are now overtime periods in the NFL to reduce the likelihood of ties. Nonetheless, the emphasis in sportswriting on wins and losses often corresponds to a lack of emphasis on the process of playing and often leads to descriptions *that* (and *how*) a team won or lost rather than to explanations of *why* that team won or lost.

In short, there is a dearth of reflection and self-reflexivity in the daily sports pages. Cheerleading about victories or whining about losses may provide emotional relief, but such journalism does little to educate readers about sport in society. Sportswriters, however, should be both reporters and analysts. As Fred Friendly (1967), former president of CBS, reminds news analysts generally, "Bear in mind that in a democracy it is important that people not only should know but should understand, and it is the analyst's function to help the listener understand" (p. 200). And it is in the analysis as well as in the display of these values that the heuristic value of sport and sportswriting for American society lies.

Note

1. Hereafter, references to newspaper articles will give the initials for the newspaper first (DMN for the *Dallas Morning News* and DTH for the *Dallas Times Herald*), followed by the article's publication date (e.g., 8/21/60 for August 21, 1960), and then the section and page, separated by a hyphen, on which the article begins (e.g., 2–1 indicates Section 2, page 1; A-3 indicates section A, page 3).

References

Carey, J. W. (1975). A cultural approach to communication. *Communication, 2*, 1–22.

Cawelti, J. G. (1965). *Apostles of the self-made man: Changing concepts of success in America.* Chicago: University of Chicago Press.

Chipman, D., Campbell, R., & Calvert, R. (1969). *The Dallas Cowboys and the NFL.* Norman: University of Oklahoma Press.

Cooley, C. H. (1889). Personal competition: Its place in the social order and effect upon individuals: With some considerations on success. *Economic Studies, 4*, 78–172.

Dowling, T. (1977, September-October). "Don't touch that dream." *Skeptic, 22.*

Duncan, H. D. (1968). *Symbols in society.* New York: Oxford University Press.

Duncan, M. C. (1983). The symbolic dimensions of spectator sport. *Quest, 35*, 29–36.

Edwards, H. (1973). *Sociology of sport.* Homewood, IL: Dorsey.

Fisher, W. R. (1973). Reaffirmation and subversion of the American Dream. *Quarterly Journal of Speech, 59*, 160–167.

Friendly, F. W. (1967) *Due to circumstances beyond our control . . . .* New York: Vintage.

Gronbeck, B. E. (1980). Dramaturgical theory and criticism: The state of the art (or science?). *Western Journal of Speech Communication, 44*, 315–330.

Guttmann, A. (1978). *From ritual to record: The nature of modern sports.* New York: Columbia University Press.

Hart, R. P. (1984). The function of human communication in the maintenance of public values. In C. C. Arnold & J. W. Bowers (Eds.), *Handbook of rhetorical and communication theory* (pp. 749–791). Boston: Allyn & Bacon.

Henderson, J. (1987). College football and the media in Texas. *Gannett Center Journal, 1*, 85–98.

Hollingshead, A. B. (1949). *Elmstown's youth.* New York: John Wiley.

Kruse, N. (1981). Apologia in team sport. *Quarterly Journal of Speech, 67*, 270–283.

Lakoff, G., & Johnson, M. (1980). *Metaphors we live by.* Chicago: University of Chicago Press.

Lipsky, R. (1975). *Sports world: An American dreamland.* New York: Quadrangle.

Lipsky, R. (1981). *How we play the game: Why sports dominate American life.* Boston: Beacon.

Maccoby, M., & Terzi, K. A. (1979). What happened to the work ethic? In W. M. Hoffman & T. J. Wyly (Eds.), *The work ethic in business: Proceedings of the third national conference on business ethics* (pp. 19–64). Cambridge, MA: Oelgeschlager, Gunn & Hain.

Michener, J. A. (1976). *Sports in America.* New York: Random House.

Michener, J. A. (1984). Foreword. In C. Stowers, *Dallas Cowboys: The first twenty-five years* (pp. vii–ix). Dallas: Taylor.

Morgan, W. J., & Meier, K. V. (Eds.). (1988). *Philosophic inquiry in sport.* Champaign, IL: Human Kinetics.

Nixon, H. L., II. (1984). *Sport and the American dream.* New York: Leisure.

Novak, M. (1976). *The joy of sports: End zones, bases, baskets, balls, and the consecration of the American spirit.* New York: Basic Books.

Orlick, T., & Botterill, C. (1975). *Every kid can win.* Chicago: Nelson-Hall.

Real, M. (1977). *Mass-mediated culture.* Englewood Cliffs: NJ: Prentice-Hall.

Rigauer, B. (1981). *Sport and work* (A. Guttmann, Trans.). New York: Columbia University Press.

Snyder, E. E., & Spreitzer, E. (1978). *Social aspects of sport*. Englewood Cliffs, NJ: Prentice-Hall.

Steele, E. D., & Redding, W. C. (1962). The American values system: Premises for persuasion. *Western Journal of Speech Communication, 26*, 83–91.

Steinbeck, J. (1962). *Travels with Charly: In search of America*. New York: Viking.

Stowers, C. (1984). *Dallas Cowboys: The first twenty-five years*. Dallas: Taylor.

Trujillo, N., & Ekdom, L. R. (1985). Sportswriting and American cultural values: The 1984 Chicago Cubs. *Critical Studies in Mass Communication, 2*, 262–281.

Weick, K. E. (1979). *The social psychology of organizing* (2nd ed.). Reading, MA: Addison-Wesley.

Whittingham, R. (1981). *The Dallas Cowboys: An illustrated history*. New York: Harper & Row.

10

Drugs and (Len) Bias on the Sports Page

Lewis Donohew
David Helm
John Haas

Although athletes have been connected with drugs since at least the seventh century B.C., when use of drugs derived from the coca leaf led to suspension of the Olympiads for 17 years, until very recently drug use in sports was largely hidden from public view. Even after development of the modern press, drug use by athletes ordinarily received little journalistic coverage (Koppett, 1981).

A number of reasons have been offered to account for this limited attention. Koppett has suggested that drug use by athletes to enhance performance or reduce pain has long been an accepted practice, and thus may not have been considered newsworthy. In fact, use of drugs specifically for these purposes has been traced back at least to the third century B.C. (Mangi & Jokl, 1981; Williams, 1974). Goldman (1984) argues that a "win at any cost" attitude pervades sports and has led to acceptance of widespread drug use to gain a competitive edge. Mangi and Jokl point out that sport is revered far beyond its true value and thus there is a reluctance to tarnish its public image.

In the last decade, the increased use of drugs by societies in general and recent deaths, arrests, and suspensions of popular athletes have brought about increased journalistic exposure of the issue of drug use in sports (Koppett, 1981). The perceived reluctance of the mass media to report on actions reflecting poorly on sports may remain, however, and in fact may have grown as a result of increased strains from what might be called the sports/media complex.

According to Wenner (1987), Real's (1975) observation that professional football "is not *like* American business; it *is* American business" can be extended to all mediated sport in America. The complex and large marketplace for mediated sports also relies heavily on the work of the sports journalists, making them servants to many, Wenner adds, responding to a variety of countervailing pressures that sometimes make them rooters rather than reporters.

How the sports press responds or does not respond to off-the-field actions discrepant with social norms such as drug use among athletes is one of the more important dimensions in defining the ideology of mediated sports, according to Wenner (1987), who notes:

> Professional ethics call on the sports journalist to report the news accurately and fairly to the audience. At the same time, the sports journalist often times reports for a media organization that may make stylistic or substantive demands on that reporting. And finally, the sports journalist must remain on good terms with sports organizations, their teams, players, coaches and other personnel. For without access to these sources, there is no access to the "inside story" that is so valued by the mediated sports audience. (p. 43)

This study examines a major dimension of journalistic coverage devoted to drug use in sports – that by print journalists, who are not on the payroll of the sports organizations. The study pays particular attention to coverage in the year before and the year and a half following the death of Len Bias. Our approach, although partly descriptive and quantitative, contrasts with much of the research on sport and communication (e.g., Melnick, 1979; Rose, 1982) in that we do not seek to present value-free data, but rather to place our observations about sports into a larger context and to offer judgments about them.

Recent History of Drug Use in Sports

Drugs taken to affect performance level that have spread through the sports community in the past include cocaine, strychnine, alcohol, amphetamines, heroin, and ether (Goldman, 1984; Strauss, 1987). These drugs were derived from naturally occurring substances and generally aided an athlete's performance by improving endurance and attentiveness. The main problem with drugs used to improve performance is that the dosage that causes mild stimulation, as in the case of strychnine, is only slightly less than the dose that causes convulsions and death (Strauss, 1987).

With the emergence of the modern sports era in the late nineteenth and early twentieth centuries, sports events became increasingly well organized. These organized sports events proved to suit the purposes of news organizations. Thus, as Koppett (1981) suggests, newspapers formed a natural alliance with organized sports events because they provided an excellent vehicle for meeting the newspapers' needs—that is, selling newspapers. However, while organized sports developed mutually beneficial relations with the media, the advent of organized competitions on a national and international scale during the late nineteenth and early twentieth centuries provided the forum in which coaches and athletes exchanged information on the use of drugs. As Goldman (1984) points out, once drugs were perceived to influence performance and information about their use was easily obtained, the practice of drug use became widespread and was almost impossible to stop. Drug use by athletes engaged in competition was first reported in 1865, when swimmers in canal races in Amsterdam were accused of drug use (Goldman, 1984). Shortly thereafter, in 1869, a number of cyclist coaches were widely known to have made available to their cyclists a heroin and cocaine mixture called "speedball" that was intended to increase endurance (Goldman, 1984). Reports of drug use among track and field athletes in the modern Olympic Games first appeared in 1904 (Goldman, 1984). Additionally, baseball and soccer players, boxers, football players, cyclists, and others were reported to have used numerous pharmaceutical agents as ergogenic aids (Williams, 1974). Drug use by athletes has been documented in all sports in which strength, weight, speed, endurance, or nerves are factors (Goldman, 1984; Strauss, 1987).

With this widespread use of drugs, instances of death and injury attributed to drug use quickly began to appear. The first reported drug-related death of an athlete engaged in competition involved a cyclist in a race in 1886 (Goldman, 1984). During the 1904 Olympic Games in St. Louis, the winner of the marathon collapsed at the conclusion of the race and nearly died from what was later revealed to be a large dose of strychnine and brandy he had taken prior to the race in an effort to boost his performance (Goldman, 1984). Injuries and deaths attributed to drug use continued to be reported until several events occurred during the 1960s that led to efforts aimed at curbing drug use.

The 1960s witnessed a considerable number of athlete deaths brought about by drug use intended to enhance performance. The prominence of the athletes and the sporting events involved began to move the issue of drug use in sports to the forefront of journalistic attention. Journalistic attention was captured during the 1960 Olympic Games in Rome by the deaths of two athletes. A Danish cyclist died as a result of taking a combination of nicotinic acid and amphetamines given him by his coach. Heroin was identified as the cause of death of 400-meter hurdler Dick Howard. Then, in 1963, welterweight boxer Billy Bello died from heroin poisoning (Goldman, 1984). These deaths and the common knowledge that the use of performance-enhancing drugs was widespread led, in 1965, to the enactment of legislation, such as that adopted in France and Belgium and in a number of sports associations, designed to curb the use of performance-enhancing drugs. While drug use was no longer officially tolerated, the widespread use of drugs continued. In 1967, cyclist Tommy Simpson died during the Tour de France of an overdose of methamphetamine (speed) while making a 6,000-foot climb up a mountain in 90-degree heat (Strauss, 1987). In 1968, cyclist Yves Mottin died from an overdose of amphetamines taken prior to a cross-country bicycle race. Additionally, amphetamines also caused the death of soccer star Jean-Louis Quadri, who collapsed during a match (Goldman, 1984).

Despite the potential harm posed by drugs traditionally used in sports, the dangers associated with them were believed to be short term. Thus when the effects of these drugs wore off, long-term effects on the body appeared to be negligible. However, the introduction of anabolic steroids posed both short-term and long-term dangers.

Anabolic Steroids

With the introduction of anabolic steroids, an entirely new class of performance-improving drug was made available to athletes. The controversy surrounding steroid use has presented a potentially fruitful area of reporting to journalists. Since the introduction of anabolic steroids following World War II, the ethics, physiological effects, and performance effects of their use have been debated.

Anabolic steroids — male testosterone and its synthetic derivatives — affect the buildup of muscle tissue mass as well as mediate the development of adult male sexual characteristics (Weiner, 1984). Synthetic steroids were developed in an effort to separate the muscle-building (anabolic) and masculinizing (androgen) effects of testosterone (Weiner, 1984). Steroids were initially used by athletes in sports that required strength, such as weight lifting. In particular, female athletes demonstrate more significant effects from anabolic steroid use because of the comparatively small amounts of testosterone their bodies produce.

Contemporary Patterns of Drug Use in Sports

The use of anabolic steroids was widespread in the late 1950s and throughout the 1960s and 1970s (Goldman, 1984; Strauss, 1987; Williams, 1974); they continue to be widely used by athletes engaged in competitive sports. However, considerable effort has been devoted in recent years to reducing the use of performance-improving drugs. Drug testing, first introduced in the 1960s and now used by virtually all international sports federations, has resulted in the revocation of titles and medals as well as suspension from competition (Goldman, 1984). The extent to which drug testing has affected organized sports was illustrated by the extensive disqualifications of athletes involved in the 1983 Pan-Am Games. In all, 15 athletes from 10 countries were suspended and stripped of 21 medals. Moreover, informed of the sensitivity of the drug tests, a number of athletes withdrew from competition (Goldman, 1984). Thus, while the use of performance-enhancing drugs appears to continue, much of the journalistic attention given this issue will likely shift to drug testing.

While the use of drugs to improve athletic performance has been a traditional concern, another form of drug use that has received recent journalistic exposure is the "recreational" use of narcotics by athletes. Although she offers little empirical evidence to support her position, Weiner (1984) has argued that the use of cocaine and other drugs is widespread among athletes. Books published by retired athletes such as *Ball Four* by Jim Bouton and *Always on the Run* by Larry Csonka and Jim Kiick tend to support the contention that alcohol and amphetamines are commonly used and abused drugs in professional sports. Reports of athletes treated for drug and alcohol abuse, such as Michael Ray Richardson, formerly of the New York Nets, or Clarence Kay of the Denver Broncos, have become increasingly common (Gwynne, 1988; Weiner, 1984). Reported drug abuse among athletes has led to the implementation of drug testing programs to detect drugs used for recreational purposes. And while journalistic coverage of the abuse of drugs in sports tends to focus on the professional level, evidence exists that some high school and college athletes also abuse drugs (see Glassner & Loughlin, 1987; Goldman, 1984; Strauss, 1987; Williams, 1974).

Although drug use in sports was recognized as a problem, the sudden cocaine-induced deaths of Len Bias and Don Rogers brought the issue of drug use in sports dramatically to the nation's attention. The newsworthiness of the Bias and Rogers deaths went beyond the mere reporting of the events. The widespread use and abuse of drugs in sports became the central issue emerging from these two deaths. Thus journalistic attention would be expected to be directed toward the larger issue of drug use by athletes. This study examines the journalistic coverage of drug use in sports prior to and following the deaths of Len Bias and Don Rogers.

Method

A purposive sample of eight newspapers was selected from cities that were home to at least two major professional sports teams. An effort was made to obtain relatively even geographic distribution. Newspapers chosen were the *Boston Globe, Washington Post, New York Times, Cleveland Plain Dealer, Chicago Tribune, St. Louis Post-Dispatch, Los Angeles Times,* and *Atlanta Constitution.*

The time frame chosen for the study began one year prior to the deaths of Bias and Rogers and ended 18 months afterward, a period of 30 months. Sampling involved random selection of dates to form a "constructed month" (Budd, Thorp, & Donohew, 1967) in two-week increments for each 6-month time period. In order to ensure distribution across days of the week, two selections were made for each of the seven days of the week, and no more than three days were chosen for each 30-day time period within each 6-month span. Within these restrictions, 70 dates were selected, and all eight papers were studied for each of these dates. For purposes of analytic comparison, the 30-month period was broken into five 6-month segments, two before the deaths and three after.

The content analysis involved only the sports sections of the papers. Stories were selected for analysis primarily on the basis of mention of drugs in headlines. Others were selected if they were displayed with illustrative material about drugs indicating that the stories also referred to drugs.

For each story, we noted the width of the headline (number of columns across) in relation to the number of columns on the page. We also noted the quadrant in which the story's headline appeared (1 = upper left, 2 = upper right, 3 = lower left, 4 = lower right), the page on which the story began (1–5, 6 or greater), its origin (locally written or syndicated article), whether it was news or commentary, the number of paragraphs, the sport (if mentioned), whether it dealt with professional or amateur sports, the referenced drugs (if mentioned), and the headline.

Another variable called "attention" was created, adapted from Budd's (1964) "attention score." Scores were assigned on the basis of headline sizes, quadrant in which displayed, page number, and total paragraphs, then summed to create the attention score. For headlines, a score of 0 was assigned if the headline covered a third or less of the total columns on the page, 1 if between one-third and two-thirds, and 2 if greater than two-thirds. For display, a score of 0 was assigned if the story began below the fold and 1 if it began above the fold. For pages, a score of 0 was assigned if the story first appeared anywhere but page one of the sports section and 1 if it began on the first page. For paragraphs, a score of 0 was given if the story was 10 or fewer paragraphs in length, 1 if between 11 and 20 paragraphs, and 2 if longer than 20 paragraphs. Hence a story's attention score could range from 0 to 6.

Findings

During the period of this study, the principal sports stories covered involving drugs (with the 6-month period in which they occurred appearing in parentheses, beginning one year before the deaths of Bias and Rogers) included the Pittsburgh drug trial implicating baseball players (1), the seeking of voluntary drug testing among baseball players by Commissioner Ueberroth (1), development of a drug plan by Football Commissioner Rozelle (1), revelation that the New York Giants' Lawrence Taylor had been committed to a drug center (2), failure of NFL drug tests by 57 college football players (2), Ueberroth's ruling in the Pittsburgh case (2), the death of Bias (3), beginning of a probe into his death (3), the death of Rogers (3), Ueberroth's banning of San Diego Padres pitcher Lamarr Hoyt (4), a drug investigation of basketball's Phoenix Suns (4), the end of drug treatment for the New York Mets' Dwight Gooden (4), and drug testing at the Pan-American Games (5). Overall, as shown in Figure 10.1, there were 112 stories in which use of a specific drug was mentioned, 82 of them concerning cocaine use. Only 12 of the stories concerned steroids.

The principal findings concern reporting on use of recreational drugs. Given our expectations about newspaper coverage of professional sports on the basis of previous commentary about the relationship of sports reporters

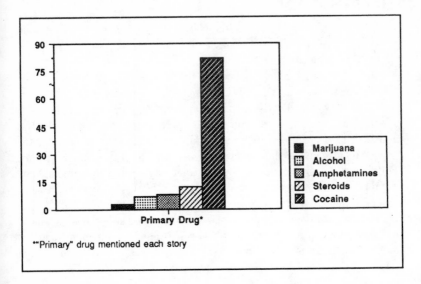

Figure 10.1. Drugs in Stories: Names of Drugs Mentioned over 30 Months

to the professional sports organizations, we might have expected a major flurry of coverage and commentary immediately after the deaths of Bias and Rogers, then a return to a normal (proportionately low) state in the months following.

Curiously, when the sample for the entire period studied is taken together, there was not even a blip of increased coverage, and the overall pattern of coverage of drug use among athletes—predominantly professional athletes—was one of decline from the period of the two sensational deaths almost up to the present. As shown in Figure 10.2, the eight major newspapers studied carried a total of 36 stories during the initial 6 months of the study, starting one year before the deaths. This increased to 63, as reports on drug violations were reported in the 6-month period immediately preceding the deaths. Following the sensational deaths of two athletes, one a professional and the other a star and number one draft pick, however, the number of stories about drug use *dropped* to 32, then to 29, and then again sharply to 12 on the observed sample days.

The proportion of commentary during the period studied is even more curious. During the initial period, from a year to 6 months before the deaths, about 14% of the coverage of drugs was devoted to editorial comment on the

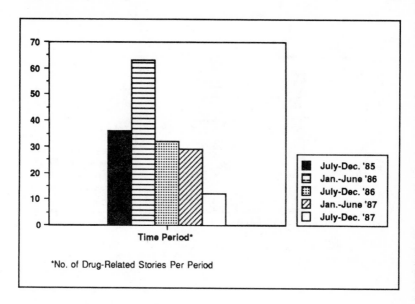

Figure 10.2. Drug Story Distribution (excluding steroid use)

sports pages, largely in sports columns. In the next period, when there was the greatest coverage of drugs, there also was the greatest proportion of commentary, 14%. In the 6 months immediately following the deaths of Bias and Rogers, however, there was *none*. It seems logical that, given that this was a sample of the period and not a count of the total number of stories and commentaries on drugs carried, there probably was *some* editorial comment. However, given that this was a *proportionate* sample, it is difficult to understand why commentary during this period was lower. It continued to be low. In the next 6 months it rose to 7%, then in the final and most recent period, it was again not a source of editorial mention among the columnists.

Other content analysis measures are generally consistent that attention to drugs has declined rather than increased since the deaths of Bias and Rogers. The "attention score" index, a composite measure involving headline size, position on the page, position in the sports section (e.g., front page or a page further back), and other measures of display given stories about drugs, generated scores (see Figure 10.3) rounded to 2.75 and 2.3 for the two 6-month periods preceding the deaths, 2.1 for the 6 months immediately following, then 2.3 again, and finally a decline to 1.8, consistent with but inde-

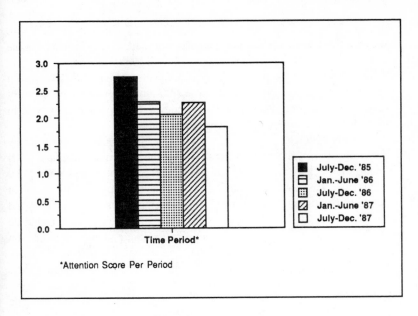

Figure 10.3. Attention Scores: Group Means (excluding steroid use)

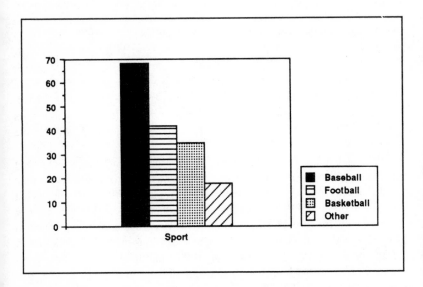

Figure 10.4. Number of Drug Stories by Sport (excluding steroid use)

pendent from reduced coverage in the most recent 6-month period. Also showing this pattern of decline are median story length and median headline size.

Most of the coverage was of baseball, football, and basketball, as shown in Figure 10.4. Across all the dates for the 30-month period, only one story concerned drugs and hockey, although hockey franchises were located in most of the cities whose newspapers were studied.

The only evidence in this entire study of an effect on sports coverage by the deaths of the two athletes was that during the 6 months immediately following their deaths, cocaine was the only drug specifically mentioned. Marijuana use was not mentioned, except when it happened to occur in connection with some other drug, such as cocaine, and even then it received the fewest mentions of all drugs covered. Alcohol, which also received little coverage throughout the first 18 months studied here, appeared to take on more interest for the sportswriters nearer the end of the study. It was mentioned in 7% of the stories in the first 6 months of the final year of the study, then in 25% of the stories in the most recent 6 months. However, this represented only three stories, two of which concerned a single incident, the arrest of Chicago Bears head coach Mike Ditka.

It would be rash to suggest that the findings reported above support a conclusion that sportswriters are protecting professional sports organizations by playing down drug use, even when it becomes a topic of national discussion. Although, as suggested, gaining access to choice information may tempt reporters to play along with the professional clubs on some matters, it is unlikely to go so far as a major cover-up. In this instance the writers are not on the payroll of the organizations and thus the lure of money is not likely to influence their sports coverage. Although play-by-play television broadcasters often are hired by the sports organizations rather than by any news medium, sportswriters and commentators by and large work only for the media.

Several explanations are possible for the pattern of stories indicating increased coverage of drugs before the deaths of Bias and Rogers, then reduced coverage afterward. One is quite simple. It reflects the underlying course of events. In the first year of the study, there was considerable activity concerning drug abuse. More and more evidence was popping up concerning drug activities. People were being arrested, some were being kicked off teams, mysterious trades were taking place, and there were various sports column suspicions about the relationship of drugs to some of these activities. The arrest of some well-known athletes, particularly, generated growing interest in drug abuse among athletes. Also prior to the deaths, the

National Basketball Association already had put a drug program in place and both the professional baseball and football leagues were working to do the same. For a large portion of this period, stories about drug-related activities were appearing with considerable frequency.

Given all this, in the post-Bias period, why was there so little coverage? Had it not been for the extensive coverage of the deaths and the activities in the aftermaths of those deaths, particularly at Maryland, where efforts were being made to put the athletic house into order, there would have been very little mention of drugs on the sports pages. Even with the coverage of these events, stories referring to drug use dropped off sharply in the 18-month period.

Were the athletes who were in a position to make the news becoming more cautious? Were their organizations covering up drug activities by their players, waiting to determine consequences of the earlier revelations? Had cocaine, clearly the most popular drug of reported misuse, become over-reported, and had reporters decided to pay more attention to something else?

It may be simply that the newsworthiness of drug use—like a rash of stories about people jumping off a bridge or being trapped in fires in tall buildings—had run its course. For a while, the category was unique, and other events fitting it became "news" and were more likely to be published. After that, however, the category became "not news." Even though other people who went through the same experiences as those reported on earlier suffered just as much, or died just as permanently or spectacularly, it was no longer news because drug use in the athletic community had come to be viewed as more commonplace.

Although in the history of drug use by athletes the stories of the deaths of Bias and Rogers are not unique, they still involve unusual ways to die, and had any more athletes died that way, undoubtedly it would have been reported. Drug-related deaths in the athletic community would continue to attract journalistic attention. But that is not what happened. The deaths of Bias and Rogers came after an extended time of concern about drugs and drug infractions by well-known sports figures. They seemed to redefine what was to be news about drugs, and to put a period after the preceding phase of coverage. After the spectacular deaths, stories of the type that had been big news in the previous six months, such as a series of revelations that the New York Giants' Lawrence Taylor had quietly undergone treatment at a drug rehabilitation center, perhaps no longer seemed as important.

What will happen next? After a period of time, will journalistic attention be captured by other sporting events, only to have drug abuse among athletes no longer considered newsworthy? Will athletes and organizations come out of the closet to be more easily reported on again? Despite the hero worship accorded athletes and despite the acknowledged influence of the clubs, in our judgment, greater reporting of drug abuse in athletics will return. Some stories, such as those dealing with the failings of stars and superstars, "demand" coverage, and they will be covered by those journalists relatively free of other ties. We think the reporting of other events, such those in which the definition of news changes for a while, will return or will be replaced by evolving new definitions. In our judgment, the study reported here, while reflecting possible changes of definition, also reflects a lull in the occurrence of events, like a dry spell in the weather that eventually will be broken by other storms.

References

Budd, R. (1964). Attention score: A device for measuring news "play." *Journalism Quarterly, 41,* 259–262.

Budd, R., Thorp, R., & Donohew, L. (1967). *Content analysis of communications.* New York: Macmillan.

Glassner, B., & Loughlin, J. (1987). *Drugs in adolescent worlds.* New York: St. Martin's.

Goldman, B. (1984). *Death in the locker room: Steroids and sports.* South Bend, IN: Icarus.

Gwynne, P. (1988). *Who uses drugs?* New York: Chelsea House.

Koppett, L. (1981). *Sports illusion, sports reality.* Boston: Houghton Mifflin.

Mangi, R. J., & Jokl, P. (1981). Drugs and sport. *Connecticut Medicine, 45,* 637–641.

Melnick, M. J. (1979). A critical look at sociology of sport. In S. Eitzen (Ed.), *Sport in contemporary society* (pp. 19–35). New York: St. Martin's.

Real, M. R. (1975, Winter). Super Bowl: Mythic spectacle. *Journal of Communication, 25,* 31–43.

Rose, D. (1982). A critique of non-normative sport sociology in the United States. *International Review of Sport Sociology, 17*(4), 73–89.

Strauss, R. H. (1987). *Drugs and performance in sports.* Philadelphia: W. B. Saunders.

Weiner, B. (1984). *Drug abuse in sports: An annotated bibliography* (CompuBibs). Brooklyn: Vantage Information Consultants.

Wenner, L. A. (1987, May). *Media, sports, and society: An agenda for communication research.* Paper presented at the annual meeting of the International Communication Association, Montreal.

Williams, M. H. (1974). *Drugs and athletic performance.* Springfield, IL: Charles C Thomas.

IV

The Audience for Media Sports

11

The Audience Experience with Sports on Television

Lawrence A. Wenner
Walter Gantz

Given the basic role sports plays in education and the socialization process, the abundance of sports on television should not be surprising. However, with such abundance, it is surprising there are so few studies of audience experiences with televised sports. Further, generalizability in these studies has been limited by experimental settings, student samples, or a focus on audiences for atypical sports events, such as the Olympic Games. A broad picture of the sports audience remains to be painted. In this study, we attempt a background sketch of audience experiences with major sports on television. We hope others will join in completing the picture.

Consistent with media gratifications research (see Palmgreen, Wenner, & Rosengren, 1985), sports viewing is seen as a complex process. We look beyond demographics and motives linked to viewing televised sports. Affective and behavioral aspects of viewing are examined, as are preparations for viewing sports and effects of that viewing. Our expectations grow from research on (1) motivations, (2) affective involvement, and (3) behaviors associated with sports viewing.

Motivations for Viewing Sports on Television

Reasons for viewing television sports are often seen to parallel reasons for spectating in the stadium. However, explanations (see Guttmann, 1986;

Sloan, 1979) about motives for sports viewing often conflict and show a reliance on supposition rather than testing (see Zillmann, Bryant, & Sapolsky, 1979). Certainly, the tensions of sporting contests may attract not only those looking to relieve boredom but those wanting to share in the stimulative stresses of an "exciting" game. Conversely, viewing sports may offer opportunities to relax, reduce tensions, and even escape. Related to either type of goal is the functionality of sports as a near universal and nonthreatening conversation topic. Further, sports viewing is often seen as a "no lose" situation. Fans often seek identification with players or teams, vicariously share in competition, and may "fantasize" competing. However, fans often do such things selectively, "basking" in "reflected glory" when "*we*" win" and disassociating when "*they* lose" (see Cialdini et al., 1976).

Sports change, becoming part of television, as they are televised (see Rader, 1984). Thus reasons for viewing sports and television in general may coincide. If one aims to kill time, escape, relax, fantasize, be stimulated, or merely spend time with someone, much television programming (including sports) may fit the bill. However, sports differs from other programs. Most nonsport entertainment programs are prerecorded, scripted stories with actors playing roles. Plot outcomes are rarely in doubt, protagonists tend to survive, and actors "bloodied" in action show no scars off the set. Most televised sport is live and unrehearsed, and "bloodied" athletes carry scars off the field. Athletes' careers hinge on their performances, and outcomes are uncertain, with the "drama" later reported as news. Reality and uncertainty in sports give its viewing a unique flavor.

Gantz's (1981) exploration of students' motives for viewing televised sports supports this view. In his study, "to thrill in victory" characterized the strongest motive for viewing sports. Here, rooting for favorites, feeling good if they won, and concern about outcome were important. Opportunities to "let loose," "get psyched," and "have a beer or drink" characterized a second strong set of priorities. Motives "to learn" about sports were less important, and viewing to "pass time" was highly unusual.

While Gantz's results show that motivational structures are similar across sports, there remain likely motivational differences by sport. Viewing motives differ by television genre and within genre (see Palmgreen et al., 1985). Similarly, differences between team and individual sports, contact and noncontact sports, and fast- and slow-paced sports should affect motives. For example, seeking stimulation should be more likely in fans of fast-paced or contact sports (e.g., basketball, football) than in fans of slower, noncontact sports (e.g., baseball, golf). Conversely, slower, noncontact sports should produce less stress, making them more attractive to viewers wanting to relax.

While avid fans should find "something to talk about" in every sports broadcast, more dominant sports (e.g., football, baseball, basketball) may have wider social applicability than less popular sports (e.g., tennis, golf, water polo). Similarly, learning about and "following" favorites should be strong motives among avid fans, but there is no reason to expect differences across sports. Also, structural differences in sports should not affect viewing to keep someone company, kill some time, engage in a parasocial relationship, or drink beer. Even though "nonfans" search for no particular sport, the availability of dominant sports may cause them to be viewed more frequently.

Affective Involvement and Television Sports Viewing

The emotions triggered in fans viewing a sports contest can be startling, even provoking riots (see Lever, 1983). Euphoria can reign in major cities after a championship has been won, and depression can set in after witnessing a disappointing loss (Zillmann et al., 1979). Enjoyment from sport is strongest where competition is seen as particularly spirited, play as "rough-and-tumble," with competitors as "hated foes" (see Bryant & Zillmann, 1983; Zillmann et al., 1979). Thus we expect fans of fast-paced or contact sports to gain the most enjoyment from a good performance by their favorites. Because distinguishing between "favorites" and "hated foes" is easier in contests where competitors are typically preordained (e.g., team sports, boxing) than in those based on tournament play (e.g., tennis, golf), where favorites may be left out of the running, we expect sports with more predictable matchups to be both more involving and more enjoyable. Similarly, the greatest disappointment should be felt by fans of "action-packed" sports where matchups are foreseeable. The related "basking in reflected glory" hypothesis (Cialdini et al., 1976) suggests that happiness with a good performance will by far outweigh disappointment with a poor one both during a sports broadcast and after it.

Just as sports may trigger different affective responses, some believe enjoyment of televised sport is influenced by the social situation in which it is viewed. Here, Zajonc's (1965) social facilitation hypothesis is invoked to support commonsense reasoning that people will enjoy and become more involved in sports when viewing in a group situation than when alone (see Sapolsky & Zillmann, 1978; Zillmann et al., 1979). Borrowing from Gantz's (1981) findings about how behaviors vary by viewing situation, we expect affective involvement not only to be stimulated by group viewing, but to be greater in groups of "friends" coming together to watch sports than in proxemically tied "family" groups that happen to watch sports together.

Behaviors Associated with Television Sports Viewing

The behaviors that accompany sports viewing are well ingrained in our culture. At a game we cheer on the home team, complain about bad calls, talk about good plays, second-guess strategies, likely consume peanuts or ice cream, and perhaps have a cold beer. Behaviors associated with sports spectating may deviate from everyday behaviors. In a game crowd, even a timid person may become vocal and challenging. After the game one may be moved to talk about it with others, watch highlights on the news, read about it in the paper, or even be inspired to go out and exercise. Further, taking time out to view a game can affect postgame responsibilities.

To what degree do these kinds of behaviors play a role in television sports viewing? Certainly, many of us have witnessed the transfer of such "stadium" behaviors to our living rooms on such special occasions as Super Bowl Sunday. Rothenbuhler (1985, 1986) shows how the viewing of the Olympic Games is a "living room celebration" where the "media event" is marked by group viewing, animated conversations about the competition, and consumption of food and drink. In less "eventful" circumstances, Gantz's (1981) findings in a student sample suggest that such behaviors accompany most sports viewing. Here, fanship behaviors (e.g., cheering, talking, complaining, pacing the floor, having a beer) were facilitated in group viewing situations, and were more likely when viewing with friends than with family. Using these results and media events research (see Rothenbuhler, 1985) to refine the social facilitation hypothesis (Zajonc, 1965), we look for viewing with friends to facilitate a more "celebrative" atmosphere than family viewing, and much more than viewing alone. Further, group viewing should inhibit noncelebrative behaviors such as doing housework or reading while viewing.

Viewing behaviors should also vary by sport. Behaviors stemming from affect (e.g., talking, cheering, pacing the floor) should be more evident in fast-paced or contact sports. On the other hand, more atypical "celebratory" behaviors may be reserved for televised sports that most approximate media events. As "event" status is inversely related to "commonness," we expect "celebratory" behaviors to be displayed most in less common, but major, sports. Of major American sports, football has the shortest season and has most play limited to weekends. Baseball has the longest season and is played almost daily. Basketball falls in between. Among these sports, celebratory behaviors should accompany football viewing most and baseball least. Event status should also stimulate previewing behaviors such as talking to others, reading predictions, tuning in early, or the likelihood of getting in the mood by having a drink. Also, event status should stimulate postexposure talking about the game as well as checking news coverage of it.

While participating in a sport raises the likelihood of spectating it (Snyder & Spreitzer, 1983), does viewing stimulate recreational activity? Using modeling theories (Bandura, 1971), we expect fans viewing sports they are likely to participate in to be most inspired. Thus viewing recreational sports (e.g., tennis, golf, bowling) should most inspire activity. Finally, we expect little difference by sport in behaviors that have little to do with fanship (e.g., doing housework or reading while viewing, keeping the set on or tending to household and family responsibilities after viewing).

Method

Telephone interviews were completed with 707 adults drawn from two random samples in Los Angeles (N = 400) and Indianapolis (N = 307). Systematic sampling from residential listings in telephone directories compensated for unlisted numbers through "add-a-digit" techniques (Frey, 1983). Indianapolis sampling was citywide, while the Los Angeles sample was drawn from the demographically diverse southwestern metropolitan area. Trained undergraduate and graduate communications students conducted interviews that typically took 10–15 minutes to complete.

Interviews were conducted over three weeks from late October to mid-November 1987. With professional and college football and basketball seasons in full swing and baseball's World Series recently completed, this is a busy time of year for sports fans. Our effort to have a sampling period where all these major sports were in season was complicated by a National Football League players' strike. To avoid deviant responses, we waited three weeks after the strike's resolution to begin interviewing.

Speaking to adults "to find out what they think about sports on television," questions about general sports interest, knowledge, activities, and media consumption opened the interview. These are detailed in our characterization of the samples in the following section. Assessment of behaviors engaged in prior to watching sports on television followed. These questions set the standard of 11-point (0–10) scales also used to assess motivations for sports viewing, behaviors and feelings concomitant with viewing, and perceived impact of sports viewing. The specific items were shaped by Gantz's (1981) study (and the sports spectatorship literature it was based on) as well as a new set of qualitative data from focused interviews (partly reported in Wenner, 1989). As we walked a fine line between asking a wide variety of questions and completing interviews in a reasonable amount of time, questions in each area were necessarily limited. However, running through these questions are foci on communicative, household, and gustatory (eating and drinking) activities, affective responses (and related behaviors) that indicate involvement, and companionship and time-killing (both indicative of viewing without involvement).

The previewing behavior question took the following form:

> People do a variety of things as they get ready to watch a game on television. Using a scale from zero to ten, where zero is just about never and ten is just about always, give me some number that tells me how often you do each of the following activities as you get ready to watch a game on TV. OK? How often do you: talk to others about the game? . . . read about what might take place? . . . tune in early so you won't miss a thing? . . . kill time until the game starts? . . . have a beer or a drink?

Questions that followed concerning motivations, concomitant behaviors and feelings, and perceived effects took a similar form (i.e., 0–10 scale) but focused specifically on the sport identified on an earlier posed interest question: "What sport on television do you spend the most time watching?" We first asked an open-ended question about the "most important reason why you watch [the identified most watched sport] on TV." This was followed by a list of "some reasons other people have given for watching sports on TV." Using the 0–10 scale, we asked how much each reason applied to watching the identified sport. The complete wording of these motives appears in Table 11.4. Communicative ("something to talk about"), gustatory ("chance to have a beer or drink"), affective ("gets me psyched up"), companionship ("because friends or family are watching"), and time-killing ("nothing going on") motives were among those inquired about. Additionally, we inquired about fanship ("see how favorite does"), learning ("about players and sport"), and parasocial ("like announcers") motives.

After assessing motives, we asked about the typical viewing situation of the most watched sport. We posed: "When you watch [most watched sport], do you usually watch it alone, with others in your family or with friends?" Based on that response, respondents used the now familiar 0–10 scale to evaluate a list of what they did (or did not do) and how they felt while watching their most watched sports in the identified viewing situation. Again, we inquired about communicative (reading, talking), household (doing or avoiding chores), and gustatory activities (with simple measures of eating and drinking, and parallel ones assessing whether these activities had been facilitated more than usual). Measures of affective involvement ("feel nervous," "get angry," "feel happy") and behavioral indicants of involvement ("yell out," "pace the floor") were also included.

After assessing these "concomitants," we posed: "Many people often are still affected by a game after it's over. After you've watched [most watched sport] using the same zero to ten scale, how often do you . . ." A list of effects items to be evaluated followed. Again, communicative activities, ranging from continuing "to watch TV even though you hadn't planned on it" to "deliberately" watching "highlights on a newscast" and reading "about the contest," were included. We also asked about the frequency of "putting off household chores" and having a "beer or drink to celebrate a win." Two items measured lingering affect: (1) staying "in a good mood after a victory" and (2) staying "in a bad mood after a defeat." Finally, we inquired about deliberately spending "time with your family" and avoiding "family because you need to recover." While not the focus of this report, we also asked married respondents about the impact of television sports on their marriages. Basic demographic questions closed the interview.

A Portrait of the Samples

The questions about sports interest and viewing that opened the interview and assessments of demographics that closed it together provide a good profile of our overall sample and the differences between samples in the two cities (see Table 11.1).

While gender difference is not significant, men (54.6%) are more prevalent in the overall sample than women (45.4%), and men dominate more in the Los Angeles sample (LA) than in the Indianapolis sample (IN). More (54%) of the overall sample were unmarried (single, divorced, or widowed) than married (46%). Here, the two samples contrasted, with IN being 59% married and LA 64% unmarried. This may be attributable to the differences in mean age in the two samples. LA's mean age was 36.6 years, compared to IN's 40.4. In LA, 68.2% were under 40, while in IN, 54.5% were under that benchmark of middle age.

Table 11.1
Summary Characteristics of Overall Sample and Contrasts
Between Indianapolis and Los Angeles Samples

Chi-Square Analyses	Overall Percentages (N = 707)	Indianapolis Percentages (N = 307)	Los Angeles Percentages (N = 400)
Gender			
male	54.6	52.3	56.3
female	45.4	47.7	43.7
Marital status*			
unmarried	54.0	40.7	64.3
married	46.0	59.3	35.7
Race*			
white	79.8	91.6	71.0
black	10.3	6.8	13.0
other	9.9	1.6	16.0
Age*			
< 40	62.3	54.5	68.2
40 +	37.7	45.5	31.8
Education*			
≤ high school	28.8	40.0	20.3
high school +	71.2	60.0	79.7
Income*			
< $20,000	21.5	22.5	20.6
$20,000–$49,000	53.0	57.2	49.6
> $50,000	25.6	20.4	29.8
TV sports interest*			
low	24.1	19.6	27.6
medium	37.2	36.9	37.5
high	38.7	43.5	34.9
Column totals		43.5%	56.5%

t-Test Analyses	Overall Means	Indianapolis Means	Los Angeles Means
Knowledge: most watched sport	3.2	3.2	3.2
Saturday–Sunday hours TV Sports*	3.0	3.4	2.6
Monday–Friday hours TV Sports	1.2	1.3	1.2
Saturday–Sunday hours TV Viewing*	5.1	5.7	4.5
Monday–Friday hours TV Viewing	3.1	3.1	3.1
TV Sportcast Attention*	3.6	3.8	3.4
Time without TV Sports until miss*	4.6	4.2	4.9
Days per week exercise*	2.6	2.0	3.0
Minutes daily read sports*	10.6	11.8	9.6
Minutes daily read newspaper	34.4	35.4	33.6

Note: Actual N for analyses may range from 634 to 707.
* significant ($p < .05$) for both chi-square and t-tests (2-tailed).

In addition, the LA group was better educated (80% having some college, as opposed to 60% for IN) and reported a higher yearly family income (30% over $50,000 per year, as opposed to 20% for IN). Racially, the overall sample was about 80% white, 10% black, and 10% "other" (primarily Hispanic or Asian). As IN was 92% white, most of the racial diversity is attributable to LA, where blacks made up 13%, Hispanics 9%, and Asians 6%.

The differences in the two samples along a number of sports interest and media consumption variables are symbolized by responses to our first question: "In general, how interested are you in watching televised sports events?" While 43.5% in IN were "very interested," only about 35% in LA were. On the other end, less than 20% of IN fell into the low-interest group (those answering "not very interested" or "not interested at all"), while over 27% in LA were not interested.

Responses to questions about sports media consumption (we asked for estimates "during fall and winter" (to control for sports season variations) show how the IN group's high interest is paralleled by comparatively high consumption. The mean for the IN group shows them watching more hours of sports on TV on an average Saturday or Sunday (3.4 to LA's 2.6), paying attention to the sports segment of a local newscast more days per week (3.8 to LA's 3.4), and on the average spending more minutes per day reading the sports pages in the newspaper (11.8 to LA's 9.6). The comparatively brisker late fall weather may explain the IN group spending more time with weekend sports viewing. However, the sports to overall TV viewing (including sports) ratios for the two cities were very similar. With 60% of weekend TV viewing spent with sports in IN and 58% in LA, it seems that viewing sports dominates television experiences over the weekend. The extended commuting times in LA may limit the audience's ability to see early evening newscasts, and hence the sports reports. The difference in sports reading may be linked to differences in the newspapers respondents are reading. It may also be partly explainable by the IN group spending more time reading the newspaper (including sports) than the LA group, although this difference is not significant. Viewed another way, 33% of IN newspaper reading was spent on sports, compared to 29% of the LA reading time.

However, there is more reason to believe that regional differences in sports consumption are not artifactual and that the IN group is more avid and dependent on mediated sports coverage. We posed the hypothetical, "Suppose there were no sports on television. How many days would have to pass before you really missed it?" Categorizing our responses (1 = less than 1 day, 2 = 1–2 days, 3 = 3–4 days, 4 = 5–7 days, 5 = a week to a

month, 6 = more than a month, 7 = never), we found the IN group mean
of near 5–7 days before missing significantly different from the week to a
month it took the LA group to miss sports.

The only measure of sports interest in which LA exceeded IN was the
number of "days a week you get a chance to exercise or participate in
sports." The LA group averaged 3 days a week of exercise to the IN group's
2 days. Whether the increased activity on the part of the LA group may
limit, and thus partly explain, its comparatively lower sports media consumption cannot be determined from these data.

The two samples were similar in some respects. They rated themselves
equally (and highly) knowledgeable about their most watched sport. Average weekday sports viewing was similar (1.2 hours), and sports dominated
weekday TV viewing (about 40%) less than was reported for weekend
viewing. Also, both estimates of overall weekday TV viewing and overall
newspaper reading were similar between the two samples.

Some Basic Differences in Fans of Different Sports

Among our 707 respondents, professional football was the sport that fans
reported spending the most time watching (N = 244, 34.5%). Next in line,
respondents most watched professional basketball (N = 96, 13.4%), baseball (N = 93, 13.2%), college basketball (N = 63, 8.9%), college football
(N = 53, 7.5%), and tennis (N = 40, 5.7%). In total, 589 respondents
(83%) in our overall sample named one of the above six sports as most
watched. Each "also ran" was named by no more than 2% of the sample.
Among these, golf (N = 14, 2.0%), auto racing (N = 11, 1.6%), gymnastics (N = 9, 1.3%), and hockey and boxing (both with N = 7, 1.0%) were
most frequently watched.

We judged that the numbers of respondents in each of the "big six" sports
groups were sufficient to analyze differences in previewing behaviors,
motivations, concomitant behaviors and feelings, and postviewing effects.
Fans of the "big six" sports that are included in further analyses are characterized in Table 11.2. As we suspected that there might be demographic and
sports interest differences among the groups, we wanted to both understand
these and control for them in later analyses. Some commonsense suspicions
about these differences were borne out. For example, in the preceding season, Indiana University had won the NCAA basketball championship and
the Los Angeles Lakers had won the NBA championship. In each sample,

Summary of Demographic Characteristics and TV Sports Interest by Most Watched Television Sport

	Baseball (N = 93)		Most Watched Television Sport Pro Football (N = 244)		College Football (N = 53)		Pro Basketball (N = 96)		College Basketball (N = 63)		Tennis (N = 40)	
	column %	row %	column %	row %	column %	row %	column %	row %	column %	row %	column %	row %
City*												
Indianapolis	43.0	14.7	45.9	41.0	52.8	10.3	26.0	9.2	93.7	21.6	22.5	3.3
Los Angeles	57.0	16.8	54.1	41.8	47.2	7.9	74.0	22.5	6.3	1.3	77.5	9.8
Gender*												
male	40.9	12.0	59.9	45.9	67.9	11.4	51.1	15.2	58.1	11.4	32.5	4.1
female	59.1	20.5	40.1	36.2	32.1	6.3	48.9	17.2	41.9	9.7	67.5	10.1
Marital status*												
unmarried	53.8	15.8	47.1	47.4	54.7	8.8	68.8	11.0	41.3	13.6	76.9	3.3
married	46.2	15.8	52.9	36.4	45.3	9.2	31.3	20.9	58.7	8.2	23.1	9.5
Race*												
white	83.3	16.5	79.8	41.9	90.2	10.1	59.4	12.6	88.5	11.9	80.0	7.0
black	3.3	4.6	9.7	35.4	7.8	6.2	31.3	46.2	6.6	6.2	2.5	1.5
other	13.3	21.0	10.5	43.9	2.0	3.2	9.4	15.8	4.9	5.3	17.5	12.3
Age*												
< 40	53.8	13.7	66.0	43.0	67.9	9.9	75.8	19.7	49.2	8.2	50.0	5.5
40 +	46.2	20.0	34.0	37.7	32.1	7.9	24.2	10.7	50.8	14.4	50.0	9.3
Education												
≤ high school	39.1	20.6	29.7	40.6	36.5	10.9	26.3	14.3	29.5	10.3	15.4	3.4
high school +	60.9	13.9	70.3	41.7	63.5	8.2	73.7	17.4	70.5	10.7	84.6	8.2
Income*												
< $20,000	30.4	21.4	18.2	35.7	18.8	8.0	34.5	26.8	6.7	3.6	14.7	4.5
$20,000–$49,000	50.6	14.1	55.0	42.6	54.2	9.2	47.1	14.4	61.7	13.0	55.9	6.7
> $50,000	19.0	11.4	26.8	44.7	27.1	9.8	18.4	12.1	31.7	14.4	29.4	7.6
TV Sports Interest*												
low	30.4	23.0	14.1	27.9	18.9	8.2	26.3	20.5	14.3	7.4	40.0	13.1
medium	34.8	14.5	43.6	47.7	37.7	9.1	31.6	13.6	28.6	8.2	37.5	6.8
high	34.8	13.2	42.3	42.1	43.4	9.5	42.1	16.5	57.1	14.9	22.5	3.7
Column totals	15.9		41.4		9.1		16.1		10.6		6.8	

NOTE: Actual N for analyses may range from 528 to 589. *Chi-square significant p < .05

the form of basketball with recent success ran second to pro football as most watched. The college basketball group is dominated by IN (94%), and the pro basketball dominated by LA (74%). We also suspected that with two Major League Baseball teams, baseball might be named more frequently in Los Angeles than in Indianapolis, where there is no Major League team. However, baseball was named by about 16% in both groups. Tennis, a warm-weather sport, was more popular in LA (77.5% of the tennis group).

As male socialization more readily condones physical resolution of conflicts, we looked for men to dominate in the contact sport groups. While men dominated football and basketball groups, women appeared more frequently in the pro basketball group (48.9%) than in the overall sample (45.4%). More women than men were in the tennis (67.5%) and baseball (59.1%) groups. Tennis, the only televised sport among the six where women are sometimes players, was more watched among women than college football and basketball.

We had little reason to believe that marital status would come into play in sport preferences. However, unmarried respondents dominated tennis (76.9%) and pro basketball (68.8%) groups. Married respondents appeared more frequently in the college basketball (58.7%) and pro football (52.9%) groups. Not surprisingly, the most married group, college basketball, also had the second oldest mean age (42.4), younger on the average only than baseball fans (42.8). Also, the unmarried plurality in the pro basketball group was reflected in their having the youngest mean age (33.5). However, the next youngest group, pro football (36.8), was mostly married. Tennis (39.0) and college football (38.2) took up the middle-age means.

In looking for racial differences in sports preferences, about the only thing we had to go on was common perception of pro basketball as a game dominated by blacks. Our groupings show that blacks make up more (31.3%) of the pro basketball group than any other, and blacks ranked this sport most watched second only to pro football. Whites most dominated the college football group (90.2%) and then the college basketball group (88.5%).

The six sports groups were not marked by differences in education. However, estimates of yearly family income did distinguish the groups. The upper income group (more than $50,000 annual income) was better represented (about one-third) in the college basketball and tennis groups. These groups also had the fewest fans from the lower income range (under $20,000). Pro basketball (34.5%) and baseball (30.4%) had the greatest percentage of lower-income fans, as well as proportionally the fewest high-income fans (about 19%).

We expected some differences in television sports interest based on differences between respondents in the two cities. The tendency of Indianapolans to be highly interested in sports and to dominate the college basketball group combines to give that sport group the greatest percentage of highly interested fans (57.1%). With about 42% of their fans highly interested, pro and college football and pro basketball trailed by quite a margin. Tennis had the most fans with low sports interest (40%), followed by baseball (30.4%). These sports also proportionally had the fewest fans with high interest. Fans who were "somewhat interested" gravitated to pro football, while low-interest respondents were a small percentage (14.1%) of that fan group.

Our findings of consistent differences among respondents in the six sport groups and just as consistent ones between our two sample populations pointed to a need to control for these differences in the analyses that follow. In order to be confident that resulting differences among the six sports in previewing behaviors, motivations, concomitant behaviors and feelings, and postviewing effects were not attributable to preexisting differences in the groups, we relied on analyses of covariance (ANCOVA) to test true group differences. As there seemed to be no pattern of differences linked to demographic variables, all were included in the covariate list. However, because it seemed differences relating to media sports consumption were traceable to basic differences in television sports interest, that variable is the only nondemographic variable in the covariate list. Some covariates—city (IN-LA), gender, marital status (unmarried-married), and race (nonwhite-white)—were dummy coded. The other covariates—age, education, income, and television sports interest—were either continuous or ordinal variables.

Behaviors Prior to Viewing Sports on Television

Five items assessed preparatory behaviors of fans as they "got ready to watch a game on TV." "Talking to others about the game" was the only item with an overall mean over 4 on the 0–10 scale. "Having a beer or drink" had the lowest overall mean at 2.6. The other items fell in the 3–4 range, with "tuning in early" at 3.6 more common than "reading" (3.3) and "killing time" (3.0). Further, "killing time" was the only previewing behavior without significant differences across sports when tested using the ANCOVA model (see Table 11.3).

Table 11.3
Summary of Means and ANCOVAs
for Previewing Behaviors and Motivations by Most Watched Sport

		Most Watched Sport				
	Baseball	Pro Football	College Football	Pro Basketball	College Basketball	Tennis
Previewing behaviors						
talk to others*	3.6	4.4	4.0	4.4	5.1a	2.8a
read predictions*	2.9a	3.5	3.7	3.0b	5.0abc	3.1c
tune in early*	2.9a	3.9	3.5	3.8	5.3ab	2.0b
kill time	2.9	3.6	3.4	3.2	2.9	2.2
have beer/drink*	2.2	3.1	3.4	1.9	2.8	2.0
Motivations						
social activity*	3.4	4.2	3.9	4.4	3.1	2.5
conversation topic	2.9	3.8	2.9	3.3	3.2	2.6
get psyched up*	2.2ab	3.7a	3.4	4.3b	3.8	2.9
let off steam	2.5	3.3	3.0	3.4	3.3	2.2
to relax/unwind	4.7	5.5	4.6	4.9	5.7	4.2
for drama/tension	4.9	6.0	5.6	5.9	6.4	5.0
nothing going on*	4.2	4.7a	3.8	4.0	2.6a	4.2
nothing else on TV*	4.0	4.4a	3.6	3.8	2.7a	4.3
not miss anything	3.3	3.0	3.0	3.6	4.3a	1.8a
excuse: beer/drink	1.0	1.0	1.1	0.9	0.7	0.4
learn: players/sport*	5.2	5.3	4.2	5.8	6.1	5.5
listen: announcers	3.3	3.0	2.3	3.6	3.1	2.2
follow favorite*	7.0	7.4a	7.2	7.2b	8.6c	5.2abc
friends/family watch	3.8	3.5	3.2	3.7	3.2	2.7

NOTE: Common lowercase letters *following* group means indicate significant Scheffé contrasts ($p < .05$) between groups within analysis. Actual N for analyses may range from 505 to 509.
*Significant ($p < .05$) main effect on item, controlling for city, gender, race, age, marital status, education, income, and sports interest.

There were differences in previewing communication behaviors by sport, and college basketball fans scored highest on all three of these items. College basketball fans' "talkative" nature (5.1) contrasted notably with the much lesser tendency of tennis fans (2.8) to engage others in conversation before viewing. Fans of both pro football and basketball were also comparatively talkative (4.4) prior to viewing.

Of the two "mediated" communication behaviors, "tuning in early" took on the above pattern of response. The pro football and basketball groups trailed college basketball fans slightly in frequently viewing early. Tennis fans were least likely to tune in early. While the college basketball group was also the most likely (5.0) to "read about what might take place," baseball, pro basketball, and tennis fans cluster low on reading (around 3.0).

With the likelihood of having "a beer or drink" before viewing their respective sports, the pattern changes. While pregame drinking is less likely than other behaviors, football fans, led by the pro fans, are the most frequent drinkers. College basketball fans trail, and baseball, tennis, and pro basketball fans are progressively less likely to so imbibe.

Motivations for Watching Sports on Television

Viewing to see how one's "favorite does" was the strongest motive (6.9 mean across sports) in each sport group (see Table 11.3). Running second, with across-sports mean of 5.8 (over 5.0 in five of six sport groups), was liking the "drama and tension involved." "Learning" (5.3) and "relaxing" (5.1) were the only two other items with overall means much above 4.0. At the bottom of the motives list (at overall 1.0) was viewing because "it's a chance to have a beer or drink." The next two least endorsed motives, "liking announcers" and "letting off steam" neared considerably stronger 3.0 overall means.

There was a relatively even split between motives that distinguished among the six sports groups and those that did not. With ANCOVA controls, 8 of the 14 showed no significant differences among fan groups. Most notably, 3 of these – "letting off steam," "relaxing," and liking "drama and tension" – involved affective motivations. Different types of fans were also as likely to have social ("talk"), parasocial ("announcers"), involvement ("not miss"), and explicit companionship ("because family/friends watch") motives as reasons for viewing. Also, seeing their viewing as "a chance for a beer or drink" was rejected equally by the different fans.

Three motives on which there were differences among sports groups concerned aspects of fanship. Tennis fans were less likely (5.2) to follow "favorites" than fans of team sports, although this was still their prime motivation for viewing. As tennis is tournament based, tennis fans may not be as confident that their favorite players will be competing.

College basketball fans were clearly the most motivated (8.6) to see how their "favorite team does." These fans also most wanted to "learn more about the players and the sport." However, the pro basketball group and even the tennis group trailed not far behind in viewing to learn. Even with the college football group lagging notably behind on the learning motive, there were no significant post hoc contrasts between groups.

While getting "psyched up" was a motive for some fans more than others, not getting "psyched up" was most telling in baseball fans. These viewers of the slower-action "grand old game" contrast with fans of pro basketball and football, who rank "getting psyched" comparatively strongly. The college basketball group also looked to "get psyched up," but post hoc tests showed no significant contrasts with other fan groups.

The three remaining motives that distinguish among sports viewing groups involve reasons having little to do with being a fan. Watching because there's nothing else "going on" or "on TV" was strongest among pro football fans, and weakest among the more purposive fans of college basketball. Fans of pro basketball and football ranked similarly high (about 4.3) viewing as "something to do with my friends or family," while tennis fans were least moved by the social occasion. While main effects were significant, post hoc contrasts were not.

Motivation Structures for Watching Sports on Television

Similarities and differences on individual motivations paint a partial picture of frequent viewers of the six sports. Factor analyses of motivations in each viewer group fill in the portrait by looking at structures underlying motivations. Varimax factor analysis procedures (SPSS principal components with iterations, eigenvalues over 1.0 for factors) were used to find solutions for the six groups. The summary in Table 11.4 focuses on motivations having (1) a highest loading on the factor, (2) a minimum factor loading of .50, and (3) no strong secondary loadings (with few exceptions primary loadings are at least two times greater than secondary loadings; see McCroskey & Young, 1979).

Three factors emerged for two largest sport groups, professional football and basketball, while motivations for the four smaller groups showed four dimensions. Also, there was a trend for accounted variance to be inversely related to group size. Variance accounted for was greatest in four factor solutions for the two smallest groups, tennis (77.1%) and college football (68.7%), and smallest in the large professional football fan group (56.9%). The variance totals for the other solutions hover in the 60% range.

Table 11.4
Summary of Factor Analyses
for Motivations by Most Watched Television Sport

	Baseball (N = 93)		Pro Football (N = 244)		College Football (N = 53)		Pro Basketball (N = 96)		College Basketball (N = 63)		Tennis (N = 40)	
Factor 1	35.5% var.		34.6% var.		35.5% var.		42.4% var.		28.0% var.		43.1% var.	
Loadings:	Learn	.87	Psych	.82	Steam	.80	Psych	.80	Steam	.76	Drama	.86
	FlwFav	.74	NoMiss	.76	Drama	.76	Drama	.79	Learn	.71	Learn	.85
	NoMiss	.67	Learn	.74	NoMiss	.75	FlwFav	.78	Psych	.71	FlwFav	.84
	Anncr	.62	Drama	.73	Learn	.73	NoMiss	.75	Talk	.69	Relax	.78
			Steam	.71	FlwFav	.71	Steam	.73	NoMiss	.63		
			Relax	.69	Psych	.66	Learn	.72	Anncr	.62		
			FlwFav	.60			Relax	.70	Drama	.60		
							Anncr	.65	Relax	.58		
Factor 2	13.9% var.		13.1% var.		16.2% var.		13.9% var.		15.5% var.		16.7% var.	
Loadings:	Steam	.78	FrdFam	.83	Talk	.76	NoOnTV	.91	NoOnTV	.86	Steam	.82
	Psych	.76	Social	.82	Relax	.74	NoToDo	.88	NoToDo	.84	Talk	.67
	Beer	.75			Anncr	.60						
Factor 3	11.4% var.		9.3% var.		9.7% var.		8.5% var.		8.9% var.		9.9% var.	
Loadings:	NoOnTV	.93	NoOnTV	.91	Social	.81	Social	.89	Social	.84	NoToDo	.93
	NoToDo	.92	NoToDo	.90	Beer	.73	FrdFam	.76			NoOnTV	.92
					FrdFam	.73						
Factor 4	7.5% var.				7.4% var.				8.4% var.		7.4% var.	
Loadings:	Social	.85			NoOnTV	.91			Beer	.82	Social	.88
	FrdFam	.84			NoToDo	.87			FlwFav	−.63		
Total	68.2% var.		56.9% var.		68.7% var.		64.9% var.		60.8% var.		77.1% var.	

NOTE: Social = it's something to do with my friends and family; Talk = it gives me something to talk about; Psych = it gets me psyched up; Steam = it's a good way to let off steam; Relax = it lets me relax and unwind; Drama = I like the drama and tension involved; NoToDo = it's something to do when there's nothing else going on; NoOnTV = it's something to watch when there's nothing else going on; NoMiss = because I don't want to miss a thing; Beer = it's a chance to have a beer or drink; Learn = it gives me a chance to learn about the players and the sport; Anncr = I like to listen to the announcers; FlwFav = to see how my favorite team (or player) does; FrdFam = because that's what my friends or family are watching.

As was the case in Gantz's (1981) study, there is much commonality to the underlying structures across sports. In each solution, two "nonfanship" factors emerge, although they are not the prime motivational force for viewers. A "time-killing" factor was generally the strongest of these two factors. Viewing because "nothing else" is "on TV" and "going on" cluster into a second factor on the two basketball solutions and a third factor for baseball, pro football, and tennis viewing. Almost as consistent in makeup, but typically less effective in explaining variance, was a "social companionship" factor that centered on viewing as a way to be with "friends and family." Only in the college football solution, where the "chance to have a beer or drink" loaded on this factor, did "social companionship" take on a character apart from spending time with friends or family.

A set of reasons defining a multifaceted "fanship" motive come together to pale "killing time" and "social companionship" as factors for viewing sports. "Fanship" is at the core of the first factor in all solutions, although aspects of it break off into other factors in some solutions. For pro football, and pro and college basketball, "fanship" items are limited to the first factor. The "chance to learn more about players and the sport" loads strongly on the first factor in all solutions. Seeing how one's "favorite" does, liking the "drama and tension involved," and wanting not to "miss a thing" load on this first factor in five of six solutions, as well. In four of the solutions, the motives to get "psyched up," to "let off steam," and to "relax and unwind" loaded on the first factor.

Those instances where these "fanship" items broke off to other factors suggest a more complex motivational structure for fans of baseball, college football, college basketball, and tennis. For baseball fans, "fanship" split between the first two factors. "Learning" and following "favorites" combine with wanting "not to miss a thing" and "liking announcers" to define "ritualistic" fanship motives on the first factor. "Letting off steam," getting "psyched," and having a "beer or drink" define a distinct secondary set of motives seemingly aimed at bringing about affective changes as a result of viewing baseball. On the secondary "fanship" factor, college football and tennis fans are both moved to view for "something to talk about." Also, the "relaxing" aspect of this factor for college football fans and the motive to "let off steam" for tennis fans gives a "mood alteration" flavor to this secondary fanship factor that is distinguishable from secondary "psych up" goals of baseball fans. Finally, worthy of note is that "a chance to have a beer or drink" is linked to *not following* "favorites" in the motivational structure of college basketball fans. More useful, however, is thinking of the avid "follower" of college basketball consistently *not* seeing the "chance for a beer or drink" as a motive for viewing.

Behaviors and Feelings Concomitant with Sports Viewing

Based on the findings of Gantz (1981) and Sapolsky and Zillmann (1978), we reasoned that behaviors and feelings accompanying sports viewing would be influenced by the viewing situation. Thus we report first (see Table 11.5) the results from tests of our ANCOVA model (demographics plus TV sports interest) on "concomitants" for viewers who identified their "usual" viewing situation as being (1) alone, (2) with family, or (3) with friends. This is followed by tests of the ANCOVA model on concomitants by "most watched sport" that parallel those reported on previewing behaviors and motivations. Finally, to isolate differences among the sports that are not attributable to the viewing situation, we add "viewing situation" to the basic ANCOVA model as a control factor that is considered after the covariate list but before main effects for the six sport groups.

The concomitants inventory comprises 10 behavioral and 3 affective items. Across sports, highest ranked among all items (overall mean 7.4) was feeling " happy when your favorite player or team does well." The two other affective items, getting "angry" when that favorite "does poorly" and feeling "nervous as the game progresses" were rated almost three mean points lower. Averaging quite a bit higher than other behavioral items (at 6.0) was having "a snack" while viewing sports. Among the higher-rated concomitant behaviors, two communicative acts — "yelling out in response to" and "talking about" the action — were the only items with overall means slightly over 5.0. The least frequent behaviors across sports were "pacing the floor" (1.1) and "drinking more beer or alcohol than you would otherwise" (1.4). Having "a beer or drink" (2.4) and "reading something" (2.9) were also comparatively infrequent behaviors across groups.

Differences by Viewing Situation

Only 5 of 13 concomitants were not influenced by viewing situation. The levels of "reading something," "feeling nervous," "feeling happy," "putting off chores," and "eating more junk food more than normal" showed no significant differences by viewing situation after controlling for covariates.

Table 11.5

Summary of Means and ANCOVAs for Concomitant Behaviors and Feelings by Viewing Situation and Most Watched Sport

Concomitants	Viewing Situation					Most Watched Sport					
	Sig*	Alone	Family	Friends	Sig*	Baseball	Pro Football	College Football	Pro Basketball	College Basketball	Tennis
Do house chores	X	3.1a	4.7ab	3.4b		4.2	3.9	4.0	3.6	2.9	3.3
Read something		2.9	3.1	2.8		3.0	2.9	2.5	2.7	2.6	3.8
Yell out response	X	4.1ab	5.3a	5.9b	YZ	4.7a	5.5	4.8	6.0	6.7ab	4.0b
Feel nervous		4.0a	4.5	4.9a	YZ	3.8a	4.6	4.3	5.4	6.0ab	3.5b
Have beer/drink	X	1.8a	1.8b	3.6ab		2.1	2.8	3.0	1.7	2.6	1.9
Pace floor	X	0.8a	0.9	1.5a	YZ	0.8	1.0	1.0	1.9	2.0	0.7
Talk about action	X	2.8ab	5.9a	6.2b	Y	4.4	5.3	5.3	5.5	5.6	4.3
Angry with poor performance	X	4.0a	4.7	5.6a	Z	4.7	5.3a	5.2	5.0	6.2b	3.2ab
Happy with good performance		7.2	7.3	7.8	YZ	7.5a	7.8b	7.7c	7.6d	8.7e	5.4abcde
Have snack	X	5.3a	5.7b	6.9ab	Y	5.6	6.4a	6.9b	6.1	6.4c	4.2abc
Put off chores		4.1a	4.0b	5.2ab		4.4	4.6	4.9	4.3	4.9	3.3
More junk food		3.2	3.5	5.1	Y	3.3	4.1a	4.5b	4.0	3.4	1.9ab
More drinking	X	0.8a	1.0b	2.2ab		1.3	1.8	1.9	1.2	1.0	0.7

NOTE: Common lowercase letters *following* group means indicate significant Scheffé contrasts ($p < .05$) between groups within analysis.

*X reports significant ($p < .05$) main effect for viewing situation on item, controlling for city, gender, race, marital status, education, income, and TV sports interest (N = 490–492). Y reports significant ($p < .05$) main effect for most watched sport on item, controlling for city, gender, race, marital status, education, income, and TV sports interest (N = 508–510). Z reports significant ($p < .05$) main effect for most watched sport on item, controlling for city, gender, race, marital status, education, income, TV sports interest, and viewing situation (N = 411–413).

260

Quite sensibly, communication behaviors such as "talking about the action" were less likely when viewing alone. While more likely than talking when alone, "yelling" a response to action was also less frequent when viewing alone. While fans viewing with friends rated these communication behaviors more likely than fans viewing with family, post hoc contrasts are not significant.

The analyses also suggest that "pacing the floor" and "getting angry when your favorite player or team does poorly" is inhibited by viewing alone and facilitated when viewing with friends. Here the spread of means between group viewing situations suggests that viewing with friends, not merely with others, encourages concomitant "pacing" and "anger."

The results also show evidence of a "friends effect" in facilitating "gustatory" behaviors. Based on responses to our scales, both "having a beer or drink" and drinking more "than you would otherwise" are twice as likely when viewing with friends than in other viewing situations. On the other hand, the increased likelihood of "having a snack," while facilitated significantly more by viewing with friends than any other viewing situation, is not so dramatic. Finally, there is evidence that viewing sports with family members most encourages one to "also work on household chores" while the contest is being televised.

Differences by Most Watched Sport

Similar to analyses of viewing situation factors, "reading" and "putting off chores" were not significantly different among the six fan groups when controlling for covariates. Further, with these controls, no differences in "doing house chores," "having a drink," "drinking more than usual," or "getting angry" were significant among the fan groups.

In reporting differences among fan groups, we will discuss results from the basic ANCOVA model (controlling for demographic and TV sports interest) and note how further controls for the viewing situation change findings. Paralleling effects by viewing situation, the communication behaviors "talking" and "yelling out" about the action differed by sport. In each instance, college basketball fans communicated the most, and baseball and tennis fans were least vocal. Differences in "yelling out" hold after controlling for viewing situation. However, differences in "talking" by most watched sport disappear when viewing situation is controlled for. A closer look reveals a significant ($p < .05$) interaction between viewing situation and sport that may be partly explained by "talkative" college basketball fans viewing more frequently in the family setting (41.2%) than other groups, and the tennis group being dominated by fans viewing alone (56.3%; overall chi-square 18.9, df $= 10$, $p < .05$).

Two affective concomitants and one demonstrative of affect have significant differences among sport groups that hold up even when viewing situation is controlled for. Feeling "happy" when a favorite does well, feeling "nervous" as play progresses, and "pacing the floor" distinguish the groups. The college basketball group was the most happy, nervous, and prone to pacing, while tennis fans were least likely to feel or do these things while viewing.

The evidence that two nonalcoholic gustatory behaviors—"having a snack" and eating "more junk food than normal"—are different in fans of different sports is mitigated by the viewing situation. College football "snackers" contrast most notably with more restrained tennis fans. While there is no significant viewing situation by sport interaction on either item, the small size of the tennis group may have inhibited significance. It remains plausible that tennis fans, more often viewing alone, are less often thrust into "celebrative" group viewing situations.

Finally, there is one anomaly to these findings. Getting "angry when your favorite player or team does poorly" did not show a significant difference ($p < .07$) among groups in the basic ANCOVA test controlling for demographics and TV sports interest. However, when viewing situation was added as a control, the further adjusted sum of squares became significant. Getting "angry" followed the general trend for college basketball fans to score highest and tennis fans the lowest, although here their lack of anger also contrasted significantly with "angry" pro football fans.

Postviewing Effects Attributed to Sports on Television

Responses to how people believe they are affected after viewing their most watched sport round out our findings about the television sports viewing process (see Table 11.6). Only 2 of the 11 effects items have overall means over 5.0. Respondents say they are most likely to "stay in a good mood for a while after a victory" (6.0) and "talk about the game" (5.4). Taken together, these more frequent behaviors support the notion of "basking in reflected glory" as outlined by Sloan (1979) and Cialdini et al. (1976).

Table 11.6
Summary of Means and ANCOVAs
for Postviewing Effects by Most Watched Sport

	Baseball	Pro Football	College Football	Pro Basketball	College Basketball	Tennis
			Most Watched Sport			
Postviewing effects						
Put off chores	2.0	2.3	2.2	2.2	2.6	1.6
More unplanned TV	3.7	3.4	3.0	3.4	2.9	2.9
Good mood with win*	5.5a	6.2	5.9	6.1	7.4ab	4.5b
Celebrate with drink*	1.2	1.9	2.4	1.2	1.5	1.5
Talk about game*	4.9	5.7	5.7	5.7	6.3	4.2
Bad mood with loss*	2.0	2.3	2.9	2.8	3.1	1.5
Go exercise more	1.2a	1.8	1.8	2.8a	1.7	2.1
View highlights	4.7a	4.7	4.8	5.2	5.4	3.8
Read about game*	3.7a	4.5	4.6	4.9	6.2ab	3.5b
More family time	4.4	4.7a	3.7	4.0	5.1b	1.9ab
Avoid family*	0.6	0.6	0.6	0.8	1.1	1.1

NOTE: Common lowercase letters *following* group means indicate significant Scheffé contrasts ($p < .05$) between groups within analysis. N = 505, except for family items, where N = 413. *Significant ($p < .05$) main effect on item, controlling for city, gender, race, age, marital status, education, income, and TV sports interest.

That "deliberately" reading "about the contest" and watching "highlights on a newscast" are next most highly rated (about 4.5) suggests that "basking" may include a mediated "reliving" of victory.

Avoiding one's family "because you need to recover" (0.7) was by far the lowest-rated effect across sports. Further, the low ratings for "have a beer or drink to celebrate a win" (1.6) and "go out and exercise more than you normally would" (1.9) suggest that drinking has no necessary role in "basking" and that immediate modeling effects are limited by entrenched exercise habits. Also under the 3.0 mark across sports were "putting off chores" (2.1) and "staying in a bad mood after a defeat" (2.3). Our results show that staying in a good mood after a win is far more likely than staying in a bad mood after a defeat. This supports the generalization that fickle fans "bask" as "we win" but avoid responsibility by explaining "they lost" (see Zillmann et al., 1979).

Controlling for covariates, viewing did not inspire "putting off chores" or spending "time with your family" differently among the six sport groups. The low "family time" rating of tennis fans is explained by their more frequent "unmarried" status. Two communications effects, viewing "highlights" on the news and unplanned viewing of "more TV," did not vary by sport. As well, "exercising" was equally uninspired across fan groups. The significant post hoc contrast between "inspired" exercisers in the basketball group and the "uninspired" baseball group is explained by the latter group being oldest and the former youngest.

Consistent with the pattern thus far, the college basketball group engaged most often, and the tennis group least often, in communicative behaviors that differentiated among groups. The college basketball group is also distinguished by purposively reading "about the contest" they viewed earlier. Baseball fans clustered with tennis fans near the bottom of both "reading" and "talking," setting them both off from college basketball fans.

The same pattern of differences emerged with respect to staying "in a good mood after a victory" and a "bad mood after a defeat." College basketball fans "bask" in the reflected glory of victory significantly more than tennis or baseball fans. They are also more affected by a loss, but the contrast with less affected groups is insignificant.

Mood "sustenance" took on a different flavor in college football viewers, who were most likely to "celebrate a win" with a "beer or drink." As drinking is highest as a previewing behavior, motivation, and concomitant behavior in college football fans, its relative availability may help make drinking part of the "basking" process for these fans. Finally, differences in the consistently low tendency to "avoid your family because you need to recover" are difficult to explain. Fans of college basketball and tennis, set apart in most analyses, are the top avoiders.

Discussion

While many of our expectations about viewing sports on television were fulfilled, others were not. Regional differences in sports preferences can be clearly seen. Indianapolans follow the Indiana tradition of supporting amateur basketball. Pro basketball's popularity with viewers in Los Angeles suggests lasting effects to a team's winning. However, viewers of college basketball, while directly contrasting with viewers of the pro game only in avidly reading prior to viewing, are clearly the most fanatic of viewers. Finally, basic climatic and life-style differences by region appear to affect interest in viewing sports such as tennis.

While pro football viewing is strong in all demographic groups, fans of different sports are fans of different sorts. Men gravitate to contact and fast-paced sports, and women to more slow-paced baseball and less brutal tennis. Of "actional" sports, women gravitate to pro basketball, a sport that also has a notably black and youthful following. The youth of pro basketball's viewers suggests it may make future gains on pro football's popularity. Conversely, baseball's older, less well-to-do audience raises questions about slow pace attracting youthful, monied viewers.

Many differences among viewers of the six major sports are foreshadowed by interest levels in television sports. College basketball fans have avid general interest in television sports, and tennis fans the least general interest, followed by baseball fans. The dominance of (especially pro) football seems traceable to strong viewing by medium interest fans. However, even when differences such as these are controlled for, audience experiences with the six major televised sports are distinctive.

Motivations for Viewing Sports on Television

Our findings support Gantz (1981) in that motivational structures are similar across sports and "fanship" motives reign supreme. However, patterned differences exist among sports. More popular sports have less clear-cut distinctions in fanship motives, as items cluster to one all-encompassing factor. Fanship motives for less popular sports are multidimensional. Popular sports may feed off their own popularity, attracting lukewarm viewers more vague in intent. For both football and basketball, fans of the less popular college game have more distinct motives than viewers of the pro game. How these structural differences in motives relate to often suggested differences between college and pro sport remains to be examined. Across sports, keeping people company and time-killing structure two distinct nonfanship motives. But only with college football do social viewing and drinking motives interrelate the "celebrative" goals Rothenbuhler (1985) poses for media events such as the Olympics.

That stimulative motives most apply to contact or fast-paced sports was confirmed in fans wanting to "get psyched," but not in seeking of "drama and tension." The mirror expectation that fans of slower or noncontact sports avoid stress was confirmed in their low desire to "get psyched," although these fans had no stronger desire to relax or let off steam. Apparently, only strong stimulative goals are affected by differences in sports, while more tempered affective goals apply equally to televised sports.

We found unexpected differences by sport in the two motives ranked highest across sports. College basketball fans most followed "favorites," but the response pattern suggests structural influences on the motive for tennis fans. Knowing "favorites" may lose in early rounds may not deter tennis fans from viewing "survivors" in tournament play. "Learning about players and the sport" was strongest in college basketball fans and weakest in college football fans. With clearly seen and fewer players to focus on, basketball may facilitate learning more than football, with its army of players and helmets masking faces. That college and pro basketball and tennis rank highest on this item supports this "numbers and visibility" argument about learning.

Unexpected differences were found in viewing sports to kill time. That "dominant" pro football is most often used to kill time speaks to its availability. But regional dominance, the cultural embeddedness of college basketball in Indiana, may prohibit nonpurposive viewing. Finally, that tennis fans do not view as "something to do with friends and family," suggests that "special interest" sports go unappreciated in proxemic circles.

Affective Involvement and Television Sports Viewing

The strongest affective involvement in sports viewing came in "feeling happy" when favorites did well. In that respondents felt nowhere near as angry or bad (both during viewing and afterward) when favorites did poorly as they did happy when favorites did well, our evidence not only supports the "basking in reflected glory" hypothesis but extends it to affect concomitant with viewing. As expected, viewers of contact or fast-paced sports felt greater amounts of both happiness and sadness in following the fate of favorites. Results for tennis viewers also support the notion that viewing sports with more predictable matchups garners more affective involvement. That fans of contact and fast-paced sports feel most nervous suggests that "action" plus "lead time" to pick sides may foster involvement. Finally, in that only communal ire among friends seems to be facilitated when things go wrong for favorites, the bounds for the viewing situation's influences on affect appear limited.

Behaviors Associated with Television Sports Viewing

A "celebratory" atmosphere pervades in sports viewing with friends. Following expectations, talking, yelling, pacing, drinking, and snacking through a televised contest happens most with friends around and least when alone. That drinking and snacking is significantly higher with friends than with family suggests a heightening of celebration outside the normative constrictions of the family. While communication behaviors are more frequent in viewing with friends than with family, the fact that such behaviors are more frequent in group viewing than in viewing alone cannot be taken as a sign of facilitation; rather, it is simply recognition of the limits of being alone.

Only two behaviors concomitant with viewing differ by sport after viewing situation is controlled for. However, as we expected, "yelling" responses to the action and "pacing the floor" were more common in contact and fast-paced sports. Contrary to our expectations concerning the relative "event status" of sports, celebratory (especially "gustatory") behaviors did not vary by sport once viewing situation was controlled for. This suggests that the "media event" is more in the viewing situation than in the event itself.

To a limited degree our expectations about "event status" were displayed in postviewing behaviors. Of major sports, viewers of college and pro basketball (with mid-range "event status") tended to score high on reading and talking about the game, and baseball fans (viewing the "nonevents" of the long summer season) less provoked to do such things. Outside the mainstream, tennis fans were affected even less to read or talk about matches on television, but more than likely were stymied more by lack of opportunity than by lack of desire to do these things after viewing. Interestingly, only in the case of "celebrating with a drink" after a victory did our media event reasoning hold true to form. Here, the fans of higher "event status" college football drank most and fans of "nonevent" baseball least. It seems as likely, however, that existing traditions of drinking accompanying sports may play as important a role in this difference as event status.

Concluding Comments

As is the case with any broad-based inquiry, this study has limitations. Our research design restricted assessments to experiences with a most watched sport. Results may differ when viewers are asked to compare their experiences with different television sports. Because we were venturing on relatively uncharted terrain, our tack was to follow a number of lines of theoretical reasoning in sketching audience experiences with sports on television. In that no one theoretical view dominates our findings, many avenues remain open to make sense of audience experiences with televised sport.

Motives for viewing major television sports seem to have both structural similarities and substantive differences. Differences are also displayed in the affective and behavioral aspects of both viewing different sports and viewing in different situations. However, just as we can safely conclude that different kinds of people view major television sports, we conclude that these people have different experiences throughout the viewing process. Media gratifications research suggests that certain theories may better explain component parts of the audience experience process. Because many aspects of audience experience with televised sport are distinct from experiences with the rest of television, we are convinced that future research needs to look beyond social psychological concerns to the subcultures behind fanship of different sports.

References

Bandura, A. (1971). *Social learning theory*. Morristown, NJ: General Learning.

Bryant, J., & Zillmann, D. (1983). Sports violence and the media. In J. H. Goldstein (Ed.), *Sports violence* (pp. 195–211). New York: Springer-Verlag.

Cialdini, R. R., Borden, R. J., Thorne, A., Walker, M. R., Freeman, S., & Sloan, L. R. (1976). Basking in reflected glory: Three (football) field studies. *Journal of Personality and Social Psychology, 34*(3), 366–375.

Frey, J. H. (1983). *Survey research by telephone*. Beverly Hills, CA: Sage.

Gantz, W. (1981). An exploration of viewing motives and behaviors associated with television sports. *Journal of Broadcasting, 25*, 263–275.

Guttmann, A. (1986). *Sports spectators*. New York: Columbia University Press.

Lever, J. (1983). *Soccer madness*. Chicago: University of Chicago Press.

McCroskey, J. C., & Young, T. J. (1979). The use and abuse of factor analysis in communication research. *Human Communication Research, 5*, 375–382.

Palmgreen, P., Wenner, L. A., & Rosengren, K. E. (1985). Uses and gratifications research: The past ten years. In K. E. Rosengren, L. A. Wenner, & P. Palmgreen (Eds.), *Media gratifications research* (pp. 11–37). Beverly Hills, CA: Sage.

Rader, B. G. (1984). *In its own image: How television has transformed sports*. New York: Free Press.

Rothenbuhler, E. W. (1985). *Media events, civil religion, and social solidarity: The living room celebration of the Olympic Games*. Unpublished doctoral thesis, Annenberg School of Communications, University of Southern California.

Rothenbuhler, E. W. (1986, May). *Media events and social solidarity: An updated report on the living room celebration of the Olympic Games*. Paper presented at the annual meeting of the International Communication Association, Chicago.

Sapolsky, B. S., & Zillmann, D. (1978). Enjoyment of a sport contest under different conditions of viewing. *Perceptual and Motor Skills, 46*, 29–30.

Sloan, L. R. (1979). The function and impact of sports for fans: A review of theory and contemporary research. In J. H. Goldstein (Ed.), *Sports, games and play: Social and psychological viewpoints* (pp. 219–262). Hillsdale, NJ: Lawrence Erlbaum.

Snyder, E. E., & Spreitzer, E. A. (1983). *Social aspects of sport.* Englewood Cliffs, NJ: Prentice-Hall.

Wenner, L. A. (1989). Therapeutic engagement in mediated sports. In G. Gumpert & S. L. Fish (Eds.), *Talking to strangers: Mediated therapeutic communication.* Norwood, NJ: Ablex.

Zajonc, R. B. (1965). Social facilitation. *Science, 149*, 269–274.

Zillmann, D., Bryant, J., & Sapolsky, B. S. (1979). The enjoyment of watching sports contests. In J. H. Goldstein (Ed.), *Sports, games and play: Social and psychological viewpoints* (pp. 297–335). Hillsdale, NJ: Lawrence Erlbaum.

12

Viewers' Enjoyment of Televised Sports Violence

Jennings Bryant

Sports Violence: A Persistent Presence

The normative, ritualized vocabulary of any subject provides important insights into its essential character. From an examination of the glossary of sports terms in *The Sports Writing Handbook* (Fensch, 1988), it is clear that sports and violence have become almost inseparable. Baseball has its "bean ball" or "knockout pitch," which has resulted in player death (p. 189). Basketball's complex system of "personal fouls" (p. 195) includes regulations to control unwarranted physical contact, such as excessive pushing, tripping, and hitting. In boxing, a "bleeder" is "a fighter who cuts easily" (p. 198); a "cauliflower ear" is "a deformed ear; caused by too many blows to the ear" (p. 198); "to knock out an opponent with one blow" is to "coldcock" him (p. 198); a "haymaker" is "a knockout punch" (p. 198); and being "punch-drunk" is "to suffer the effects of taking too many punches to the head" (p. 200). The list could go on and on.

Additional indices are readily available from a variety of archival media sources and reveal a great deal about the persistent presence of violence in sports. For example, comparison of a sample of sports headlines from the 1981–1982 popular press with a similar sample from 1987–1988 reveals sports journalists' continued preoccupation with sports violence. Bryant and Zillmann (1983) list 1981–1982 headlines that include the following:

- PLAYING FOR BLOOD
- BALL GAMES OR BRAWL GAMES?
- TAKE THE BODY!
- WATCHING OUT FOR THE HIT MAN?
- YES, YOU CAN CALL HIM THE ASSASSIN

A sample of today's headlines paints a highly similar picture:

- HOW DIRTY A GAME!
- FINESSE IS OUT, PHYSICAL IS IN
- THE PAIN IS PLAIN
- TODAY'S SPORTS PAGES FILLED WITH THE GRISLY
- A BLOODY MESS
- FANS WITH AN AFFECTION FOR VIOLENCE

The persistence of these themes is perhaps even more clearly revealed in the title of a recent *Sports Illustrated* article on violence in professional ice hockey: "The *Never-Ending* Story" (Neff, 1988; emphasis added). That article includes the following indictment of sports violence, embellished with highly revealing statistics:

> If you had six or eight free hours, you might have been able to watch an NHL playoff game last week. There were so many fights and infractions that the contests seemed interminable, and most postgame statistical summaries read like police blotters. . . . The brawlers from Boston and Buffalo racked up 474 penalty minutes in the first *three* games of their Adams Division semifinal; the NHL playoff record is 611 penalty minutes set in a *six*-game Quebec-Hartford series a year ago. (pp. 21, 24; emphasis added)

From time to time, the NHL has attempted to gloss over if not dismiss the gravity of player violence by arguing that the frequent brawls that occur before, during, and after play are just "spontaneous combat" that comes from the frustrations inherent in the sport. But not all of the players and managers see it that way. Some, such as Calgary Flyers general manager Cliff Fletcher, readily admit that the preeminent purpose of player violence is *intimidation*; and "intimidation is probably the major factor in hockey" (Swift, 1986, p. 14). The Flyers' designated "enforcer," Dave Brown, has even gone so far as to confess that his primary job is to intimidate opponents via gratuitous physical abuse. Does he administer his beatings in the heat of anger? No! Brown admits, "I don't know if I ever really get all that mad" (Swift, 1986, p. 15). Is Brown and his kin's violence merely expressive behavior (Zillmann, 1979), intended less to inflict harm or injury than to communicate that worse is yet to come if the opponents do not exercise restraint? Again, no. It is genuine aggression, that is, an "activity by which a person seeks to inflict bodily damage or physical pain" on another (Zillmann, 1979, p. 33). Brown freely admits it, saying, "There's no sense getting into a fight if you're not going to hurt them" (Swift, 1986, p. 15).

Increasing levels of violence in sports paralleled by enhanced concern about the impact of sports violence are in no way unique to professional ice hockey. Technically, basketball is classified as a noncontact sport, yet,

> In 1987–88 the NBA had more fist fights than Mike Tyson. It also had spectacles like 6-foot-10, 255-pound Rick Mahorn of the Detroit Pistons catching Chicago's Michael Jordan in midair and throwing him onto the floor. To which Jordan said later, "No doubt, Mahorn was trying to injure me." . . .
> Mahorn's bruising physicality last season left deep imprints on foes— mentally and physically. But it helped lift the Pistons all the way to the NBA finals and earn a reputation as *the team of tomorrow.* (DelNagro, 1988, p. 19; emphasis added)

Such perceptions of increased violence in NBA play have caused the league to utilize a third official for the 1988–1989 season. However, as New York Knicks general manager Al Bianchi has said, "Fouls are fouls, but the overall unwritten indelible code for NBA officials is 'Let Them Play! . . . Less fouls, more fun'" (DelNagro, 1988, p. 19). Evidently Bianchi is right: The NBA is "coming off its fifth straight year of record attendance and TV ratings. . . . TV coverage has expanded" ("Edge Gel Presents," 1988, p. 4).

Headlines and articles may be revealing, but today's medium of authority seems to be the television sound bite. Head coach Chuck Knox of the NFL's Seattle Seahawks has provided what is perhaps the perfect sports violence sound bite: "Football, remember, is combat" (quoted in Durslag, 1988a, p. 21).

The past and present seem to be perfectly clear: Sports and violence have thrived in their common-law marriage, whether consummated on grass, artificial turf, hardwood, or ice, but especially on television. What about the foreseeable future? Sports journalism expert Thomas Fensch (1988) lists "violence" (e.g., "excess violence," "spectator violence," "individual acts of violence by athletes"; p. 180) as one of the "10 major topics that will continue to be key areas of concern into the 1990s" (p. 179). Similar projections are offered by many sources. Remember, the physically abusive Detroit Pistons are touted as the NBA "team of tomorrow." In a recent telecast of an NFL game involving the Houston Oilers, on no less than six occasions the sportscasters noted that the Oilers had become increasingly "aggressive," "physical," and even "ferocious." Near the end of the telecast, one of the commentators added, "This may well be the team of the 90s. I think we'll be covering them more and more." As if to cement the importance of violence to the Oilers' television coverage, only a few weeks later, during a telecast of the Oilers-Dallas Cowboys Thanksgiving 1988 game, a halftime feature examined the incredible number of face masks that the Oilers had destroyed during the current season—a most telling, sensationalistic statistic. Further sports violence histrionics were provided in the dramatized visual coverage of that game: Time after time, especially following a particularly rough tackle, a camera would linger on signs held by Oiler fans that proclaimed that the Astrodome had become the "House of Pain."

There seems to be little doubt of the intricate and symbiotic interrelationships among sports, violence, and the media. Certainly one dimension of those relationships is clear: If a team's performance and public relations image indicate that the team plans to raise sports violence to new heights, the media will be there. When it comes to media coverage, violence does pay.

Purpose of This Chapter

A half decade ago, the first relatively comprehensive scholarly examination of this topic was published as a chapter titled "Sports Violence and the Media" (Bryant & Zillmann, 1983) in an edited book titled *Sports Violence* (Goldstein, 1983). The purpose of the present chapter is to provide an update on this topic and to extend the discussion along lines suggested by several recent empirical investigations into spectators' enjoyment of televised sports violence.

Four questions will guide the present treatment: Why do the media persist in presenting and covering sports violence? Do viewers of sports on television really enjoy sports violence? If they do, why do they? Does spectators' enjoyment of sports violence have no limits?

Why Do the Media Present and Cover Sports Violence?

A sports fan might answer this question tersely: "Because violence is such a big part of today's sports!" A media marketing expert or a network executive might refocus the answer and reassign the "blame": "Because it's what sports fans want!" In fact, because television has become "Almighty TV" as far as sports is concerned and has been allowed, if not encouraged, to reshape sports in its own image (Durslag, 1988b), the former claim has become inexorably intertwined with the latter. But the composite claim is perhaps more truism than truth. Although it is obvious that sports producers and directors are convinced that all their viewers lust after violence in sports, evidence to support the common contention that sports spectators want and demand violence is less than consistent. In fact, a review of the literature on the appeal of televised sports violence reveals that producers of televised sporting events would appear to be somewhat more confident in their claims for the uniform drawing power of violence than the scant evidence might support. On the other hand, for many hard-core sports viewers—"Super Spectators" (Johnson, 1971)—the producers' gut reactions of what it takes to keep them (us) glued to their (our) screens may be more correct than most critics of sports violence would care to admit.

Does "Super Spectator" Really Enjoy Sports Violence?

Several recent studies on the enjoyment of watching televised sports contests have shed light on the question of whether all sports fans like sports violence. The first study examining the effects of sports violence on viewer enjoyment was conducted by Comisky, Bryant, and Zillmann (1977). In this investigation, examples of what casually appeared to be rough play versus normal play were selected from a professional ice hockey match. Systematic examinations of specific audio and video properties of the telecast revealed a fortuitous occurrence. For one segment in which rather rough and violent play was visually present, the sportscasters had let the video channel carry the action, providing only extremely bland commentary. In contrast, during a segment in which minimal rough and no violent play had occurred, the announcer and color commentator had tried to "juice up" the action by embellishing the play with commentary that stressed how rough and tough the play had become, even threatening to turn into a brawl at any second. This variation during a naturally occurring broadcast permitted tests of (a) broadcast commentary's effects on viewers' perceptions of the roughness of the action, and, more important for our purposes, (b) the effects of viewers' perceptions of the roughness of play on their enjoyment.

In a quasi-experimental design, spectators viewed one of the two segments either with or without commentary and rated their enjoyment of the segment and how rough or violent they perceived the segment to be. The commentary significantly altered viewers' perceptions of the roughness of play. In the rough-action condition, the bland commentary that failed to emphasize the visually present violence made play appear less violent and more normal. In contrast, in the normal-action condition, the commentary that emphasized the roughness and viciousness of play made the normal play seem rough, actually rougher than the visually rough play. Most critically, viewers' enjoyment of play was in direct correspondence to how rough they *perceived* the play to be. Enjoyment did not follow actual violence; rather, it resulted from viewers' perceptions of rougher and more violent play. This provides evidence for what is purely a medium effect on enjoyment – the impact of sports commentary. Clearly, enhancing viewers' perceptions of roughness and violence via commentary can contribute to their enjoyment of a televised sports contest.

In a second investigation, Bryant, Comisky, and Zillmann (1981) selected and pretested plays from professional football telecasts that varied in their degree of roughness or violence (low, intermediate, high) yet were equated on other stimulus dimensions. Male and female viewers watched all plays, rating each immediately after watching it. The enjoyment of televised football plays was found to increase with the degree of roughness and violence; however, this relationship was reliable for male viewers only. The authors interpret the findings as suggesting that, "at least for male viewers, a high degree of aggressiveness is a critical ingredient of the enjoyment of watching sports contests" (Bryant et al., 1981, p. 256).

Two recent theses have added to our understanding of viewers' enjoyment of sports violence. Rapaport (1984) investigated the normative contents of another of television's unique contributions to viewer's enjoyment of sporting events – the instant reply. One conclusion drawn from this investigation is that television network executives act as if they abide by an implicit theory that the viewing (and re-viewing) of particularly violent plays adds significantly to audiences' pleasure, because an exceptionally large proportion of replays repeat the roughest and most violent aspects of play. These findings were interpreted as providing support for George Orwell's view of the place of violence in the enjoyment of sports: "Serious sports . . . has nothing to do with fair play. It is bound up with hatred, jealousy, boastfulness, disregard for all rules, and *sadistic pleasure in witnessing violence*: In other words, it is war minus the shooting" (quoted in Rapaport, 1984, p. 60; emphasis added).

Sullivan (1987), a professional sports journalist, returned to the focus of the investigation by Comisky et al. (1977) – the effects of television sports commentary on viewers' perceptions of play and their enjoyment of play that is perceived to be violent. Commentary from a televised basketball game between Big East collegiate foes Georgetown and Syracuse was manipulated by professional sportscasters so as to create three commentary conditions (commentary stressing Syracuse player aggression, neutral commentary, no commentary). Among several other variables employed were subject gender and subjects' degree of sports fanship. Viewers' perceptions of the degree of roughness and violence of play were assessed, as was their appreciation of the telecast. Once again, commentary was found to influence significantly viewers' perceptions of the degree of aggressiveness of the sports contest. In this instance, viewers of the manipulated commentary condition saw the Syracuse players as being significantly more aggressive than did the viewers in either the neutral commentary or no commentary condition, precisely in line with the stimulus manipulation. As has been found in other investigations, men enjoyed the aggressive play more than did women. Surprisingly, experienced sports fans' perceptions of play were as vulnerable to the commentary manipulation as were those of less avid fans. Unfortunately, the appreciation variables were confounded in this investigation, as the commentary merely shifted the locus of the aggression from one team to the other, rather than systematically accentuating or diminishing viewers' perceptions of the overall level of aggressiveness of play. However, trends in patterns of means scores for enjoyment would seem to support the author's contention that "commentary . . . can facilitate enjoyment of player violence" (Sullivan, 1987, p. 3).

Recent and significant advances in our understanding of the importance of television viewers' *perceptions* of violence also have been made in areas other than in sports. Gunter (1985) conducted a series of investigations into television viewers' perceptions of violence in entertainment programming and, in line with the sports-specific findings of Comisky et al. (1977), concludes that "*perceptions of programmes as 'violent' did not depend on the actual number of violent incidents*" (p. 36). Moreover, Gunter found that the subjective *salience* of the televised violence was a critical determinant of how audiences perceived and reacted to violent television content. Numerous *individual differences* were also found to mediate viewers' perceptions of television violence, one of the most potent of which was the viewer's history of *personal aggressiveness*. Atkin, Greenberg, Korzenny, and McDermott (1979) had previously reported related findings; they found that physical aggressiveness was a good predictor of preferences for violent television programs among boys, while for girls verbal aggressiveness was a reliable predictor of selectively viewing violent fare. Atkin (1985), after reviewing this and related research, noted in summary fashion that viewers do select "entertainment television programming that is compatible with their [aggressive] predispositions" (p. 78). Extensive research by Huesmann and Eron (e.g., 1986; Eron & Huesmann, 1980; Huesmann, 1982) provides strong cross-national support for the contention that aggressive predispositions and behavior patterns are reliable predictors of the selection of violent viewing fare. This mounting evidence from several areas suggests that research into the enjoyment of sports violence should consider viewers' personal propensity for aggression as well as their subjective perceptions of sports violence.

Bryant and Brown (1988) built on these findings and propositions and conducted an investigation assessing the effects of viewers' personal propensity toward aggression on their enjoyment of sports violence. Following Gunter (1985), viewers' personal propensity toward aggression was assessed using the Buss-Durkee Hostility Inventory. Several weeks prior to the study, subjects — adult learners in one of four college continuing-education classes — completed this inventory as a portion of a battery of what they were told were "general aptitude tests." Male adults who were found to be either extremely high or extremely low in propensity for aggression were selected for participation in a subsequent sports viewing study, although the connection between the screening tests and the study was not indicated and apparently was not suspected by the subjects.

A second, related factor involved an induced sensitivity toward the functions and dysfunctions of aggression in sports, designed to assimilate sports viewers' various moral and social sensibilities toward the effects of sports violence. In this study, viewer sensibilities were manipulated rather than assessed. Approximately 45 minutes prior to the sports viewing portion of the study, subjects watched one of three 5-minute, specially produced videotaped intervention treatments presented in the form of journalistic *sports features*. The manipulated segment was embedded in six other short segments, all involving interviews of various sorts, that subjects viewed, ostensibly in order to assess several technical aspects of interviews, none of which was related to the variables under consideration.

One version of the sports feature offered an apologia for extreme roughness and even violence in sports. In it, an interviewee professed that it was absolutely essential to be physically rough in sports in order to succeed (sports violence justified). Two film clips were used to embellish the interview. In the first, the interviewee, a burly tackle on a collegiate football team, was shown playing with young children and talking with them about the fact that "being physical" was a noble part of the game and was something players had to accept if a team was to succeed. The second film clip, taken from a college football game, purportedly showed the player delivering a bone-jarring tackle to an opposing halfback, and then helping him up in an obvious show of sportsmanship. In a final portion of the interview, the tackle embellished his earlier position on sports violence, emphasizing that roughness was part of giving the best that one has, and that willingness to give one's all in contact sports is a good predictor of personal achievement in later life.

The second version of the sports feature utilized an identical format and the same talent. However, this version presented sports violence as being unnecessary aggression and emphasized all the harm that such gratuitous violence has caused (sports violence condemned). The first film clip featured the interviewee teaching the children how to use "dirty tricks" to hurt their opponents and to "take them out of the game." In this version, the game clip featured the same bone-jarring tackle, but via electronic editing the play was seen to result in serious injury to the halfback who had been tackled. In the subsequent interview, the interviewee indicated without remorse that the halfback had been "wiped out" for that season, and he cruelly and insensitively talked about how much pleasure he personally received from making such "vicious" tackles.

The third version served as a control segment. Again using an identical format and the same talent, it featured a relatively innocuous "up close and personal" look at the same tackle; but neither roughness nor violence was mentioned in any portion of the interviews, and the game clip featured a very mild play emphasizing the tackle's skills.

In addition to the factors of viewers' propensity for aggression and sensibilities toward sports violence, a message variable of degree of roughness/violence of play was included. The stimulus materials were those employed by Bryant et al. (1981), a sample of plays from numerous NFL telecasts selected and pretested to create a three-level differentiation in roughness/violence of play. A $2 \times 3 \times 3$ factorial design was employed, with two independent factors—viewers' measured propensity for aggression (low, high) and viewers' manipulated sensibilities toward sports violence (violence justified, violence condemned, control)—along with a repeated measures factor—roughness/violence of play (low, intermediate, high). As in the study by Bryant et al. (1981), viewers rated their enjoyment of each play immediately after viewing it. After this assessment had been completed, subjects viewed each play again, this time rating how rough and violent they perceived each play to be. Perceived roughness/violence ratings for each play yielded a pattern of differentiation identical to that found in the ratings of the pretest, which had been performed by expert judges. Following all other assessment procedures, subjects rated their own degree of sports fanship and reported their personal experiences in playing various types of sports.

Enjoyment of play varied both as a function of assessed personal propensity for aggression and induced sensibilities toward violence. Statistically significant main effects occurred for all three factors. To summarize: (a) Viewers who had been assessed as being more prone to aggressive behavior enjoyed the football plays more than did those viewers low in aggression propensity. (b) Similarly, viewers who had watched the segment designed to legitimize sports violence reported higher overall enjoyment of play than did those viewers receiving the treatment condemning sports violence, who, in turn, enjoyed the plays less than did those subjects in the control condition. (c) As in the study for which the stimulus materials were originally prepared (Bryant et al., 1981), the viewers (all males, in this instance) enjoyed the roughest and most violent plays the most and the least rough plays the least.

More revealing, however, were several significant interactions. To illustrate a few of the more interesting of these findings: (d) For viewers who had been assessed as low in aggression propensity, the effect of roughness of play did not yield a significant differentiation in mean scores. In fact, viewers who were low in aggression propensity liked the moderately rough plays slightly but insignificantly more than the violent plays. (e) In contrast, aggression-prone viewers rated the violent plays as more than twice as enjoyable as the moderately rough plays and nearly 10 times as enjoyable as the mild plays, which they enjoyed less than did viewers low in aggression propensity. (f) Moreover, the significant three-way interaction revealed that viewers who were evaluated as being predisposed toward interpersonal violence plus who had received the intervention treatment that justified sports violence enjoyed the extremely rough plays significantly more than subjects in any other combination of treatment and assessment conditions. (g) In contrast, viewers high in propensity for aggression reported the lowest overall level of enjoyment for the plays that were devoid of violence, regardless of which intervention treatment they had received.

As might be expected, (h) the violence legitimization or condemnation treatment had lesser effects on viewers' enjoyment of mild than of violent plays. Moreover, (i) although low-aggression-propensity viewers' enjoyment of plays of intermediate levels of roughness was effected by the intervention treatment, this treatment was of little moment for aggression-prone subjects' enjoyment of moderately rough play. (j) Only for highly violent plays did the intervention treatment yield the anticipated effect among subjects with a high high propensity for aggression.

In summary, although it seems that viewers do enjoy extremely rough football plays more than they do milder plays, such general reports mask substantial viewer differences. Among more aggression-prone subjects, sports violence may indeed yield maximal enjoyment. Among their more mild-mannered peers, however, excessive violence in sports may be somewhat of a turn-off. In this context it is important to note that subjects who were found to have more extensive experience with sports, especially with contact sports, and who reported being more avid sports fans, were more frequently found among viewers with a high propensity for violence. In contrast, relatively few of the viewers who were assessed as being low in propensity for aggression reported being avid fans of contact sports. Therefore, producers of televised sporting events may be safe and even sage in continuing to emphasize and thereby potentially accelerate sports violence, *if* their primary goal is to please their already most avid fan—Super Spectator. That same strategy would appear to be highly risky if the attraction of the typically less fanatic sports viewer is desired. Once again, catch-22.

It is also important to note that both aggression-prone and less aggressive viewers can be sensitized to the merits or demerits of sports violence via the viewing of carefully crafted televised features on sports violence. This traditional sports journalism format apparently has great potential for subtle persuasion, possibly because it is part "news"—from which source it obtains credibility—and part entertainment—from which it receives and retains its audience. Moreover, in this instance the direction of sensitization via the sports features was clearly found to affect the enjoyment of subsequently viewed rough play. Once again, viewers' perceptions and predispositions have been found to be critical ingredients of their enjoyment of watching sports contests.

Why Do Viewers Like Violence in Their Televised Sports?

Since it now seems clear that many of television's most avid sports viewers do enjoy sports violence, a most appropriate question would seem to be, Why? Theories of the enjoyment of aggression in sports have been presented and reviewed extensively elsewhere (Bryant & Zillmann, 1983; Zillmann, Bryant, & Sapolsky, 1979) and will not be repeated here in any detail. To summarize, however, typically one of three theories is offered to explain why sports violence is so popular. The most widely cited of these rationales, especially among laypersons and by writers in the popular press, is the notion of *symbolic catharsis*. In this view, sports violence offers viewers a golden opportunity to purge themselves of destructive energies by vicariously participating with their sports heroes who regularly perform aggressive acts under the guise of "play." This purgation is seen to provide relief, which is enjoyable. The more violence, the greater the relief, and the more intense the enjoyment. In a second view, sports violence is seen as offering an ideal means for viewers to *assert power and dominance* by siding with a sports hero who viciously "sticks it" to the opponent, thereby asserting mastery and control via legitimized play. Extreme violence symbolizes powerful dominance, which in this view is seen to be highly enjoyable. Therefore, the more vicious the violence, the greater the viewers' enjoyment. The third commonly employed rationale stems from the propositions of entertainment theory, which assert that *competition and conflict are the heart and soul of drama*. We seem to enjoy conflict of various sorts in almost all of our popular entertainment fare, and sports television is, after all, entertainment fare. Sports violence is conflict at its extreme and serves to indicate to viewers that the players in this reality drama are giving all that they have to the contest, even at the risk of sustaining serious injury to themselves. The more violent the contest, the clearer the indication that the battle is being bitterly fought, and the greater the drama and the viewers' enjoyment.

Other theories can also be called upon or construed to explain at least a portion of the appeal of sports violence. In fact, Sullivan (1987) presents eight different theories—the aforementioned plus five others—that can be employed to this end. To date, no investigation has specifically addressed the comparative validity of these various explanations for the enjoyment of sports violence. Until such time as this potentially valuable theory testing and refinement is undertaken, scholars' epistemological biases and the more objective general criteria normally called upon to judge the soundness of theory must be employed to select one or several reasons for the popularity of sports violence. But good reasons do abound.

Are There Limits to the Amount of Violence Sports Viewers Will Enjoy?

We have seen that violence in sports television occurs and is featured for a very good reason: It is enjoyed by many viewers, especially by many extremely avid sports fans, who presumably are among the most loyal audience for televised sports events. We have also seen that many potentially legitimate explanations exist as to why viewers enjoy high levels of sports violence. Some of the most popular of these explanations would seem to predict that the more violence the better, as far as viewer enjoyment is concerned. Can that be true? Bryant and Zillmann (1983) have speculated about limits to the enjoyment of sports violence:

> The truism appears to be correct: At least within certain limits, sports spectators do love aggression. The limits are unclear, however. Does sports enjoyment thrive on fierce competitiveness? Or need the competition entail blood and gore, incapacitation and mutilation, even death—as some sports writers and analysts apparently believe? . . . It takes a low view of human nature, indeed, to suggest that they would. Notwithstanding speculation, research fails us at this point. The effect of injurious play in sports on spectators' enjoyment is simply not known at present. (p. 203)

Two recent investigations have shed light on these speculations. However, it should be noted at the outset that both were conducted utilizing fictionalized sports presentations, due to obvious difficulties in creating controlled stimulus materials from actual televised sporting events in which injury or death result. By employing sports fiction, generalizations to the enjoyment of live or videotaped actual sporting events are tenuous.

Bryant (1988a) attempted to create what might be described as a "worst (or best) case scenario" for the enjoyment of extreme sports violence; in this case, death. Relying on elements of entertainment theory, a number of factors that have been shown to intensify the enjoyment of violence were incorporated into the sports research purview: (a) an extremely dangerous sport, (b) viewers with a high propensity for personal violence, and (c) a hated foe. The dangerous sport employed was stock car racing. The primary footage utilized was from the movie *Greased Lightning*, starring Richard Pryor. A segment in which "redneck" race spectators demonstrate obvious contempt and hatred for Pryor's character, Wendell Scott, whom they label and scorn as "nigger," was employed as an "establishing scene." Race footage from this film was then professionally edited together with segments from two other stock car racing films to create a segment in which "the thrill of the chase" occurred and in which the outcome could be manipulated. During the race, a pileup and fiery crash were seen to occur. In one version, Scott's car was destroyed, and he obviously suffered a painful, violent death. In the second version, Scott's car miraculously emerged from the fiery crash, and he was seen alive and well.

A significant ingredient in the enjoyment of most drama is what frequently is called "disposition toward the protagonist" (e.g., Zillmann, 1980; Zillmann & Bryant, 1986). This factor has been demonstrated to be as critical to the enjoyment of sports as to that of any other entertainment fare (e.g., Zillmann et al., 1979). According to Zillmann et al. (1979), the two essential propositions of the disposition theory of sports fanship are "1. Enjoyment derived from witnessing the success and victory of a competing party increases with positive sentiments and decreases with negative sentiments toward that party. 2. Enjoyment derived from witnessing the failure and defeat of a competing party increases with negative sentiments and decreases with positive sentiments toward that party" (p. 312).

To achieve a wide range of dispositions toward the black protagonist Wendell Scott (and, likewise, toward the "redneck" opposing drivers and spectators), behavioral indices were employed initially. The study was conducted between 1985 and 1988 in four states—Alabama, North Carolina, Tennessee, and Texas. Black and white adult males, drawn predominantly from lower- and lower-middle-class populations (because of the nature of the sporting event examined), were sampled so as to form a tentative dispositional continuum: (a) whites who were active members of racist, white supremacist organizations (extremely negative disposition), (b) whites who exhibited some separatist behaviors (e.g., who enrolled their children in "white flight" private schools) but who did not belong to any active racist organizations (e.g., moderately negative disposition), (c) a mixture of whites and blacks who lived in mixed neighborhoods, whose children played in interracial groups, and so on (neutral disposition), (d) black members of black support but nonseparatist organizations such as the NAACP (moderately positive disposition), and (e) members of black separatist and supremacist organizations (extremely positive disposition).

Posttests evaluated respondents' actual dispositions toward the character Wendell Scott and toward actor Richard Pryor as well as general racial attitudes, and subjects whose self-reported dispositions differed from their preliminary assignments based on the behavioral indices (13% of the sample) were replaced prior to inspection of the data. Other tests administered to the subjects included assessments of personality factors of interest, subjects' degree of overall sports fanship, their liking for stock car racing, their personal experience in playing various sports, and their prior exposure to any of the stimulus materials employed.

Included in the various personality assessments was the Buss-Durkee Hostility Inventory. Contrary to the procedures of the investigation by Bryant and Brown (1988), a median split was performed on these data. Subjects scoring above the median were identified as "more aggression prone"; those scoring below the median were considered "less aggression prone."

A $5 \times 2 \times 2$ factorial design was employed, with independent factors of disposition toward the stock car driver (extremely negative, moderately negative, neutral, moderately positive, extremely positive), proclivity for aggression (less aggression prone, more aggression prone), and outcome for the protagonist (violent death, escape). Subjects were tested independently in whatever appropriate test sites could be arranged in their locale. In all, 16 different test sites were employed. All subjects viewed five different video-taped movie segments and rated their enjoyment of each segment. The fourth segment was one of the four versions of the stimulus materials. In this instance, since affect in response to the stimulus materials might conceivably be either negative or positive, a bipolar scale was employed on which viewers responded to the question, "How much did you enjoy the segment you just watched?" Response options ranged from "hated it" (-10) through "neither hated nor loved it" (0) to "loved it" (10). Additional entertainment-related items were also included but will not be reported at this time.

The potential main effects from this investigation are confounded conceptually and will not be considered. However, several of the significant interaction effects are meaningful and important, as can be seen from a sampling of the results. If the conditions featuring the archetypical popular entertainment scenario of a liked protagonist in a conflict situation are isolated in this investigation—accomplished by considering only the neutral, moderately positive, and extremely positive levels of disposition toward the protagonist—the findings on enjoyment fit the classic pattern of results from research on entertainment theory. Viewers in these conditions reported substantial enjoyment in response to the segment in which the race car driver escaped harm, and they disliked the version in which the hero was killed. Moreover, the more positive the disposition toward the driver, the greater the enjoyment of the "happy ending" and the greater the despair at the "sad ending." The personality variable of propensity for aggression also was involved in significant interactions, as less aggression-prone viewers liked the happy ending and disliked the sad ending more than did their more aggressively disposed peers. Indeed, viewers who reported feeling only mildly negative toward the race car driver responded with a similar pattern of mean enjoyment ratings, although the differentiation in mean scores was not significant under this disposition condition.

It was only when true hatred occurred that the pattern of results changed; and then it changed dramatically. The white supremacists whose self-reports verified that they truly hated blacks, including Wendell Scott, actually reported positive affective responses (i.e., enjoyment) after viewing the version of the race in which Scott was seen to die a violent death (mean = +2.6). In contrast, not only did they fail to enjoy, they actually disliked the version in which Scott escaped the fiery crash (mean = −3.8). White supremacists who were scored as being more aggression prone in real life were particularly intense in their hatred for the version of the race in which the black driver escaped (mean = −5.4) as well as in their enjoyment of the version in which he suffered his fiery death (mean = +3.5). In all, 10 of the 15 viewers in this latter experimental and experiential condition reported enjoyment reactions significantly greater than zero.

These findings indicate that under the right conditions, certain viewers will enjoy and even rejoice in the death of an athlete who voluntarily engages in a televised sporting event involving great risk. The conditions that permit pleasure from an athlete's death certainly may not be normative, but they are not all that rare either: What it seems to take is viewers who hate the victim intensely, although having viewers with a predilection for personal aggression is a bonus. For these viewers, it seems that sports may truly be "war minus the shooting." The only difference seems to be that in sports we legitimize the enjoyment of violent destruction by calling it entertainment.

Actually, the question of legitimizing the enjoyment of violence is very interesting in its own right. In Bryant's (1988a) investigation, the participant's death came about "within the rules of the game." In this sense, the violence might best be defined as "sanctioned aggression," because the behavior leading to death was "performed within socially agreed-upon confines" (Zillmann, 1979, p. 43). By getting into the stock car and entering of his own volition into a race that he knew involved great risks, the driver chose to place himself in jeopardy within a certain set of commonly observed conventions of what other participants in the sporting event could or could not do. Since the driver's death came about within parameters that might be expected to circumscribe viewers' perceptions of what was appropriate for this event, no intuitive notion of injustice should have been called forth that would potentially impair viewers' enjoyment of the accident, if they were so inclined via their negative dispositions toward Scott to enjoy his destruction in the first place. On the other hand, if one of the other drivers, or even a spectator, had intentionally and viciously caused the driver's wreck, viewers — even normally aggressive and bigoted viewers — might perceive this as unfair or at least something of a violation of propriety, and their enjoyment might have been bridled.

Bryant (1988b) has recently investigated the mediation by moral judgmental processes of the enjoyment of sports violence. In this investigation, special stimulus materials were produced once again, this time in an audiotape format. Because the variables were operationalized in this form, it should be noted at the outset that it is possible that the findings may not generalize to the enjoyment of televised sporting events. However, since similar events and treatments occur in television programs and even in films, such potential lack of generality is unlikely.

In science fiction books, movies, and television programs (e.g., *Max Headroom*), many writers' and directors' visions of sports in the future are filled with images of paired contestants who engage in fierce but sportive combat in which savagery is just as important to winning as are various skills. Moreover, most such futuristic games seem to conclude only when the defeated opponent is injured or killed. For the present investigation, such a futuristic sports drama was created by producing a series of original and carefully manipulated audiotaped "sportscasts." The sports event was called "screamball," and the skills required for proficiency were said to be speed skating, hurling of a steel sphere, and prowess in a fictional form of martial arts called Kwin Struk, primary functions of which could be either self-defense or aggression, specifically to injure, maim, or kill an opponent with one's bare hands.

Three independent message factors were included and manipulated so as to form a $2 \times 2 \times 4$ factorial design. The first factor was disposition toward the sports protagonist. The study was conducted in Houston, Texas, and the dispositional variation was accomplished by varying the identity of the victor/victim as being a loyal son and the city screamball champion of Houston/Dallas or of Dallas/Houston. The second factor was a moral judgmental factor that was created by having the violent defeat accomplished by sanctioned versus unsanctioned means. It was made clear to the listeners that the violence was either well within the rules of the game (sanctioned) or a flagrant and patently illegal violation of the rules (unsanctioned). The severity of the consequences of violence were varied so that the victim (a) was uninjured, (b) received a temporary injury, (c) received a crippling injury, or (d) was brutally killed.

Subjects were undergraduate males who were residents of Houston, who claimed Houston as their home, and who had reported in a pretest that they liked Houston intensely and just as intensely disliked Dallas. They listened to one version of the 12-minute stimulus materials under the pretext of evaluating a dramatized pilot radio sportscast. Enjoyment was assessed in several ways, although only ratings of enjoyment will be reported at this time.

A significant main effect for disposition indicated, in line with findings from prior sports research, that versions in which the Houston athlete defeated the Dallas foe were enjoyed far more than those featuring the opposite results; but any Rockets, Astros, or Oilers fan could tell us that! A significant main effect for the moral judgmental factor was also found: Listeners reported greater liking for the version in which the outcome was accomplished via sanctioned means than for the same outcome brought about illegally. No main effect for level of severity of the outcome of the violence was found.

The more important findings can be seen in the several significant interactions, from which only a couple of key results will be examined at present. The highest level of reported enjoyment was in response to the versions of the "sportscast" in which the Houston star *legally* bestowed either transitory injury or permanent injury on his Dallas opponent. When *illegal* means were employed, the Houston fans actually reported greater enjoyment in response to having their own player defeated noninjuriously than in hearing that the Dallas opponent was viciously maimed or killed by their star. Moral judgment clearly seems to play a major role in mediating the enjoyment of sports violence, although much remains to be done to clarify these processes and the conditions under which they occur.

Summary of Findings and Conclusions

Taken together, the findings from the research that has been presented and reviewed seem to reveal several general features of the enjoyment of viewing sports violence:

(1) It has been reaffirmed that sports telecasts can be presented and manipulated to create different levels of enjoyment for viewers and listeners. Message factors in sportscasts and other sports presentations must be taken seriously, since it is so obvious that they can have robust effects on sports fans' perceptions and on their enjoyment.

(2) Sports fans are not all alike. For example, viewers with a propensity for personal aggression tend to be particularly fond of sports violence. Those who are personally less aggression prone tend to have their enjoyment dampened by excess violence, or they may just not watch in the first place.

(3) The disposition of fans toward teams and players is consistently a potent predictor of their enjoyment of sports violence. Violence, and particularly the harm resulting from violence, must happen to the right people if

it is to be enjoyed to the fullest. In this vein, hatred is a particularly potent fuel that can propel viewers to enjoy extreme violence, even that resulting in mutilation or death, as long as a hated foe is the victim. (This may or may not be a valid claim for "real" sportscasts; it certainly seems to be so for fictionalized sports.)

(4) Moral judgmental factors are important mediators of the enjoyment of sports violence. Unsanctioned sports violence tends to result in impaired enjoyment, even if a disliked opponent is defeated via such unfair aggressive tactics.

(5) Most avid sports fans seem to enjoy extremely rough, even violent, televised sporting events, so long as dispositional factors are aligned correctly, the viewers' moral judgment is not violated, and "macho" personality factors prevail.

However, although entertainment factors seem to favor the inclusion and even the escalation of violence in sports, this does not mean that sports violence should receive an entirely clean bill of health. Critical social impact issues still have to be addressed. If player violence begets spectator and viewer violence, as is frequently claimed, and if "crowd control" and domestic violence continue to be vital issues, it will behoove social critics, entertainment theorists, and sports scholars to attempt to determine if alternative tactics to violence can be employed, especially by the media, to enable Super Spectator to wring every possible bit of pleasure from watching games without simultaneously creating latent social problems.

References

Atkin, C. K. (1985). Informational utility and selective exposure to entertainment media. In D. Zillmann & J. Bryant (Eds.), *Selective exposure to communication* (pp. 63–91). Hillsdale, NJ: Lawrence Erlbaum.

Atkin, C. K., Greenberg, B., Korzenny, F., & McDermott, S. (1979). Selective exposure to televised violence. *Journal of Broadcasting, 23,* 5–14.

Bryant, J. (1988a). [Genuine hatred and aggression-proneness as factors in the enjoyment of death and destruction in televised sports fiction]. Unpublished raw data.

Bryant, J. (1988b). [Moral judgmental factors in the enjoyment of injury and death in televised sports fiction]. Unpublished raw data.

Bryant, J., & Brown, D. (1988). [The effects of aggression-proneness and sensibilities toward sports violence on viewers' enjoyment of football]. Unpublished raw data.

Bryant, J., Comisky, P., & Zillmann, D. (1981). The appeal of rough-and-tumble play in televised professional football. *Communication Quarterly, 29,* 256–262.

Bryant, J., & Zillmann, D. (1983). Sports violence and the media. In J. H. Goldstein (Ed.), *Sports violence* (pp. 154–221). New York: Springer-Verlag.

Comisky, P., Bryant, J., & Zillmann, D. (1977). Commentary as a substitute for action. *Journal of Communication, 27*(3), 150–153.

DelNagro, M. (1988, November 12). Sports view: Quick whistle? *TV Guide*, p. 19.

Durslag, M. (1988a, October 22). Sports view: Pancakes and other rituals. *TV Guide*, p. 22.

Durslag, M. (1988b, December 3). Almighty TV. *TV Guide*, p. 27.

Edge Gel presents: The 1988-89 NBA preview. (1988, November 7). *Newsweek*, p. 4.

Eron, L., & Huesmann, L. (1980). Adolescent aggression and television. *Annals of the New York Academy of Sciences, 347*, 319–331.

Fensch, T. (1988). *The sports writing handbook*. Hillsdale, NJ: Lawrence Erlbaum.

Goldstein, J. H. (Ed.). (1983). *Sports violence*. New York: Springer-Verlag.

Gunter, B. (1985). *Dimensions of television violence*. Hants, England: Gower.

Huesmann, L. (1982). Television violence and aggressive behavior. In D. Pearl, L. Bouthilet, & J. Lazar (Eds.), *Television and behavior: Ten years of scientific progress and implications for the eighties* (pp. 126–137). Rockville, MD: U.S. Department of Health and Human Services.

Huesmann, L. R., & Eron, L. D. (Eds.). (1986). *Television and the aggressive child: A cross-national comparison*. Hillsdale, NJ: Lawrence Erlbaum.

Johnson, W. O., Jr. (1971). *Super Spectator and the electric Lilliputians*. Boston: Little, Brown.

Neff, G. (1988, April 18). The never-ending story. *Sports Illustrated*, pp. 21, 24.

Rapaport, D. (1984). *T.V. sports violence: Factors which influence the replay of violence in televised sports*. Unpublished master's thesis, San Francisco State University.

Sullivan, D. B. (1987). *The effects of sports television commentary on viewer perception of overt player hostility*. Unpublished master's thesis, University of Hartford, CT.

Swift, E. M. (1986, February 17). Hockey? Call it sockey. *Sports Illustrated*, pp. 12–17.

Zillmann, D. (1979). *Hostility and aggression*. Hillsdale, NJ: Lawrence Erlbaum.

Zillmann, D. (1980). Anatomy of suspense. In P. H. Tannenbaum (Ed.), *The entertainment functions of television* (pp. 133–163). Hillsdale, NJ: Lawrence Erlbaum.

Zillmann, D., & Bryant, J. (1986). Exploring the entertainment experience. In J. Bryant & D. Zillmann (Eds.), *Perspectives on media effects* (pp. 313–324). Hillsdale, NJ: Lawrence Erlbaum.

Zillmann, D., Bryant, J., & Sapolsky, B. S. (1979). The enjoyment of watching sports contests. In J. H. Goldstein (Ed.), *Sports, games and play: Social and psychological viewpoints* (pp. 297–335). Hillsdale, NJ: Lawrence Erlbaum.

13

Sex Typing, Sports Interests, and Relational Harmony

Michael E. Roloff
Denise H. Solomon

> They [men] baffle me. They'll send in a whole list of every sport they either play or are interested in, saying that they're looking for a woman with the same interests and who is very good-looking and slender. Now how many women are into rugby, handball, curling, hockey, football, baseball, squash and basketball?
>
> —Pam Berns,
> publisher of *Chicago Life* (a magazine focused on personal ads for singles; *Chicago Tribune*, February 14, 1988, p. 7 of TempoWoman)

The observation expressed in the opening quotation is consistent with the popularly held belief that sports are by and large a masculine domain (Harris, 1980). Moreover, it implies that this sexual segregation is a source of relational incompatibility. A similar idea is evidenced in such terms as "football widow" and "golf widow."

Empirical evidence supports the notion that males are more likely than females to participate in sports (Szalai, Converse, Feldheim, Scheuch, & Stone, 1973), to prefer watching them on television (Gantz, 1981, 1985; Prisuta, 1979; Zuckerman, Singer, & Singer, 1980), and to seek a relational partner who shares such an interest (Bolig, Stein, & McKenry, 1984). While some scholars have speculated that this differential interest may lead to relational divisiveness (Loy, McPherson, & Kenyon, 1978), there is scant empirical documentation addressing this issue (see Gantz, 1985, as an exception).

The dearth of scholarly activity is both surprising and regrettable given the consuming role sports appear to play in the lives of some males (Smith, Patterson, Williams, & Hogg, 1981), the importance of *shared interests* as a source of relational satisfaction (Argyle & Furnham, 1983), and societal interest in identifying the sources of relational disharmony and instability. To address this deficiency, we will advance a series of arguments that link sports to the dynamics of interpersonal relationships and report the results of an exploratory study that tested hypotheses emerging from our perspective.

The Role of Sports in Interpersonal Relationships

In addition to the scarcity of empirical research examining the role of sports in relationships, there has been no attempt to link sports and relational activities conceptually; therefore, there is no basis from which to deduce testable hypotheses. In this section, we will explicate our perspective and derive a series of predictions from it.

We define sports broadly as athletic activity performed for pleasure, exercise, and/or competition. Sports may vary in the degree to which they are organized, team or individually oriented, or rule governed. Interest in a given sport may be manifested in direct participation or vicarious involvement, such as attending sporting events or viewing the activity on television (Redekop, 1984). Although direct and vicarious involvement may differ in some respects, there is evidence that individuals who enjoy watching and reading about sports also directly participate in sports on a regular basis (Smith et al., 1981). Consequently, we start with the simplifying assumption that direct and vicarious involvement are equivalent indicators of interest.

Our perspective is embodied in five arguments. *First, we believe that interpersonal relationships are important sources of rewards.* People are attracted to and stay in relationships because they accrue benefits and gratifications that are superior to those derived from solitary existence. This assumption is consistent with relational perspectives derived from social exchange theories (Roloff, 1981) and symbolic interactionism (McCall & Simmons, 1978), and supported by empirical research documenting the association between rewards and increased interpersonal attraction (Davis, 1981) and relationship satisfaction (Berg, 1984; Cate, Lloyd, Henton, & Larson, 1982; Hays, 1985; Michaels, Edwards, & Acock, 1984; Rettig & Bubolz, 1983; Rusbult, 1980).

Second, we argue that shared interests in activities are primary bases of relational rewards. While some rewards can be achieved through individual action (e.g., satisfaction gained from attending a play by oneself), engaging in a rewarding activity with someone who also finds it enjoyable may add to the pleasure resulting from the activity, especially if the other person is someone to whom we are attracted. Conversely, being involved with someone who does *not* share our interests may detract from an enjoyable activity and may be particularly unpleasant. When interests diverge, relational partners may have to sacrifice involvement in a pleasurable activity, persuade/coerce the reluctant partner to participate, or engage in the activity without the partner.

The empirical support for our argument is impressive and suggests that shared interests are a source of satisfaction across a variety of interpersonal relationships (Argyle & Furnham, 1983; Berg, 1984; Birchler, Weiss, & Vincent, 1975; Jacobson, Waldron, & Moore, 1980; La Gaipa, 1977), are better predictors of interpersonal attraction than similar attitudes (Davis, 1981; Werner & Parmelee, 1979), and are utilized as a strategy to increase attractiveness (Bell & Daly, 1984). Furthermore, having dissimilar interests is frequently cited as a reason for a failed dating (Hill, Rubin, & Peplau, 1976) or marital relationship (Kitson & Sussman, 1982). Thus common interests are critical bonds in interpersonal relationships.

Third, we argue that because of sex typing, sports constitute a source of both conflicting and similar interests within opposite-sex relationships. Sports have traditionally embodied masculine ideals such as strength, bravery, aggressiveness, and competitiveness (King & Chi, 1979), and some scholars have argued that interest and success in sports are seen as proof of one's masculinity (e.g., Stein & Hoffman, 1978) and the absence of femininity (e.g., Harris, 1980). This masculine orientation has created a situation in which male interest in sports and identification with sports ideals is not only more likely (Stensaasen, 1981), but also more socially acceptable than female involvement.

Their primarily masculine nature suggests that sports will not be a shared interest within heterosexual relationships. Supporting this, Gantz (1981) found that females reported watching televised sports only when nothing else was on, there was nothing else to do, or family and friends were also watching. By contrast, males watched TV sports "to have a few beers, to let off steam, to get psyched, to experience some additional excitement—as well as to pick up additional information about players" (p. 267). Females appear "trapped" into watching, whereas males seem to be sincerely interested and derive enjoyment from it.

These differences imply that sports-related conflict may be a natural by-product of opposite-sex relationships. For example, Gantz (1985) reports that husbands had greater interest in watching televised sports than did wives, and wives perceived their husbands enjoyed watching sports programs more than they did. More important, the greater the discrepancy between the spouses' interests in sports programming, the more likely TV was perceived to interfere with leisure time, the greater the annoyance when only one spouse watched TV, the more one spouse felt ignored when the other was watching, and the less likely TV was viewed as a shared activity or basis of discussion. These latter findings are consistent with those of Smith et al. (1981), who discovered that 26% of a sample of avid male sports fans reported that their interests were a source of friction with their family and that their wives complained the family was neglected, time was wasted, and the TV was monopolized.

While the evidence suggests sports promote relational dissimilarity, research has focused primarily on televised sports that tend to be masculine (A. C. Nielsen Company, 1976) and mainly involve male athletes (deVarona et al., 1987). Therefore, it is not possible to determine whether all sports or only those that are typically perceived to be masculine are sources of dissimilarity.

Matteo (1986) found that not all sports are viewed as masculine. When a college sample was asked to rate the gender orientation of 68 sports, 30 were considered masculine, 26 neutral, and 12 feminine. When reporting their participation in the sports, *both* males and females indicated the most experience and commitment to neutral sports followed by sex-appropriate (e.g., males playing masculine sports) and sex-inappropriate sports (e.g., males playing feminine sports). While males reported greater prior activity with neutral sports than did females, these gender-neutral activities may constitute a source of relational commonality rather than friction. Given that neutral sports have no identification with either gender, males and females may jointly participate in them with less fear of the social pressures associated with engaging in sex-inappropriate sports (Harris, 1980). Moreover, prior experience with and interests in gender-neutral sports make them activities that may be shared throughout the course of relational development (dating through marriage), rather than ones that must be acquired or tolerated as a condition of the relationship. Unfortunately, we found no research testing this notion.

Our fourth argument is that a person's sex role orientation will also affect whether sports are a source of conflict or similarity. While Matteo (1986) discovered that, in general, males evidenced greater commitment to masculine sports than did females, and females expressed greater commitment to feminine sports than did males, this relationship was tempered by the sex role orientation of the individual. Using Bem's (1981) gender schema theory as a base, Matteo (1986) discovered that males who are androgynous (high in masculinity and femininity) or undifferentiated (low in both masculinity and femininity) reported significantly greater experience and commitment to feminine sports than did sex-typed males (high in masculinity and low femininity). Also, androgynous (high in masculinity and femininity) and cross-sex (high in masculinity and low in femininity) females reported greater commitment to masculine sports than did sex-typed females (high in femininity and low in masculinity). Consistent with research indicating that female athletes score higher in androgyny than their nonathletic counterparts (Harris, 1980; Marsh & Jackson, 1986), androgynous and cross-sex females in Matteo's sample reported greater experience with feminine, neutral, and masculine sports.

Matteo's (1986) research suggests that sex typing may be related to the role sports play in opposite-sex relationships. Males with flexible sex role orientations have interests in a variety of sports, including those considered feminine; hence their female partners' interests in sports may be a source of similarity rather than conflict. Moreover, androgynous and cross-sex females seem more likely to share interests in masculine sports (and sports in general) with their male partners. Therefore, only sex-typed males and females may find sports to be a source of relational conflict. While this is a plausible speculation, we found no research testing it.

Our final argument is that shared interests in sports promote relational satisfaction and stability, while dissimilarity in the sports domain is a source of relational disharmony. As noted earlier, shared interests are important sources of rewards for interpersonal relationships. To the extent that such shared interests are absent and/or dissimilar interests are present, relational difficulties may emerge.

Again, limited research has investigated this possibility. Chadwick, Albrecht, and Kunz (1976) found that among both husbands and wives marital satisfaction was positively correlated with spouse's conformity to expectations about recreational activities, and the frequency of disagreement about recreational activity was negatively related to the likelihood they would marry their partners again if given a choice. A similar pattern was observed in Gantz's (1985) study, where discrepant interests in watching televised sports were positively related to seeing TV as a relational irritant. However, neither of these studies found a significant relationship between frequency of disagreement about sports or recreational activities and marital satisfaction. This is not entirely surprising, since marital satisfaction may be a function of a variety of factors (e.g., Rettig & Bubolz, 1983) and the decision to stay in a marriage is a function not only of relational benefits but also of economic and social costs associated with divorce (Booth, Johnson, White, & Edwards, 1985; Levinger, 1976). Thus, while divergent sports interests will be negatively correlated with satisfaction and stability, the magnitude of the association may not be large.

To summarize, we believe that sports can be a source of relational satisfaction or discord, and the influence of sports depends upon the sex typing of the activity and gender role orientation of the individuals. Since we found no research directly testing our speculation, we conducted an exploratory test of hypotheses derived from our arguments.

We clustered the hypotheses into three groups. The first set focuses on sports as a source of conflict in heterosexual relationships. These hypotheses are based upon the observation that *in general*, interest in sports is higher among males than among females and therefore increased involvement by males is a primary source of relational conflict about sports. Furthermore, we noted that sex-inappropriate sports are more frequent irritations than are neutral or sex-appropriate ones. Finally, we speculated that individuals who are sex-typed would be especially likely to view sports as a source of relational conflict. The hypotheses are as follows:

H1: When describing sports that they enjoy but their relational partners do not, males will list significantly more sports than will females.

H2: When describing sports that they enjoy but their relational partners do not, males will list significantly more masculine sports than neutral or feminine sports.

H3: When describing sports that they enjoy but their relational partners do not, females will list significantly more feminine sports than neutral or masculine sports.

H4: When describing sports that they do not enjoy but their relational partners do, females will list significantly more sports than will males.

H5: When describing sports that they do not enjoy but their relational partners do, females will list significantly more masculine sports than neutral or feminine sports.

H6: When describing sports that they do not enjoy but their relational partners do, males will list significantly more feminine sports than neutral or masculine sports.

H7: Among males, masculinity will be positively related to (a) the number of sports males enjoy but their partners do not, (b) the number of masculine sports males enjoy but their partners do not, (c) the number of sports their partners enjoy but males do not, and (d) the number of feminine sports their partners enjoy but males do not.

H8: Among females, femininity will be positively related to (a) the number of sports the females enjoy but their partners do not, (b) the number of feminine sports the females enjoy but their partners do not, (c) the number of sports their partners enjoy but they do not, and (d) the number of masculine sports their partner enjoy but they do not.

H9: Among males and females, androgyny will be negatively related to the number of sports that only one relational partner enjoys.

The second set of hypotheses focuses on similarity of interests in sports. Based upon our belief that gender-neutral sports are a basis of similar interests and that androgynous individuals have a broader range of interests in sports, we hypothesize the following:

H10: For both males and females, when describing sports that both relational partners enjoy, more neutral than masculine or feminine sports will be listed.

H11: Among both males and females, androgyny will be positively related to the number of sports both relational partners enjoy.

The final set of hypotheses deals with the effects of similar or conflicting sports interests on the relationship:

H12: The greater the number of sports that *only one* partner enjoys, the lower the relational satisfaction and the less stable the relationship.

H13: The greater the number of sports that *both* partners enjoy, the higher the relational satisfaction and the more stable the relationship.

Methods

Sample

A total of 103 individuals (39 males and 64 females) participated in this study. All were enrolled in undergraduate communication courses at Northwestern University. While participants ranged in age from 18 to 35, 97% of the sample was 18 to 22 years of age. With reference to sports experience,

89% indicated current or previous participation on at least one organized sports team. While males reported participation on more teams ($M = 3.02$, $SD = 1.92$) than did females ($M = 2.52$, $SD = 1.84$), this difference was not statistically significant ($t = 1.32$, df $= 100$, $p < .19$). Matteo (1986) also found a nonsignificant difference in overall sports participation in a college sample.

Procedure

Students in communication courses were invited to participate in this study in exchange for extra course credit. Questionnaires were distributed in group settings, and participants were verbally directed to our definition of sports. That definition was also presented at the beginning of the questionnaire in the following manner:

> We view a sport as any athletic activity performed for pleasure, exercise, and/or competition. Hence, it may be performed at the team (e.g., football) or individual level (e.g., racquetball), may be primarily for exercise (e.g., aerobics) or competition (e.g., basketball) and may have many rules (e.g., baseball) or few (e.g., jogging).

The remaining portion of the questionnaire consisted of two counterbalanced sets of items. One set assessed the respondent's sex role orientation, and the second focused on the role of sports in the respondent's romantic relationship. On the questionnaire, a romantic relationship was defined as at *least* casual dating. If a participant had no current romantic involvement, that individual could report on the most recent romance. The one respondent indicating *never* having been romantically involved was deleted from all analyses. Most participants (93%) described their current or past relationships as either steady or casual dating; the remainder indicated that they were engaged to, living with, or married to their partners.

Measures

Conflict. Deutsch (1973) defines conflict as the occurrence of incompatible activities. Our three measures of interpersonal conflict reflect an emphasis on conflicting preferences for involvement in sports-related activities. Specifically, respondents were asked to identify on three separate questions up to five sports that (1) the partner enjoyed, but the respondent did not; (2) the respondent enjoyed, but the partner did not; and (3) the respondent and the partner both enjoyed, but did not enjoy together. The presence of all three types of conflict was assessed across three levels of sports involvement: actual participation, TV viewing, and attendance at sporting events. For descriptive purposes, the frequency of arguing about different sports preferences (the first two types of conflict) was assessed on two 7-point scales (1 = infrequently, never; 7 = frequently, all the time). Alphas for the sum of the two items exceeded .96. Respondents were also asked if they had told their partners that they did not enjoy playing, watching on TV, or attending a sporting event the partner enjoyed.

For exploratory purposes, we asked about the frequency of involvement in sports listed as sources of conflict. All assessments were made on two 7-point scales (1 = infrequently, never; 7 = frequently, all the time). Respondents indicated the frequency of their involvement in sports that their partners enjoyed but they did not and sports they enjoyed but their partners did not (alphas > .62), the frequency of partner involvement in sports the respondent did not enjoy but the partner did (alphas > .95), and the frequency with which they and their partners engaged in sports-related activity they both enjoyed but not together (alphas > .75).

Similarity. To assess the degree of compatible joint sports involvement, we asked participants to identify up to five sports that they and their partners enjoyed together. Similarities were measured across the three levels of sports involvement noted earlier: actual participation, TV viewing, and attendance at sports events. The frequency of joint participation was assessed for all levels of involvement by two 7-point scales (1 = infrequently, never; 7 = frequently, all the time). Alphas for the summed index exceeded .92.

Gender orientation of sports. Because some of our hypotheses focused on sports having different gender orientations, we conducted a supplementary study to assess the masculinity/femininity of *each* sport listed as a source of conflict *or* similarity. A total of 22 individuals (11 males and 11 females) were recruited for extra class credit from the aforementioned student population. The 60 sports identified as sources of conflict or similarity in the main study were rated by each respondent on a 9-point scale (1 = strongly masculine; 5 = neutral; 9 = strongly feminine).

The 60 sports were divided into masculine, feminine, and neutral categories according to the following scheme: Sports with mean ratings between 1.0 to 3.9 were considered masculine, between 4.0 and 6.9 were considered neutral, and between 7.0 and 9.0 were feminine. After this categorization, t-tests contrasted the masculine and feminine sports from the neutral point (and midpoint) of the scale (5). Using an alpha level of .01, we found that all the masculine and feminine sports were significantly different from the neutral point of the scale. As a further check, we discovered that the ratings of the sports were generally unaffected by the respondent's gender (only 1 out of 60 t-tests was significant) or their sex role orientation as measured by Bem Sex Role Inventory (only 5 out of 60 correlations were significant). These tests suggest sports are viewed by all respondents in similar fashion.

Sex role orientation. Participants completed the Bem Sex Role Inventory (Bem, 1974), which includes 20 self-report items measuring masculinity and 20 assessing femininity. Respondents indicated on 7-point scales the extent to which each item was an accurate self-descriptor. The alphas were .85 for masculinity and .78 for femininity. For our sample, there was significantly greater ($t = 2.58$, df = 101, $p < .01$) masculinity among males ($M = 108.31$, $SD = 13.29$) than among females ($M = 101.86$, $SD = 11.69$), and significantly greater femininity ($t = 4.24$, df = 101, $p < .001$) among females ($M = 100.08$, $SD = 10.26$) than among males ($M = 91.13$, $SD = 10.61$).

Relational stability. Participants not currently involved in a romantic relationship were instructed to describe sports conflict and similarity that occurred in a *lapsed* relationship. We used current romantic involvement as our measure of stability. Of the total sample, 60 respondents were currently involved in the relationships they described; the remaining 43 referred to past romantic involvements.

Relational satisfaction. The 60 respondents currently involved in romantic relationships were asked to indicate their feelings about the relationships on five 7-point scales (1 = not satisfied at all, very angry, not content at all, not happy at all, not stable at all; 7 = very satisfied, not angry at all, very content, very happy, very stable). Coefficient alpha for the sum of these items was .93.

Results

The results are divided into sections corresponding to the three sets of hypotheses: conflict, similarity, and relational effects. Within each section, we will report descriptive data about the occurrence and nature of sport involvement in relational life as well as specific tests of the thirteen hypotheses.

Conflict

Originally, we included three types of interpersonal conflict over sports; however, conflicts in which both parties enjoyed a sport but did not enjoy playing, watching, or attending together occurred so infrequently that they could not be reasonably analyzed. Therefore, all analyses focused on conflicts due to different preferences.

Table 13.1 contains descriptive data about conflict over sports. Several patterns are apparent. First, roughly half of the sample reported at least one sport that one partner enjoyed playing or watching on TV but the other partner did not. This proportion is much lower when reporting different preferences for attending sporting events. Perhaps attending athletic events together is primarily considered dating activity, and the athletic nature of the specific event is overshadowed by and incidental to being together. The data also indicate that half of the respondents reporting different sports preferences report having told their partners they dislike participating in, watching on TV, or attending a sports event the other likes. Argument about different sports preferences, however, was infrequent. Finally, when only one partner enjoyed a sport, his or her levels of participation, TV viewing, and attendance at sports events were moderate. When the respondent did not find the sport enjoyable, minimal involvement was reported. Unfortunately, we cannot ascertain from these data whether the differing degrees of involvement represent exclusion or deliberate avoidance by the less interested partner.

Table 13.2 contains data illustrating the total number of sports that only one partner enjoys as reported by males and females. When comparing the number of sports respondents say they enjoy but their partners do not, a significant multivariate F for gender was observed. Consistent with H1, males report more sports they enjoy playing, watching on TV, and attending than do females. It should be noted that the univariate F for participation only approached significance ($p < .08$) and the one for attendance was clearly not significant ($p < .50$). Thus gender differences were more strongly evidenced for TV watching than other indicators of sports interest.

Stronger evidence is found when examining sports that the respondent's partner enjoys but the respondent does not. Again, a significant multivariate effect for gender was observed. Consistent with H4, females report more sports their partners enjoy playing, watching on TV, and attending than do males. The univariate Fs indicate significant differences ($p < .05$) for participation and TV viewing but not attendance at sports events ($p < .59$). As before, attending sporting events is a weak source of conflict.

We also predicted that conflict over sports would vary with both the gen-

Table 13.1
Descriptive Statistics About Sports Conflicts

	Sports the Respondent Enjoys but Partner Does Not	Sports the Partner Enjoys but Respondent Does Not
Proportion who		
listed at least one sport played	.72	.58
listed at least one TV sport	.54	.45
listed at least one sport attended	.31	.15
told partner about playing	not asked	.69
told partner about TV sport	not asked	.96
told partner about attendance	not asked	.69
Frequency of		
arguing about playing	3.09	3.25
	(1.86)	(2.01)
arguing about TV sports	3.47	4.52
	(2.28)	(3.04)
arguing about attending	4.09	3.06
	(2.98)	(2.26)
self sport participation	10.67	2.44
	(3.19)	(.70)
self TV sport viewing	8.67	3.35
	(3.46)	(1.97)
self attendance	7.62	3.44
	(3.41)	(2.48)
partner's sport participation	not asked	9.73
		(3.26)
partner's TV sport viewing	not asked	9.00
		(3.47)
partner's sport attendance	not asked	8.12
		(4.21)

NOTE: Standard deviations are in parentheses. Other than the proportions, all scales ranged from 2 (low frequency) to 14 (high frequency).

der of the person and the gender orientation of the sport. Before describing the tests of these hypotheses, we need to explain our choice of statistics. The distribution of masculine, neutral, and feminine sports listed for participation, TV watching, and attendance suffered from nonnormality. Moreover, some of these variables had unequal variances for males and females and transformations did not alleviate these occurrences. Coupled with unequal cell sizes, these factors made the use of analysis of variance inappropriate. Therefore, we tested the hypotheses using nonparametric statistics.

Table 13.2

Multivariate Analysis of Number of Sports Listed on Conflict Measures

Dependent Variables	Independent Variables				
			Univariate		Multivariate
	Male	Female	F	Eta^2	F
Sports respondent enjoys but partner does not					3.83**
playing	1.55	1.41	3.13	.03	
	(1.22)	(1.08)	$p < .08$		
TV viewing	1.37	.70	9.40**	.08	
	(1.15)	(1.00)			
attending	.45	.36	< 1		
	(.72)	(.63)			
Sports partner enjoys but respondent does not					10.40**
playing[a]	1.01	1.20	4.79*	.05	
	(.37)	(.44)			
TV viewing[b]	.69	.84	30.15***	.23	
	(.10)	(.14)			
attending[a]	.78	.81	< 1		
	(.21)	(.26)			

NOTE: Cell entries are means with standard deviations in parentheses. Degrees of freedom for multivariate Fs = 3.97 and for univariate Fs = 1.99.
a. Due to unequal cell variances, this variable was transformed into square roots.
b. Due to unequal cell variances, this variable was transformed into the sine of its square root.
*$p < .05$; **$p < .001$; ***$p < .0001$.

Table 13.3 contains the data indicating the number of masculine, neutral, and feminine sports listed by males and females as sources of conflict for each of the three levels of involvement. For males and females separately, we conducted Friedman two-way analysis of variance for ranked data on the number of masculine, neutral, and feminine sports reported as sources of conflict for participation, TV watching, and attendance. Specific cell contrasts reflecting the hypotheses were done through Wilcoxon matched-pairs signed rank tests. Both of these nonparametric tests have statistical power roughly equivalent to their parametric counterparts (Siegel, 1956).

Consistent with H2, males report significantly more masculine relative to neutral and feminine sports they enjoy participating in, watching on TV, and attending but their partners do not. However, there is no support of H3. Instead of reporting conflicting enjoyment of feminine sports, females indicated more *neutral* rather than feminine or masculine sports they enjoyed

Table 13.3
Friedman Two-Way Analysis of Variance for Ranked Data
on Conflict About Masculine, Neutral, and Feminine Sports
Among Males and Females

| | *Mean Ranks* | | | |
	Masculine Sports	*Neutral Sports*	*Feminine Sports*	*Chi-Square*
Male Sample				
Sports respondent enjoys but partner does not				
playing	2.34_a	2.18_a	1.47_b	16.26***
TV viewing	2.49_a	1.95_b	1.57_c	16.27***
attending	2.30_a	1.87_b	1.83_b	5.25
				$p < .07$
Sports partner enjoys but respondent does not				
playing	1.89_a	2.09_a	2.01_a	.75
TV viewing	2.05_a	1.97_a	1.97_a	.16
attending	2.08_a	1.92_a	2.00_a	.47
Female Sample				
Sports respondent enjoys but partner does not				
playing	1.71_a	2.23_b	2.05_c	9.05**
TV viewing	1.95_a	2.23_b	1.82_a	5.77*
attending	2.02_a	2.05_a	1.93_a	.78
Sports partner enjoys but respondent does not				
playing	2.31_a	2.09_b	1.59_c	17.37***
TV viewing	2.47_a	1.87_b	1.66_c	22.41***
attending[a]	2.15_a	1.94_b	1.91_b	2.17

NOTE: Common subscripts indicate that the magnitude of the mean rank of the two cells did not differ significantly ($p < .05$) as tested by Wilcoxon matched-pairs signed-ranks test.
*$p < .05$; **$p < .01$; ***$p < .001$.

playing and watching on TV. No significant differences were observed for attendance at sports events.

There is support for H5. When reporting sports their partners enjoy but they do not, females listed significantly more masculine than neutral or feminine sports at each of three levels of involvement. However, there is no support for H6. Males did not differ in the number of masculine, feminine, or neutral sports they felt their partners enjoyed but they did not.

Thus far, male preferences for masculine sports and, to a lesser extent, female enjoyment of neutral sports appear to be sources of conflict; however, we hypothesized that this pattern should be affected by the sex role orientation of the males and females. As advocated elsewhere (Bem, 1977; Taylor & Hall, 1982), our analysis retained the continuous nature of the masculinity, femininity, and androgyny measures, rather than following the more popular route of creating nominal indicators of each. When analyzing the data, we employed a hierarchical regression approach advocated by Cohen and Cohen (1975) in which the masculinity and femininity scores were entered on the first step of a regression followed by their interaction term (the product of the two measures) on the second. The correlation between masculinity and femininity was small and nonsignificant ($r = -.09$), making the test of the interaction appropriate.

Because multiple regressions are also sensitive to the patterns found in our data (nonnormality, heteroscedasticity of variance), we created new measures that contained fewer biases. For each subject, we created three variables by subtracting (1) the number of neutral sports from the number of masculine sports, (2) the number of feminine sports from the number of masculine sports, and (3) the number of feminine sports from the number of neutral sports. Examination of their distributions yielded lower levels of skewness than the individual indicators of enjoyment of masculine, neutral, and feminine sports.

Our regressions yielded *no* support for H7, H8, and H9. Masculinity among males, femininity among females, and androgyny in the total sample did *not* account for statistically significant portions of variance in the total number of sports in which there was divergent interest of any kind. Thus only part of our perspective is accurate. Males and females do differ in their enjoyment of masculine sports participation and TV viewing, but sex role orientation plays no role.

Similarity

Our similarity hypotheses were focused on shared enjoyment of mutual involvement with sports. We found greater similarity than conflicting interests in sport. In this sample, 72% of the respondents listed at least one sport they both enjoyed participating in together, 63% indicated at least one sport they both enjoyed watching together on TV, and 73% reported at least one sporting event they both enjoyed attending together. They also reported

Table 13.4

Friedman Two-Way Analysis of Variance for Ranked Data
on Similar Interests in Masculine, Neutral, and Feminine
Sports Among Males and Females

| | Mean Ranks | | | |
	Masculine Sports	*Neutral Sports*	*Feminine Sports*	*Chi-Square*
Male Sample				
Sports both parties enjoy playing together	1.91_a	2.54_b	1.55_c	18.98***
Sports both parties enjoy watching on TV together	2.22_a	2.14_a	1.63_b	7.85**
Sports both parties enjoy attending together	2.62_a	1.75_b	1.63_c	22.06***
Female Sample				
Sports both parties enjoy playing together	1.88_a	2.59_b	1.52_c	37.98***
Sports both parties enjoy watching on TV together	2.49_a	1.95_b	1.55_c	28.33***
Sports both parties enjoy attending together	2.70_a	1.73_b	1.57_c	47.27***

NOTE: Common subscripts indicate that the magnitude of the mean rank of the two cells did not differ significantly ($p < .05$) as tested by Wilcoxon matched-pairs signed-ranks test.
*$p < .05$; **$p < .01$; ***$p < .001$.

moderate levels of joint participation ($M = 8.62$, $SD = 3.13$), TV viewing ($M = 9.05$, $SD = 3.08$), and attendance ($M = 7.59$, $SD = 3.25$).

As before, the distribution of reported sports forced us to analyze H10 through the same nonparametric statistics reported earlier. Table 13.4 contains the relevant data. Only partial support is found for H10. Both males and females report more neutral than masculine or feminine sports that they both enjoy playing together. On the TV viewing measure, both males and females listed more neutral than feminine sports, but this pattern occurred only for females on the attendance measure. However, on *both* the TV watching and attendance measures, more or equal numbers of masculine sports were listed than neutral ones.

H11 was tested using the same regression techniques employed earlier. We found absolutely no support for the hypothesis. Androgyny was not significantly related among males or females to the number of sports both part-

THE AUDIENCE FOR MEDIA SPORTS

ners enjoy together at any of the three levels of involvement. Contrary to the hypothesis, femininity among females was positively related to the number of sports both parties enjoyed participating in together (beta = .37, $p < .003$), watching on TV (beta = .29, $p < .01$), and attending (beta = .24, $p < .054$). These relationships were of lower magnitude and not statistically significant for males.

Relational Effects

Through exploratory analysis, we discovered that neither gender nor sex role orientation was significantly related to our measures of relational satisfaction or stability; therefore, we report the tests of H12 and H13 on the total sample.

When examining the six bivariate correlations between the total number of sports only one partner enjoyed and relational satisfaction, *no* support for H12 is found. Relational satisfaction was, however, positively correlated with the total number sports both parties enjoy participating in together ($r = .41, p < .05$), watching on TV together ($r = .42, p < .05$), and attending together ($r = .27, p < .05$). This is consistent with H13. When all nine of the sports enjoyment indicators were analyzed with a stepwise multiple regression procedure, *only* the total number of televised sports both enjoy watching together was significantly correlated with relational satisfaction.

To test whether the sports indicators could predict current or lapsed romantic involvement, we examined the bivariate correlations among each of the six conflict measures, three similarity measures, and the current romantic status of the relationship being reported (currently involved was coded 1 and lapsed was coded 2). Only one of the six correlations involving conflict measures even approached significance, and it was in the wrong direction. The greater the number of sports the respondent's partner enjoyed playing but the respondent did not, the more likely the partners were still involved ($r = -.169, p < .08$). Of the three similarity measures, only the number of televised sports both partners enjoyed watching together was significantly and positively related to still being romantically involved ($r = -.195, p < .05$).

Discussion

The results provide support for some portions of our perspective. Greater male interest in sports is a more frequent source of conflict than female preferences, and this divergence centers on masculine rather than neutral or feminine sports. On the other hand, gender-neutral sports are frequent sources of similarity between the sexes when compared with feminine sports, while masculine sports are important bases of similarity for watching televised sports and attendance at sporting events. There is strong evidence that enjoyment of similar sports is positively related to relational satisfaction, and weaker support that it facilitates relational stability.

These data also indicate that our perspective needs revision in some areas and is clearly wrong in others. We advanced several hypotheses that predicted that female interests in feminine sports would be a source of conflict. That was not the case. The disconfirmation may be due to the relative lack of feminine sports. Matteo (1986) found only 12 of 68 (17.6%) sports were perceived by college students as feminine, while 26 of 68 (38%) were perceived to be gender neutral. Our data indicate that when conflict occurs over female involvement, the more common gender-neutral sports appear as sources.

We also expected that the sex role orientation of the respondent would play a role in sports conflict or similarity. Overall, none of the hypothesized relationships was observed among androgyny, masculinity, and sports preferences. More important, we found a pattern among females clearly opposite to our perspective. Among females, femininity was positively related to the number of sports both parties enjoyed together. A supplementary analysis found that femininity among the females was positively related to mutual enjoyment of masculine relative to feminine sports (playing, $r = .19$, $p < .12$; TV viewing, $r = .23$, $p < .06$; attending, $r = .22$, $p < .07$) and neutral relative to feminine sports (playing, $r = .35$, $p < .005$; TV viewing, $r = .36$, $p < .004$; attending, $r = .11$, $p < .20$). While not all correlations are statistically significant, a positive trend is evident. There was no evidence that femininity was related to preferring either masculine or feminine sports over the other.

Perhaps this unexpected pattern resulted from a redefinition of sports by feminine females. Redekop (1984) reports that wives appear to see sports as activities to be shared with family members; hence their involvement (especially TV viewing and sport attendance) occurs primarily with other family members rather than alone or with nonfamily members. We can only speculate that sports enjoyment among feminine females may stem from joint participation with their male partners, rather than from the characteristics of the sports themselves.

We also found no support for the notion that conflict over sports aversely affects relational quality. Indeed, while we have evidence that such conflict exists, and most of our sample reported having told their partners about sports they do not enjoy, argument about these differences remains infrequent.

Perhaps the ability to control the conflict stems from the stage of relationship most common in our sample. Most reported being involved in casual or steady dating. In such cases, communication about divergent interests may be avoided so as to maintain the illusion of similarity and the potential for relational escalation (Baxter & Wilmot, 1985). Therefore, while partners may have been told about differing levels of enjoyment, the avoidance of argument reduced the importance of such dissimilarity. Different results might have been found had our sample been composed of more mature relationships. Swensen, Eskew, and Kohlhepp (1981) found that spouses in marriages at later stages of relational development were less tolerant of unpleasant aspects of their loved ones. In long-term relationships, conflict avoidance may be less likely, disagreements about sports more important, and open argument about sports more frequent.

Finally, our initial assumption that all types of sport involvement are the same appears incorrect. Examination of the overall pattern of results indicates that differences and similarities related to watching televised sports are more significant than either participation or attendance. Perhaps the primary focus of television on masculine sports makes it a likely manifestation of divergent interests. Also, the relative ease with which one can become involved in televised sport (and thereby exclude the partner) could increase its saliency. As noted by respondents in Gantz's (1985) sample, when the interested party is focused on televised sports, the other feels ignored.

Future research should examine two issues. First, we urge researchers to focus on the dyad rather than the individual as the unit of analysis. Our study asked only one partner about sources of conflict and similarity in the relationship. While we believe that such information is valid for understanding the individual's perception of the relationship, that perception may not be shared by the partner (see Jacobson & Moore, 1981). Second, while we believe our data to be informative, researchers should move to longitudinal designs (see Berg, 1984; Hays, 1985) to avoid potential bias in retrospective accounts of activities in past relationships and to rule out the possibility that relational quality creates shared sport interest.

Overall, this chapter suggests a direction for studying sports in relational life. Our preliminary work leads to the tentative conclusion that under specifiable conditions, sports are sources of both divergent and convergent interests. Moreover, shared sports involvement is a characteristic of satisfied relationships. The data analysis also highlights the role of televised sports viewing as a source of significant relational differences and similarities.

References

Argyle, M., & Furnham, A. (1983). Sources of satisfaction and conflict in long-term relationships. *Journal of Marriage and the Family, 45,* 481-493.

Baxter, L. A., & Wilmot, W. W. (1985). Taboo topics in close relationships. *Journal of Social and Personal Relationships, 2,* 253-269.

Bell, R. A., & Daley, J. A. (1984). The affinity-seeking function of communication. *Communication Monographs, 51,* 91-115.

Bem, S. L. (1974). The measurement of psychological androgyny. *Journal of Consulting and Clinical Psychology, 42,* 155-162.

Bem, S. L. (1977). On the utility of alternative procedures for assessing psychological androgyny. *Journal of Consulting and Clinical Psychology, 45,* 196-205.

Bem, S. L. (1981). Gender schema theory: A cognitive account of sex typing. *Psychological Review, 88,* 354-364.

Berg, J. H. (1984). Development of friendship between roommates. *Journal of Personality and Social Psychology, 46,* 346-356

Birchler, G. R., Weiss, R. L., & Vincent, J. P. (1975). Multimethod analysis of social reinforcement exchange between maritally distressed and nondistressed spouse and stranger dyads. *Journal of Personality and Social Psychology, 31,* 349-360.

Bolig, R., Stein, P. J., & McKenry, P. C. (1984). The self-advertisement approach to dating: Male-female differences. *Family Relations, 33,* 587-592.

Booth, A., Johnson, D. R., White, L. K., & Edwards, J. N. (1985). Predicting divorce and permanent separation. *Journal of Family Issues, 6,* 331-346.

Cate, R. M., Lloyd, S. A., Henton, J. M., & Larson, J. H. (1982). Fairness and reward level as predictors of relationship satisfaction. *Social Psychology Quarterly, 45,* 177-181.

Chadwick, B. A., Albrecht, S. L., & Kunz, P. R. (1976). Marital and family role satisfaction. *Journal of Marriage and the Family, 38,* 431-440.

Cohen, J., & Cohen, P. (1975). *Applied multiple regression/correlation analysis for the behavioral sciences.* Hillsdale, NJ: Lawrence Erlbaum.

Davis, D. (1981). Implications for interactions versus effectance as mediators of the similarity-attraction relationship. *Journal of Experimental Social Psychology, 17,* 96-116.

Deutsch, M. (1973). *The resolution of conflict.* New Haven, CT: Yale University Press.

deVarona, D., Auchincloss, E., DeFrantz, A., Grant, C., Harris, D., & Visser, L. (1987). Women's sports and the media. *Gannett Center Journal, 1,* 56-75.

Gantz, W. (1981). An exploration of viewing motives and behaviors associated with television sports. *Journal of Broadcasting, 25,* 283-286.

Gantz, W. (1985). Exploring the role of television in married life. *Journal of Broadcasting and Electronic Media, 29,* 65-78.

Harris, D. V. (1980). Femininity and athleticism: Conflict or consonance? In D. F. Sabo & R. Rubola (Eds.), *Jock: Sports and male identity* (pp. 222-239). Englewood Cliffs, NJ: Prentice-Hall.

Hays, R. B. (1985). A longitudinal study of friendship development. *Journal of Personality and Social Psychology, 48,* 909-924.

Hill, C. T., Rubin, Z., & Peplau, L. A. (1976). Breakups before marriage: The end of 103 affairs. *Journal of Social Issues, 32,* 147-168.

Jacobson, N. S., & Moore, D. (1981). Spouses as observers of the events in their relationship. *Journal of Consulting and Clinical Psychology, 49*, 269–277.

Jacobson, N. S., Waldron, H., & Moore, D. (1980). Toward a behavioral profile of marital distress. *Journal of Consulting and Clinical Psychology, 48*, 696–703.

King, J. P., & Chi, P.S.K. (1979). Social structure, sex-roles, and personality: Comparisons of male-female athletes/nonathletes. In J. H. Goldstein (Ed.), *Sports, games, and play* (pp. 115–148). Hillsdale, NJ: Lawrence Erlbaum.

Kitson, G. C., & Sussman, M. B. (1982). Marital complaints, demographic characteristics, and symptoms of mental distress in divorce. *Journal of Marriage and the Family, 44*, 87–101.

La Gaipa, J. J. (1977). Testing a multidimensional approach to friendship. In S. Duck (Ed.), *Theory and practice in interpersonal attraction* (pp. 249–270). New York: Academic Press.

Levinger, G. (1976). A social psychological perspective on marital dissolution. *Journal of Social Issues, 32*, 21–42.

Loy, J. W., McPherson, B. D., & Kenyon, G. (1978). *Sports and social systems*. Reading, MA: Addison-Wesley.

Marsh, H. W., & Jackson, S.A. (1986). Multidimensional self-concepts, masculinity, and femininity as a function of women's involvement in athletics. *Sex Roles, 15*, 391–415.

Matteo, S. (1986). The effect of sex and gender-schematic processing on sport participation. *Sex Roles, 15*, 417–432.

McCall, G., & Simmons, J. (1978). *Identities and interactions: An examination of human associations in everyday life* (rev. ed.). New York: Macmillan.

Michaels, J. W., Edwards, J. N., & Acock, A. C. (1984). Satisfaction in intimate relationships as a function of inequality, inequity, and outcomes. *Social Psychology Quarterly, 47*, 347–357.

A. C. Nielsen Company. (1976). *Let's look at sports*. Chicago: Author.

Prisuta, R. H. (1979). Televised sports and political values. *Journal of Communication, 29*, 94–102.

Redekop, P. (1984). Sport and the masculine ethos: Some implications for family interaction. *International Journal of Comparative Sociology, 25*, 262–269.

Rettig, K. D., & Bubolz, M. M. (1983). Interpersonal resource exchanges as indicators of quality of marriage. *Journal of Marriage and the Family, 45*, 497–509.

Roloff, M. E. (1981). *Interpersonal communication: The social exchange approach*. Beverly Hills, CA: Sage.

Rusbult, C. E. (1980). Satisfaction and commitment in friendships. *Representative Research in Social Psychology, 11*, 96–105.

Siegel, S. (1956). *Nonparametric statistics for the behavioral sciences*. New York: McGraw-Hill.

Smith, G. J., Patterson, B., Williams, T., & Hogg, J. (1981). A profile of the deeply committed male sports fan. *Arena Review, 5*, 26–44.

Stein, P. J., & Hoffman, S. (1978). Sports and male role strain. *Journal of Social Issues, 34*, 136–150.

Stensaasen, S. (1981). Sport ideal and sport involvement among adolescents. *International Review of Sport Sociology, 4*, 63–79.

Swensen, C. H., Eskew, R.W., & Kohlhepp, K. A. (1981). Stage of family life cycle, ego development, and the marriage relationship. *Journal of Marriage and the Family, 43*, 841–853.

Szalai, A., Converse, P. E., Feldheim, P., Scheuch, E., & Stone, P. J. (1973). *The use of time-daily activities of urban and suburban populations in twelve countries.* The Hague: Mouton.

Taylor, M. C., & Hall, J. A. (1982). Psychological androgyny: Theories, methods, and conclusion. *Psychological Bulletin, 92,* 347–366.

Werner, C., & Parmelee, P. (1979). Similarity of activity preferences among friends: Those who play together stay together. *Social Psychology Quarterly, 42,* 62–66.

Zuckerman, D. M., Singer, D. G., & Singer, J. L. (1980). Children's television viewing, racial and sex-role attitudes. *Journal of Applied Social Psychology, 10,* 281–294.

About the Contributors

Robert V. Bellamy, Jr. (Ph.D., University of Iowa, 1985) is Associate Professor of Communication at Duquesne University in Pittsburgh. A program consultant and former program director, he has research interests in programming, media history, and economic relationships between media institutions and other industries. His work has appeared in such publications as the *Journal of Broadcasting & Electronic Media* and the *Journal of Communication*.

Jennings Bryant (Ph.D., Indiana University, 1974) is Professor and holds the Ronald Reagan Chair of Communication in the College of Communication at the University of Alabama. His research interests are in the areas of mass communication theory, processes, and effects.

Lewis Donohew (Ph.D., University of Iowa) is Professor of Communication at the University of Kentucky. He is currently principal investigator on a National Institute on Drug Abuse-funded study on the effects of drug abuse prevention messages. He is coeditor of *Communication, Social Cognition, and Affect* (Erlbaum) and a special issue of *American Behavioral Scientist* on communication and affect.

Susan Tyler Eastman (Ph.D., Bowling Green University) is Associate Professor of Telecommunications at Indiana University, Bloomington. She is senior author/editor of *Broadcast/Cable Programming* (Wadsworth, 1989) and *Strategies in Broadcast and Cable Promotion* (Waveland, 1988), and contributing author to *Broadcasting in America* (Houghton Mifflin, 1987), as well as author of other books, chapters, and scholarly articles. Her research interests include broadcast programming and economics, new technologies, computers and writing, and sports communication.

Walter Gantz (Ph.D., Michigan State University, 1975) is Associate Professor of Telecommunications and Director of the Institute for Communication Research at Indiana University, Bloomington. His research focuses on the uses and impact of media in everyday life, with special interests in the impact of sports in marital life and the diffusion of news events. He teaches courses on media effects and advertising. A former collegiate cross-country coach and marathon runner, he remains an avid runner today.

Richard Gruneau teaches communication and cultural studies at Simon Fraser University. He has written widely in both fields and his publications include *Popular Cultures and Political Practices* (Garamond), *Class, Sports, and Social Development* (University of Massachusetts Press), *Sport, Culture, and the Modern State* (University of Toronto Press), and *Canadian Sport: Sociological Perspectives* (Addison-Wesley).

John Haas is a doctoral student in organizational communication at the University of Kentucky. His research interests focus on communication and social cognition, and his publications include a chapter on that subject in *Communication, Social Cognition, and Affect*.

David Helm is a doctoral student in mass communication at the University of Kentucky and a research assistant on a National Institute on Drug Abuse project. His research interests focus on media uses and effects, including expectancy-value approaches to the moviegoing experience.

Sut Jhally is Associate Professor of Communication at the University of Massachusetts at Amherst. He is author of *The Codes of Advertising*, coauthor of *Social Communication in Advertising*, and coeditor of *Cultural Politics in Contemporary America*.

Robert W. McChesney is Assistant Professor of Journalism and Mass Communication at the University of Wisconsin – Madison. He has published in several journals and yearbooks on media history, broadcast policy, and issues relating to free expression and the exercise of democracy under the conditions of modern capitalism. A former publisher of a weekly newspaper and rock magazine, he also served as a sports stringer for United Press International from 1979 to 1986.

Timothy P. Meyer is Rosenberg Professor at the University of Wisconsin – Green Bay. He has authored more than 100 books, book chapters, and journal articles. He recently coauthored *Mediated Communication: A Social Interaction Approach* (Sage, 1988). His research interests include the process and impact of mediated communication, programming and audience research, advertising and consumer behavior, and management and organizational communication.

Michael R. Real (Ph.D., University of Illinois) is Professor and Chair of Telecommunications and Film at San Diego State University. He is the author of *Super Media: A Cultural Studies Approach* (Sage, 1989) and *Mass-Mediated Culture* (Prentice-Hall, 1977). He has also authored numerous studies of mass media and contemporary culture in the *Journal of Communication, Journal of Popular Culture, Media Development, Journalism Quarterly, American Quarterly, Newsday*, and other places. In addition, he has produced television series on the problems of science and technology and issues of aging.

Michael E. Roloff (Ph.D, Michigan State, 1975) is Professor of Communication Studies at Northwestern University. His research interests include social exchange in intimate relationships, interpersonal conflict resolution, bargaining and negotiation, and persuasion. He is the author of *Interpersonal Communication: The Social Exchange Approach* and coeditor of *Persuasion: New Directions in Theory and Research*; *Interpersonal Processes: New Directions in Communication Research*; and *Social Cognition and Communication* (all from Sage Publications).

Denise H. Solomon is a doctoral student in communication studies at Northwestern University. Her research interests include coping strategies in distressed relationships, intercultural interaction, and gender differences in communication.

Nick Trujillo (Ph.D., University of Utah, 1983) is Assistant Professor in the Center for Communication Arts at Southern Methodist University. He has published numerous books chapters and articles in such journals as *Communication Monographs, Critical Studies in Mass Communication, Management Communication Quarterly*, and *Public Relations Review*. He recently authored a case study on the Texas Rangers baseball organization (Guilford, 1989).

Leah R. Vande Berg (Ph.D., University of Iowa, 1981) is Assistant Professor and Graduate Director in the Center for Communication Arts at

Southern Methodist University. She has published in such journals as *Critical Studies in Mass Communication, Journalism Quarterly,* and *Western Journal of Speech Communication.* She recently coauthored *Organizational Life on Television* (Ablex, 1988) with Nick Trujillo. Her research interests include television criticism, sports communication, and ethics in news.

Lawrence A. Wenner is Associate Dean of the College of Arts and Science and Professor of Communication Arts at the University of San Francisco where he holds the Louise M. Davies Chair of Contemporary Values in America for 1989–90. Formerly he was Director of the Media Studies and Management Programs at Loyola Marymount University, a University Fellow at the University of Iowa (Ph.D., University of Iowa, 1977), and a coeditor of *Media Gratifications Research* (Sage, 1985). He serves on the editorial board of a number of journals and his research has appeared in such journals as *Communication Research, Communication Monographs,* and the *Journal of Broadcasting and Electronic Media.* His current research combines media criticism and audience experience, with a special focus on media-based subcultures and interpretations of media texts in sport, rock and roll music, and other areas of popular culture.

NOTES

NOTES

NOTES